Culture *and* Competence

Culture *and* Competence

CONTEXTS OF LIFE SUCCESS

EDITED BY

Robert J. Sternberg and Elena L. Grigorenko

AMERICAN PSYCHOLOGICAL ASSOCIATION
WASHINGTON, DC

Published by
American Psychological Association
750 First Street, NE
Washington, DC 20002
www.apa.org

To order
APA Order Department
P.O. Box 92984
Washington, DC 20090-2984
Tel: (800) 374-2721; Direct: (202) 336-5510
Fax: (202) 336-5502; TDD/TTY: (202) 336-6123
Online: www.apa.org/books/
E-mail: order@apa.org

In the U.K., Europe, Africa, and the Middle East, copies may be ordered from
American Psychological Association
3 Henrietta Street
Covent Garden, London
WC2E 8LU England

Typeset in Goudy by Stephen McDougal, Mechanicsville, MD

Printer: Sheridan Books, Inc., Ann Arbor, MI
Cover Designer: Berg Design, Albany, NY
Technical/Production Editor: Dan Brachtesende

The opinions and statements published are the responsibility of the authors, and such opinions and statements do not necessarily represent the policies of the American Psychological Association.

Library of Congress Cataloging-in-Publication Data

Culture and competence : contexts of life success / edited by Robert J. Sternberg and Elena L. Grigorenko.
    p. cm.
Includes bibliographical references and index.
   ISBN 1-59147-097-8
   1. Cognition and culture. I. Sternberg, Robert J. II. Grigorenko, Elena.

BF311.C845 2004
153.9—dc22   2003016804

British Library Cataloguing-in-Publication Data
A CIP record is available from the British Library.

Printed in the United States of America
First Edition

CONTENTS

CONTRIBUTORS

Hiroshi Azuma, PhD, Seisen Jogakuin College, Tokyo, Japan

John W. Berry, PhD, Department of Psychology, Queen's University at Kingston, Kingston, Ontario, Canada

Stephen J. Ceci, PhD, Department of Human Development, Cornell University, Ithaca, NY

Sean Duffy, PhD, Research Center for Group Dynamics, Ann Arbor, MI

Patricia Greenfield, PhD, Department of Psychology, University of California, Los Angeles

Elena L. Grigorenko, Yale University PACE Center, New Haven, CT

Susanna A. Hayes, PhD, Western Washington University, Bellingham, WA

Brenda Pitts Haynes, PhD, Department of Education, University of Maryland Baltimore County, Baltimore

Shinobu Kitayama, PhD, Graduate School of Human and Environmental Studies, Kyoto University, Japan

Kimberly A. Kopko, PhD, Department of Human Development, Cornell University, Ithaca, NY

Walter J. Lonner, PhD, Department of Psychology, Western Washington University, Bellingham,

David Matsumoto, PhD, Department of Psychology, San Francisco State University, San Francisco, CA

Joan G. Miller, Department of Psychology, New School University, New York, NY

Paul A. O'Keefe, University of Wisconsin, Madison

Ype H. Poortinga, PhD, Faculty of Social and Behavioral Sciences, Universiteit van Tilburg, Tilburg, The Netherlands

Robert Serpell, PhD, Department of Psychology, University of Maryland Baltimore County, Baltimore, MD

Lauren J. Shapiro, PhD, Stanford University, Stanford, CA

Robert J. Sternberg, PhD, Yale University PACE Center, New Haven, CT

Fons J. R. Van de Vijver, PhD, Faculty of Social and Behavioral Sciences, Universiteit van Tilburg, Tilburg, The Netherlands

Qi Wang, PhD, Department of Human Development, Cornell University, Ithaca, NY

Wendy M. Williams, PhD, Department of Human Development, Cornell University, Ithaca, NY

Isabel Zambrano, PhD

PREFACE

In certain rural Kenyan villages, the most competent children are often those viewed as having the broadest and most accurate knowledge regarding natural herbal medicines that are used to treat parasitic and other illnesses.[1] Such knowledge is important, because almost all of the children suffer from parasitic infections (such as hookworm, whipworm, malaria, and schistosomiasis). In contrast to views in many developed Western countries, in these villages, academic skills are viewed as only a relatively minor part of cognitive and other forms of competence.[2]

In many rural Alaskan Yup'ik villages, the most competent children are often those viewed as having the most superior hunting and gathering skills.[3] Hunting, in particular, is a major part of the culture and of the means for gaining sustenance, and a poor hunter is viewed not only as less competent, but also as compromising the family's food resources.

In Taiwan, Chinese people's conceptions of intellectual competence are quite a bit broader than the notion of IQ. Taiwanese Chinese view traditional cognitive skills as important. But they also emphasize interpersonal and intrapersonal competence,[4] as well as knowing when to show one's abilities and when not to, as important to intellectual competence.

These examples illustrate that just as there are differences in conceptions of competence within a culture,[5] so are there differences across cul-

---

[1]Sternberg, R. J., Nokes, K., Geissler, P. W., Prince, R., Okatcha, F., Bundy, D. A., & Grigorenko, E. L. (2001). The relationship between academic and practical intelligence: A case study in Kenya. *Intelligence, 29,* 401–418.

[2]Grigorenko, E. L., Geissler, P. W., Prince, R., Okatcha, F., Nokes, C., Kenny, D. A., et al. (2001). The organisation of Luo conceptions of intelligence: A study of implicit theories in a Kenyan village. *International Journal of Behavioral Development, 25,* 367–378.

[3]See note 2 above.

[4]Gardner, H. (1983). *Frames of mind.* New York: Basic Books.
Gardner, H. (1999). *Reframing intelligence.* New York: Basic Books.

[5]Sternberg, R. J., & Kolligian, J., Jr. (Eds.). (1990). *Competence considered.* New Haven, CT: Yale University Press.

tures. What are such differences, and why should we care about them? The answers to these and related questions form the basis for this book.

We believe that in an age in which more and more emphasis is being placed on biological bases of competencies, it is particularly important to discuss cultural issues and their relations to biological ones. Many psychologists, educators, and others are interested in cultural issues but, increasingly, do not know where to turn for fresh points of view and information.

The goal of this book is to provide reflections on what, if anything, is common to intellectual and social competence across cultures, and what is not. Is there a common core, or do different cultures simply value different competencies? And whatever may be the answer to this question, what can people learn from the diverse conceptions of competencies that exist around the world?

As society and the technology underlying (and sometimes, driving) it become more complex, the role of cognitive and social competencies in society increases. The number of unskilled and semiskilled jobs has been decreasing and can be expected to continue to decrease. Hence society needs competent, skilled workers. But what does it mean for a worker, a student, or really, anyone else to be competent?

Many views of competency date back to the early 20th century, when the technologies of ability and achievement testing first developed. But are the skills measured by these tests adequate to today's world? And do these skills apply globally, or do they apply more to some societies and not to others?

The authors in this book have been asked to address five questions:

1. What are core competencies, if there are such things, and what are competencies that are culturally unique?
2. How does one identify and study these various types of competencies? What forms do the competencies take?
3. What kind of theoretical framework can be used to understand and organize these competencies?
4. What empirical results are available to support your views?
5. How do your views relate to those of others, and why might the data tend to favor yours?

The chapters in the book have been written in a way that is interpretable to first-year graduate students in psychology with no specialized background. But we believe that the book will appeal to diverse audiences: psychologists specializing in educational, developmental, cultural, cross-cultural, cognitive, social, personality, and differential psychology; educators; anthropologists; and laypeople interested in issues relating culture to competence.

The contributors to this volume include many of the most distinguished psychologists in the field of culture and competence and come from around the world. They form a who's who of theorists and researchers in the field of culture and competence. We hope you enjoy reading this book as much as we have enjoyed editing it.

Culture *and* Competence

1

AN ECOCULTURAL PERSPECTIVE ON THE DEVELOPMENT OF COMPETENCE

JOHN W. BERRY

This chapter begins by outlining a general framework for linking the development and display of human behavior to the contexts (ecological and cultural) in which an individual lives. I adopt a universalist perspective, within which the assumption is made that basic psychological processes are shared, species-wide phenomena on which cultural experiences create behavioral variations. I further propose that these variations are adaptive to habitat, in that they permit effective operation in the environment in which a person develops. I then focus on competence as one psychological feature that is both universal and adaptive, drawing on concepts and empirical research from the field of cross-cultural psychology. The chapter ends with a proposal for designing studies of competence in various cultural contexts that are both context-sensitive and comparative, allowing for an evaluation of the universalist assumption.

ECOCULTURAL PERSPECTIVE

For many years, I have advocated an ecocultural perspective (Berry, 1966). It has evolved through a series of research studies devoted to understanding similarities and differences in cognition and social behavior (Berry, 1967, 1976, 1979; Berry, Bennett, & Denny, 2000; Berry et al., 1986; Mishra, Sinha, & Berry, 1996) to a broad approach to understanding human diversity. The core ideas have a long history (Jahoda, 1995) and have become assembled into conceptual frameworks (Berry, 1975, 1995) used in empirical research and in coordinating textbooks in cross-cultural psychology (Berry, Poortinga, Segall, & Dasen, 2002; Segall, Dasen, Berry, & Poortinga, 1999). Similar ideas and frameworks have been advanced both by anthropologists (e.g., Whiting, 1974) and psychologists (e.g., Bronfenbrenner, 1979), who share the view that human activity can only be understood within the context in which it develops and takes place.

The ecocultural perspective is rooted in two basic assumptions, both deriving from Darwinian thought. The first (the universalist assumption) is that all human societies exhibit commonalities (cultural universals) and that basic psychological processes are shared, species-common characteristics of all human beings on which culture plays infinite variations during the course of development and daily activity. The second (the adaptation assumption) is that behavior is differentially developed and expressed in response to ecological and cultural contexts. This view allows for comparisons across cultures (on the basis of the common underlying process), but makes comparison worthwhile (using the surface variation as basic evidence). Whether derived from anthropology (e.g., Murdock, 1975) or sociology, (e.g., Aberle et al., 1950), there is substantial evidence that groups everywhere possess shared sociocultural attributes. For example, all peoples have language, tools, social structures (e.g., norms, roles) and social institutions (e.g., marriage, justice). It is also evident that such underlying commonalities are expressed by groups in vastly different ways from one time and place to another. Similarly, there is parallel evidence, at the psychological level, for both underlying similarity and surface variation (Berry et al., 1997). For example, all individuals have the competence to develop, learn, and perform speech, technology, role–playing, and norm observance. At the same time, there are obviously vast group and individual differences in the extent and style of expression of these shared underlying processes. This combination of underlying similarity with surface expressive variation has been given the name *universalism* by Berry and Bennett (1992) to distinguish it from two other theoretical views: *absolutism*, which denies cultural influence on behavioral development and expression, and *relativism*, which denies the existence of common underlying psychological processes. Of course, whereas variations in behavioral expression can be directly observed, underlying commonalities are a theoretical construction and cannot be observed directly (Troadec, 2001). Paradoxically, this search for our common humanity can only be pursued by observing our diversity. This dual task is the essence of cross-cultural psychology (Berry, 1969, 2000).

EPISTEMOLOGICAL ISSUES

Two basic assumptions of the ecocultural approach were articulated at the outset: universalism and adaptation. Although no claim can be made that these two assumptions have been verified, they have served as a useful and important heuristic in the field (see Troadec, 2001). One other theoretical issue has not yet been addressed. This is the question: Is culture conceptualized as an *independent* or as an *organismic* variable in the framework? My answer (Berry, 2000) is that it is both.

To justify this view, it is helpful to recall the argument (Kroeber, 1917) that culture is "superorganic," *super* meaning above and beyond, and *organic* referring to its individual biological and psychological bases. Kroeber presented two arguments for the independent existence of culture at its own level. First, particular individuals come and go, but cultures remain more or less stable. This is a remarkable phenomenon; despite a large turnover in membership with each new generation, cultures and their institutions remain relatively unchanged. Thus, a culture does not depend on particular individuals for its existence but has a life of its own at the collective level of the group. The second argument is that no single individual "possesses" all of the culture of the group to which one belongs; the culture as a whole is carried by the collectivity, and indeed is likely to be beyond the biological or psychological capacity (to know or to do) of any single person in the group. For example, no single person knows all the laws, political institutions, and economic structures that constitute even this limited sector of one's culture.

For both these reasons, Kroeber considered that cultural phenomena are collective phenomena, above and beyond the individual person, and hence his term "superorganic." This position is an important one for cross-cultural psychology because it permits us to use the group–individual distinction in attempting to link the two, and possibly to trace the influence of cultural factors on individual psychological development.

From the superorganic perspective, which also proposes that culture exists prior to any particular individual, we can consider culture as "lying in wait" to pounce on newcomers (be they infants or immigrants) and to draw them into its fold by the processes of cultural transmission and acculturation (see Figure 1.1). Hence, we can claim that culture is, in important ways, an *independent variable* (or more accurately, a complex set of interrelated independent variables).

However, these same two transmission processes lead to the incorporation of culture into the individual; hence culture also becomes an *organismic variable*. It is simultaneously outside and inside the individual. Being both "out there" and "in here" (Berry, 2000), the interactive, mutually influencing, character of culture–behavior relationships becomes manifest. This view is indicated by the feedback loop shown in Figure 1.1, in which individuals

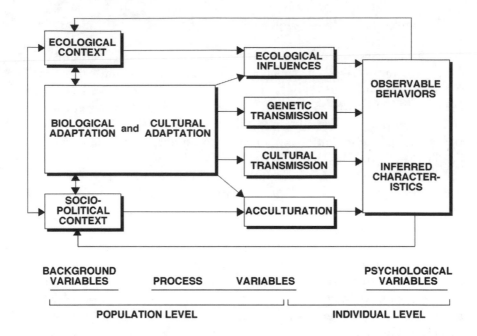

Figure 1.1. Ecocultural framework linking ecology, cultural adaptation, and individual behavior (From Berry et al., 2002).

are in a position to influence, change, and even destroy their ecosystem and cultural accomplishments.

Cross-cultural psychology examines the relationship between cultural context and human behavior. There are three distinguishable conceptualizations of these relationships (Berry et al., 2002): *absolutism*, *relativism*, and *universalism*. The absolutist position is one that assumes that human phenomena are basically the same (qualitatively) in all cultures: honesty is honesty and depression is depression, no matter where one observes it. From the absolutist perspective, culture is thought to play little or no role in either the meaning or display of human characteristics. Assessments of such characteristics are made with standard instruments (perhaps with linguistic translation) and interpretations are made easily, without alternative culturally based views taken into account.

In sharp contrast, the relativist approach assumes that all human behavior is culturally patterned. It seeks to avoid ethnocentrism by trying to understand people on their own terms. Explanations of human diversity are sought in the cultural context in which people have developed. Assessments are typically carried out with the values and meanings that a cultural group gives to a phenomenon. Comparisons are judged to be problematic and ethnocentric, and are thus virtually never made.

A third perspective, one that lies somewhere between the first two positions, is that of universalism. Here it is assumed that basic human characteristics are common to all members of the species (i.e., constituting a set of psychological givens), and that culture influences the development and display of them (i.e., culture plays different variations on these underlying themes). Assessments are based on the presumed underlying process, but measures are developed in culturally meaningful versions. Comparisons are made cautiously, with a wide variety of methodological principles and safeguards, and interpretations of similarities and differences are attempted that take alternative culturally based meanings into account.

ECOLOGICAL AND CULTURAL ADAPTATION

One continuing theme in cultural anthropology is that cultural variations may be understood as adaptations to differing ecological settings or contexts (Boyd & Richerson, 1983). This line of thinking, usually known as *cultural ecology* (Vayda & Rappoport, 1968), *ecological anthropology* (Moran, 1982; Vayda & McKay, 1975), or the *ecosystem* approach (Moran, 1990) to anthropology, has a long history in the discipline (see Feldman, 1975). Its roots go back to Forde's (1934) classic analysis of relationships between physical habitat and societal features in Africa, and Kroeber's (1939) early demonstration that cultural areas and natural areas covary in aboriginal North America. Unlike earlier simplistic assertions by the school of "environmental determinism" (e.g., Huntington, 1945), the ecological school of thought has ranged from "possiblism" (in which the environment provides opportunities and sets some constraints or limits on the range of possible cultural forms that may emerge) to an emphasis on resource utilization (in which active and interactive relationships between human populations and their habitat are analyzed).

Of particular interest to psychologists was Steward's (1955) use of what was later called the *cognized environment*; this concept refers to the "selected features of the environment of greatest relevance to a population's subsistence" (p. 186). With this notion, ecological thinking moved simultaneously away from any links to earlier deterministic views and toward the more psychological idea of individuals actively perceiving, appraising, and changing their environments.

The earlier ecological approaches have tended to view cultural systems as relatively stable (even permanent) adaptations as a *state*, largely ignoring adaptation as a *process*, or adaptability as a system characteristic of cultural populations (Bennett, 1976). However, it is clear that cultures evolve over time, sometimes in response to changing ecological circumstances, and sometimes because of contact with other cultures. This fact has required the addition of a more dynamic conception of ecological adaptation as a continuous as well as an interactive process between ecological, cultural, and psychological variables. It is from the most recent position that I approach the topic.

It is a view that is consistent with more recent general changes in anthropology, away from a "museum" orientation to culture (collecting and organizing static artifacts) to one that emphasizes cultures as constantly changing and is concerned with creation, metamorphosis, and recreation.

Over the years, ecological thinking has influenced not only anthropology but also psychology. The fields of ecological and environmental psychology have become fully elaborated (see Werner, Brown, & Altman, 1997), with substantial theoretical and empirical foundations. In essence, individual human behavior has come to be seen in its natural setting or habitat, in terms of both its development and its contemporary display. The parallel development of cross-cultural psychology (see Berry et al., 1997) has also "naturalized" the study of human behavior and its development. In this field, individual behavior is accounted for to a large extent by considering the role of cultural influences on it. In my own approach, ecological as well as cultural influences are considered as operating in tandem; hence the term *ecocultural approach*.

AN ECOCULTURAL FRAMEWORK

The current version of the ecocultural framework (see Figure 1.1) proposes to account for human psychological diversity (both individual and group similarities and differences) by taking into account two fundamental sources of influence (ecological and sociopolitical) and two features of human populations that are adapted to them: cultural and biological characteristics. These population variables are transmitted to individuals by various transmission variables such as enculturation, socialization, genetics, and acculturation. Our understanding of both cultural and genetic transmission has been greatly advanced by work on culture learning (e.g., Tomasello, Kruger, & Ratner, 1993) and on the human genome project (e.g., Paabo, 2001). The essence of both these domains is the fundamental similarity of all human beings (at a deep level), combined with variation in the expression of these shared attributes (at the surface level). Work on the process and outcomes of acculturation has also been advancing (e.g., Marin, Balls-Organista, & Chung, 2001), necessitated by the dramatic increase in intercultural contact and change.

In summary, the ecocultural framework considers human diversity (both cultural and psychological) to be a set of collective and individual adaptations to context. Within this general perspective, it views cultures as evolving adaptations to ecological and sociopolitical influences and views individual psychological characteristics in a population as adaptive to their cultural context, as well as to the broader ecological and sociopolitical influences. It also views (group) culture and (individual) behavior as distinct phenomena at their own levels that need to be examined independently (see discussion below).

Within psychology researchers in the burgeoning field of environmental psychology have attempted to specify the links between ecological context and individual human development and behavior. Cross-cultural psychologists have tended to view cultures (both one's own and others one is in contact with) as *differential contexts* for development, and view behavior as adaptive to these different contexts.

The ecocultural approach offers a "value neutral" framework for describing and interpreting similarities and differences in human behavior across cultures (Berry, 1994). As adaptive to context, psychological phenomena can be understood "in their own terms" (as Malinowski [1944] insisted), and external evaluations can usually be avoided. This is a critical point, because it allows for the conceptualization, assessment, and interpretation of culture and behavior in nonethnocentric ways (Dasen, 1993). It explicitly rejects the idea that some cultures or behaviors are more advanced or more developed than others (Berry, Dasen, & Witkin, 1983; Dasen, Berry, & Witkin, 1979). Any argument about cultural or behavioral differences being ordered hierarchically requires the adoption of some absolute (usually external) standard. But who is so bold, or so wise, to assert and verify such a standard?

Finally, the sociopolitical context brings about contact among cultures, so that individuals have to adapt to more than one context. If many cultural contexts are involved (as in situations of culture contact and acculturation), psychological phenomena can be viewed as attempts to deal simultaneously with two (sometimes inconsistent, sometimes conflicting) cultural contexts. These attempts at understanding people in their multiple contexts is an important alternative to the more usual pathologizing of colonized or immigrant cultures and peoples. Of course, these intercultural settings need to be approached with the same nonethnocentric perspective as cross-cultural ones (Berry, 1985).

CULTURAL TRANSMISSION

A core feature of the ecocultural framework is the process of cultural transmission: How do features (ecological and cultural) of one's groups become transmitted and incorporated into the day-to-day behavior of individuals who develop in a particular habitat? One proposal (Berry, 1980) is rooted in the ecological thinking of Egon Brunswik's "probabilistic functionalism" (1956), which uses an arc model that links contexts to behavior through features of populations and individuals. The goals of the scheme (see Figure 1.2) are to link psychological effects or outcomes (on the right) to their contexts (on the left) across the scheme; to do so at four distinct levels (down the scheme) ranging from naturalistic (at the top) to controlled (at the bottom) forms of research; and to link the four levels of contexts by "nesting" each one in the level above it.

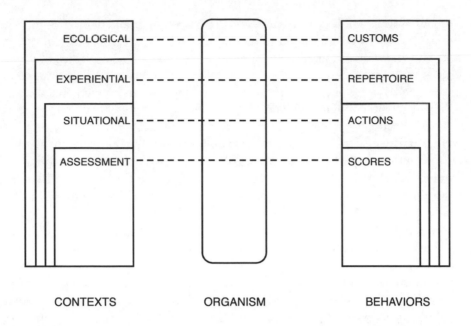

| CONTEXTS | ORGANISM | BEHAVIORS |

Figure 1.2. Cultural transmission: Linkages between contexts and outcomes.

Psychologists have traditionally attempted to comprehend behavior as a function of stimuli impinging on an individual. Ecological psychologists (e.g., Barker, 1969; Brunswik, 1956) have noted that the stimuli usually used in psychology represent only a very narrow range of all possible stimuli and that they are excessively artificial in character. As a result, ecological psychologists have emphasized the need to study behavior in more naturalistic contexts. Similarly, as I have mentioned frequently, cross-cultural psychology proposes that we should be attending to broad ranges of situations drawn from a cross-section of cultures. Sampling from new cultures also means sampling from the new physical environmental contexts in which the cultures are situated. Thus, it is essential that the extension of research cross-culturally be accompanied by increased attention to the natural environmental settings of the cultures studied, a position similar to that espoused by ecological psychology and presented in our general framework (Figure 1.1). Figure 1.2 represents four relationships (perhaps sometimes causal linkages) between environmental contexts and behavioral outcomes. Toward the top of the model are natural and holistic contexts and outcomes, whereas at the bottom they are more experimental (controlled and reductionistic).

Looking in more detail at the environmental contexts, the *ecological context* is the "natural–cultural habitat" of Brunswik (1956) or the "preperceptual world" of Barker (1969). It consists of all the relatively stable and permanent characteristics of the habitat that provide the context for human action and includes the population-level variables identified in Figure 1.1: the ecological context, the sociopolitical context, and the general cultural and biological adaptations made by the group.

Nested in this ecological context are two levels of the "life space" or "psychological world" of Lewin (1936). The first, the *experiential context*, is that pattern of recurrent experiences that provides a basis for individual learning and development; it is essentially the set of independent variables present in a particular habitat during the development of behavioral characteristics. These variables include such day-to-day experiences as child-rearing practices, occupational training, and education. The other, the *situational context*, is the limited set of environmental circumstances (the "setting" of Barker, 1969) that may be observed to account for particular behaviors at a given time and place. They include features such as specific roles or social interactions that can influence how a person will respond to that setting.

The fourth context, the *assessment context*, represents those environmental characteristics, such as test items or stimulus conditions, that are designed by the psychologist to elicit a particular response or test score. The assessment context may or may not be nested in the first three contexts; the degree to which it is nested represents the ecological validity of the task.

Paralleling these four contexts are four behavioral outcomes. The first, *customs*, refers to the complex, long-standing, and developed behavior patterns in the population or culture that are in place as a traditional response to the ecological context. Customs include established, collective, and shared patterns of behavior exhibited by a cultural group.

The second, *repertoire*, is the relatively stable complex of behaviors that have been learned over time in the recurrent experiential or learning context. Included are the skills, traits, and attitudes that have been nurtured in particular roles or acquired by specific training or education, whether formal or informal. The third effect, *actions*, connotes those behaviors that appear in response to immediate stimulation or experience. In contrast to repertoire, they are not so much a function of role experience or long-term training but appear in reply to immediate situational experiences.

The fourth effect, *scores*, comprises those behaviors that are observed, measured, and recorded during psychological assessment (experiments, interviews, or testing). If the assessment context is nested in the other contexts, the scores will be representative of the repertoire of the organism and the customs of the population.

Relationships can be traced between the environmental contexts and the behavioral outcomes across the scheme (dotted lines in Figure 1.2). The first level is concerned with the life situation (in physical, environmental, and cultural terms) and its relationship to daily customs and practices of the population. It is here that other disciplines (such as anthropology and ecology) can supply valuable information to cross-cultural psychology. The second level is concerned with tying together recurrent experiences of individuals with their characteristic repertoire of behaviors. The third level is interested in more specific acts as a function of immediate and current experience. And the fourth level is devoted to the systematic study of relationships between stimuli and the scores obtained by individuals.

A recurrent problem for general psychology, in terms of this scheme, has been the difficulty of contributing to an understanding of relationships at the three higher levels while collecting data almost exclusively at the lowest level. The problem facing cross-cultural psychology is more complex. Rather than ascend the reductionistic–holistic dimension to achieve ecological validity, cross-cultural psychologists have typically failed to work systematically at all levels to achieve a specification of context variables that are responsible for task performance and behavioral variation across natural habitats. In our view only when tests and experimental tasks and outcomes (scores) are understood in terms of their relationships with variables in the upper levels of the scheme will cross-cultural psychologists be able to grasp the meaning of their data.

COMPETENCE IN CONTEXT

Because there is no culture-free behavior, there can be no culture-free competence. This view is central to the proposal made by Ferguson (1956) that "[c]ultural factors prescribe what shall be learned and at what age; consequently different cultural environments lead to the development of different patterns of ability" (p. 121). Embedded in this "Law of Cultural Differentiation" (as it was named by Irvine & Berry, 1988) is the distinction between a species-shared *process* (learning) and cultural-variable *outcomes* (abilities). As I have argued, the existence of process commonality and outcome variability characterizes the *universalist* approach. In this section, I examine some implications of this distinction for understanding human cognition in context.

Process, Competence, and Performance

The process–competence distinction parallels the one made by Hebb (1949) between *Intelligence A* and *Intelligence B*. The former is a person's "innate potential" or "capacity for development" (cf. processes within the organism in Figure 1.2). In contrast, the latter is a person's actual level of (cf. "repertoire" in Figure 1.2). As noted by Bors (1994), Hebb considered Intelligence A to be "independent of time and place" but not accessible to direct measurement (cf. genotype), whereas Intelligence B is a product of A interacting with the cultural environment (cf. phenotype). As Hebb stated,

> [Intelligence B] is quite measurable, with relatively short steps of inference by tests which in effect sample a cultural product, to determine the

extent to which the person being tested has mastered the ideas, modes of thought and of solving problems, ways of perceiving, and the store of information characteristic of the society of which the test is standardized. (1980, p. 74)

A further distinction was proposed by Vernon (1969), who had carried out extensive cross-cultural work. He proposed the concept of *Intelligence C*, which is the result of an assessment procedure (testing, observation, interview) that usually only samples Intelligence B (cf. actions and scores in Figure 1.2). If the test is culturally appropriate, then Intelligence C will be a reasonably valid sample of B, but if it is not, or the situation is unfamiliar or unmotivating, then Intelligence C will be a poor representation of B.

In these distinctions between Intelligence A, B, and C there is a parallel between the process–competence–performance distinction (see Gelman, 1994): *Processes* are those basic operations available to a person; *competence* is what a person knows (intellectual, social, practical), and *performance* is what a person actually does with this knowledge (cf. organism, repertoire, actions in Figure 1.2). From the universalist perspective, processes are considered to be culturally invariant; they are not shaped or altered by cultural experience but remain as basic psychological qualities that can be nurtured into development (competence) and expressed during performance. Such fundamental processes as learning, analysis, synthesis, memory, induction, and deduction are viewed as being available to all people everywhere. What varies is the extent to which these processes are used, how they are used, and to which kinds of problems they are addressed. Thus, cultural experience is viewed as a variable input (on the left of Figure 1.2) that results in the development of variable output (on the right of Figure 1.2). Cultural differences are also viewed as source of error (or bias) in assessing competence, thus yielding performance assessments that vary in their representativeness of the underlying competence.

Developmental Goals

"You can't tell how far a person has progressed unless you know where he is going" (Berry, 1987). In this old adage lies the core of the issue addressed in this and the next (indigenous) section. In the general developmental literature, work on parental ethotheories has revealed that all societies espouse developmental goals for their children, which then become socialized by parents and others responsible for nurturing (see Segall et al., 1999, chap. 3). The concept of the *developmental niche* (Super & Harkness, 1997) incorporates this basic idea as one of its core components, as well as the early work by Barry, Child, and Bacon (1959) on emphases in socialization.

Because societies vary in their ecological demands, and in their cultural adaptations to these demands (including their socialization emphases), there is a solid basis for studying variations in developmental goals. Societies do not all share the same adaptive challenges, and hence it is unlikely that they would all direct development toward the same goals.

In the ecocultural framework, there is a second context (the sociopolitical) that imposes new challenges for developing individuals and their societies. The process of acculturation following culture contact may interfere with those developmental goals that have been adaptive to the ecological context. If so, two sets of demands may conflict; and if the new set dominates (e.g., in schooling or employment settings) previously adaptive competencies may no longer be the most appropriate ones. However, in acculturation theory (Berry, 2003) such domination is not the only way to deal with contact and change, nor is it the most functional. Assimilation (loss of heritage culture, combined with the imposition of the dominant culture) is less functional than integration (selected maintenance of heritage culture, combined with learning useful features of the dominant culture). In essence, assimilation replaces heritage developmental goals with those of the dominant society, whereas integration values both and seeks to balance them so that competence in both societies is permitted, sought, and developed. Thus the study of developmental goals during acculturation requires concepts that provide alternatives to the common assumption that all groups in a society should share the same competencies. In this way, we can avoid the inevitable labeling of cognitive *differences* as cognitive *deficiencies* (McShane & Berry, 1988).

Indigenous Cognition

The study of cultural variations in cognitive competence has come to be known as *indigenous cognition* (Berry, Irvine, & Hunt, 1987). It is important to remind ourselves that the search for indigenous cognition is both an important enterprise in its own right and a necessary step toward achieving a universal understanding of cognitive competence (Berry, 1984). Numerous studies have been carried out that attempt to identify the cognitive goals of peoples in Africa (e.g., Grigorenko et al., 2001; Wober, 1974), among aboriginal peoples in North America and India (e.g., Berry & Bennett, 1992; Mishra, Sinha, & Berry, 1996; Stern, 1999), and in Asia (e.g., Das, 1994; Keats, 1979; Yang & Sternberg, 1997), as well as general populations (Sternberg et al., 1981). One central finding characterizes this literature: The notion of competence in most societies extends well beyond the narrow definitions that are typically adopted by Western Academic Scientific Psychology. Most frequently, moral and social features appear as well as those that are specifically adaptive to a particular group (e.g., developed spatial abilities among hunters; Berry & Bennett, 1989, 1992; Stern, 1999).

TABLE 1.1
Two Levels of Observation and Two Levels of Analysis of the Data

LEVEL OF ANALYSIS	LEVEL OF OBSERVATION	
	CULTURAL	INDIVIDUAL
CULTURAL	1. HOLOCULTURAL (e.g., HRAF)	2. AGGREGATION (e.g., values)
INDIVIDUAL	4. ECOCULTURAL (e.g., cognitive style)	3. INDIVIDUAL DIFFERENCE (e.g., traits, abilities)

TOWARD UNIVERSALS

As noted above, studies of indigenous competence both highlight cultural variations, even uniquenesses, and are also necessary to provide evidence in our search for universals. If we search for patterns of similarities, we need to attend to some distinctions among kinds of studies.

Research Designs

Two pairs of distinctions are important. These are between two levels of observation (cultural and individual) and between two levels of analysis of the data obtained by such observations (also cultural and individual). In Table 1.1 these two distinctions are presented in relation to each other. For each, the distinction between the cultural (population) level and the individual level is made, producing a classification of four methodological types of cross-cultural studies.

In the first type, holocultural, the data are collected at the cultural level, usually by anthropologists using ethnographic methods, and are interpreted at that level, leading to the typical ethnographic report. These cultural observations can also be related to each other, comparing various customs or institutions with other factors across cultures, leading to holocultural studies (e.g., using the human relations area files [HRAF]). Such studies have revealed broad patterns of covariation among elements of culture. For example, the early study by Barry and colleagues (1959) showed that child-rearing practices, ranging on a dimension from those emphasizing "assertion" to emphasizing "compliance," correlate with ecological factors (such as subsistence economy) and with social structural factors (such as hierarchy in social relationships). Although no individual psychological data are collected in this type of study, they serve the important role of providing basic contextual information for studies in cross-cultural psychology.

In the second type, aggregation, the data are collected at the individual level (e.g., with interviews, questionnaires, etc.) with samples of people in a population. These data are then used to create scores for each culture, by aggregation, from the individual responses. Here the level of observation is the individual, but the level of analysis is the culture. Culture (or country) scores can claim to represent the population if individual data are from representative samples of individuals. Such country scores can be related to other aggregated scores, or to independent country indicators such as gross national product. They can also be related to other independent cultural descriptions obtained with holocultural research methods (Type 1). These aggregated country scores are sometimes used in correlations with individual scores on very similar scales (e.g., in countries with a high collectivism score, individuals usually score high on a collectivism scale). That is, the same set of data is used twice in the correlation, once at the individual level of observation and once at the cultural level of analysis. This practice may lack sufficient independence in conceptualization and measurement to be entirely valid.

In the third type of study, individual difference, data are collected at the individual level and remain at that level for analysis. These are the common and basic kinds of study used by psychologists more generally. Usually, mean scores are calculated for a particular test, and the relationships among scores are correlated or factor-analyzed. The vast majority of these individual difference studies are not used in cross-cultural comparisons and remain focused on distributions and relationships among variables within one population. However, when cross-cultural comparisons are made, they are usually of these mean scores, sometimes taken to represent only the sample, but also sometimes taken to represent the culture as a whole. If factors are produced, comparisons of the factors are made, usually to establish equivalence or provide evidence of bias. These cross-cultural comparisons remain at the individual level of observation and analysis; cultural factors are not usually invoked in any attempt to explain mean score differences that may be obtained. Occasionally post hoc "cultural" explanations are proposed to account for mean score differences. Studies of personality traits, emotions, or other behaviors (e.g., conformity; Bond & Smith, 1996) are of this type.

The fourth type, ecocultural, represents a hybrid, combining elements of the first and third types. Here, cultural-level findings (the first type, from ethnographic sources) are taken and examined for their relationships with individual-level data (from the third type, individual-difference studies). Sampling of cultures can provide a range of variation in contexts, and allow the prediction of variation (similarities and differences) in individual psychological development and behavior. Because the two sets of data are independent of each other (because of their different levels of observation and analysis), it is valid to examine relationships between them. Examples of these are the ecocultural studies of cognitive style (e.g., Berry, 1976), mentioned earlier, in which ecological and cultural information was used to select cultural groups as contexts for development, followed by predictions and assessment of individual behavior in these various settings.

Universal Framework

To approach universals, I have proposed a comparative framework (Berry, 1984) that incorporates the various aspects of competence that have been identified in studies of indigenous cognition. These may be assessed in a number of cultures, with tasks that are rooted in the underlying process but are rendered accessible through the use of indigenous materials and instructions. Figure 1.3 illustrates how to comparatively examine these aspects of competence with culturally appropriate tasks. Down the left-hand side are the areas of cognitive competence that may eventually emerge from folk and psychologists' conceptions, such as reasoning, spatial, vocabulary, and social; the list is extendable until all culturally identified and valued cognitive activities are included, representing the first part of our prescription—the emic inclusion strategy. Across the top of Figure 1.3 is a dimension that provides a rationale for comparing individuals in cultures on that particular cognitive competence, such as the language basis for vocabulary competence, or the ecological basis for spatial competence; along this dimension, societies may be sampled to provide a good cross-cultural representation of cultural variation in, for example, linguistic families (not all Indo-European) or ecological engagement (not all agriculturalists).

Empirical studies guided by the framework may proceed in a variety of ways. If one wishes to search for a universal in a particular cognitive function, one would work across a single line, across cultures; integrating these findings would say something about the universality of, for example, competence in reasoning. If one wishes to understand the cognitive competencies of people in a particular culture, one would work down a single column; integrating these findings would say something about the "societal psychology" of cognitive competence in a particular culture.

It should be obvious that only by working both across and down can one be in a position to achieve anything close to a universal psychology of cognitive competence. Such a two-way integration is demonstrably different, in this framework, from what has been so far achieved—a single societal psychology for Western, European American cognitive competence—and from what is being attempted occasionally, such as the tracing of a particular cognitive competence across a few cultures.

If, in the end, all information in the framework can be neatly integrated in the lower right-hand corner, then we will have evidence for a universal general cognitive competence (all abilities cohere similarly in all cultures); if integration is not possible in either direction (no cross-cultural pattern, nor intracultural pattern), then we will have evidence to support a specific abilities approach; and if coherent patterns appear across competence areas within cultures (that is, not a single general competence) and these patterns vary according to the cultural context, then we will have evidence for a cognitive styles approach. Thus, the framework serves the dual

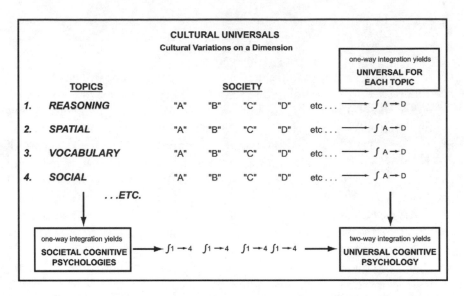

Figure 1.3. Framework for pursuing universals of cognitive competence.

purpose of outlining a strategy for comparative research and for evaluating the validity of each of the current conceptualizations.

REFERENCES

Aberle, D. F., Cohen, A., Davis, A., Levy, M., & Sutton, F. (1950). Functional prerequisites of society. *Ethics, 60,* 100–111.

Barker, R. (1969). *Ecological psychology.* Stanford: Stanford University Press.

Barry, H., Child, I., & Bacon, M. (1959). Relations of child training to subsistence economy. *American Anthropologist, 61,* 51–63.

Bennett, J. (1976). *The ecological transition.* London: Pergamon.

Berry, J. W. (1966). Temne and Eskimo perceptual skills. *International Journal of Psychology, 1,* 207–229.

Berry, J. W. (1967). Independence and conformity in subsistence-level societies. *Journal of Personality and Social Psychology, 7,* 415–418.

Berry, J. W. (1969). On cross-cultural comparability. *International Journal of Psychology, 4,* 119–128.

Berry, J. W. (1975). An ecological approach to cross-cultural psychology. *Nederlands Tijdschrift voor de Psychologie, 30,* 51–84.

Berry, J. W. (1976). *Human ecology and cognitive style: Comparative studies in cultural and psychological adaptation.* New York: Sage/Halsted.

Berry, J. W. (1979). A cultural ecology of social behaviour. In L. Berkowitz (Ed.), *Advances in experimental social psychology* (Vol. 12, pp. 177–206). New York: Academic Press.

Berry, J. W. (1980). Ecological analyses for cross-cultural psychology. In N. Warren (Ed.), *Studies in cross-cultural psychology* (Vol. 2, pp. 157–189). London: Academic Press.

Berry, J. W. (1984). Towards a universal psychology of cognitive competence. *International Journal of Psychology, 19*, 335–361.

Berry, J. W. (1985). Cultural psychology and ethnic psychology. In I. Reyes Lagunes, & Y. Poortinga (Eds.), *From a different perspective* (pp. 3–15). Lisse, The Netherlands: Swets & Zeitlinger.

Berry, J. W. (1987). Cognive values among the bricoleuts. In J. W. Berry, S. H. Irvine, & E. B. Hunt (Eds.), *Indigenous cognition* (pp. 2–9). Dordrecht, The Netherlands: Nijhoff.

Berry, J. W. (1994). An ecological approach to cultural and ethnic psychology. In E. Trickett (Ed.), *Human diversity* (pp. 115–141). San Francisco: Jossey-Bass.

Berry, J. W. (1995). The descendants of a model. *Culture & Psychology, 1*, 373–380.

Berry, J. W. (2000). Cross-cultural psychology: A symbiosis of cultural and comparative approaches. *Asian Journal of Social Psychology, 3*, 197–205.

Berry, J. W. (2003). Conceptual approaches to acculturation. In K. Chun, P. Balls-Organista, & G. Morin (Eds.), *Acculturation: Advances in theory, measurement, and applied research* (pp. 17–37). Washington, DC: American Psychological Association.

Berry, J. W., & Bennett, J. A. (1989). Syllabic literacy and cognitive performance among the Cree. *International Journal of Psychology, 24*, 429–450.

Berry, J. W., & Bennett, J. A. (1992). Cree conceptions of cognitive competence. *International Journal of Psychology, 27*, 73–88.

Berry, J. W., Bennett, J. A., & Denny, J. P. (2000, July). *Ecology, culture and cognitive processing.* Paper presented at the International Association for Cross-Cultural Psychology Congress, Pultusk, Poland.

Berry, J. W., Dasen, P. R., & Witkin, H. A. (1983). Developmental theories in cross-cultural perspective. In L. Alder (Ed.), *Cross-cultural research at issue* (pp. 13–21). New York: Academic Press.

Berry, J. W., Irvine, S. H., & Hunt, E. B. (Eds.). (1987). *Indigenous cognition: Functioning in cultural context.* Dordrecht, The Netherlands: Ninjhoff.

Berry, J. W., van de Koppel, J. M. H., Sénéchal, C., Annis, R. C., Bahuchet, S., Cavalli-Sforza, L. L., & Witkin, H. A. (1986). *On the edge of the forest: Cultural adaptation and cognitive development in Central Africa.* Lisse, The Netherlands: Swets and Zeitlinger.

Berry, J. W., Poortinga, Y. H., Pandey, J., Dasen, P. R., Saraswathi, T. S., Segall, M. H., et al. (1997). *Handbook of cross-cultural psychology* (Vol. 1–3). Boston: Allyn & Bacon.

Berry, J. W., Poortinga, Y. H., Segall, M. H., & Dasen, P. R. (2002). *Cross-cultural psychology: Research and applications* (Rev. 2nd ed.). New York: Cambridge University Press.

Bond, R., & Smith, P. (1996). Culture and conformity: A meta-analysis. *Psychological Bulletin, 119*, 111–137.

Bors, D. (1994). Hebb's theory of intelligence. In R. J. Sterberg (Ed.), *Encyclopedia of human intelligence* (pp. 527–528). New York: Macmillan.

Boyd, R., & Richerson, P. (1983). Why is culture adaptive? *Quarterly Review of Biology, 58*, 209–214.

Bronfenbrenner, U. (1979). *The ecology of human development*. Cambridge: Harvard University Press.

Brunswick, E. (1956). *Perception and the representative design of psychological experiments*. Berkely: University of California Press.

Das, J. P. (1994). Eastern views of intelligence. In R. J. Sternberg (Ed.), *Encyclopaedia of human intelligence* (pp. 387–391). New York: Macmillan.

Dasen, P. R. (1993). Theoretical/conceptual issues in development research in Africa. *Journal of Psychology in Africa, 1*, 151–158.

Dasen, P. R., Berry, J. W., & Witkin, H. A. (1979). The use of developmental theories cross-culturally. In L. Eckensberger, W. Lonner, & Y. Poortinga (Eds.), *Cross-cultural contributions to psychology* (pp. 69–82). Lisse, The Netherlands: Swets & Zeitlinger.

Feldman, D. (1975). The history of the relationship between environment and culture in ethnological thought. *Journal of the History of the Behavioural Sciences, 110*, 67–81.

Forde, D. (1934). *Habitat, economy and society*. New York: Dutton.

Ferguson, G. (1956). On transfer and the abilities of man. *Canadian Journal of Psychology, 10*, 121–131.

Gelman, S. (1994). Competence versus performance. In R. J. Sternberg (Ed.), *Encyclopedia of human intelligence* (pp. 283–286). New York: Macmillan.

Grigorenko, E. L., Geissler, P. W., Prince, R., Okatcha, F., Nokes, C., Kenny, D. A., et al. (2001). The organisation of Luo conceptions of intelligence: A study of implicit theories in a Kenyan village. *International Journal of Behavioral Development, 25*, 367–378.

Hebb, D. O. (1949). *The organisation of behaviour*. New York: Wiley.

Hebb, D. O. (1980). *Essays of mind*. Hillsdale: Erlbaum.

Huntington, E. (1945). *Mainsprings of civilization*. New York: Wiley.

Irvine, S. H., & Berry, J. W. (1988). The abilities of mankind. In S. H. Irvine & J. W. Berry (Eds.), *Human abilities in cultural context* (pp. 3–59). New York: Cambridge University Press.

Jahoda, G. (1995). The ancestry of a model. *Culture & Psychology, 1*, 11–24.

Keats, D. (1979). Cross-cultural studies in cognitive development and language in Malaysia and Australia. *Educational Research and Perspectives, 6*, 46–63.

Kroeber, A. (1917). The superorganic. *American Psychologist, 19*, 163–213.

Kroeber, A. (1939). *Cultural and natural areas of native North America*. Berkeley: University of California Press.

Lewin, K. (1936). *Principles of topological psychology*. New York: McGraw-Hill.

Malinowski, B. (1944). *A scientific theory of culture*. Chapel Hill: University of North Carolina Press.

Marin, G., Balls-Organista, P., & Chung, K. (Eds.). (2001). *Acculturation*. Washington, DC: American Psychological Association.

McShane, D., & Berry, J. W. (1988). Native North Americans: Indian and Inuit abilities. In S. H. Irvine & J. W. Berry (Eds.), *Human abilities in cultural context* (pp. 385–426). New York: Cambridge University Press.

Mishra, R. C., Sinha, D., & Berry, J. W. (1996). *Ecology, acculturation and psychological adaptation: A study of Advasi in Bihar*. Delhi, India: Sage.

Moran, E. (1982). *Human adaptability: An introduction to ecological anthropology*. Boulder, CO: Westview Press.

Moran, E. (Ed.). (1990). *The ecosystem approach in anthropology*. Ann Arbor: University of Michigan Press.

Murdock, G. P. (1975). *Outline of cultural materials*. New Haven, CT: Human Relations Area Files.

Paabo, S. (2001, February 19). The human genome and our view of ourselves. *Science, 291*, 1219–1220.

Segall, M. H., Dasen, P. R., Berry, J. W., & Poortinga, Y. H. (1999). *Human behaviour in global perspective: An introduction to cross-cultural psychology* (Rev. 2nd ed.). Boston: Allyn & Bacon.

Stern, P. (1999). Learning to be smart: An exploration of the culture of intelligence in a Canadian Inuit community. *American Anthropologist, 101*, 502–514.

Sternberg, R. J., Conway, B., Ketron, J. & Bernstein, M. (1981). People's conception of intelligence. *Journal of Personality and Social Psychology, 41*, 37–55.

Steward, J. (1955). The concept and method of cultural ecology. *Theory of culture change*. Urbana: University of Illinois Press.

Super, C., & Harkness, S. (1997). The cultural structuring of child development. In J. W. Berry, P. R. Dasen, & T. S. Saraswathi (Eds.), *Handbook of cross-cultural psychology* (Vol. 3, pp. 1–39). Boston: Allyn & Bacon.

Tomasello, M., Kruger, A., & Ratner, H. (1993). Culture learning. *Behavioral and Brain Sciences, 16*, 495–552.

Troadec, B. (2001). Le modèle écoculturel: Un cadre pour la psychologie culturelle comparative [The ecocultural model: A framework for comparative psychology]. *International Journal of Psychology, 36*, 53–64.

Vayda, A. P., & McKay, B. (1975). New directions in ecology and ecological anthropology. *Annual Review of Anthropology, 4*, 293–306.

Vayda, A. P., & Rappoport, R. (1968). Ecology, cultural and non-cultural. In J. Clifton (Ed.), *Cultural anthropology* (pp. 477–497). Boston: Houghton Mifflin.

Vernon, P. E. (1969). *Intelligence and cultural environment*. London: Methuen.

Werner, C., Brown, B., & Altman, I. (1997). Environmental psychology. In J. W. Berry, M. H. Segall, & C. Kagitcibasi (Eds.), *Handbook of cross-cultural psychol-*

ogy: *Vol. 3. Social behaviour and applications* (pp. 253–290). Boston: Allyn & Bacon.

Whiting, J. W. M. (1974). A model for psychocultural research. *Annual Report.* Washington: American Anthropological Association.

Wober, M. (1974). Towards an understanding of the Kiganda concept of intelligence. In J. W. Berry & P. R. Dasen (Eds.), *Culture and cognition* (pp. 261–280). London: Methuen.

Yang, R. J., & Sternberg, R. J. (1997). Taiwanese Chinese conceptions of intelligence. *Intelligence, 25,* 21–36.

2

WHAT DO CHILDREN DO WHEN THEY CANNOT GO TO SCHOOL?

ELENA L. GRIGORENKO AND PAUL A. O'KEEFE

We live in a world populated by more than 6 billion people.[1] Approximately 2.15 billion (39%) of them are children under the age of 18. Of these children, 1.89 billion (approximately 88% of all children) live in developing countries. In developing countries, children constitute approximately 39% of these countries' population. In more developed countries, this number is approximately 25%. One might ask why the word *approximately* appears next to these figures. Why not just count the people through their birth certificates? The answer is because it is virtually impossible: Every year approximately one third of all births (approximately 40 million births) are not registered. The overwhelming majority of these unregistered births take place in developing countries, raising the estimates of the number of children living there even higher.

Preparation of this chapter was supported by Grant REC-9979843 from the National Science Foundation. Grantees undertaking such projects are encouraged to express freely their professional judgment. This chapter, therefore, does not necessarily represent the position or policies of the National Science Foundation, and no official endorsement should be inferred. The authors are thankful to Robyn Rissman for her assistance in preparing the final version of the manuscript. Correspondence should be sent to Elena L. Grigorenko, PACE Center, Yale University, Box 208358, New Haven, CT 06520-8358.
[1]The figures for this chapter were drawn primarily from *The State of the World's Children 2002* (UNICEF, 2002).

Moreover, population growth trends indicate that the situation will be even more dramatic in the future. The growth of human population has been, is now, and in the future will be almost entirely determined in the world's less-developed countries (Bureau of the Census, 1999). Ninety-nine percent of global natural increase (the difference between number of births and number of deaths) now occurs in the developing regions of Africa, Asia, and Latin America. Projections of the U.S. Census Bureau indicate that at the beginning of this century the numbers of deaths will exceed the numbers of births in the world's more developed countries, and *all* of the net annual gain in global population will, in effect, come from the world's developing countries. This projection means that, in the near future, even more children will be living in the developing world.

Here are a few other facts that set up the context of the following chapter (United Nations International Children's Emergency Fund [UNICEF], 2002). Between 1990 and 2000, the rate of infant mortality was reduced by 14% (from 94 to 81 per 1,000 live births), meaning that 3 million more children a year are now surviving beyond their fifth birthday than was the case a decade ago. However, there is a massive disparity in infant mortality between regions. The range of change is impressive: from 9 to 6 per 1,000 live births in industrialized countries to 180 to 172 per 1,000 live births in sub-Saharan Africa. The latter figure reflects, among other causes, the tragedy of the HIV/AIDS epidemic in Africa. Having survived, however, the majority of children in the world have to face other tremendous challenges. Approximately 30% of the children in developing countries (149 million) are underweight. In Asia, where more than two thirds of the world's malnourished children live, the drop in child malnutrition rates was relatively small, from 36% to 29%, whereas in sub-Saharan Africa the absolute number of malnourished children has actually increased. Throughout their lives, only about 82% of the world's population has universal access to safe drinking water and only about 60% have universal access to sanitary means of human waste disposal. Needless to say, most of those people who do not have access to safe drinking water and sanitary means of human waste disposal live in the developing world.

Most psychologists live and work in industrialized countries. Some of them do research and writing about children in the developing countries. Thus, most of what is known about child development has been observed, registered, and experimentally scrutinized on or with children growing up in industrialized countries, where almost all children go to school, help at home, and play in between. However, in 2000, only 82% of the world's children had universal access to basic (primary, lasting usually three to four years) education. In developing countries, the net primary school enrollment in 1998 was 60% for sub-Saharan Africa, 74% for South and West Asia, 76% for Arab States/North Africa, 92% for Central Asia, 94% for Latin America and the Caribbean, and 97% for East Asia and Pacific Islands. Note, however, that these figures do not reflect dropout and absenteeism rates, both of which can be as high as 40% to 50%. And, although precise figures are not known, only about 10% of children in developing countries make it through 10 to 11 years of study. Thus, although the majority of the world's children do experience at least some schooling, approximately 20% of them never go to school, and for the majority schooling is very limited. And of those who do go to school, the quality of schooling is extremely variable.

The main objective of this chapter is to survey the literature on "other than school" activities carried out by children around the world. We do not intend to survey after-school activities (i.e., the activities of children who attend school and then do something else—play, participate in sports, or do chores at home after school) of children who go to school. Here we are interested primarily in out-of-school children. What do children do if they are not enrolled in school? What competencies do their societies expect them to acquire, and how do children acquire them?

The chapter is divided into three sections. First, we discuss a developmental model of competencies and their mastery. Second, we summarize the literature on competencies in children living in nonindustrialized countries whose salient developmental tasks differ from those of their peers in industrialized societies. Finally, we argue for the importance of studying competencies in a wide variety of contexts in which children grow up. We state that the presented model is generic, and as long as the children interiorize models of successful life adjustment through developing competencies, they are able to transfer this model into new contexts and formulate new developmental tasks by detecting the key competencies to be mastered to adjust successfully.

CHILDREN'S COMPETENCIES:
A DEVELOPMENTAL PERSPECTIVE

The concept of children's competencies has attracted the attention of many developmental psychologists (e.g., Cicchetti & Cohen, 1995; Cicchetti & Toth, 1995; Denham & Holt, 1993; Masten & Coatsworth, 1995; Waters & Sroufe, 1983). Defined as "possession of required skill, knowledge, qualification, or capacity" (Webster's New Universal Unabridged Dictionary, 1996), the concept of competency is characterized both by the breadth (ranging from skill to capacity) and the developmentally transient nature (required by a given developmental period, by a certain situation) of its meaning. Thus, the concept of competence covers a cluster of constructs related to successful (adaptive) functioning at a given age and in a given cultural and historical environment (Masten & Coatsworth, 1995). What is particularly valuable about this concept, from our point of view, is that it does not have an evaluative connotation. That is, unlike the ability–disability concept, the concept of competence does not have the connotation of the given; quite on the contrary, it assumes that competence can be acquired. However, what matters is whether the available competencies are suitable for the management of a given developmental situation.

Although not well defined formally, a succession of competencies—the mastery of which is expected of a child growing in the industrialized world—is implicitly present in expectations of parents and teachers. It is commonly accepted that children who fail to meet these implicit expectations are of concern to the society and should be referred for evaluations and interventions (Masten & Curtis, 2000). Moreover, a rich literature addresses consequences of the failure to acquire developmentally required competencies: Failure to develop secure infant attachment has been found to be associated with higher risk for later behavior problems (e.g., Easterbrooks & Goldberg, 1990; Erickson, Sroufe, & Egeland, 1985); failure to master basic linguistic capacities is likely to correlate with later cognitive, social–emotional, and behavioral problems (e.g., Sameroff & Haith, 1996); failure to acquire adaptive peer-relationship skills is related to risk for poor social–emotional adjustment later in life (e.g., Cicchetti, 1984; Dodge & Murphy, 1984; Ladd, Huot, Thrivikraman, & Plotsky, 1999; Sroufe, 1979; Sroufe & Rutter, 1984); and failure to master self-regulation and socially accepted behaviors can result in later school adaptation and academic achievement problems (e.g., Parker, Rubin, Price, & DeRosier, 1995; Rubin, Bukowski, & Parker, 1998; Sroufe & Rutter, 1984).

Although these findings form a basis of modern developmental psychology, it is important to acknowledge that the overwhelming majority of research on the nature and process of the acquisition of various competencies at different developmental stages has been conducted in industrialized countries, where the primary indicator of life adjustment is school adjustment (school competence). But, as we demonstrated above, less than 15% of the world's children grow up in industrialized countries. In addition, for children growing up in developing countries, the experience of schooling and, therefore, school competence, are rather distal to the fulfillment of their immediate needs of safety and well-being. The question, then, is if schooling is not central to these children, what is?

The general assertion, derived from studies in industrialized countries, is that acquiring "key" competence in stage-salient tasks increases the likelihood of later success in mastering other required skills (e.g., gaining other competence) and minimizes the risk of emergence and persistent presence of maladaptive patterns (Keenan & Shaw, 1997; Masten & Coatsworth, 1995, 1998). If this claim is correct then we should be able to identify such "key" competencies in developing societies as well. The content of "key" competencies most likely will be different in children in the industrialized and unindustrialized worlds, but the general structure underlying the relationships between competencies and life adjustment should be the same across different cultures and societies.

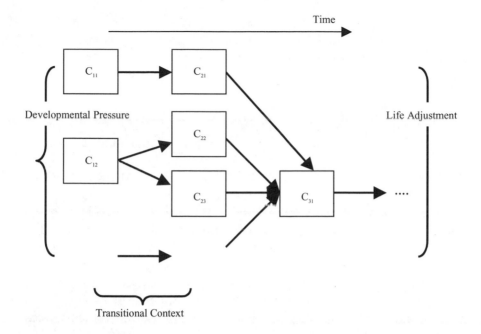

Figure 2.1. The model of the development of competencies over time. The letter *C* is used as abbreviation for competencies. The letters are indexed so that the first index signifies the time (we depict three times points) and the second index signifies a given competence.

Here we present a general model linking competencies and life adjustment (see Figure 2.1). The model assumes the development of competencies across time and is oriented toward successful life adjustment and unfolding under developmental pressure. In more detail, we assume that one of the roles of developmental socialization is the acquisition of a set of competencies that are necessary for successful life adjustment. Although this model is embedded in and derived from the literature on competence (e.g., Havighurst, 1972; Masten & Coatsworth, 1995, 1998; White, 1959), we think that a number of issues important for understanding child development in nonindustrialized countries are stressed in this model.

First, the concept of life adjustment, by its nature, reflects the culture, society, and community in which the child develops. The dimensions of life for the Masai people of rural Kenya are different from those of people elsewhere. For example, according to one Masai adult, the tribe picks out the brightest children, the ones with the most potential, and sends them away with the goats. As a father of two sons says, it takes brains to identify every animal, find water, and ward off cattle rustlers. Therefore, he sends his smarter son away with the goats and sends his not-so-smart son to school ("No Swots, Please, We're Masai," 2002). Clearly, the life, community, and family demands and expectations of the Masai boy herding sheep are different from that of a child of a Harvard professor attending a prep school in New England. Yet, their success of life adjustment might be comparable: both boys need to meet the expectations of their societies, as expressed by expectations of their fathers, and for that they need to master corresponding competencies. Thus, although the content of the competencies is very different (how to herd goats in remote areas of Kenya versus how to succeed in a New England prep school), the developmental tasks are similar: The boys need to learn what is expected of them culturally.

Second, we would like to stress how important it is, from our point of view, to consider more than merely Westernized approaches to studying children's competencies in nonindustrialized cultures. Specifically, what we mean is the following. For the past 30 years in industrialized countries, the concept of *resilience*, usually defined as the child's ability to develop required competencies in spite of growing up in the context of disadvantaged or threatening environments, has attracted a lot of attention (Masten, 1999a, 1999b). The underlying assumption of this research is that there are children who can somehow develop typically in atypical (disadvantaged or threatening) environments; thus, if we understand what drives their development, we can prevent or treat negative outcomes that are usually observed in such atypical environments. The important issue here is that, by the standards of the industrialized world, most of the children in the developing world live and grow up in atypical (disadvantaged and threatening) environments. What we argue here is that their development cannot be studied and understood with the list of Western-world required competencies in mind; we need to understand the critical competencies for successful lives in their cultures, and how such competencies are acquired.

The success of life adjustment is determined by how well a child is able to master the competencies necessary for prospering in life, including meeting the demands of culture, society, community, and family. The mastery of these competencies occurs over time and assumes some sequence (e.g., for a child to be able to hunt, as is required by Bushman society, he needs to know how to read animal tracks in the sand, how to interpret the environment so as not to lose the sense of direction, how to shoot a bow, and so on). Moreover, often, prior to mastery of a structurally complex competency (e.g., C_{31} in the figure), the child needs to become competent performing easier tasks (e.g., C_{22}, C_{23}, and C_{24}). For example, before a 6- or 7-year-old girl in a slum of Delhi is left alone to care for her baby brother, the girl should know how to carry the boy around, what to do if the boy cries, and so on.

The third and fourth issues with regard to Figure 2.1 relate to the question of how the child selects competencies to master and how the transition to higher-level (more complex) competencies is insured. With regard to the third issue, selecting competencies to master, this selection, especially at early stages of development, is done for the child through mechanisms of socialization. For example, a street boy on the streets of Nairobi (see below) does not have much choice but to learn how to make some money by the age of 8 or 9 so that he can support himself, because his parents do not want to support him anymore, and bring some income back to his mother's house, because she expects him to help them support his younger siblings. Similarly, a child soldier in the National Mozambican Resistance may not have much choice but to master weapons to save his or her life. We refer to this necessity of acquiring competencies that ensure the child's survival and the sense of belonging as *developmental pressure*. With this concept we attempt to signify (a) the demand embedded in the need to gain competencies in doing things that are crucial for the child's well-being at a given moment and (b) the temporal nature of this pressure—a given competency lays a foundation for mastery of new competencies but does not warrant by itself a successful life adjustment.

Regarding the fourth issue, the transition to higher-order competencies always assumes the presence of the transitional context. Typically, this transitional context is created by adults who survey the level of acquisition of the lower-level activities and judge whether the child is competent enough at the lower-level activity (e.g., handling a fishing net) to attempt mastering a new, higher-level activity (e.g., going fishing on a boat alone). This transitional context can also be created by more knowledgeable peers or even by strangers who can be used as models for the child. One way or another, the transitional context assumes the presence of a person (or some other agent of socialization—a manual, a legend, a movie, a book, or a symbol) more competent than the child (e.g., Goodnow, 2001). The structure of the transitional context is such that it permits (a) the formulation of the child's developmental task (explicitly, by the child him- or herself—e.g., I want to become a soldier, or implicitly, by the surrounding adults—e.g., we need you to become a good fighter); (b) the creation of the motivational structure underlying the accomplishment of this developmental task (i.e., the establishment of the system of praises and punishments allowing the mastery of the skill); and (c) the delivery of the tools necessary for the mastery of the new competency (e.g., of fishnets for young fishermen or weapons for young soldiers).

Finally, it is important to know that competencies themselves do not have values attached to them; they are not "good" or "bad." A competent thief is as much a master of the competencies required for stealing something without being caught as a scoring soccer player is a master of the competencies required for success in a soccer game and an A-student is a master of competencies required in successful schooling. Although the contents of the activity of stealing, the activity of playing soccer, and the activity of succeeding at school are different, the model of acquiring them is generic.

In this chapter, we argue that the field of psychology collectively has put much emphasis on understanding competencies in children living in industrialized countries, with the central competency there being that of successful school adjustment. However, there is very little theory and research regarding acquisition of competencies by children who never experience the task of school adjustment as their developmental task simply because they do not go to school at all or go to school briefly and asystematically (with schooling a rather peripheral activity in their lives). Therefore, having presented the general model linking competencies and social adjustment at multiple levels, below we attempt to discuss examples of competencies whose acquisition appears to be important for the life of out-of-school children. In general, we will attempt to answer the following question: What are developmentally salient competencies that are expected to be acquired by children who grow up in environments where schooling does not play the central role and school adjustment is not the salient developmental task?

OTHER THAN SCHOOL AND PLAY

In this section of the chapter, we briefly review literature on children's competencies around the world as presented by researchers, social workers, and journalists. Here we are interested in competencies acquired outside of school and play settings. Specifically, we survey settings of (a) war and armed civil conflicts; (b) street childhood; and (c) large poor households.

All subsections of this part of the chapter will follow the same structure. First, we will present the known statistics on the number of children observed in the described settings. Second, we will offer several hypotheses on why children enter a setting and how they function in a given setting. Third, we will summarize what is known in the literature with regard to competencies children acquire in these settings and the transferability of these competencies to other competencies.

War and Armed Civil Conflicts and Children

Over the past two decades, war and armed civil conflicts have killed more than 6 million people worldwide. Lives of millions and millions of people have been affected by war. For example, the Congo's war has affected some 16 million people (*Economist*, December 9, 2000, p. 27). Most wars and armed civil conflicts devastate the countries in which they unfold. Wars jeopardize food supplies, damage agricultural infrastructure, and destroy crops and domestic animals. Of the 10 countries with the highest rates of infant and toddler death, 7 are affected by armed conflict.

Various world peace organizations have developed a number of provisions to influence parties involved in conflicts and urge them to find peaceful solutions to disputes (Machel, 2000). The international laws of war pay special attention to the involvement of children in the armed conflicts. Specifically, the norms of humanitarian law found in the 1977 Protocols I and II to the Geneva Conventions of 1949 forbid the use of children under the age of 15 as soldiers and urge states to give priority to the oldest children when recruiting children between the ages of 15 and 18. The United Nations Convention on the Rights of the Child contains similar language. A broad international accord of more than 80 countries prohibits the use of child soldiers in war and establishes 18 as the minimum age for sending soldiers into combat (Myers, 2000). However, practice shows that when there is a war, these regulations are usually disregarded.

In recent decades, the proportion of civilian war victims has leaped dramatically, from 5% to more than 90%. Of the 35 million refugees and displaced people in the world, 80% are women and children. Between 1990 and 2000, 2 million children were slaughtered, 6 million injured or permanently disabled, and 12 million left homeless because of conflict. Conflict has orphaned or separated more than 1 million children from their families in the last decade of the 20th century (UNICEF, 2002). Half of all Rwanda's children have witnessed a massacre (UNICEF, 1996). A study carried out in Mozambique during the war involved a survey of a large group of girls and boys and reported that, of those surveyed, 77% witnessed assassinations, usually in large numbers, 88% witnessed physical abuse and torture, 51% were physically abused or tortured, 63% witnessed kidnapping and sexual abuse, 64% were kidnapped from their families, 75% of the kidnapped children were forced to serve as couriers, and 28% of the kidnapped children (all boys) were trained for combat (Boothby, 1992). It is estimated that more than 500,000 children under age 18 are in armies and guerilla groups around the world, with 300,000 of them in actual combat (Crossette, 2001).

There is evidence documenting the involvement of children as soldiers in Afghanistan, Angola, Burma, Congo, El Salvador, Ethiopia, Guatemala, Israeli-occupied territories, Liberia, Mozambique, Sri Lanka, and Sudan (Cohn & Goodwin-Gill, 1994). The details of this evidence are both heartbreaking with regard to what difficult times children go through in these conflicts and astonishing with regard to competencies children acquire through these conflicts. For example, Uganda's National Resistance Army, which took power in January 1986 after the overthrow of President Obote, contained an estimated 3,000 children under 16, including 500 girls (Dodge & Raundalen, 1991). Data indicate that, at the end of the war in Mozambique, 27% (about 25,498) of the demobilized soldiers were at the time younger than 18 years of age; of these numbers, about 16,553 belonged to the governmental army, whereas 8,945 belonged to the National Mozambican Resistance (Máusse, 1999). According to the UNICEF estimates, the war in Liberia involved 6,000–8,000 children under age 15 as soldiers in various military groups. Since the involvement of the Taliban in the Afghanistan civil war in 1994, it has been estimated that at least 108,000 children were involved in fighting the Soviets in Afghanistan (ECPAT, 1999). There are an estimated 25,000 child soldiers in the armed forces in the Burma military (ICFTU, October 1996). And the list can go on, indicating that the presence of an armed conflict almost inevitably results in the recruitment of children as soldiers. Currently, more than 50 countries recruit child soldiers into the armed forces (Global March Against Child Labour, n.d.).

There are many reasons why children get engaged in armed conflicts. The generic description of these many reasons amounts to a reference to the ecologies (or developmental niches) of their lives. Such ecologies encompass children's religion, ideology, and indoctrination, and their social, community, and family values, as well as their peers' pressure. However, the majority of these reasons can be clustered into two large groups: involuntary and voluntary recruitment.

Involuntary recruitment is coercive and usually originates from a shortage of manpower and the need to raise and train new skilled soldiers to replace the dead ones. In a number of countries, however, involuntary recruitment into the military was used as a means of population control, that is, children were taken away from their families to control the size of a growing minority population (e.g., ethnic and religious conflicts in Sudan; Sudan Update, n.d.). There are many documented ways of coercive recruitment. Examples are threat to the child ("Under-age Killers," 1998, on the war in Sierra Leone), threat to the child's family or community ("Kalashnikov Kids," 1999, on child soldiers), even bribes to the child's family or community (e.g., Department of Foreign Affairs and International Trade, Canada, n.d.), or "simple" abduction ("Call Off the Dogs of War," 1999, on the war in Uganda; Human Rights Watch, n.d., on the civil conflicts in Peru). For example, between the late 1980s and 1992 some 12,500 Sudanese boys wandered across 2,000 kilometers of desert between Sudan, Ethiopia, and Kenya. It was suspected that they had been taken away from their families at a very young age by Sudanese rebel forces, the Sudanese People's Liberation Army, trying to ensure a future supply of fighters; the boys appeared to receive paramilitary training, although there was no documentation of it (Moumtzis, 1992).

However, many children join one of the two (or many) fighting sides voluntarily. The literature contains quite a number of qualitative descriptions of reasons leading children to join the armed forces. Here we will mention only selected reasons. First, several developing countries use a type of schooling modeled after militarized education, in which children are educated and disciplined in a style resembling that of the military (e.g., militarized education in Afghanistan; Center for Defense Information, 2001). Second, it has been documented that in societies in which physical and structural violence are ruling forces of everyday life, violent behavior is often rewarded and, therefore, children develop a "taste" for violence. For example, young fighters surveyed while in the army have reported that they joined the army because being a part of it gives them power and allows them to be "the strong one" or because they see themselves as fighting for a good cause (e.g., UNICEF, n.d.). Third, while living in war, joining military forces might be among the better of the not-so-good or bad choices. If children's homes are destroyed and their caregivers are killed, children who are left without any means of supporting themselves may join a fighting side as a means of survival (e.g., UNICEF, n.d.).

The great majority of a rather limited number of publications on the issue of children caught in armed and civil conflicts view children as victims of these conflicts. In general, these works concentrate on trying to find an answer to the question of whether war disrupts the emotional adaptation and social–emotional development of the victimized children, no matter what country the research took place in (e.g., Day & Sadek, 1982— Lebanese children; Dodge, 1986—Ugandan children; Macksoud & Aber, 1996—Lebanese children; Macksoud, Aber, & Cohn, 1996—Kuwaiti children; Mandour & Hourani, 1989—Palestinian children; Povrzanovic, 1997—Croatian and Bosnian children; Protacio-Marcelino, 1989— children of the Philippines; Punamäki, 1987—children of Israel and Palestine; Rousseau, Drapeau, & Platt, 1999—Cambodian children; Salman, ten Bensel, & Maruyama, 1993—Palestinian and Israeli-Arab children; Shirmer, 1986—children of Chile; Yule, 2000—Bosnian children; Ziv & Israel, 1973—Israeli children; Zvizdic & Butollo, 2001—children of Bosnia and Herzegovina). Invariably, the conclusion of these studies is that war is a direct causal factor of social–emotional maladjustment of children witnessing or participating in the conflict and the increase of war stress is related to the increase in psychopathology (e.g., Ager, 1996; Jensen, 1996; Wessells, 1998).

Two issues have to be mentioned here. One is that the primary focus of research on children engaged in war conflicts has been on psychological outcomes of armed conflicts, specifically, posttraumatic stress symptoms (e.g., Boehnlein, Kinzie, Rath, & Fleck, 1985; Hubbard, Realmuto, Northwood, & Masten, 1995; Kinzie, 1985; Nader, 1997; Weine, Becker, & McGlashan, 1995; Zivcic, 1993) or response to chronic stress (Stichick, 2001; Terr, 1991). The second issue is that, although 65 of the 79 countries that have been involved in armed conflicts since 1993 are in the developing world, only a handful of investigations consider the mental health of children drawn into armed conflicts in these countries (Stichick, 2001), indicating the field's lack of understanding of the psychology of children's passive and active participation in armed conflicts.

Needless to say, war endangers many aspects of child development. However, there is another, less-explored aspect of the children's involvement in armed conflicts. As stated by Garbarino and colleagues (Garbarino, Kostelny, & Dubrow, 1991), children growing up in dangerous environments such as those involving armed conflicts have to demonstrate remarkable psychological adjustment skills in coping with chronic violence. Such skills can be both adaptive and maladaptive and, correspondingly, may result in both positive and negative alterations in behavior and attitudes.

There is virtually nothing known about the competencies a child serving as a soldier should master simply to stay alive in such an adverse environment as the front line of a war. What are these competencies and how do children master them?

To our knowledge, there has been very little systematic research on the competencies of a child soldier. Roles and duties of children involved in armed conflicts have been reported to include running errands, carrying ammunition, acting as bodyguards, acting as spies, acting as informants, manning checkpoints, checking documents and packages, carrying out ambushes, fighting on the front lines, and serving as executioners of suspected enemies (Human Rights Watch, 1994).

In Uganda, child soldiers were described as disciplined, reliable, and trustworthy: They were assigned military tasks requiring high-level skills of handling weapons and maneuvering at the front lines and in enemy territory (Dodge & Raundalen, 1991). Interviews with Irish, Palestinian, and Israeli children involved in conflicts revealed "positive" aspects of children's participation in a state of war. It was reported by children that war gave child participants a mission in life, order, hierarchy, physical fitness, a sense of importance, of being essential to both a particular goal and an abstract idea, true friendship, and the sense of stability (Rosenblatt, 1983). Children of South Africa were not directly involved in military actions, but participated in a rather unusual "war" fought in the streets of many communities throughout the country. These children were soldiers as well as schoolchildren. They combined roles of football players, torturers, township *kwaito* dancers, killers, and demolition machines (Nina, 1999).

UNICEF reports on the involvement of children in military operations describe the following competencies mastered by "good soldiers": handling and caring for weapons, having minimal medical and hygiene skills in handling wounds and personal needs, reading and interpreting maps, navigating unknown terrains, assuming leadership roles at checkpoints, accepting and issuing orders, detecting enemies, cooking, and so on. On the top of these competencies crucial for the child's survival, there have been reports on psychological features of successful young soldiers. For example, a child soldier from Sudan reported that for a child to be a successful soldier, he or she needs to learn how to battle the feelings of helplessness and vulnerability, how to relate to personal experiences with the enemy to feel the desire for revenge, how to identify with the army, and how to not fear death (Santoro, 2000). Furthermore, as described above, particular "positive" feelings experienced by child soldiers, chiefly patriotism, self-pride, and unit-pride, have been shown to contribute to the prevention of posttraumatic stress disorder often experienced by children caught in an armed conflict (Armfield, 1994).

Some additional information can be drawn from related reports that have studied the impact of armed conflicts on children. For example, Rofe and Lewin (1982) showed that children living in Israeli towns that were shelled more frequently because of their proximity to the border experienced fewer sleep disturbances than children whose towns were shelled less frequently. The relevant hypothesis here is that a prolonged exposure to an adverse environment results in the development of an adaptive style that permits more-or-less adequate functioning even in high-stress situations. Extending this hypothesis further, living and growing up in environments with high levels of threat results in developing competencies that are essential for successful adjustment to this environment and are not required at all for living in a no-threat environment.

Again, virtually nothing is known about the ways children acquire competencies required of a soldier. Throughout reports of aid organizations and mass media, one can find multiple references to the militarized schooling environment of those schools from which the military or guerilla forces draw their recruits. However, given that the recruitment from these schools is relatively low in comparison to the overall number of children involved in armed crises, it is clear that most of the relevant competencies are mastered by these children on the spot without proper training. We assume that, similar to mastering any skill, adult and peer supervision plays a crucial role in mastering competencies of a warrior, but no published evidence supports this hypothesis.

Armed conflicts have orphaned or separated more than 1 million children from their families in the last decade of the 20th century. Approximately one third of these children ended up being a part of military formations, fighting shoulder-to-shoulder with adults. Much attention has been given to the detrimental impact of the war on the psychological development of these children. Significantly less attention has been given to wide ranges of competencies acquired by these children, their resourcefulness in developing themselves, mastering necessary activities, and adjusting to the harsh lives they live. Although the image of a child as a passive victim of armed conflict is well justified, we cannot underestimate the importance of understanding the active involvement of children in war and the mechanisms of their successful adjustment and survival in adverse conditions of armed conflicts. What is called a developmental success here refers to the child's ability to "detect" the components of the competency chain that provide him or her with tools for survival, acquire these competencies, and then, it is hoped, be able to transfer the acquired competencies to a new, after-war situation. This active role of a child is well expressed by Farid Dadashev, an 11-year-old boy from Azerbaijan, who said that if children are involved in the war they often can do nothing but learn how to fight; but if children need peace they must do something to make the peace happen (UNICEF, 2002).

Street Childhood

Large urban centers in developing countries have a rather special subpopulation that can be easily "registered" as living on the streets; the members of this subpopulation can be seen, primarily in downtowns, wearing shabby, dirty clothing, begging, performing menial chores, working, or just wandering apparently without a purpose. This subpopulation usually comprises children younger than 18. These children are often collectively referred to as *street children*.

The United Nations defines a street child as

> any boy or girl . . . for whom the street (in the widest sense of the word, including unoccupied dwellings, wasteland, and so on) has become his or her habitual abode and/or source of livelihood; and who is inadequately protected, supervised, or directed by responsible adults. (quoted in Lusk, 1992, p. 24)

Clearly, this definition refers collectively to heterogeneous groups of children including runaway, homeless, orphaned, and throwaway children and adolescents.

To understand this heterogeneous population, researchers have attempted to subdivide the collective entity of street children in several different ways. The broadest classification forms two groups: *children of the streets* (children who actively live on the street and do not have stable family ties) and *children in the streets* (children who live with their families and may attend school but spend all or part of their time on the streets, trying to make money for themselves or their families; Barker & Knaul, 1991; Campos et al., 1994). Other researchers have proposed other classifications, but these are usually closely related to the specific samples studied. For example, Felsman (1985) identified three different groups of street children in Calí, Colombia: (a) children who were orphaned or abandoned by their families; (b) children who apparently made an "active, willful departure from home" to live on the streets, and (c) those who "actively maintained family ties" (p. 4). In another classification, Martins (1996) classified street children in São José, Brazil, using dimensions of school attendance, occupation on the streets, and family ties.

The number of street youth worldwide is unknown, and the estimates range from several million to more than 100 million (UNICEF, 1989, 1993). Similar to the youth involved in armed conflicts, street youth have been largely excluded from the realm of developmental research. Children and adolescents living on streets can be found in virtually any country and any nation. However, there is a geographical variability in causes of their street childhood. Specifically, in India and most of Latin America, the major force leading children to the streets is poverty. More than half a billion children live on less than $1 U.S. a day. More than 100 million children are out of school because of poverty, discrimination, or lack of resources (UNICEF, 2002).

The existence of street children is an urban phenomenon, and this fact, on its own, requires attention of sociologists and psychologists. It is interesting to note that parentless and homeless children either get "incorporated" by rural communities or leave rural communities and go to urban centers. The reasons for the presence of the population of street children vary across different times and nations. In the developing world, there are three main reasons for the children ending up on the streets: poverty, armed conflicts, and diseases. In industrialized countries, the majority of youngsters found on city streets appear to be escaping dysfunctional family or peer relationships (e.g., Whitbeck & Hoyt, 1999).

Below we provide a selective capsule review of the literature on street children in Asia, Latin America, and Africa.

Asia

In India, many street children come from second- and third-generation migrant families of lower, socially disadvantaged castes. These families usually migrate to urban areas from rural areas affected by drought or flood, trying to find employment. In such families, children start working on the streets very young, working 8–12 hours a day (Rane & Shroff, 1994). It has been estimated that almost half of Indian street children do not have a roof over their heads and lack access to basic amenities (Rane & Shroff, 1994). Not all children live independently; quite a few children live on the streets with their families (Arimpoor, 1992; Verma & Dhingra, 1993).

Seventy percent of children working on the streets of India make approximately 10 rupees (21 cents) per day (Verma, 1999). Ten rupees in India will buy a low-quality loaf of bread. They are usually willing to do any kind of chores; the luckier children find jobs selling newspapers or lottery tickets, or working as teashop attendants or helpers in automobile repair shops (Mathur, 1993). If nothing is available, children beg, steal, peddle drugs, engage in prostitution, and scrounge from the garbage (Koushik & Bawikar, 1990; Varma & Jain, 1992). In addition to sparse work opportunities, children face other difficulties, such as difficulties with the police (who both exploit and abuse them), weather (many children move from Delhi to Bombay during winter, and from Bombay to Delhi during monsoons; Panicker & Nangia, 1992), and health problems (cholera, typhoid, gastroenteritis, amoebic dysentery, tetanus, tuberculosis, intestinal parasites, scabies, rickets, malnutrition, anemia, and night blindness).

To investigate Indian street children's daily experiences, Verma and colleagues (Verma, 1999; Verma & Dhingra, 1993) studied a sample of 100 children aged 11–18 years living in the city of Chandigarh, who were working on the streets as beggars, vendors, ragpickers, and in other occupations. The researchers collected data on daily experiences (what street children do) and time spent on daily activities (how street children spend their time). The researchers reported that the activities could be divided into three major groups: (a) household work; (b) income-earning activities; and (c) leisure-time activities.

The interviewed children reported child care, cleaning, cooking, washing, fetching water, and collecting wood or fuel, among other things, as household activities. Child care is often combined with other activities, so that an older street child (from about the age of 6 years!) is often seen with an infant or toddler while performing a street chore or begging. There is a large gender difference, with girls spending four times as much time on these activities compared with boys (Verma, 1999; Verma & Dhingra, 1993).

With regard to income-earning activities, children engage in a wide variety of marginal economic activities and their repertoires vary depending on the weather, season, and other factors. Children reported spending 8 to 10 hours on the streets every day at various points of day and night depending on the chore they are engaged with on a particular day. Often, to support each other and to protect their "borders," children will form a gang. Any violation of the gang rules invites violent collisions and social ostracism (Pande, 1992; Verma & Dhingra, 1993).

The following presents a true story of Ashok,[2] a boy from a Lucknow slum who works.

> At the age of 7, Ashok Kumar got his first "career break" while sneaking into a nearby clinic to watch television. An employee noticed the boy and offered him two choices: work or leave. Ashok has worked at the homeopathic clinic—6 days and 40 hours per week—ever since.
>
> For 2 years Ashok has been an assistant compounder. His job is to crush medicine and to roll it into little balls. Once in ball-form, he packs the medicine into glass vials. If a powder is required, Ashok measures the medicine into paper packets. He likes his boss, Dr. R. Diverma, and enjoys earning 100 rupees ($2.07) each month. After a year of training, the work is now easy and Ashok works without complaint. He acknowledges that each member of the Kumar household of 12 is expected to work outside of the home to fulfill his or her familial duty.
>
> Ashok's mother, Savitri, has been a part of the workforce for 21 years. She is a *sahika* (assistant) at the local Anganwadi Center, where she earns 250 rupees ($5.16) per month. Her duties include distributing morning porridge and conducting classes for preschool children. Recently, Savitri was involved in the movement to vaccinate the nation's children against polio. On a predesignated weekend, the government sent medical technicians into all of the Anganwadi Centers (among other places) and gave children mouth-drops containing the vaccine. Savitri proudly announces that she has helped India to become polio-free.
>
> The older siblings work as well, but it is Ram, Ashok's father, who earns most of the family income. Ram makes 800 rupees ($16.52) per month as a *rickshaw-wallah* (rickshaw-man); he pedals a bicycle attached to a carriage, and delivers customers to their desired destinations. The job is physically demanding, and Ram is exhausted at the end of each day. So it is the children and Savitri who do all the work in the household.

---

[2]The story was written down by Elisa Meier, a research assistant on one of the PACE Center projects in Lucknow, India. Included with permission.

Street children's leisure activities are interwoven with their chores. Typically, the leisure activities include chatting, playing games, roaming around, dancing, singing, watching television, listening to transistor radios, playing video games in market areas, and watching movies. Younger children often make their own toys and engage in role-playing by separating rags, fetching water, and cooking using tiny containers, thus imitating elder siblings and mothers.

There are no accurate and consistent estimates of the percentage of time children spend on any particular type of activity. What is known, however, is that street children in India have very little leisure time. The days are spent mostly in earning money or finding food and a place to sleep. Thus, from these accounts, the main factor that drives children out to the streets is poverty (Pande, 1992; Verma, 1999; Verma & Dhingra, 1993).

Latin America

It has been estimated that the number of street children in Brazil ranges from 7 million to 30 million (Barker & Knaul, 1991; Lusk, 1992; Sanders, 1987; UNICEF, 1989). There are different reasons that put children on the streets (Raffaelli, 1997), but, similar to the situation in Asia, most of them are underwritten by poverty. First, some children are sent to downtown streets by their families to find food, money, or clothes. Second, some children come to the streets on their own hoping to help their families and themselves; these children are not encouraged to go on the streets, but they have silent support from their families. Third, some children are thrown away by their parents, who cannot afford to support them. Finally, some children run away from their families (often driven away by frequent violence at home).

It is important to mention that the competencies of street children in Latin America are formally the most studied. There are multiple reasons for that. One, and probably the most important, is that prior to the AIDS epidemic in Africa (see below), Latin America had the largest number of street children in the world. In addition, many street preadolescents and teenagers engage in or develop their own "street business," selling such snack foods as roasted peanuts, popcorn, coconut milk, or corn on the cob. For example, in the Brazilian cities of Fortaleza and Salvador, 2.2% and 1.4%, respectively, of street vendors in 1980 were aged 14 or under, and 8.2% and 7.5%, respectively, were aged 15–19 (Cavalcanti & Duarte, 1980a, 1980b).

Another very important reason is that a number of researchers in Latin America, especially in Brazil, have developed interesting paradigms engaging street children in scientific research. One such paradigm of research is on street mathematics (e.g., Guberman, 1996; Nuñes, Schleimann, & Carraher, 1993). The Brazilian researchers (for a review, see Nuñes, Schleimann, & Carraher, 1993) referred to street mathematics as an example of informal math—mathematics practiced outside school. Their initial studies were based on the observation that street business boys and girls have to solve a large number of mathematical problems without applying any tools such as a pencil, paper, or a calculator. The review of the street operations revealed that these children and adolescents carry out operations of multiplication, addition, subtraction, and division. The researchers designed a series of parallel tasks, one set of which was administered to the young vendors in street settings, as if they were doing their everyday jobs, whereas a comparable set of tasks was administered to the same children in school-like settings, in which problems were formalized and presented in abstract terms. It turned out that young vendors demonstrated competent problem solving in street settings, but their performance dropped significantly in school-like settings.

This line of research on comparative performance in street (or some other "applied") settings versus school-like settings has been developed further through work with apprentices of farmers, carpenters, builders, and fisherman. Different mathematical operations have been considered (including operations with decimals and proportions), but the pattern of results remained the same: There is a discrepancy between applied (trade-related) and formalized (school-like) performance of children and adolescents with lack of formal education. Specifically, if presented with comparable tasks in different applied and school-like settings, they tend to do much better on tasks relevant to their everyday trades (for a review, see Nuñes, Schleimann, & Carraher, 1993).

This research has indicated that street mathematics has a great social significance in cultures that do not provide either formal training or official recognition to the mathematical abilities required for success in various trades. Moreover, this research has shown that street mathematics in particular and informal mathematics in general, often considered as "lesser mathematics," is a complex type of cognition (and, correspondingly, cognitive development) that can be referred to as "cognition in practice" (Lave, 1988). From this point of view, street mathematics is a type of cognitive operation that is embedded in a social situation and, therefore, constrained by cultural, social, empirical, and logical rules and a specific target (e.g., conducting measurement, determining change, calculating distance). In other words, becoming competent in street mathematics is as important a developmental task for a youngster engaged in a street trade as a mastery of abstract mathematical concepts and rules for a youngster attempting to become a successful school student. In terms of our model, the developmental pressures for a young street vendor and a school student are different, but the developmental tasks of adjusting to street life or school life are comparable: both require mastery of competence, street mathematics in the former and formal mathematics in the latter.

Africa

Although there are many more boys on the street than girls all over the world, in Kenya this imbalance is even more pronounced: 9 out of 10 street children in Kenya were reported to be male (Onyango, Suda, & Orwa, 1991). There are multiple hypotheses of why there are more boys on the streets than girls, with the underlying assumption of these differences being different socialization of boys and girls. It has been argued that boys are driven to the streets by their parents' expectation to be independent at a rather early age, specifically, by the age of 10–12 (Aptekar & Stocklin, 1996). On the contrary, the girl-like way of coping with poverty is by staying at home and helping with household chores; thus girls who come to the street either lose their homes or leave home because of abuse or family dysfunction. For example, it has been reported that 80% of street girls came from homes with only a single room (Undugu Society of Kenya, 1990–1991). It has been stated that, given the rather loose family structure frequently observed among lower-socioeconomic status Kenyans, it is common for a woman with children to have multiple partners sequentially, forming short-lasting, common-law unions. Thus, children can grow up with multiple sequential men in the household. Often housing is an issue, so the mother, her children, and the men in the household have to share one room. It has been reported that 80% of the street girls in Nairobi have been sexually abused (Onyango, Suda, & Orwa, 1991) and the major reason found for girls to leave home was because they could no longer sleep without the fear of being violated by a nonrelated man living in the house (Aptekar & Ciano-Federoff, 1999).

The epidemic of AIDS has been slowly changing this balance, with extended families being overwhelmed with the number of orphaned child relatives and unable to care for them anymore. The AIDS epidemic has now become the major factor in the phenomenon of street youth (Rutayuga, 1992). Eighty percent of children under the age of 15 living with HIV are children living in Africa. Many African children die of AIDS before the age of 5. In Botswana this figure is devastating, reaching 64%—thus, the majority of Botswana children born with AIDS die before the age of 5. Figures in other African nations range from 17–50%. In addition, more than 13 million children aged 14 or younger have been orphaned by AIDS, and 80% of these children live in Africa (UNICEF, 2002).

The AIDS crisis has overwhelmed the already weak African economies and has thrown millions and millions of children on the street (Guest, 2001). In 2001, 12 countries in sub-Saharan Africa contained 70% of the AIDS orphans; the three countries with the largest number of orphans were Nigeria, Ethiopia, and the Democratic Republic of Congo (UNICEF, 2002). All developmental agencies agree that today's prevalent rates of HIV infection will largely determine the pattern of orphaning for the next decade—in essence, the number of orphans will continue to rise. For example, according the estimates by an American aid organization (USAID), in the year 2010, the Eastern African country of Tanzania will have 4.2 million orphans.

However, similar to the situation with the research on children affected by the armed conflicts, existing psychosocial research on AIDS orphans has concentrated primarily on children from industrialized societies (e.g., Dansky, 1997; Geballe, Gruendel, & Andiman, 1995). The central themes of this research are children living with uncertainty about their future, dealing with the impact on family relationships, dealing with disclosure and grief, and finding adequate social support. Although all these themes are essential to understanding the impact of the AIDS epidemic on humanity, our literature search has not resulted in any publications on the development of adaptive competencies in orphans of AIDS. But these millions of children must adapt to survive and they do, so how do they do this?

Naturally, the most serious efforts in coping with the problem of AIDS orphans in Africa have to do with the issues of infection prevention and taking the children off the streets and bringing them into the more ordered and stable environments of orphanages and special schools. Thus, similar to the stories of successful young soldiers (i.e., those children who master the competencies related to being a soldier, survive armed conflict, and grow up to be a well-adjusted adult), the stories of "beating the fate" by orphan children in Africa and growing up into a well-adjusted adult are not told and, therefore, not heard.

The brief overviews of the literature generated on the three different continents are strikingly similar. The similarity lies in the devastating nature of the situations in which street children grow up, the "roughness" of the world in which they live, and in the remarkable resourcefulness, adaptive skills, and creativity they demonstrate to survive. Researchers (Aptekar & Ciano-Federoff, 1999; Lucchini, 1996; Muraya, 1993; Suda, 1994; Tyler, Tyler, Tommasello, & Connolly, 1992) indicate that street children master the skill of approaching people and relating to them (reading a customer and trying to figure out what, if anything, can be sold to him or her); negotiation; stress management; personal safety; dealing with and protecting themselves from abuse and aggression; finding ways of making money; finding ways of sending some money back to their families; finding and benefiting from social services; finding ways to meet their medical needs; maneuvering the legal system (e.g., giving the officers different names at each arrest and obtaining lighter sentences as first offenders); navigating large geographic areas (buying things at cheaper prices and selling them at higher prices); making deals with restaurants and food stores to get leftovers; finding safe sleeping arrangements; detecting danger "in the air"; finding places to meet personal hygiene needs (e.g., to shower); trying on different social roles (figuring out what works and what does not while trying to find work or beg); and staying away from or negotiating relationships with drug dealers, pimps, and police. All these and many other skills are needed for survival on the streets and developing a way to deal with life.

Clearly, even from the brief descriptions presented above, it is obvious that the most important developmental task faced by street children is the urgency and immediacy of daily survival, and that these kids show intelligence and a wide range of competencies in adapting to their immediate environments (Tyler, Tyler, Tomasello, & Connolly, 1992) and trying to figure out their place in society and use it to their advantage (Aptekar & Ciano-Federoff, 1999; Lucchini, 1996; Muraya, 1993; Suda, 1994). As indicated in our model above, and in concordance with Kagitçibasi (1996), we stress the importance of mastering skills up to the degree of competence by these children. Arguably, what matters most developmentally is creating the model of how to negotiate any novel situation and determine skills that need to be mastered for competent behavior in the situation; when the task is clear and the child knows what to do, he or she can, mostly likely, master the needed skill. Kagitçibasi (1996) refers to these skills of negotiating new situations as *generalizable* competencies, arguing that they are much more important and transfer much further than task-specific competencies. Having mastered generalizable competencies, a street child (or any child) can, most likely, master task-specific competencies. It is the reverse movement that is much more difficult to make.

Child Labor

Traditionally, the UNICEF annual reports on the state of the world's children contain citations from girls and boys around the world collected, translated, and compiled by UNICEF-affiliated adults around the world. Here are a few selected quotes from the 2002 report (p. 72) with which we would like to start this section of the chapter.

> *"How can I continue education without having enough to eat?"*
>
> Zewdi, 14, Eritrea
>
> *". . . child labor is more profitable in the eyes of their parents, because they will be making money for the family instead of studying. Studying would be an investment for families, which would not be affordable in many cases."*
>
> Deepti, 17, India
>
> *"Even if I could enroll in standard one for free, there would be no money for supplies."*
>
> Piana, 13, Lesotho
>
> *"I live in roofless and damaged former government building with my 14-year-old sister, and my three children—one son and two girls (twins). The oldest is my 4-year old son and the twins are one-and-a-half years old. When I go begging, I take my children with me. My sister goes begging. We eat together what we get."*
>
> Refugee girl, 16, Somalia

It has been estimated that 90% of domestic workers, the largest group of child workers in the world, are girls between the ages of 12 and 17 (UNICEF, 2002). The overwhelming majority of these girls are born into large poor families in developing countries. These girls are often sent away from their families to richer households where they work as housemaids for room and board. Children also work to pay off the debts of their parents (or other rela-tives). However, often getting out of debt is difficult and the children might be sold on. This very shaky arrangement of working for food or for debt can turn into commercial slavery. For example, children from multibirth families of poor African countries Mali and Benin have been reported to be "bor-rowed," "lent," "sent away for better life," or simply kidnapped and trans-ported to the somewhat richer country of Côte d'Ivoire to work unpaid on farms or plantations, beaten if they try to run away, or forced into prostitu-tion or drug-pushing ("Slave Ships in the 21st Century?" 2001).

Needless to say there are no accurate figures indicating exactly how many children live lives of slavery or near-slavery. The International Labour Organization estimates that 250 million children between the ages of 5 and 14 work as slaves, mainly in Asia and Africa. In this section of the chapter, we will review the rather scarce literature on developmental circumstance and competencies of child domestic workers.

In general, the literature on children as domestic workers stresses several points of interest. First, the main focus of the majority of the surveyed studies is the physical rather than psychological outcome of child labor (Caesar-Leo, 1999; Wooley & Fisher, 1915). Second, there is an apparent lack of theorization with regard to the place and meaning of child labor, especially domestic labor, as one of the factors of child development (Goodnow, 1988; Hobbs & Cornwell, 1986). Third, the parents send their children away to other people's houses for pay because they see immediate financial relief for themselves and a better long-term outcome for the child (stating a very low or no return to the family or the child for sending the child to school; Aderinto & Okunola, 1998; Buchmann, 2000; Wilson-Oyerlaran, 1989). Fourth, there is much support for domestic child labor among both the parents and the "employers": both sides argue that this type of early experience better pre-pares the child for future life, gives the child more independence, provides them with a taste of urbanization, and allows him or her to have some sav-ings (e.g., Agarwal et al., 1997; Drenovsky, 1992; Khan & Lynch, 1997). Fifth, it appears that in the nonindustrialized world, preventing children from working is likely to make their lives more difficult and their problems worse unless the societies and local communities are able to substitute sources of income and welfare (Mehta, Prabhu, & Mistry, 1985).

In sum, it appears that child labor for pay is yet another understudied domain of child development. Obviously, the importance of this domain in nonindustrialized countries is much greater than in the developed world. Also apparent is the fact that, given the economic situation of the develop-ing world, the issue of child labor will not dissolve in the near future—quite the contrary. The ratio of the speed of the natural growth of the population in the developing world versus the availability of food to support this popula-tion suggests that there are going to be even more children forced to live in other people's homes and work for room and board or work for pay than there are now. And, to get fed or to get paid, these children need to acquire competencies that are required at the job. The questions are how they do this, whether the skill of acquiring competencies is transferable from one domain to another, and whether success at the child's job predicts the overall adjustment later in life.

CONCLUSION

The majority of the research on human competence has been carried out in the industrialized world, with the major criterion of life success being that of successful schooling, job placement, and job performance. In nonindustrialized countries (i.e., the majority of the world), however, successful life adjustment often has little, if anything, to do with academic and career success. Consequently, the content of competencies acquired by children in the developing world has to do with what constitutes successful life adjustment in their cultures. In this chapter we attempted to highlight some of these competencies and stress the importance of studying and understanding them. The main point we wanted to make is that the developmental context of acquired competencies is extremely important, and that the competence of a child soldier in Africa to handle a rifle might be developmentally comparable to the academic competence of a child in England. The ultimate life adjustment outcome is determined by a transformational chain of competencies in which the functional meaning of a given competence in a given culture is much more important and developmentally predictive than absolute content of a given competence.

Do we imply, then, that the values attached to traditional competencies related to schooling, job placement, and career success considered to be "key" in industrialized societies and central to the function of many social institutions (e.g., families, child-care centers, schools, and labor institutions) are nontransferable to the developing world? Not at all. Quite the contrary, what we want to do is join with Kagitçibasi (2002) in stressing the importance of advocacy for early enriched child care and schooling—the social inventions designed to develop competencies valued by industrialized societies. We do, however, want to make a cautionary remark: From our point of view, such social inventions will work only if developmental pressure in the societies in which they are established is *for* rather than *against* the manifestations of competencies developed by these institutions. For example, we recognize that many families in developing countries expect their children to work, whether domestically or for pay, often instead of attending school, so that they can contribute to the well-being of the family. Therefore, educational progress can only be accomplished if the value of schooling can become universal, and this can happen only when the developmental pressure imposed on children by their societies is such that academic competencies are commonly appreciated and accepted. From what the statistics at the beginning of this chapter show, many children in the developing world are not pressured to succeed academically—they are pressured to survive. Thus, it is the positive functional nature of their survival competencies, whether it is handling a rifle, running a street business, or being a servant, that we need to study and understand.

REFERENCES

Aderinto, A. A., & Okunola, R. A. (1998). Push, pull, and sustaining factors of child labour in Nigeria. *Ife Psychologia: An International Journal, 6,* 173–184.

Agarwal, S., Attah, M., Apt, N., Grieco, M., Kwakye, E. A., and Turner, J. (1997). Bearing the weight: The kayayoo, Ghana's working girl child. *International Social Work, 40,* 245–263.

Ager, A. (1996). Children, war, and psychological intervention. In S. C. Carr & J. F. Schumaker (Eds.), *Psychology and the developing world* (pp. 162–173). Westport, CT: Praeger.

Aptekar, L., & Ciano-Federoff, L. M. (1999). Street children in Nairobi: Gender differences in mental health. In M. Raffaelli & R. W. Larson (Eds.), *Homeless and working youth around the world: Exploring developmental issues* (pp. 35–46). San Francisco, CA: Jossey-Bass.

Aptekar, L., & Stocklin, D. (1996). Growing up in particularly difficult circumstances: A cross-cultural perspective. In J. Berry, P. R. Dasen, & T. S. Saraswathi (Eds.), *Handbook of cross-cultural psychology: Vol. 2. Basic processes and development psychology* (2nd ed., pp. 377–412). Boston: Allyn & Bacon.

Arimpoor, J. (1992). *Street children of Madras: A situational analysis.* Noida, India: Child Labour Cell, National Labour.

Armfield, F. (1994). Preventing post-traumatic stress disorder resulting from military operations. *Military Medicine, 159*(12), 739–746.

Barker, G., & Knaul, F. (1991). *Exploited entrepreneurs: Street and working children in developing countries.* New York: Childhope USA.

Boehnlein, J. K., Kinzie, J. D., Rath, B., & Fleck, J. (1985). One-year follow-up study of posttraumatic stress disorder among survivors of Cambodian concentration camps. *American Journal of Psychiatry, 142*(8) 956–960.

Boothby, N. (1992). Displaced children: Psychological theory and practice from the field. *Journal of Refugee Studies, 5,* 106–122.

Buchmann, C. (2000). Family structure, parental perceptions, and child labor in Kenya: What factors determine who is enrolled in school? *Social Forces, 78,* 1349–1379.

Bureau of the Census. (1999). *World population at a glance: 1998 and beyond.* U.S. Department of Commerce. (International Brief 98-4. REPRINTS Bureau)

Caesar-Leo, M. (1999). Child labour: The most visible type of child abuse and neglect in India. *Child Abuse Review, 8,* 75–86.

Call off the dogs of war. (1999, December 11). *The Economist*.

Campos, R., Antunes, C. M., Raffaelli, M., Halsey, N., Ude, W., Greco, M., et al. (1994). Social networks and daily activities of street youth in Belo Horizonte, Brazil. *Child Development, 65*, 319–333.

Cavalcanti, C., & Duarte, R. (1980a). *A procura de espaço na economia urbana: O setor informal de Fortaleza* [The search for space in the urban economy: The informal sector of Cortaleza]. Recife: Sudan.

Cavalcanti, C., & Duarte, R. (1980b). *O setor informal de Salvador: Dimensões, natureza, significação* [The informal sector of Salvador: Dimensions, nature, meaning]. Recife: Sudan.

Center for Defense Information. (2001, October 15). *Children on the front line. Child soldiers in Afghanistan*. Retrieved September 14, 2002 from http://www.cdi.org/terrorism/childsoldiers.cfm

Cicchetti, D. (1984). The emergence of developmental psychopathology. *Child Development, 55*, 1–7.

Cicchetti, D., & Cohen, D. (1995). Perspectives on developmental psychopathology. In D. Cicchetti & D. Cohen (Eds.), *Handbook of developmental psychopathology theory and methods* (Vol. 1, pp. 3–22). New York: Wiley.

Cicchetti, D., & Toth, S. (1995). Developmental psychopathology and disorders of affect. In D. Cicchetti & D. Cohen (Eds.), *Developmental psychopathology: Vol. 2. Risk, disorder, and adaptation* (pp. 369–420). New York: Wiley.

Cohn, I., & Goodwin-Gill, G. S. (1994). *Child soldiers: The role of children in armed conflict*. Oxford, England: Clarendon Press.

Crossette, B. (2001, June 14). Wars enlist young legions, report says. *The New York Times*, p. A14.

Dansky, S. (1997). *Nobody's children: Orphans of the HIV epidemic*. New York: Haworth Press.

Day, R. C., & Sadek, S. (1982). The effect of Benson's relaxation response on the anxiety levels of Lebanese children under stress. *Journal of Experimental Child Psychology, 34*, 350–356.

Denham, S. A., & Holt, R. W. (1993). Preschoolers' likeability as cause or consequence of their social behavior. *Developmental Psychology, 29*, 271–275.

Department of Foreign Affairs and International Trade, Canada. (n.d.). *Child Soldiers*. Retrieved September, 2002, from http://www.dfait-maeci.gc.ca/cfp-pec/NationalForum/elementary/childSoldiers-en.asp#q3

Dodge, C. P. (1986). Child soldiers in Uganda: What does the future hold? *Cultural Survival Quarterly, 10*, 31–33.

Dodge, C. P., & Raundalen, M. (1991). *Reaching children in war: Sudan, Uganda, and Mozambique*. Soreidgrend, Norway: Sigma Forlut.

Dodge, K. A., & Murphy, R. R. (1984). The assessment of social competence in adolescents. *Advances in Child Behavioral Analysis & Therapy, 3*, 61–96.

Drenovsky, C. K. (1992). Children's labor force participation in the world system. *Journal of Comparative Family Studies, 23*, 183–195.

Easterbrooks, M. A., & Goldberg, W. A. (1990). Security of toddler–parent attachment: Relation to children's sociopersonality functioning during kindergarten. In M. T. Greenberg, D. Cicchetti, & E. M. Cummings (Eds.), *Attachment in the preschool years* (pp. 221–244). Chicago: University of Chicago Press.

ECPAT International Newsletters. (1999). *A step forward: The third report on the implementation of the agenda for action adopted at the world congress against commercial sexual exploitation of children.* Issue 29, 28 August 1996. Bangkok, Thailand: ECPAT.

Erickson, M. F., Sroufe, L. A., & Egeland, B. (1985). The relationship between quality of attachment and behavior problems in preschool in a high-risk sample. In I. Bretherton & E. Waters (Eds.), *Monographs of the Society for Research in Child Development*, 50(1/2, Serial No. 209), 147–166.

Felsman, J. K. (1985). *Abandoned children reconsidered: Prevention, social policy, and the trouble in families.* ERIC Document Reproduction Service No. ED268457.

Garbarino, J., Kostelny, K., & Dubrow, N. (1991). *No place to be a child.* San Francisco: Jossey-Bass.

Geballe, S., Gruendel, J., & Andiman, W. (1995). *Forgotten children of the AIDS epidemic.* New Haven, CT: Yale University Press.

Global March Against Child Labour. (n.d.). *Worldwide report on child soldiers.* Retrieved September 2002, from http://www.globalmarch.org/worstformsreport/world/childsoldiers.html

Goodnow, J. J. (1988). Children's household work: Its nature and functions. *Psychological Bulletin, 103,* 5–26.

Goodnow, J. J. (2001). Directions of change: Sociocultural approaches to cognitive development. *Human Development, 44,* 160–165.

Guberman, S. R. (1996). The development of everyday mathematics in Brazilian children with limited formal education. *Child Development, 67,* 1609–1623.

Guest, E. (2001). *Children of AIDS: Africa's orphan crisis.* London: Pluto Press.

Havighurst, R. J. (1972). *Human development and education* (3rd ed.). New York: McKay.

Hobbs, S., & Cornwell, D. (1986). Child labour: An underdeveloped topic in psychology. *International Journal of Psychology, 21,* 225–234.

Hubbard, J., Realmuto, G. M., Northwood, A. K., & Masten, A. S. (1995). Comorbidity of psychiatric diagnoses with posttraumatic stress disorder in survivors of childhood trauma. *Journal of the American Academy of Child and Adolescent Psychiatry, 34,* 1167–1173.

Human Rights Watch. (n.d.). *On the civil conflicts in Peru.* Retrieved September 2002 from http://www.hrw.org/americas/peru.php

Human Rights Watch/Africa and Human Rights Watch Children's Rights Project. (1994). *Easy prey: Child soldiers in Liberia.* New York: Human Rights Watch.

In the heart of darkness. (2000, December 9). *The Economist,* 27–29.

International Conference of Free Trade Unions. (1996, October). *Free labour world.* Brussels, Belgium: Author.

Jensen, J. P. (1996). War-affected societies and war-affected children: What are the long-term consequences? *Childhood: A Global Journal of Child Research, 3*, 415–421.

Kagitçibasi, C. (1996). *Family and human development across cultures*. Mahwah, NJ: Erlbaum.

Kagitçibasi, C. (2002). Psychology and human competence development. *Applied Psychology, 51*, 5–22.

Kalashnikov kids. (1999, July 10). *The Economist*.

Keenan, K., & Shaw, D. (1997). Developmental and social influences on young girls' early problem behavior. *Psychological Bulletin, 121*, 95–113.

Khan, N. Z., & Lynch, M. A. (1997). Recognizing child maltreatment in Bangladesh. *Child Abuse & Neglect, 21*, 815–818.

Kinzie, J. D. (1985). Cultural aspects of psychiatric treatment with Indochinese refugees. *American Journal of Social Psychiatry, 5*(1), 47–53.

Koushik, S. S., & Bawikar, R. (1990). *Street children of Pune City: A status report, 1990*. Pune, India: Karve Institute of Social Service.

Ladd, C. O., Huot, R. L., Thrivikraman, K. V., & Plotsky, P. M. (1999). Reversal of the maternal separation phenotype by reboxetine. *Society for Neuroscience Abstracts, 2*, 1456.

Lave, J. (1988). *Cognition in practice: Mind, mathematics and culture in everyday life*. Cambridge, England: Cambridge University Press.

Lucchini, R. (1996). The street and its image. *Childhood: A Global Journal of Child Research, 3*, 235–246.

Lusk, M. (1992). Street children of Rio de Janeiro. *International Social Work, 35*, 293–305.

Machel, G. (2000, September). *The impact of armed conflict on children: A critique review of progress made and obstacles encountered in increasing protection for war-affected children*. Paper presented at the International Conference on War-Affected Children, Winnipeg, Canada.

Macksoud, M. S., & Aber, J. L. (1996). The war experiences and psychosocial development in children in Lebanon. *Child Development, 67*, 70–88.

Macksoud, M. S., Aber, J. L., & Cohn, I. (1996). Assessing the impact of war on children. In R. J. Apfel & B. Simon (Eds.), *Minefields in their hearts: The mental health of children in wars and communal violence* (pp. 218–230). New Haven, CT: Yale University Press.

Mandour, M., & Hourani, I. (1989). Effects of the uprising on the psychological development of Palestinian children in the occupied territories. *Arab Journal of Psychiatry, 1*, 7–11.

Martins, R. A. (1996). Censo de crianças e adolescentes em situação de rua em São José do Rio Preto [A census of street children and adolescents in São José do Rio Preto]. *Psicologia Reflexão e Crítica, 9*, 101–122.

Masten, A. S. (1999a). Resilience comes of age: Reflections on the past and outlook for the next generation of research. In M. D. Glantz & J. L. Johnson (Eds.),

Resilience and development: Positive life adaptations (pp. 281–296). New York: Kluwer Academic/Plenum Publishers.

Masten, A. S. (1999b). Commentary: The promise and perils of resilience research as a guide to preventive interventions. In M. D. Glantz & J. L. Johnson (Eds.), *Resilience and development: Positive life adaptations* (pp. 251–257). New York: Kluwer Academic/Plenum Publishers

Masten A. S., & Coatsworth, D. J. (1995). Competence, resilience, and psychopathology. In D. Cicchetti & D. Cohen (Eds.), *Developmental psychopathology: Vol. 2. Risk, disorder, and adaptation* (pp. 715–752). New York: Wiley.

Masten, A. S., & Coatsworth, D. J. (1998). The development of competence in favorable and unfavorable environments. *American Psychologist, 53,* 205–220.

Masten, A. S., & Curtis, W. J. (2000). Integrating competence and psychopathology: Pathways toward a comprehensive science of adaptation in development. *Development and Psychopathology, 12,* 529–550.

Mathur, M. (1993). Mapping socioeconomic realities of street children in Jaipur, India. In K. Ekberg & P. E. Mjaavatn (Eds.), *Children at risk: Selected papers.* Trondheim, Norway: University of Trondheim.

Máusse, M. A. (1999). *The social reintegration of the child involved in armed conflict in Mozambique.* Pretoria, South Africa: Institute for Security Studies.

Mehta, M. N., Prabhu, S. V., & Mistry, H. N. (1985). Child labor in Bombay. *Child Abuse & Neglect, 9,* 107–111.

Moumtzis, P. (1992, July). Children of war. *Refugees (UNHCR Quarterly Report),* 30–32.

Muraya, J. (1993). *Street children: A study of street children in Nairobi, Kenya.* Swansea, Wales: Center for Development Studies, University College of Swansea.

Myers, S. L. (2000, January 22). Agreement bars using children as soldiers. *The New York Times,* p. A8.

Nader, K. (1997). Treating traumatic grief in systems. In C. R. Figley, B. E. Bride, & N. Mazza (Eds.), *Death and trauma: The traumatology of grieving* (pp. 159–192). London: Taylor & Francis.

Nina, D. (1999). *Children involved in South Africa's wars: After Soweto 1976.* Pretoria, South Africa: Institute for Security Studies.

No swots, please, we're Masai. (2002, March 23). *The Economist.*

Nuñes, T., Schleimann, A. D., & Carraher, D. W. (1993). *Street mathematics and school mathematics.* New York: Cambridge University Press.

Onyango, P., Suda, C., & Orwa, K. (1991). *A report on the Nairobi case study on children in especially difficult circumstances.* Florence, Italy: UNICEF.

Pande, R. (1992). *Street children of Kanpur.* Noida, India: Child Labour Cell, National Labour.

Panicker, R., & Nangia, P. (1992). *Working and street children of Delhi.* New Delhi, India: National Labour Institute.

Parker, J. G., Rubin, K. H., Price, J. M., & DeRosier, M. E. (1995). *Peer relationships, child development, and adjustment: A developmental psychopathology perspective.* In

D. Cicchetti & D. J. Cohen (Eds.), *Developmental psychopathology: Vol. 2. Risk, disorder, and adaptation* (pp. 96–161). New York: Wiley.

Povrzanovic, M. (1997). Children, war, and trauma: Croatia 1991–1994. *Childhood: A Global Journal of Child Research, 4*, 81–102.

Protacio-Marcelino, E. (1989). Children of political detainees in the Philippines: Sources of stress and coping patterns. *International Journal of Mental Health, 18*, 71–86.

Punamäki, R. L. (1982). Childhood in the shadow of war: A psychological study on attitudes and emotional life of Israeli and Palestinian. *Current Research on Peace and Violence, 5*, 26–41.

Raffaelli, M. (1997). The family situation of street youth in Latin America: A cross-national review. *International Social Work, 40*(1), 89–100.

Rane, A. J., & Schroff, N. (1994). Street children in India: Emerging need for social work intervention. In A. J. Rane (Ed.), *Street children*. Bombay, India: Tata Institute of Social Sciences.

Rofe, Y., & Lewin, I. (1982). The effect of war environment on dreams and dream habits. In N. A. Milgram (Ed.), *Stress and anxiety* (Vol. 8, pp. 67–79). Washington, DC: Hemisphere.

Rosenblatt, R. (1983). *Children of war*. New York: Anchor Press.

Rousseau, C., Drapeau, A., & Platt, R. (1999). Family trauma and its association with emotional and behavioral problems and social adjustment in adolescent Cambodian refugees. *Child Abuse & Neglect, 23*, 1263–1273.

Rubin, K. H., Bukowski, W., & Parker, J. G. (1998). Peer interactions, relationships, and groups. In W. Damon (Series Ed.) & N. Eisenberg (Vol. Ed.), *Handbook of child psychology: Vol. 3. Social, emotional, and personality development* (5th ed., pp. 619–700). New York: Wiley.

Rutayuga, J. B. (1992). Assistance to AIDS orphans within the family/kinship system and local institutions. *AIDS Education and Prevention, 4*(Suppl.), 57–68.

Salman, E., ten Bensel, R., & Maruyama, G. M. (1993). Children at risk: Psychological coping with war and conflict in the Middle East. *International Journal of Mental Health, 22*, 33–52.

Sameroff, A. J., & Haith, M. (Eds.). (1996). *The five to seven year shift: The age of reason and responsibility*. Chicago: University of Chicago Press.

Sanders, T. (1987). *Brazilian street children: Who they are* (United Field Service International Report No. 17: Latin America). Indianapolis, IN: United Field Service.

Santoro, L. (2000, July 31). The sons of carnage. *Newsweek*.

Shirmer, J. (1986). Chile: The loss of childhood. *Cultural Survival Quarterly, 19*, 40–42.

Slave-ships in the 21st century? (2001, April 19). *The Economist*.

Sroufe, L. A. (1979). The ontogenesis of emotions. In J. Osofsky (Ed.), *Handbook of infant development* (pp. 462–516). New York: Wiley.

Sroufe, L. A., & Rutter, M. (1984). The domain of developmental psychopathology. *Child Development, 55*(1), 17–29.

Stichick, T. (2001). The psychosocial impact of armed conflict on children: Rethinking traditional paradigms in research and intervention. *Cultural and societal influences in child and adolescent psychiatry, 10*, 797–814.

Suda, C. (1994). *Report of a baseline survey on street children in Nairobi.* Nairobi, Kenya: Institute of African Studies, University of Nairobi.

Sudan Update. (n.d.). Untitled report on religious and ethnic conflicts in Sudan. Retrieved September 2002 from http://www.sudanupdate.org/REPORTS/mrgintro.html

Terr, L. (1991). Childhood traumas: An outline and overview. *American Journal of Psychiatry, 148*, 10–20.

Tyler, F., Tyler, S., Tommasello, A., & Connolly, M. (1992). Huckleberry Finn and street youth everywhere: An approach to primary preventions. In G. Albee, L. Bond, & T. Monsey (Eds.), *Improving children's lives: Global perspective on prevention* (pp. 200–212). Thousand Oaks, CA: Sage.

Under-age killers. (1998, December 12). *The Economist.*

Undugu Society of Kenya. (1990–1991). *Experiences in community development.* Nairobi, Kenya: Undugu Society of Kenya.

UNICEF. (n.d.). *Children as soldiers.* Retrieved September 2002 from http://www.unicef.org/sowc96/2csoldrs.htm

UNICEF. (1989). *Annual report.* New York: United Nations.

UNICEF. (1993). *Annual report.* New York: United Nations.

UNICEF. (1996). *Annual report.* New York: United Nations.

UNICEF. (2002). *Annual report.* New York: United Nations.

Varma, A. P., & Jain, M. (1992). *Situation of working children in Uttar Pradesh.* Noida, India: Child Labour Cell, National Labour.

Verma, S. (1999). Socialization for survival: Developmental issues among working street children in India. In M. Raffaelli & R. W. Larson (Eds.), *Homeless and working youth around the world: Exploring developmental issues* (pp. 5–18). San Francisco: Jossey-Bass.

Verma, S., & Dhingra, G. (1993). Who do they belong to? A profile of street children in Chandigarh. *People's Action, 81*, 22–25.

Waters, E., & Sroufe, L. A. (1983). Social competence as a developmental construct. *Developmental Review, 3*, 79–97.

Webster's New Universal Unabridged Dictionary. (1996). New York: Random House.

Weine, S. M., Becker, D. F., & McGlashan, T. H. (1995). Psychiatric consequences of "ethnic cleansing:" Clinical assessments and trauma testimonies of newly resettled Bosnian refugees. *American Journal of Psychiatry, 152*, 536.

Wessells, M. G. (1998). The changing nature of armed conflict and its implications for children: The Grace Machel/U.N. study. *Peace and Conflict: Journal of Peace Psychology, 4*, 321–334.

Whitbeck, L. B., & Hoyt, D. R. (1999). *Nowhere to grow: Homeless and runaway adolescents and their families*. New York: Aldine de Gruyter.

White, R. W. (1959). Motivation reconsidered: The concept of competence. *Psychological Review, 66*, 297–333.

Wilson-Oyerlaran, E. B. (1989). The ecological model and the study of child abuse in Nigeria. *Child Abuse & Neglect, 13*, 379–387.

Wooley, H. T., & Fisher, C. R. (1915). Mental and physical measurements of working children. *Psychological Monographs, 18*, 1–247.

Yule, W. (2000). From program to "ethnic cleansing": Meeting the needs of war-affected children. *Journal of Child Psychology and Psychiatry and Allied Disciplines, 41*, 695–702.

Ziv, A., & Israel, R. (1973). Effects of bombardment on the manifest anxiety level of children living in kibbutzim. *Journal of Consulting and Clinical Psychology, 40*, 287–291.

Zivcic, I. (1993). Emotional reactions of children to war stress in Croatia. *Journal of the American Academy of Child and Adolescent Psychiatry, 32*, 709–713.

Zvizdic, S., & Butollo, W. (2001). War-related loss of one's father and persistent depressive reactions in early adolescents. *European Psychologist, 6*, 204–214.

3

CULTURAL COMPETENCE—TACIT, YET FUNDAMENTAL: SELF, SOCIAL RELATIONS, AND COGNITION IN THE UNITED STATES AND JAPAN

SHINOBU KITAYAMA AND SEAN DUFFY

There are many cultural competences. Some are very explicit and obvious: For example, using chopsticks is a special skill quite well suited for some cuisines but not for others. Less obviously, there also exist myriad other competences, both social and nonsocial, that are highly tacit (Polyani, 1957). People rarely recognize these competences—in fact, it is not until a surge of careful cross-cultural experimental studies on self, social relations, and cognition in the past decade (e.g., Fiske, Kitayama, Markus, & Nisbett, 1998; Heine, Lehman, Markus, & Kitayama, 1999; Markus & Kitayama, 1991; Nisbett, Peng, Choi, & Norenzayan, 2001) that this point was brought to the attention of many researchers in psychology, anthropology, and other related disciplines (see Gay & Cole, 1967; Rivers, 1901; Titchener, 1916; Witkin, 1967, for earlier work on the issue). Whereas explicit practices, customs, and imperatives of culture can be intentionally followed, imitated, and sometimes resisted, implicit skills, abilities, and competences are much more difficult to identify, let alone to modify or improve. Yet, they are fundamental prerequisites for successfully engaging in and effectively carrying out culturally sanctioned modes of being human, relating to others, and perceiving and thinking about the social and nonsocial worlds. In the present chapter, our primary focus is on these tacit competences for cultural adaptation.

In examining tacit cultural competences, we draw on the cultural psychological literature. Cultural psychology is an interdisciplinary study of the ways in which cultural practices and meanings and psychological processes and structures relate to each other (Bruner, 1990; Cole, 1996; Fiske et al., 1998; Shore, 1996; Shweder, 1991). As argued by some theorists in anthropology (Boyd & Richardson, 1985; Durham, 1991), economics (Aoki, 2001), and psychology (Kitayama & Markus, 1999), culture and the psyche are likely to coevolve to form a mutually reinforcing state of equilibrium. Relatively recent research in this and adjacent topics has covered many domains, ranging from in-depth ethnographic descriptions of sociocultural activities of daily life (Cole, 1996), experimental studies on self (Markus & Kitayama, 1991), emotion (Kitayama, Karasawa, & Mesquita, in press), and cognition (Nisbett et al., 2001), to systemic analyses of coevolutionary processes (Aoki, 2001; Boyd & Richardson, 1985; Durham, 1991). Altogether, these studies have demonstrated the mutual constitutive relationship between culture and psychological processes. Thus, culture is best understood as being constantly motivated, directed, and co-opted by the collective functioning of individual psychological processes; at the same time, psychological processes are also best understood as embedded, reinforced, and constrained by the structuralized field of culture.

During the course of the past two decades, the literature has demonstrated that very different forms of self are constructed across different cultures (Markus & Kitayama, 1991; Sampson, 1988; Shweder & Bourne, 1984; Triandis, 1989). Many theorists have contrasted the notion of the autonomous, independent self, which is widespread in the West, with the notion of the relational, interdependent self of the East. Moreover, these selves are fostered, encouraged, and maintained by a variety of cultural practices and lay theories. For example, whereas the independent, autonomous, egocentric self is associated with the practices of free choice, market economy, self-expression, and associated ideas and folk beliefs, the interdependent, embedded, sociocentric self is associated with cultural practices of conformity and adjustment, obligation to others, and associated folk beliefs and cultural icons. These respective sets of cultural practices and meanings constitute very different fields for action—the field called *behavioral environment* by Hallowell (1955) and *action field* by Lewin (1936). Because psychological functions are often inseparable from their behavioral environment, it is often more illuminating to analyze these divergent selves as embedded in the specific behavioral environment of culture. The notion of selves-in-actual-behavioral-environment is close to what Bourdieu (1977) meant by his notions of *habitus* and *modus operandi*. We refer to it as *modes of being* (Markus & Kitayama, in press).

Although the distinction between the two notions of selves or the two corresponding modes of being might strike one as an oversimplification, it has served a reasonable heuristic function for generating testable hypotheses. Moreover, many theorists have been quite explicit in cautioning that these selves or associated modes of being should be seen as prototypes or models (Shweder & Sullivan, 1993). That is to say, they are not designed to describe each and every individual engaged within a given culture. The prototypes are used to summarize the nature of ideational resources distributed, often quite unevenly, within and over any given geographic region or historical time (Adams & Markus, 2001; Kitayama, 2002). Regardless of the specific focus of any given research, the hypothesis regarding the two forms of the self—or more fine-grained varieties—is not designed to reduce individuals to the corresponding types of personality, although allegations to the contrary have occasionally been made (e.g., Takano & Osaka, 1999). Fortunately, in recent years, there have been an increasing number of studies that explicitly examine regional and subgroup differences (Nisbett & Cohen, 1996; Plaut, Markus, & Lachman, 2002; Sampson, 2000; Sanchez-Burks, 2002).

In distilling the most significant contributions from this emerging literature, two points stand out. First, the two forms of self that are postulated to be more or less dominant across different cultures do not exist in a social vacuum. To the contrary, the different forms of self are assumed to be both antecedents and consequences of correspondingly divergent forms of social relationship, institutionalized practices, and publicly shared meanings (Kitayama & Markus, 1999, 2000). These selves are grounded significantly in a number of biologically prepared psychological tendencies or epigenetic rules for psychological functions that, as a whole, define the human species (Rozin & Schull, 1988; Seligman, 1970; Wilson, 1999). Yet, they are also culturally and collectively constructed. That is, they are given specific shapes and functions, in that they are animated and mobilized by means of a number of sociocultural artifacts, practices, meanings, tools, and devices. As suggested by Tomasello (1999) and other thinkers of culture and evolution (e.g., Boyd & Richardson, 1985; Durham, 1991; Sperber, 1985, 1996), humans have evolved to attain and use culture—its symbolic resources in particular—for the purpose of biological adaptation. Hence, to analyze and understand the forms and functions of each self, researchers need to attend to the self's surroundings, especially to the social relations of which it is part and other sociocultural practices and systems of socially shared meanings.

The second significant contribution of the cultural psychological literature concerns questions about the fundamental building blocks of the human mind. For the most part, cognitive processes traditionally have been conceptualized as basic building blocks of the mind that are used in managing all forms of self and social relations. According to this analysis, basic cognitions are held to be constant and little influenced, if at all, by the social or the cultural. Yet if psychological processes are designed to be shaped through culture, cognitive processes may also be shaped in the same way. If so, the boundary between domains of basic cognition and more social domains such as self and social relationships may prove to be much fuzzier than has thus far been assumed in psychology. Indeed, some significant parameters of basic cognitive processes may be significantly modified by practices, strategies, and routines that are brought to bear on the construction of both self and social relationships. Hence, even some of the very basic cognitive competences may be best seen as part and parcel of the socioculturally constituted modes of self and social relationship. The two are mutually constitutive.

In what follows, we first review evidence pertaining to the cross-culturally divergent forms of the self and social relations. Next, we move on to review recent evidence on cultural variations in cognition. The cultural competences suggested throughout this chapter are quite tacit and often automatic and spontaneous. Moreover, they are quite systematic. In fact, we point out that they can be summarized in terms of a relatively simple parameter of allocating differential weights to "object" or "context." In the closing section of this chapter, we indicate directions of future research by raising a number of questions regarding the malleability, variability, and origins of this particular dimension that cut across many cultural competences.

SELF AND SOCIAL RELATIONS IN DIFFERENT CULTURAL CONTEXTS

In this section, we review evidence supporting the divergent *independent* and *interdependent* forms of the self and social relations across cultures. We illuminate divergent social worlds, selves, and social relations that are held in place in different cultural contexts. First we discuss the concepts of independence and interdependence and then discuss the acts of self-enhancement and self-criticism and influence and adjustment in relation to these concepts.

Independence and Interdependence

Markus and Kitayama (1991, 1998; Kitayama, Markus, & Matsumoto, 1995; Kitayama & Markus, 1999) have proposed that in North American middle-class culture, the idea of the self as independent is quite widespread and often taken for granted. This and other related ideas, such as individual choice, freedom, self-expression, and the notion of market as the prototype for social interactions in general, are also involved in creating and maintaining myriad practices and customs that permeate this culture. Accordingly, the personal is defined as relationship-independent because the personal is conceptualized prior to the social and, furthermore, it is imagined to be bounded and separate from the latter. Obviously, social relations are also important; but they are often structured in terms of each person's choice to enter into such relations. In fact, social relations themselves are often grounded in the independence of each participating individual. These cultural practices and meanings as a whole reinforce and maintain the personal self. Although many elements of the independent mode of being can be found across cultures, they are assumed to be especially widespread, both elaborated and institutionalized, in many domains of social life of North American cultures.

In contrast, East Asian cultures are committed to the contrasting idea of the self as interdependent (Markus & Kitayama, 1991). Ideas such as interpersonal or societal obligations, hierarchical social order, and interpersonal adjustment and fitting-in are involved in creating and maintaining many central practices and customs that permeate these cultures. Obviously, personal selves are also important and often just as salient as social obligations and duties. However, the personal is largely defined vis-à-vis the expectations and demands of the surroundings. In some cases, personal desires and needs are more or less congruous with social expectations, as may be the case in identification and spontaneous role obligation; whereas in some other cases they may go against one another, as may be true in many cases of youth rebellion against authority figures. Whichever form it might take, the personal in these cultural contexts may then be best conceptualized as highly context- or relationship-dependent and, thus, fully embedded and connected.

Many elements of the interdependent mode are widely distributed across many cultures and, in nearly all of them, some domains such as intimate relationships or family may lend themselves to interdependence. At the same time, many domains of social life can be construed and constructed on the foundation of either one or even both of the two models of the self. In these cases, interdependence may be more instrumental in organizing these domains in some cultures (e.g., East Asian) than in others (e.g., North American).

Both the independent and the interdependent modes of being can be analyzed at a variety of different levels. Certain characteristic psychological tendencies are embedded in corresponding styles of interpersonal interactions, which, in turn, are included in customs and institutions at larger community and society levels. By way of illuminating the multifaceted nature of the two modes of being, we focus on two specific areas of research. First, one personal-level characteristic of the two modes of being that has been carefully studied in the current literature is a set of biases in perceiving and judging the self. Whereas self-enhancing tendencies are typically associated with the independent mode of being, self-critical tendencies are often associated with the interdependent mode of being. Second, these personal-level biases in self-perception are associated with a set of interpersonal-level processes. Whereas independent, self-enhancing selves form social relations by seeking to influence one another, interdependent, self-critical selves often do so by adjusting themselves to one another.

Self-Enhancement and Self-Criticism

In the independent mode of being, internal attributes of the self such as motives, abilities, talents, and personality traits are assumed to be central to defining the nature of the self. Construing the self as highly competent, resourceful, and thus, autonomous, is quite self-affirming. It therefore carries considerable significance to confirm and express such desirable internal attributes of the self. Individuals are often highly motivated to maintain and pursue a high sense of self-esteem (Taylor & Brown, 1988), autonomy and choice (Iyengar & Lepper, 1999), rationality (Miller, 1999), competence (Deci & Ryan, 1995), and efficacy (Bandura, 1997). For those engaged in the independent mode of being, it is an important cultural competence to maintain a positive view of the personal self because it facilitates the ever-important cultural mandates of self-expression, choice, and autonomy.

In contrast, in the interdependent mode of being, social connectedness as actualized in social obligations, duties, and responsibilities, constitutes the central theme of self-definition. Construing the self as fully embedded and appreciated in a meaningful social relation is highly self-affirming. It therefore carries a premium to pay close attention to the surroundings and fit in. "Standing out" by boosting the positivity of the self can hardly be seen as mature or respectable. Instead, to "stand in" by focusing on one's relatively negative aspects is better accepted and encouraged and is seen as a sign of maturity. As may be expected, the tendencies for self-enhancement, which are quite widespread in North America, are hardly as pronounced and, often times, barely observed in any consistent fashion in Japan and other East Asian cultures (Heine et al., 1999). In fact, in many cases, Japanese draw self-critical appraisals of themselves. Moreover, this self-criticism is the case even if there is no chance of public scrutiny of their responses (Karasawa, 2001). For those engaged in the interdependent mode of being, it is an important cultural competence to maintain a self-critical attitude toward one's self because it promotes the ever-important goal of fitting-in.

The divergent psychological tendencies of self-enhancement and criticism are mediated by myriad collective, society-level processes. For example, in a recent study, American and Japanese respondents were asked to remember what they did when something either good or bad happened to their friends (Kitayama, Nakama, & Saitoh, 2003). They were also asked to remember how many days ago the event occurred, as a proxy measure of the frequency of the behaviors. The median recentness of the latest acts of such support showed a dramatic cross-cultural difference. Whereas in the United States such acts of support occurred fairly recently, regardless of the state of the friends being positive or negative (the average median recentnesses were four and three days, respectively), in Japan, similar acts of support were offered fairly recently if the friends were in a negative state (the average median recentness was three days). However, such acts of support must have, in all likelihood, been very rare if the friends were in a positive state. The mean median recentness was 60, which is longer than the corresponding number for Americans by factor of 12. These numbers imply, then, that in the United States, but not in Japan, friends tacitly encourage and reinforce the positivity of one another.[1]

It is likely that there are many similar cultural patterns that collectively maintain the psychological tendencies of self-enhancement and self-criticism. Indeed, the collective foundation for these psychological tendencies may be both very subtle and highly pervasive. For example, a study suggests that the very ways in which mundane social situations are defined and constructed are systematically different across cultures so that these situations themselves foster and reproduce the respective psychological biases in self-perception (Kitayama, Markus, Matsumoto, & Norasakkunkit, 1997). This work was composed of two phases. In the first phase, both American and Japanese college students were asked to remember and describe as many situations as they could in which their self-esteem increased or decreased (called the success and the failure situations, respectively). The researchers then sampled 400 situations from the much larger set of situations thus generated. The sampling was entirely random except that there were equal numbers of success and failure situations generated by the American and Japanese respondents (100 each × 4 = 400). These situations were translated, back-translated, and prepared in both languages. In the second phase, new groups of American and Japanese students were asked to read each situation carefully and to report the degree to which their own self-esteem would increase or decrease in the situation.

Are Americans really self-enhancing, in that their self-esteem is more likely to increase in success situations than it decreases in failure situations? Alternatively, are Japanese really self-critical, in that their self-esteem is more likely to decrease in failure situations than to increase in success situations? To address these questions, the researchers averaged both the degree of estimated increase in self-esteem in the success situations and the degree of estimated decrease in self-esteem in the failure situations. The average estimate for the decrease in self-esteem in the failure situations was then subtracted from the average estimate for the increase in self-esteem in the success situations to yield an index of relative self-esteem change. Positive scores on this index indicate that self-esteem is more likely to increase with success than it decreases with failure (self-enhancement), whereas negative scores indicate an opposite tendency (self-criticism). This index was computed separately for both Americans and Japanese when they were presented with either American- or Japanese-made situations.

---

[1]This occurrence happens either because there are a greater number of positive events in North America than in Japan, because Americans are more likely to offer well-intended acts when a good event happens to their friends, or both. We suspect that both of these mechanisms are involved.

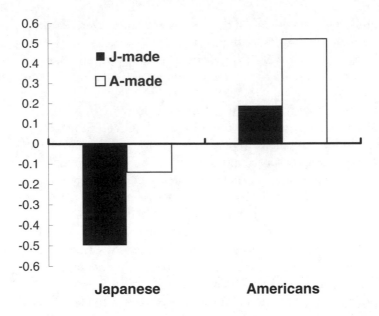

Figure 3.1. Self-enhancement in the United States and self-criticism in Japan: Whereas Americans were more likely to feel an increase of self-esteem in success (relative to a decrease of self-esteem in failure), Japanese were more likely to feel a decrease of self-esteem in failure. Moreover, these culture-contingent biases in self-perception are more pronounced when individuals are presented with situations that are commonly available in their own cultural contexts. From the data reported in Kitayama, Markus, Matsumoto, and Norasakkunkit, 1997.

The results are summarized in Figure 3.1. First, consider cases in which the respondents were presented with situations that had been sampled from their own respective cultural contexts. As can been seen, Americans (when responding to the American-made situations) showed a massive self-enhancing effect. Indeed, in this condition, nearly 90% of the respondents showed a varying degree of the same tendency, hence replicating earlier research in this area. In contrast, Japanese (when responding to the Japanese-made situations) showed an equally robust self-critical effect. Again, nearly 90% of the respondents showed the same effect to a varying extent. Second, the remaining two conditions fell between the two extremes. Thus, when responding to the Japanese-made situations, Americans were less self-enhancing and, likewise, when responding to the American-made situations, Japanese were less self-critical. This pattern of results strongly suggests that the psychological tendencies of self-enhancement and self-criticism are grounded importantly in the actual social situations of the respective cultures. Specifically, it is likely that American situations are constructed in such a way that they encourage individuals to attend to, elaborate, and express the positivity of the self while ignoring, suppressing, or discounting negativity of the self. Likewise, Japanese situations may be constructed to carry a reversed pattern of affordances for self-perception.

Influence and Adjustment

The two modes of being may also be associated with equally divergent interpersonal functions. Weisz, Rothbaum, and Blackburn (1984) have proposed that there are two ways of relating to others (or, more generally, to the external environment). One is to influence and cause changes to happen to others in accordance with one's own wishes, desires, and needs. This strategy is called *primary control*. The other is to adjust the self to others or, more generally, to external contingencies. This strategy is called *secondary control*. Although some researchers have suggested that the first strategy of influence is literally more dominant and primary and, thus, taken prior to the second strategy of adjustment (e.g., Heckhausen & Schulz, 1995), the present analysis suggests that deployment of the two social coping strategies is contingent on a variety of factors including, among others, the predominant cultural views of the self as independent or interdependent (e.g., Gould, 1999; Kitayama, 2002; Morling, Kitayama, & Miyamoto, 2002, in press).

In the independent mode of being, in accordance with the positivity, competence, and abilities of each personal self, social relations are organized in terms of each person's choice to enter into them. Furthermore, individuals exercise primary control or influencing strategies in relating to others. They therefore seek mutual fulfillment of each other's positive self-images. In this form of social relationship, it is important to carefully attend to and even manage each other's self-esteem so as to continue a positive relationship with others. Hence, to be generous (i.e., to offer supportive acts even when there is no obvious need) may become an important virtue. It may be recalled that American friends extended supportive acts to one another regardless of the other's state being positive or negative. Thus, individuals must have acquired important competences to form relationships and to maintain them in a way that is most satisfactory to them.

An analogous argument can be made for the interdependent mode of being. Within this mode of being, social relations are likely to be relatively stable and, more often than not, assigned and prearranged for each individual (e.g., as in arranged marriages or in social networks in a school classroom). The primary task of fitting-in and adjustment, then, goes hand-in-hand with these forms of social relationship. Fitting into these social relations often, if not always, involves finding, creating, and returning obligations. It is a social responsibility, for example, to help someone in need, which in turn produces an obligation to return the favor when the roles are reversed. Therefore, it is an important moral imperative never to fail to help someone in distress. In the absence of such obligations, helping someone is "strange" or "unnatural," interpreted accordingly with suspicions about ulterior motives.

In short, dependability is required to assure a respectable membership in a social relationship like this. Remember, Japanese friends extended supportive acts only when the other was in trouble. Thus, individuals must have acquired important competences to be attentive to others in a relationship and to coordinate themselves in accordance with others' expectations.

Recent research by Morling, Kitayama, and Miyamoto (2002) has provided initial support for the hypothesis on the relational functions associated with the two modes of being. These researchers asked both American and Japanese college undergraduates to describe as many situations as possible in which they either "influenced things in their surroundings in accordance with their own wishes and desires" or "adjusted themselves to things in their surroundings." The respondents were asked to report only those situations that had actually happened to them. They also indicated how long ago each situation took place. The first important finding concerns the recentness of the reported situations. This finding yielded a reliable cross-cultural difference. Thus, when asked to generate situations involving influencing acts, Americans reported much more recent situations than did Japanese (4 days ago versus 14 days ago). But when asked to generate situations involving adjustment, Japanese reported more recent situations than did Americans (1 day ago versus 7 days ago). Thus, as hypothesized, in the United States, acts of influencing were more commonly constructed and, thus, cognitively more elaborate and hence more available in memory. They are, in fact, primary. But in Japan, acts of adjusting are more common, more elaborate, and more available in memory. Hence, in Japan, it is these acts of adjustment—secondary control (Weisz et al., 1984)—that are arguably more primary.

According to our analysis of the two modes of being, however, the acts of influencing and adjusting are likely to be not only different in prevalence and mnemonic availability but also defined or framed in very different ways across the two cultures. In the United States, influencing is assumed to be a means of both keeping one's own self-esteem high and forging a meaningful social relationship. One typical example of this form of influence is persuasion. In contrast, in Japan, adjusting is assumed to be a means for creating and maintaining a meaningful social relationship. One typical example is sympathy and compassion extended to someone in need or distress. In this cultural context, self-esteem in the sense of perceived efficacy, power, and competence, is not central and, therefore, is unlikely to be implicated in many social domains and activities, including the main cultural task of adjustment.

To investigate these ideas, Morling and colleagues selected 320 acts from the entire set of acts that had been generated in the first phase of the study. The selection was constructed randomly with the constraint that equal numbers of influencing and adjusting acts were sampled from both the United States and Japan. These acts were subsequently translated and back-translated and prepared in both languages. These acts were then presented to new groups of American and Japanese college students. The respondents were asked to imagine that they had engaged in each act and to report both how efficacious, competent, or powerful they would feel (−4 = *very inefficacious and incompetent*; +4 = *very efficacious and competent*) and how connected and close they would feel to others (who are present in actuality or in imagination) in the situation (−4 = *quite separate and independent*; +4 = *quite connected and close*).

It is reasonable to assume that acts sampled from one's own culture are ecologically and culturally more valid. More often than not, Americans are likely to find themselves engaging in acts that are sampled from the United States, whereas Japanese are likely to find themselves engaging in acts that are sampled from Japan. Only those ecologically or culturally valid cases are discussed here. The culturally foreign cases (where the participants respond to foreign-made situations) are omitted.[2] Figure 3.2-A shows the increase in self-esteem estimated by both American and Japanese respondents in the influence and the adjustment conditions. First of all, it is clear that acts of adjustment have virtually nothing to do with self-esteem. Second, and more important, the respondents reported that engaging in acts of influence would be quite effective in increasing their self-esteem. Moreover, this effect was substantially stronger for Americans than for Japanese. Consistent with our analysis, this finding demonstrates that influencing serves as a booster of self-esteem and, moreover, that this is especially true in the United States.

Next, Figure 3.2-B shows the estimated increase in interpersonal connectedness. As predicted, Japanese reported much more connectedness when engaging in acts of adjusting than when engaging in acts of influencing. This finding is quite consistent with the hypothesis that in the Japanese cultural context, interpersonal adjustment is the culturally sanctioned means for creating and maintaining social relationships. It is important to note that when Americans were engaging in acts of adjustment, they experienced little or no sense of interpersonal connectedness. Instead, Americans experienced a strong sense of connectedness to others when engaging in acts of influencing. This finding lends support to the hypothesis that mutual influence is the culturally sanctioned mode of relating to one another in the United States. Note again that the Japanese reportedly experienced little or no sense of connectedness when engaging in comparable acts of influencing.

Summary

Along with other relevant research findings (e.g., Fiske et al., 1998; Heine et al., 1999; Kitayama & Markus, 1999; Markus & Kitayama, in press, for reviews), the two studies examined in some detail here (Kitayama et al., 1997; Morling et al., 2002) suggest that the way in which the notion of self

---

[2]By examining the responses to acts sampled from the culture different from the respondents'.

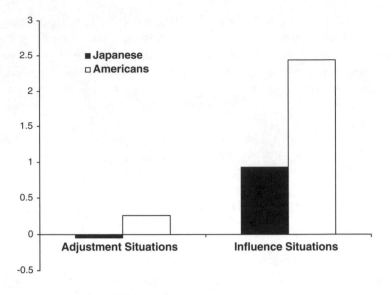

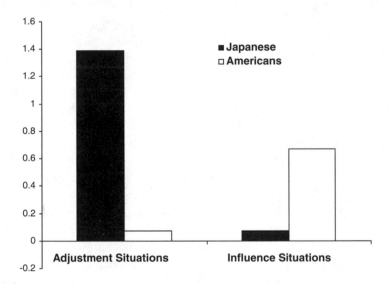

Figure 3.2. Perceived levels of self-esteem (Figure 3.2-A) and connectedness (Figure 3.2-B) for Americans and Japanese during the acts of either influencing or adjusting. From the data reported in Morling, Kitayama, and Miyamoto (2002).

and social relations are constructed varies across cultures. In the independent mode, which is more common in the United States, attending to one's self-esteem-related concerns is primary. Moreover, acts of influencing others serve the functions of both maintaining high self-esteem and forging social relations. The associated skills and psychological tendencies constitute a significant cultural competence.

In contrast, in the interdependent mode, which is more common in Japan, adjusting to others and, thus, feeling embedded in a social relationship constitute much more central concerns. Furthermore, skills and psychological tendencies that promote this mode of being (such as self-criticism and adjustment) constitute a significant cultural competence. As may be expected, interpersonal adjustment serves the function of enhancing social connectedness. But little or no self-esteem appears to be involved in this process. This set of findings strongly suggests that forms of self-in-social-context vary considerably across cultures and correspondingly divergent sets of cultural competences are called for.

CULTURAL VARIATIONS IN COGNITION

The cross-culturally divergent forms of self and social relations, along with the associated personal and interpersonal skills and competences, are likely to be related to cognitive competences. In differently organized social worlds, individuals are likely to (a) think differently because very different beliefs, schemas, and folk assumptions about the nature of the person and his or her surroundings are encouraged, vividly revealed in cultural icons, media, and other cultural artifacts of daily life, and made highly accessible in memory; (b) attend differently because quite different pieces and configurations of stimuli or quite different parts of the social world are held to be relevant and informative; and, moreover, (c) perceive differently because of varying informativeness and relevance of different parts of the perceptual world. These considerations suggest that there should be considerable variations not only in the domains of self and social relations, but also in the domains of basic cognition and perception.

The notion that cultural factors may influence perception is related to a set of ideas first proposed by Jerome Bruner and his colleagues in the 1950s under the name of the *New Look*. The basic thesis of the New Look is that perception relies not only in part on sensory information but that percepts are also significantly modified by factors endogenous to the perceiver, such as value, expectation, needs, desire, and emotion (Bruner, 1957; Bruner & Goodman, 1947; Higgins & Bargh, 1987). Exogenous factors such as the physical properties of a stimulus or the resulting sensory impression do not fully explain the experienced percept.

If value, need, expectation, desire, and emotion affect perception, it is relevant to ask whether culture may be an important source of these endogenous factors. Individuals constantly engage themselves in the institutions, practices, technologies, and rituals of their culture and rely on these cultural resources to create meaning from their experiences. Thus, culture may be an important source of the kinds of endogenous factors that modify perception. Given the variability in the practices and beliefs maintained by different cultures, it is likely that these cultural resources maintain and encourage divergent attentional and perceptual capacities.

Folk Beliefs and Social Inference

In the independent mode of being, each individual is held to be independent and separate from her or his context and, moreover, she or he is assumed to guide her or his own behaviors to influence and cause changes to happen in her or his surroundings. In other words, the prevailing assumption is that each person has her or his own disposition, which is causally related to her or his own overt behaviors. This belief, called *lay dispositionism* by Ross and Nisbett (1991), has been suggested to be responsible, at least in part, for fundamental attribution error namely, the tendency to estimate an undue causal power in the actor. One of the most discussed cases of fundamental attribution error is the effect called *correspondence bias*. A number of studies have shown that when observing another person making a statement on an issue, North Americans attribute the corresponding attitude to the person even if the person's behavior is heavily constrained by external factors (e.g., being pressured by an authority figure to make the statement; see Gilbert & Malone, 1995; Jones, 1979, for reviews).

In the interdependent mode of being, by contrast, individuals are held to be interconnected through a web of obligations and, moreover, it is assumed that they will adjust themselves to expectations, needs, and desires of people in their surroundings. In other words, the prevailing assumption is that social surroundings often solicit, induce, encourage, and guide each person to behave one way or the other. This assumption does not deny individual agency because the agency itself is conceptualized as inclusive of the individual's surroundings and thus as conjoint rather than as disjoint. That is, each person is assumed to be attentive to his or her social surroundings, actively incorporating cues available in those surroundings, and eventually coordinating their wills and desires in accordance with situational expectations and inducements. However, beliefs in interdependence may not give rise to a simplified notion that every behavior is likely to have a cause in the corresponding disposition of the actor. Other factors such as situational constraints and affordances are equally likely to be taken into account.

An increasing number of cross-cultural studies have suggested that dispositional biases and errors in causal inference and attitude attribution may not be as robust in the Asian cultures of India (Miller, 1984), Hong Kong (Lee, Hallahan, & Herzog, 1996; Morris, Menon, & Ames, 2001), China (Morris & Peng, 1994), Korea (Choi & Nisbett, 1998), and Japan (Miyamoto & Kitayama, 2002). This finding, however, should not be taken to suggest that there is no dispositional understanding in East Asia. East Asians do take dispositional factors into account. However, they are also likely to weigh the situational factors as heavily as the dispositional factors. Their decision rules about the degree to which to give weight to disposition versus situation might prove to be more complex than the lay dispositionism that is demonstrably more common in North America.

Specifically, according to the lay belief in interdependence, when behavior takes place, it is placed in a web of many factors, including the disposition of the actor himself or herself and certain situational factors that are impinging on the actor. Under this scheme of social understanding, it is crucial to find out how diagnostic behavior is in respect to the actor's corresponding disposition. If, for example, the actor is making a very lengthy, passionate, and more or less coherent argument for a certain position, the behavior is highly diagnostic of his own attitude. Unless motivated by his conviction, it is hard to imagine why the person is acting the way he does. If, however, the actor's argument is emotionless, quite short, and unpersuasive, it may seem that the person is acting out of other, external concerns. Under these conditions, the individuals will weigh possible situational factors quite seriously. If so, they may not exhibit any correspondence bias.

To investigate these possibilities, Miyamoto and Kitayama (2002) manipulated attitude diagnosticity of behavior and examined whether correspondence bias would diminished if the diagnosticity were quite low (see also Masuda & Kitayama, 2002). Both American and Japanese college students were given an essay that was allegedly composed by a fellow student. It was explained to them that the student was asked by his political science instructor to write an essay. The position to be taken in the essay, so the explanation continued, was decided on by the instructor and, thus, the student had no choice. The stimulus essay either supported or argued against capital punishment. Furthermore, the essay was either highly diagnostic of the writer's attitude (i.e., it was quite long and persuasive) or utterly nondiagnostic (i.e., it was quite short and unpersuasive). After reading the essay, the participants estimated the true attitude of the essay writer. Correspondence bias would be indicated if the estimated attitude was more pro-capital punishment in the "pro" essay condition than in the "anti" essay condition.

Miyamoto and Kitayama (2002) found that American respondents showed a quite strong correspondence bias regardless of the attitude diagnosticity of the stimulus essay. Along with other findings indicating a strong dispositionism of Americans, this finding demonstrates a strong cognitive bias that favors dispositional attributions for these individuals. In contrast, Japanese showed an equally strong correspondence inference when the stimulus essay was highly diagnostic of the attitude of the essay writer. However, when the essay was nondiagnostic and, therefore, there was reason to suspect outside influences on behavior, Japanese no longer showed any correspondence bias.

The extra weight devoted to verbal content by Americans can be found at the level of more spontaneous attention. In a recent series of studies,

Kitayama, Ishii, and Reyes have applied a Stroop-type paradigm to examine spontaneous attention to verbal content and vocal tone (Ishii, Reyes, & Kitayama, 2003; Kitayama & Ishii, 2002). In one study, Ishii and colleagues (2003) prepared a number of English words and their translation equivalents in Japanese. Half of the words had positive verbal content (e.g., grateful, warm) and the remaining half had negative content (e.g., tasteless, sly). Furthermore, the words were spoken in either a positive (smooth and round) or a negative (harsh and constricted) tone of voice, which are recognized to be either pleasant or unpleasant, respectively. The researchers exercised some necessary controls over the stimuli. First, several English–Japanese bilinguals served as speakers to create both the English and the Japanese stimuli. Second, a series of pretests were conducted on low-pass filtered stimuli (with verbal meanings made indiscernible) to make sure that the pleasantness or unpleasantness of the verbal content and the vocal tone was equivalent in the two languages.

The respondents were presented with each word one at a time and asked either to judge whether the verbal meaning of the word was pleasant or unpleasant while ignoring the attendant vocal tone, or to judge whether the vocal tone of the word was pleasant or unpleasant while ignoring the attendant verbal meaning. Using this Stroop-type procedure, it was possible to examine the degree to which attention was automatically captured to either vocal tone or verbal meaning when respondents were instructed to ignore the respective channels of information. To the extent that the to-be-ignored channel automatically captures attention, it should interfere with the required judgment. Hence, the time required to make this judgment should be longer if the to-be-ignored channel carries incongruous information than if it carries congruous information.

Response times of both Americans and Japanese showed a significant interference effect in both judgments, indicating that regardless of languages, both verbal content and vocal tone are automatically processed. As predicted, however, the size of the interference effect varied substantially between the two judgments and, moreover, the direction of the effect was diametrically opposite in the two cultures or languages. Thus, as predicted, Americans showed a stronger interference effect in vocal tone judgment, indicating that they processed verbal content more automatically than they processed vocal tone. In contrast, Japanese showed a stronger interference effect in the verbal content judgment than in vocal tone judgment, hence indicating that they spontaneously attended more to vocal tone than to verbal content. Thus, this data indicates that Americans are much more likely than Japanese to concentrate their attention on the focal aspect of what the person is saying (i.e., verbal content). We should hasten to add, however, that the relative sensitivity to word versus tone is most likely to vary across different social settings. For example, Sanchez-Burks (2002) used a similar vocal Stroop-type paradigm and showed a reliable preference for tone over word (the pattern observed for Japanese in the Ishii et al. study) for Americans when they were placed in a family context.

Perceiving an Object and Its Context

Whenever individuals are exposed to a configuration of stimuli, they are likely to segregate the environment into an object and its context (Kahneman, 1973). The findings reviewed so far suggest that a major cross-cultural difference lies in the weight given to the object vis-à-vis its context in perceiving, recognizing, and drawing inferences about the stimulus configuration. If greater weight is given to the object (with its context relatively ignored), the perception becomes quite narrowly focused on the object. In this sense, the perception may be said to be *field-independent* (Witkin et al., 1954). Moreover, any reasoning and inferences generated from the perception are bound to be linearly derived. Inferences, in other words, become more rule-based (Norenzayan, Smith, Kim, & Nisbett, 2002). In this sense, the associated style of thought may be said to be *analytic* (Nisbett et al., 2001).

By contrast, if greater weight is given to the context in lieu of the attendant object, perception becomes quite broadly encompassing. Particularly when there is an imminent need or requirement to ignore any stimuli in the context, individuals might have serious difficulty ignoring them. Hence, the perception may be said to be *field-dependent* (Witkin et al., 1954), although, as we shall note below, failure to ignore context can also be seen as an important competence under conditions in which context provides critical information for judgments. Moreover, any reasoning and inferences generated from context-oriented perception may become more gestalt-like: They may be difficult to articulate in linear logic, but may be more readily subjected to iconic images and ideographic configurations. Inferences, in other words, will become more similarity-based (Norenzayan et al., 2002). In this sense, the style of thought may be characterized as *holistic* (Nisbett et al., 2001).

It is debatable whether divergent phenomena encompassed in the rubric of field-independence and field-dependence and analytic–holistic mode of thought is reducible to the abilities to either include or exclude context. Yet, it is clear that both of these theoretical distinctions have these attentional competences as their integral parts. As we shall see, growing evidence suggests that the ability to weigh in context varies systematically across cultures even at nonsocial, largely unconscious levels of information processing.

Framed Line Test

Several recent studies suggest that East Asians place greater attentional resources on contextual information, whereas Americans attend to object features and characteristics. Masuda and Nisbett (2001) showed Japanese and American participants computerized vignettes of underwater scenes with various objects such as fish, bubbles, and seaweed. In a subsequent recognition task that included objects from the scene in similar and unique settings, Japanese made more references to contextual information and relationships within the environment and were more accurate in recognizing previously seen objects in their original settings than Americans. American participants were equally accurate regardless of whether a previously seen object was shown in its original setting or in a novel setting. Moreover, they provided more descriptions of individual object features than relationships within the environment.

Ji, Peng, and Nisbett (2000) explored differences in context sensitivity by testing American and Chinese participants on Witkin's (Witkin et al., 1954) rod-in-frame task, which was designed to test individual differences in the construct of field-dependence and field-independence. Participants were presented with a tilted frame, at the center of which was a rotating line. The participants rotated the line to be orthogonal to the earth's surface while ignoring the frame. Context-sensitive individuals tended to be influenced by the titled frame, while context-independent individuals tended to be more accurate at the task. Ji and colleagues (2000) found that Americans were more accurate at the task than Chinese, suggesting that Chinese were unable to ignore the contextual information provided by the tilted frame. Kato (1965) reported a similar effect of greater context dependency among Japanese compared with Westerners as measured by the rod-in-frame task.

The Ji and colleagues (2000) study demonstrates that East Asians are influenced by contextual information to a greater extent than Americans in a perceptual task. One limitation of the task, however, is that the rod-in-frame task only measures the ability to ignore context. This ability may be separate from the ability to incorporate context. This limitation is partly due to the general bias of the cognitive literature, which views human and cultural development as a progression from an ontogenetically primitive field-dependence to a rational, field-independent cognitive style (Witkin, 1967). Yet a variety of cognitive and perceptual mechanisms depend on the ability to incorporate context effectively and accurately into judgments. For example, the spatial scaling involved in using a model or map requires accurately encoding the relation among a variety of objects and encoding proportional distances among symbolically represented objects (Uttal, 1994). Thus, it is possible that the ability to include contextual information may often be extremely adaptive if these abilities are called for by the task at hand.

If we are to be able to test the hypothesis that those engaging in the independent and the interdependent mode of being are more capable of excluding and including context, respectively, it is important to measure the ability to include context in perception separately from measurement of the ability to exclude context in perception. Moreover, the two measurement tasks must be directly comparable. To address these issues, Kitayama, Duffy, Kawamura, and Larsen (2003) have developed a new task called the *framed*

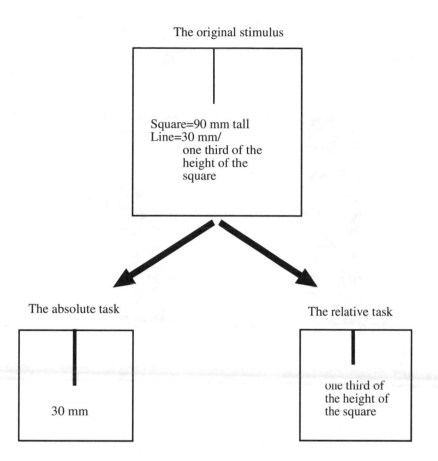

The original stimulus

Square=90 mm tall
Line=30 mm/
      one third of the
      height of the
      square

The absolute task

30 mm

The relative task

one third of
the height of
the square

Figure 3.3. The original stimulus, the absolute task, and the relative task from the framed line test. From "Perceiving an Object and its Context in Different Cultures: A Cultural Look at New Look," by S. Kitayama, S. Duffy, T. Kawamura, & J. T. Larsen (2003), *Psychological Science, 14*, p. 201. Copyright by Blackwell. Reprinted with permission.

line task. As illustrated in Figure 3.3, participants are shown a line in a square frame. Participants are then presented with another square frame of the same or different size and asked to draw a line in it. In the *absolute task*, participants are instructed to draw a line that is identical in absolute length to the original line in the first frame. In the *relative task*, participants are instructed to draw a line in the second frame so that it has the same proportion to the new frame as the original line in the original frame. The absolute task requires ignoring the contextual information provided by the original frame while the relative task requires incorporating the context provided by the initial frame in reproducing the line.

    In their first experiment, Kitayama and colleagues (2003) applied the framed line task to both Americans and Japanese. The size of the errors in the two tasks is reported in Figure 3.4. As shown, Japanese were more accurate in the relative task whereas Americans were more accurate in the abso-

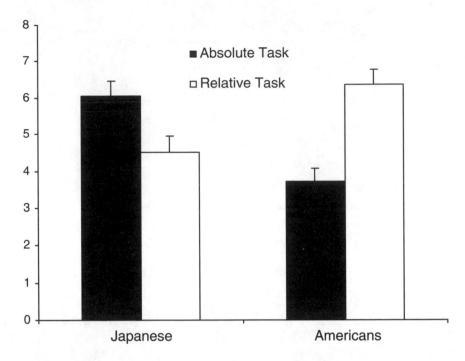

Figure 3.4. Mean error (mm) for the absolute and relative tasks of the framed line test for Japanese and Americans. From "Perceiving an Object and its Context in Different Cultures: A Cultural Look at New Look," by S. Kitayama, S. Duffy, T. Kawamura, & J. T. Larsen (2003), *Psychological Science, 14*, p. 201. Copyright by Blackwell. Reprinted with permission.

lute task. This finding suggests that Japanese were better able to incorporate context into their judgments, but less able to ignore context, whereas Americans were better at ignoring context, but less capable at incorporating context into their reproductions.

In their second experiment, Kitayama and colleagues tested Americans engaged in Japanese culture (Americans studying in Japan) and Japanese engaged in American culture (Japanese studying in the United States). Kitayama and colleagues found that individuals engaged in a host culture demonstrated an effect that mimicked the effect normally observed in the host culture. Moreover, this was the case even for those who stayed in the host culture only for a few months.

There are at least two alternative interpretations for the finding. First, the attentional bias may be malleable enough to become readily adjusted to the new attentional demands of a host culture. Such an acculturation effect has been observed in attitudes and other social psychological measures such as self-esteem (Heine et al., 1999). Second, the perceptual orientations may be analogous to a personality trait that is stable and static over time once acquired, perhaps, quite early in socialization (e.g., Lucy & Gaskins, 2000). According to this interpretation, the above finding may be due to selection bias, whereby people are attracted to a culture that promotes the orientation they themselves have. To tease apart these two interpretations will entail quite significant implications for the malleability and stability of these competences, as well as for the specific role that bias might have in cultural adaptation.

Preliminary evidence suggests that the acculturation effect might happen in the nonsocial cognitive competence of excluding and including context, but this effect might be weak at most. In a recent study, Kawamura, Kitayama, Greenholtz, and Lehman (2003) applied framed line task to a group of Japanese college students who participated in a six-month exchange program with a Canadian university. Whereas half of the students were tested right before the departure to Canada, the remaining half were tested right before the return to Japan from Canada at the end of the program period. Before the departure to Canada, the ability to include context was much higher than the ability to exclude it. Indeed, the performance of these participants on the framed line task was no different than other Japanese students. If there were any substantial acculturation effect, their cognitive competence would show a reversed pattern at the end of the six-month period. An earlier study by Heine and Lehman (reported in Heine et al., 1999) suggested that this period is long enough to produce a substantial increase in self-esteem of the Japanese students who participated in the same program. However, the Kawamura and colleagues study revealed that the acculturation effect, as measured by performance on the framed line task, was discernible but quite marginal both in actual magnitude and in terms of statistical significance. Hence, acculturation in social psychological domains does happen within the short period of time, but cognitive acculturation might not. Further work is necessary to determine whether longer periods of acculturation are required to reverse these cognitive orientations.

Perceptual Base Rate in Judgment of Object Size

Although context is generally conceptualized as information that physically surrounds a target object within a perceptual field, context may be more broadly construed as information that conceptually surrounds or encompasses a focal object. For example, when individuals hear someone speak, some may be more inclined than others to engage in memory search for potentially useful contextual information to identify the true speech intent (Sperber & Wilson, 1986). Or, when one sees someone on the street, generic knowledge associated with the person, such as race, gender, and age, might be recruited in constructing the conscious representation of the person. For example, if specified as Black, the person might be perceived in terms of the associated stereotypes of Black people as, say, athletic or aggressive (e.g., Wittenbrink, Judd, & Park, 2001). Likewise, if presented with any given perceptual focal object, say, a particular fish, some individuals may be more inclined than others to engage in memory search to locate pertinent generic knowledge associated with fish in general, and to use the information from stored knowledge to develop a conscious representation of the fish (Huttenlocher, Hedges, & Vevea, 2000).

We suggest that generic knowledge activated in this way constitutes a *cognitive context* for the focal object. Thus, those engaging in the interdependent mode of being (e.g., East Asians) might be predicted to assign a greater weight to the context than might those engaging in the independent mode of being (e.g., North Americans). In a recent study (Duffy & Kitayama, 2003), we investigated whether this possibility might be true in a perceptual domain by using an experimental procedure developed by Huttenlocher and colleagues (2000) with Japanese and North Americans.

Participants were presented with a number of trials in which they reproduced lines of varying lengths. On each trial, participants saw a target line for one second, and after a short delay they adjusted a reproduction line to have the same length as the target line. There were 192 trials of 24 distinct lines that varied in length from 48 pixels (1.5 cm) to 432 pixels (14 cm) in 16 pixel (.5 cm) increments. Under these conditions, Huttenlocher and colleagues suggested that individuals automatically develop a representation of the average (prototypic) line, which in this study was a line length of 240 pixels (8 cm). Once this generic representation is developed after exposure to several lines of varying lengths, the estimation of subsequent lines is influenced by this generic representation. Specifically, the final representation of any individual line is an integration of both the actual sensory input for that specific line and the stored generic representation of the average line length. This integration of sensory information and generic knowledge results in a biased response in which smaller lines are overestimated and longer lines are underestimated.

It has been shown that individuals assign varying weights to the sensory input versus the generic representation in performing this integration on estimation. For instance, if the memory for a particular instance is very inexact, people generally rely more heavily on a stored generic knowledge to reconstruct the instance than if the memory for the particular instance is very exact (Huttenlocher, Hedges, & Duncan, 1991). Over the long run, the use of generic information is likely to enhance the accuracy of perception, especially if sensory information is relatively impoverished. This adaptive function of the prototype, however, may be differentially used in different cultural contexts. To the extent that East Asians are more likely than Americans to strongly weigh cognitive context, the effect of generic knowledge in perception should be more pronounced for the former than for the latter.

The results of this study are presented in Figure 3.5. Bias (the average difference between the participant's estimate of the line length and its actual length) is plotted against the actual line length. Both Japanese and North Americans bias their responses toward the average line length, as indicated

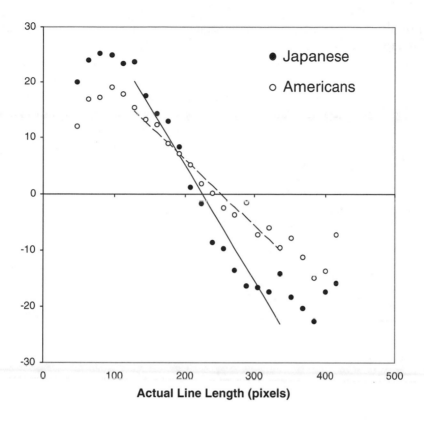

Figure 3.5. Bias (in pixels) as a function of actual stimulus values by culture in a line-estimation task. The steeper the slope for the regression line for Japanese participants suggests that a greater incorporation of cognitive context. From Duffy and Kitayama (2003).

by the negative slope of the line. However, the bias toward the prototype was significantly stronger for Japanese participants than for North American participants. We replicated this cross-cultural difference in another study that drew a comparison between Americans and Chinese. In both studies, the East Asian participants were influenced by the context provided by the prior distribution of lines to a greater extent than the North Americans. These results are consistent with the findings of Kitayama and colleagues (2003), which show that East Asians incorporate context in their judgments of a target object to a greater extent than North Americans. However, in the present task, the context is not a physical frame that surrounds a focal stimulus but a conceptual "frame" in the form of average information that influences the estimation of a focal object's features.

It remains to be seen whether analogous effects of generic knowledge or schema effects in general, including some of the vicious effects of stereotypes, might also be stronger and more persistent among East Asians or those engaging in the interdependent mode of being than among Americans or those engaging in the independent mode of being. On the one hand, such a cross-cultural difference is the most straightforward extrapolation from the study reported above (Figure 3.5). On the other hand, different domains—say, domains of racial stereotyping—do carry many extraneous factors such as strength and mnemonic accessibility of relevant stereotypes, severity of consequences associated with such knowledge, and associated discourse patterns and social institutions. These factors, in turn, make any simple extrapolation from a nonsocial domain to the social domains seriously premature. It is only through careful comparative empirical work that any believable answers can be suggested and, at present, such studies have yet to be conducted.

IMPLICATIONS FOR FUTURE RESEARCH ON CULTURAL COMPETENCE

In this chapter, we have summarized, in broad strokes, the two divergent modes of both being a self and relating to others. We have further delineated some consequences of these social dynamics on cognitive processes. In this section we summarize the findings of the chapter.

Cultural Modes of Being

Within the independent mode of being, individuals are quite motivated to establish desirable internal attributes and use them to regulate their own behaviors and influence others. This general schema for self and social relations serves as a cognitive template for interpreting and drawing inferences about another person. Hence, the causes of another's behavior are first searched for in the person himself or herself, resulting in fundamental attribution error or correspondence bias. In all these social instances of cultural influence, major bias occurs in the assignment of a greater weight to a focal object such as person and verbal content. Indeed, this bias for object has been demonstrated even in some domains that are arguably nonsocial, such as determining the length of a line presented in varying contexts.

In contrast, within the interdependent mode of being, individuals are quite motivated to adjust themselves to others, thereby maintaining and managing social ties and mutual obligations. This general schema for self and social behavior serves as a cognitive template for social perception and inference. Hence, the cause of another's behavior is often distributed relatively evenly to both dispositional and situational factors. As may be expected, the fundamental attribution error or the correspondence bias is demonstrably attenuated. In all these instances of cultural influence, an appreciably greater weight is assigned to context rather than to the object. Moreover, this bias for including context has also been established in nonsocial domains.

It must be kept in mind that although the modes of being are associated, from a broad cross-cultural perspective, with general cultural regions such as North America and East Asia, there may be many exceptions to this general association. In fact, it may be predicted that cultural biases may be quite variable within any single culture, depending on the specific mode of being that is evoked in any given situation. For example, it is entirely possible that North Americans show interdependent patterns of social behavior and cognitive biases if placed in close friendship relationships (Kitayama & Uchida, 2003) or within a family context (Sanchez-Burks, 2002). Conversely, East Asians may exhibit independent patterns if placed in anonymous social settings that encourage the pursuit of self-interest (Yamagishi, 1986). More generally, any cultural biases may be contingent on specific social situations that subtly, yet powerfully, prime and highlight one or the other mode of being. Given the evidence reviewed earlier (Kitayama et al., 1997; Morling et al., 2002) on the effect of exposure to situations sampled from different cultures, it would seem entirely possible that any given cultural biases are most vividly observed on the home cultural turf. Temporarily activating alternative cultural frames or situations might effectively induce the correspondingly different cultural biases. The studies on priming effects have suggested that this possibility is quite plausible at least in some social and cognitive domains (e.g., Brewer & Gardner, 1996; Hong, Morris, Chiu, & Benet-Martinez, 2000; Kuhnen, Hannover, & Schubert, 2001; Kuhnen & Oyserman, 2002).

Malleability and Variability of Cultural Competences

Our analysis suggests that engagement in the specific modes of being that organize and animate an individual's social world nurture a myriad of cultural competences. These competences are constantly encouraged and reinforced so that many of them may ultimately form an integral part of the psychological system of regulating attention, perception, cognition, emotion, motivation, and action. Although these specific competences are quite unique and variable in detail, one unmistakable theme cuts across these various domains. The work we have reviewed suggests that whereas the independent mode of being fosters a competence for focusing on focal objects and excluding contextual information, the interdependent mode of being fosters a competence for incorporating context in thinking about focal objects.

Future research must explore a number of issues pertaining to the differential weighing of focal versus contextual information. Given the degree to which modern technologies and economies promote and foster individual engagement within international contexts and settings, it is of utmost significance to determine the degree of stability or malleability of the independent and interdependent modes of being and their consequent effects on cognition and perception. Research on priming (e.g., Kuhnen & Oyserman, 2002) suggests that these social and cognitive processes may temporarily change by activating constructs associated with an alternative mode of being. However, in view of the many difficulties immigrants have in coping with the norms and customs of a new host culture, the cultural competences we have described may not be nearly as malleable as the priming studies suggest. Thus, there is reason to suspect that the kinds of cultural competences we have reviewed—especially those that are nonsocial and, hence, relatively dissociated from the specific details of daily social activities—represent deeply entrenched and fundamentally divergent ways of thinking and interacting within fundamentally different sociocultural worlds.

Developmental Time Course

Indeed, most nonsocial competences within the domains of cognition and perception are likely to be established fairly early in life (Arterberry & Kellman, 2000; Spelke, 1990). Hence, as we suggested earlier, it seems unlikely that cultural competences within these domains may be mutable through minimal exposure to an alternative mode of being. Phonemic learning is a case in point. Although neonates are born with the capacity to discriminate all the phonemes used in all human languages, by age nine months exposure to the phonemes in the language environment fixes the categorical boundaries so that nonnative distinctions become indiscriminable (Werker & Tees, 1984). Once brought up in Japan, the phonemic distinction between the /l/ and the /r/ sound, which is absent in Japanese, becomes totally blurred and recoverable only after extensive training (McCandliss et al., 2002; Miyawaki et al., 1975). Likewise, the cultural bias in the allocation of weight to "object-in-general" versus "context-in-general" may also have a relatively early origin, which, in turn, provides a constant constraint over all matters of cognitive, emotional, and motivational functions that begin to unfold in every corner of social life. This constraint and the resulting bias on the emerging social competences may be relatively easy to overcome with self-conscious effort, but will, in all likelihood, be impossible to totally nullify or, much less, to ignore. Moreover, the bias itself may be relatively difficult to change.

Once acquired, these nonsocial cognitive competences are likely to channel higher-order thought and action in social domains in certain systematic directions. And yet, they are unlikely to be directly challenged or compromised by demands and requirements of social tasks and activities. These considerations raise an important possibility that nonsocial cognitive competences, which are variable across cultures, might prove to be relatively easy to acquire fairly early in life and, yet, might be quite stable afterward. If so, these nonsocial cognitive competences might be good candidates for a mechanism for the durable maintenance and reliable cross-generational reproduction of culture (see also Sperber, 1985, 1996, for a related analysis of cognitive basis of culture). This possibility is schematically illustrated in Figure 3.6. This preliminary model of cultural competence highlights the potentially important role played by nonsocial competences that are acquired

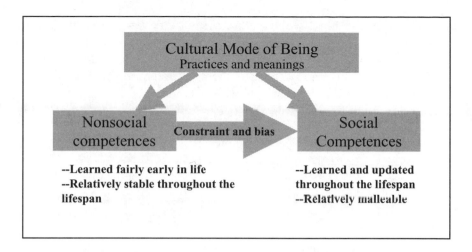

Figure 3.6. A preliminary model of cultural competences: The critical role of nonsocial competences acquired early in life.

early in life and that remain relatively stable throughout the lifespan. Here we might be able to locate a significant psychological underpinning of cultural traditions, which fluctuate, to be sure and, yet, are extremely unlikely to change in any drastic ways over a very short time.

To the extent that this conjecture has any merit, future research in this area will benefit from a concerted effort to explore the critical period when such weight assignment in nonsocial domains is acquired (Lucy & Gaskins, 2000; Minoura, 1990). Moreover, it is also important to examine what kinds and extent of training or experience might be required to challenge and even reverse habitual modes of focusing on object or context in perception and cognition. A systematic program of empirical work addressing these questions will have very important practical bearings in helping people to adapt to new cultural environments if they move across cultural boundaries.

Final Thought

Aside from some of the practical implications of the nonsocial cultural competences we noted above, we are well aware of one enormous challenge the relevant findings pose to the theories of cultural psychology. The challenge has to do with the origins of these competences. The past two decades of research has shown, or at least has strongly suggested, that the origins of nonsocial cultural competences are in the sociocultural worlds or, more specifically, in the culturally constituted practices and meanings available in given regions and groups (e.g., Fiske et al., 1998; Markus & Kitayama, in press; Nisbett et al., 2001). Yet, to argue for this cultural constructionist view only begs the question of where culture comes from: How have the very practices, customs, and meaning systems that make up culture been developed, selected, and institutionalized? To make the matter even more complicated, it would seem likely that the very cultural competences at issue, say, divergent weighting of object versus context, are significantly implicated in the selection and development of the attendant cultural customs, practices, and their configurations. Exploring the process of emergence is a significant new direction for future research.

REFERENCES

Adams, G., & Markus, H. R. (2001). Culture as patterns: An alternative approach to the problem of reification. *Culture & Psychology, 7,* 283–296.

Aoki, M. (2001). *Toward a comparative institutional analysis.* Cambridge, MA: MIT Press.

Arterberry, M. E., & Kellman, P. J. (2000). *Cradle of knowledge: Development of perception in infancy.* Cambridge, MA: MIT Press.

Bandura, A. (1997). *Self-efficacy in changing societies.* New York: Cambridge University Press.

Bourdieu, P. (1977). *Outline of a theory of practice.* Cambridge, England: Cambridge University Press.

Boyd, R., & Richardson, P. J. (1985). *Culture and the evolutionary process.* Chicago: University of Chicago Press.

Brewer, M. B., & Gardner, W. L. (1996). Who is this "we"? Levels of collective identity and self representations. *Journal of Personality and Social Psychology, 71,* 83–93.

Bruner, J. (1957). On perceptual readiness. *Psychological Review, 64,* 123–152.

Bruner, J. (1990). *Acts of meaning.* Cambridge, MA: Harvard University Press.

Bruner, J., & Goodman, C. C. (1947). Value and need as organizing factors in perception. *Journal of Abnormal and Social Psychology, 42,* 33–44.

Choi, I., & Nisbett, R. E. (1998). Situational salience and cultural differences in the correspondence bias and the actor-observer bias. *Personality and Social Psychology Bulletin, 24,* 949–960.

Cole, M. (1996). *Cultural psychology: A once and future discipline.* Cambridge: Harvard University Press.

Deci, E. L., & Ryan, R. M. (1995). Human autonomy: The basis for true self-esteem. In M. H. Kernis (Ed.), *Efficacy, agency, and self-esteem* (pp. 31–49). New York: Plenum Press.

Duffy, S., & Kitayama, S. (2003). [Japanese, Chinese, and American responses in a line estimation task]. Unpublished raw data.

Durham, W. H. (1991). *Coevolution: Genes, culture and human diversity.* Palo Alto, CA: Stanford University Press.

Fiske, A., Kitayama, S., Markus, H. R., & Nisbett, R. E. (1998). The cultural matrix of social psychology. In D. Gilbert, S. Fiske, & G. Lindzey (Eds.), *The handbook of social psychology* (4th ed., pp. 915–981). San Francisco: McGraw-Hill.

Gay, J., & Cole, M. (1967). *The new mathematics and an old culture*. New York: Holt, Rinehart & Winston.

Gilbert, D. T., & Malone, P. S. (1995). The correspondence bias. *Psychological Bulletin, 117,* 21–38.

Gould, S. J. (1999). A critique of Heckhausen and Schultz's (1995) life-span theory of control from a cross-cultural perspective. *Psychological Review, 106,* 597–601.

Hallowell, A. I. (1955). *Culture and experience*. Philadelphia: University of Pennsylvania Press.

Heckhausen, J., & Schulz, R. (1995). A life-span theory of control. *Psychological Review, 102,* 284–304.

Heine, S. J., Lehman, D. R., Markus, H. R., & Kitayama, S. (1999). Is there a universal need for positive self-regard? *Psychological Review, 106,* 766–794.

Higgins, E. T., & Bargh, J. A. (1987). Social cognition and social perception. *Annual Review of Psychology, 38,* 369–425.

Hong, Y., Morris, M., Chiu, C., & Benet-Martinez, V. (2000). Multicultural minds: A dynamic constructivist approach to culture and cognition. *American Psychologist, 55,* 709–720.

Huttenlocher, J., Hedges, L., & Duncan, S. (1991). Categories and particulars: Prototype effects in estimating spatial location. *Psychological Review, 95,* 471–484.

Huttenlocher, J., Hedges, L., & Vevea, J. (2000). Why do categories affect stimulus judgment? *Journal of Experimental Psychology: General, 129,* 220–241.

Ishii, K., Reyes, J. A., & Kitayama, S. (2003). Spontaneous attention to word content versus emotional tone: Differences among three cultures. *Psychological Science, 14*(1), 39–45.

Iyengar, S. S., & Lepper, M. R. (1999). Rethinking the value of choice: A cultural perspective on intrinsic motivation. *Journal of Personality and Social Psychology, 76,* 349–366.

Ji, L. J., Peng, K., & Nisbett, R. E. (2000). Culture, control, and perception of relationships in the environment. *Journal of Personality and Social Psychology, 78,* 943–955.

Jones, E. E. (1979). The rocky road from act to disposition. *American Psychologist, 34,* 107–117.

Kato, N. (1965). The validity and reliability of new rod frame test. *Japanese Psychological Research, 4,* 120–125.

Kahneman, D. (1973). *Attention and effort*. Englewood Cliffs, NJ: Prentice-Hall.

Karasawa, M. (2001). A Japanese perception of self and others: Self-critical and other-enhancing biases. *Japanese Journal of Psychology, 72,* 195–203.

Kawamura, T., Kitayama, S., Greenholtz, J., & Lehman, D. (2003). *Framed line test and acculturation effect: A preliminary study*. Unpublished data, Kyoto University.

Kitayama, S. (2002). Cultural and basic psychological processes: Toward a system view of culture. *Psychological Bulletin, 128,* 89–96.

Kitayama, S., Duffy, S., Kawamura, T., & Larsen, J. T. (2003). Perceiving an object and its context in different cultures: A cultural look at New Look. *Psychological Science, 14*, 201–206.

Kitayama, S., & Ishii, K. (2002). Word and voice: Spontaneous attention to emotional utterances in two languages. *Cognition and Emotion, 16*, 29–59.

Kitayama, S., Karasawa, M., & Mesquita, B. (in press). Collective and personal processes in regulating emotions: Emotion and self in Japan and the U.S. In P. Philippot & R. S. Feldman (Eds.), *The regulation of emotion.* Hillsdale, NJ: Erlbaum.

Kitayama, S., & Markus, H. R. (1999). Yin and yang of the Japanese self: The cultural psychology of personality coherence. In D. Cervone & Y. Shoda (Eds.), *The coherence of personality: Social cognitive bases of personality consistency, variability, and organization* (pp. 242–302). New York: Guilford Press.

Kitayama, S., & Markus, H. R. (2000). The pursuit of happiness and the realization of sympathy: Cultural patterns of self, social relations, and well-being. In E. Diener & E. Suh, (Eds.), *Subjective well-being across cultures* (pp. 113–116). Cambridge, MA: MIT Press.

Kitayama, S., & Markus, H. R., & Matsumoto, H. (1995). Culture, self, & emotion: A cultural perspective on "self-conscious" emotions. In J. P. Tangney & K. W. Fisher (Eds.), *Self-conscious emotions: The psychology of shame, guilt, embarrassment, and pride.* (pp. 439–464). New York: Guilford Press.

Kitayama, S., Markus, H. R., Matsumoto, H., & Norasakkunkit, V. (1997). Individual and collective processes in the construction of the self: Self-enhancement in the United States and self-criticism in Japan. *Journal of Personality and Social Psychology, 72*, 1245–1267.

Kitayama, S., Nakama, D., & Saitoh, K. (2003). *Culture, self, and social support.* Unpublished data, Kyoto University.

Kitayama, S., & Uchida, Y. (2003). Explicit self-criticism and implicit self-regard: Evaluating self and friend in two cultures. *Journal of Experimental Social Psychology, 39*, 476–482.

Kuhnen, U., Hannover, B., & Schubert, B. (2001). The semantic-procedural-interface model of the self: The role of self-knowledge for context-dependent versus context-independent modes of thinking. *Journal of Personality and Social Psychology, 80*, 397–409.

Kuhnen, U., & Oyserman, D. (2002). Thinking about the self influences thinking in genera: Cognitive consequences of salient self-concept. *Journal of Experimental Social Psychology, 38*, 492–499.

Lee, F., Hallahan, M., & Herzog, T. (1996). Explaining real life events: How culture and domain shape attributions. *Personality and Social Psychology Bulletin, 22*, 732–741.

Lewin, K. (1936). *Principles of topological psychology* (1st ed.). New York: McGraw-Hill.

Lucy, J., & Gaskins, S. (2000). Grammatical categories and the development of classification preferences: A comparative approach. In S. Levinson & M. Bowerman

(Eds.), *Language acquisition and conceptual development* (pp. 257–283). Cambridge, England: Cambridge University Press.

Markus, H. R., & Kitayama, S. (1991). Culture and the self: Implications for cognition, emotion, and motivation. *Psychological Review, 98,* 224–253.

Markus, H. R., & Kitayama, S. (1998). The cultural psychology of personality. *Journal of Cross-Cultural Psychology, 29,* 32–61.

Markus, H. R., & Kitayama, S. (in press). Models of agency: Sociocultural diversity in the construction of action. In *Nebraska Symposium on Motivation.*

Masuda, T., & Kitayama, S. (2002). *Culture and correspondence bias.* Unpublished manuscript, University of Michigan.

Masuda, T., & Nisbett, R. A. (2001). Attending holistically versus analytically: Comparing the context sensitivity of Japanese and Americans. *Journal of Personality and Social Psychology, 81,* 922–934.

McCandliss, B. D., Fiez, J. A., Protopapas, A., Conway, M., & McClelland, J. L. (2002). Success and failure in teaching the [r]-[l] contrast to Japanese adults: Predictions of a Hebbian model of plasticity and stability in spoken language perception. *Cognitive, Affective, and Behavioral Neuroscience, 2,* 89–108.

Miller, D. T. (1999). The norm of self-interest. *American Psychologist, 54,* 1053–1060.

Miller, J. G. (1984). Culture and the development of everyday explanation. *Journal of Personality and Social Psychology, 46,* 961–978.

Minoura, Y. (1990). A sensitive period for the incorporation of a cultural meaning system: A study of Japanese children growing up in the United States. *Ethos, 20,* 304–339.

Miyamoto, Y., & Kitayama, S. (2002). Cultural variation in correspondence bias: The critical role of attitude diagnosticity of socially constrained behavior. *Journal of Personality and Social Psychology, 83,* 1239–1248.

Miyawaki, K., Strange, W., Verbrugge, R., Liberman, A., Jenkins, J. J., & Fujimura, O. (1975). An effect of linguistic experience: The discrimination of [r] and [l] by native speakers of Japanese and English. *Perception & Psychophysics, 18,* 331–340.

Morling, B., Kitayama, S., & Miyamoto, Y. (2002). Cultural practices emphasize influence in the U.S. and adjustment in Japan. *Personality and Social Psychology Bulletin, 28,* 311–323.

Morling, B., Kitayama, S., & Miyamoto, Y. (in press). American and Japanese women use different coping strategies during normal pregnancy. *Personality and Social Psychology Bulletin.*

Morris, M. W., Menon, T., & Ames, D. R. (2001). Culturally conferred conceptions of agency: A key to social perception of persons, groups, and other actors. *Personality and Social Psychology Review, 5,* 169–182.

Morris, M. W., & Peng, K. (1994). Culture and cause: American and Chinese attributions for social and physical events. *Journal of Personality and Social Psychology, 67,* 949–971.

Nisbett, R. E., & Cohen, D. (1996). *Culture of honor: The psychology of violence in the South.* Denver, CO: Westview Press.

Nisbett, R. E., Peng, K., Choi, I., & Norenzayan, A. (2001). Culture and systems of thought: Holistic vs. analytic cognition. *Psychological Review, 108,* 291–310.

Norenzayan, A., Smith, E. E., Kim, B. J., & Nisbett, R. E. (2002). Cultural preferences for formal versus intuitive reasoning. *Cognitive Science, 26,* 653–684.

Plaut, V., Markus, H. R., & Lachman, M. E. (2002). Place matters: Consensual features and regional variation in American well-being and self. *Journal of Personality and Social Psychology, 83,* 160–184.

Polanyi, K. (1957). *The great transformation: The political and economic origins of our time.* Boston: Beacon Press.

Rivers, W. H. R. (1901). Physiology and psychology. In A. C. Haddon (Ed.), *Report of the Cambridge anthropological expedition to the Torres Straits* (Vol. 2). Cambridge, England: Cambridge University Press.

Ross, L., & Nisbett, R. E. (1991). *The person and the situation: Perspective of social psychology.* New York: McGraw-Hill.

Rozin, P., & Schull, J. (1988). The adaptive-evolutionary point of view in experimental psychology. In R. C. Atkinson, R. J. Hernstein, G. Lindzey, & R. D. Luce (Ed.), *Handbook of experimental psychology* (pp. 503–546). New York: Wiley.

Sampson, E. E. (1988). The debate on individualism: Indigenous psychologies of the individual and their role in personal and societal functioning. *American Psychologist, 43,* 15–22.

Sampson, E. E. (2000). Reinterpreting individualism and collectivism: Their religious roots and monologic versus dialogic person-other relationship. *American Psychologist, 55,* 1425–1432.

Sanchez-Burks, J. (2002). Protestant relational ideology and (in)attention to relational cues in work settings. *Journal of Personality and Social Psychology, 83,* 919–929.

Seligman, M. A. (1970). On the generality of the laws of learning. *Psychological Review, 77,* 406–418.

Shore, B. (1996). *Culture in mind: Cognition, culture and the problem of meaning.* New York: Oxford University Press.

Shweder, R. A. (1991). *Thinking through culture: Expeditions in cultural psychology.* Cambridge, MA: Harvard University Press.

Shweder, R. A., & Bourne, E. J. (1984). Does the concept of the self vary cross-culturally? In R. A. Shweder & R. A. Levine (Eds.), *Culture theory: Essays on mind, self, and emotion* (pp. 158–199). New York: Cambridge University Press.

Shweder, R. A., & Sullivan, M. A. (1993). Cultural psychology: Who needs it? *Annual Review of Psychology, 44,* 497–523.

Spelke, E. (1990). Principles of object perception. *Cognitive Science, 14*(1), 29–56.

Sperber, D. (1985). Anthropology and psychology: Towards an epidemiology of representations. *Man, 20,* 73–89.

Sperber, D. (1996). *Explaining culture: A naturalistic approach*. Oxford, England: Blackwell.

Sperber, D., & Wilson, D. (1986). *Relevance, communication and cognition*. New York: Academic Press.

Takano, Y., & Osaka, E. (1999). An unsupported common view: Comparing Japan and the U.S. on individualism/collectivism. *Asian Journal of Social Psychology, 2*, 311–341.

Taylor, S. E., & Brown, J. D. (1988). Illusion and well-being: A social psychological perspective on mental health. *Psychological Bulletin, 103*, 193–210.

Titchener, E. H. (1916). On ethnological tests of sensation and perception with special reference to the Cambridge University expedition to the Torres Straits. *Proceedings of the American Philosophical Society, 55*, 204–236.

Tomasello, M. (1999). *The cultural origins of human cognition*. Cambridge, MA: Harvard University Press.

Triandis, H. C. (1989). The self and social behavior in differing cultural contexts. *Psychological Review, 96*, 506–520.

Uttal, D. (1994). Preschoolers' and adults' scale translation and reconstruction of spatial information acquired from maps. *British Journal of Developmental Psychology, 12*, 259–275.

Weisz, J. R., Rothbaum, F. M., & Blackburn, T. C. (1984). Standing out and standing in: The psychology of control in America and Japan. *American Psychologist, 39*, 955–969.

Werker, J., & Tees, R. C. (1984). Cross-language speech perception: Evidence from the first year of life. *Infant Behavior and Development, 7*(1), 49–63.

Wilson, E. O. (1999). *Consilience: The unity of knowledge*. New York: Vintage Books.

Witkin, H. A. (1967). A cognitive-style approach to cross-cultural research. *International Journal of Psychology, 2*, 233–250.

Witkin, H. A., Lewis, H. B., Kertzman, M., Machover, K., Meissner, P. B., & Karp, S. A. (1954). *Personality through perception*. New York: Harper.

Wittenbrink, B., Judd, C. M., & Park, B. (2001). Spontaneous prejudice in context: Variability in automatically activated attitudes. *Journal of Personality and Social Psychology, 81*, 815–827.

Yamagishi, T. (1986). The provision of a sanctioning system as a public good. *Journal of Personality and Social Psychology, 51*, 110–116.

4

UNDERSTANDING THE COGNITIVE AND SOCIAL ASPECTS OF INTERCULTURAL COMPETENCE

WALTER J. LONNER AND SUSANNA A. HAYES

Ted and Clifford are in their mid-20s. Separated in age by only 15 months, they grew up in the same intact family in a Toronto, Canada, suburb. Their father is a successful insurance agent, and their mother was and still is a caring and devoted "stay-at-home Mom". Both have Scottish–Welsh heritage. The family can be described as "typical," and their neighborhood has for years been moderately multiethnic. Any ethnic or racial prejudice in their community, if it ever existed, was well hidden. A friendly Asian family lives across the street and their next-door neighbors, a family of five from Montreal, speak as much French as they do English. The deputy mayor is Black. In recent years there has been a striking influx of immigrant families in the broader community. Consequently, the local schools have become increasingly multiethnic. The local high school has a significant number of Asian and Middle Eastern students enrolled.

Considering this generally positive background and the many commonalities in their formative years, Ted and Clifford are quite a contrast. All of his life Ted showed an affinity for people who are "different" in such things as skin color, language, type of family, and overall cultural characteristics. He befriended many of them and continues to nurture the relationships he has established with a wide range of people. Moreover, he has been abroad twice in his young life, both times for nearly a year in student exchange programs. Ted says that he would like to get into an occupation in which he can be stimulated by a good mixture of cultures and ethnicities. He reports being comfortable and fulfilled when he is among students from many different backgrounds. He actually thrives on the interesting differences. It is a win–win situation: The students from other parts of the world like him as much as he likes them.

Clifford, however, is almost uncannily different from Ted in this regard. He readily admits that he never had much of an interest in people who are different because of their cultures or ethnicities. In fact, he often pokes fun at them, sometimes to the point of stimulating serious frictions and occasional threats. Clifford has been involved in several scuffles with foreign students. He openly expresses a distaste for "those people" and claims to feel intimidated by them as well as emotionally distant. He often chides Ted for not staying with his "own kind." He has blasted several men in the community for marrying people he sometimes calls "mongrels" or members of the "mud races" (a pernicious reference to darker skin color). He has often expressed an interest in joining a group whose intent it is to set strict limits on immigration. One wonders if he may be affiliated with an active hate group.

The scenario cited above raises many questions. Why are Ted and Clifford so different with respect to their tolerance for and interest in people who are culturally different? In the context of this chapter, why is Ted so genuinely and proudly competent in his intercultural interactions whereas Clifford is so seemingly incompetent, with no intention to do anything about it? How can these differences be explained? Psychologists who study individual differences in such behavior are hard pressed to come up with easy answers to paradoxes like these. However, there are various ways to help answer such questions, and this chapter will focus on several of the relevant ways to consider individual differences in cultural competence.

One must recognize and expect that coming up with solid answers to such questions is immediately clouded by a stark reality: There are few terms in any language as complex in meaning as *culture* and *competence*. When these two terms are combined to form *cultural competence*, complexities are compounded. In this chapter, various meanings of these two terms will be operationally defined as they relate to cognitive and social functioning across the life span and across cultures. It is interesting that the *Oxford English Dictionary* (2nd ed., 1989) offers the literal meaning of competence as the suitability, adequacy, or appropriateness of means to live in comfort or easy circumstances. There is no suggestion of excellence but there is the connotation of competition to meet a standard of adequacy and sufficiency. It can be presumed that anyone who cannot compete or demonstrate adequacy has little choice but to experience the consequences of being regarded as incompetent and all of the negative traits this may suggest.

We must be candid about the concept of culture as well as cautious about what we mean by that term. Much has been written about what it is, is not, or may be. One must remember that half a century ago Kroeber and Kluckhohn (1952) found some 160 definitions of culture in the extant literature. The situation seems to be consistent, over time, with further insight and analysis of the term. Indeed, the debate about what culture may or may not be remains quite active (e.g., Jahoda, 2002). Different camps of psychologists—those who identify more strongly with either cultural psychology, cross-cultural psychology, or indigenous psychology—often treat this "nebulous construct" (Lonner & Adamopoulos, 1997, p. 62) somewhat differently. In short, some important questions to keep in mind are these: What does it mean if someone is competent in a particular culture? What are some of the common expectations in particular cultures that someone must fulfill before he or she is considered competent? And what are the criteria that must be used to christen someone as culturally competent as he or she meets cultural norms across the life span from childhood to adulthood? Indeed, who determines when a good level of cultural competence has been reached? These are heady questions, the answers to which may be as difficult to reach as it is to define both culture and competence. We merely ask readers to keep them in mind as they read this and other chapters in this book.

TWO DIFFERENT APPROACHES TO THE STUDY OF INTERCULTURAL COMPETENCE

We are also faced with yet another reality. In this chapter we restrict our discussion of intercultural competence to individuals who, for one or more reasons, are required or want to reach a higher level of intercultural effectiveness than they currently enjoy (even if they have reached an acceptable or adequate level of competence). Such individuals may be sojourners, Peace Corps or International Red Cross volunteers, students, tourists, business persons, military personnel, educators, and even anthropologists or cross-cultural psychologists. Our interest in this group of individuals is guided by such questions as (a) what accounts for variations in intercultural effectiveness, (b) what are the consequences of ineffectiveness, and (c) what are some of the techniques used to teach or train people to become more competent in their interaction with people in other societies? Generally, such individuals are under little pressure to become comfortably or even superbly competent in other parts of the world. In a sense, we are concerned here with what might be called intercultural–interpersonal intelligence. This perspective can be explained by using three highly related concepts. *Contextual intelligence*, the third leg in Sternberg's triarchic theory of intelligence (Sternberg, 1985,

1988b), concerns the ways in which intelligent behavior is displayed in specific contexts. It has sometimes been called "street smarts," and is qualitatively different from traditional views of intelligence. The idea of *social intelligence* has been used by many psychologists to explain the extent to which an individual is competent in a specific social context. Walters (1986) and Gardner (1993), for instance, have suggested that *interpersonal intelligence* should be recognized as a legitimate type of intelligence, on par with several other manifestations of competence in different domains. *Emotional intelligence* (Goleman, 1995; Salovey & Mayer, 1990), which is closely related to social intelligence, has received considerable attention. Those who are emotionally intelligent may be characterized as sympathetic, as in the Italian expression *multo simpatico*, the French *sympathique*, the Spanish *sympatia*, the German *sympatisch*, and in, no doubt, thousands of terms in other languages. However, these basically identical words may well have varying connotations in their respective languages.

Nevertheless, taking these concepts together, one sees an emerging picture of a person who is emotionally caring yet controlled, sensitive to interpersonal dynamics, and genuinely perceptive when in complex and highly interactive situations. Most important, those who witness such behavior would call it the mark of someone who is socially competent. Such a person may be described more generically with such phrases as a "cool people person," a "comfortable person to be around," and an "admirable, confident, and trustworthy leader."

The other way to look at intercultural competence is from the perspective of adjustment to other cultures, often subsumed under the broad title of acculturation (e.g., Ward, 2001). In this domain one must be concerned with such phenomena as the forced or required adjustment of others because they are running from religious persecution, seeking political asylum, escaping from desperate economic conditions or natural disasters, adjusting as foreign students during exchange programs, and so on. If one studies the interactions between aboriginal communities and colonizing peoples who intend to occupy the land of the aboriginals, questions about acculturation and cultural change or even survival abound. Research in this area is undoubtedly prolific, perhaps because so many more people are involved and because both the mental and the physical health of so many more individuals are at stake.

Both forms of intercultural competence share much of the same literature, and researchers who study either or both perspectives will likely continue to find positive but weak correlations among variables related to this second kind of intercultural competence. For instance, in their extensive review of the intercultural competence literature, Dinges and Baldwin (1996, p. 114) reported the results of much research in this area. Among numerous synopses, researchers have found that higher levels of ethnocentrism were related to less culture-general understanding, greater degrees of perceived knowledge of specific cultures were associated with greater culture-general understanding, and the culture-general dimension was positively correlated with perceived social distance. Dedicated researchers in this area have even developed scales and inventories to measure individual variations in adjustment. One of the most commonly used devices is the Behavioral Assessment Scale for Intercultural Communication Effectiveness (Koester & Olebe, 1988). Throughout this chapter we occasionally mention this type of research, insofar as it relates to the type of intercultural competence we have chosen to highlight.

WHY CROSS-CULTURAL COMPETENCE?

In any culture it would be hard to argue with the proposition that it is good for a person to be competent or effective and to be viewed as such by others. One suspects the obvious: Regardless of culture, a competent person is quite likely viewed very positively as a responsible, trustworthy, and effective person (despite the fact that there can also be competent pickpockets and other criminals, who would be evaluated negatively by most). Whether it is manifested in school achievements and peer relationships, music, athletics, farming, cooking, or raising children, it is rewarding to both the individual and the culture to strive for sufficiency, for basic and enduring competence, in such activities. But why *cultural* competence? Is it not enough to be competent in one's own milieu? Might it not be too much to expect people to be competent in, or with, other cultures as well?

People anywhere would benefit from being culturally competent if for no other reason than it would tend to influence positive interpersonal relationships in an increasingly globalized, mobile, and multicultural world. But for psychologists there are many reasons—professional, ethical, scholarly, humanitarian, and even legal —to be competent within such diversity. Consider, for example, four reasons why intercultural competence would pay off handsomely for anyone in the social and behavioral sciences:

1. A licensed psychologist is hired by a mental health clinic in a community that is rich in cultural, age, and linguistic diversity. Unless the psychologist makes an effort to understand the people in the community, he or she will not be effective. Indeed, his or her job will be a daily grind of confusion and frustration, brought on by incompetence. It would be incumbent for this person to become familiar with relevant literature in multicultural counseling (e.g., Pedersen, Draguns, Lonner, & Trimble, 2002).
2. An instructor of psychology is employed in a community college in which students from many ethnic groups are enrolled.

A failure to understand the lives and cultures of these students would likely lead to ineffective teaching, poor evaluations, and poor professional advancement.

3. A neuropsychologist is employed in a medical setting that serves a broad cultural constituency. For accurate diagnosis followed by recommendations for proper treatment, such a psychologist would be considered professionally incompetent (ethically questionable as well) if he or she was not aware of the many subtle cultural nuances that could affect both diagnosis and treatment (Fletcher-Janzen, Strickland, & Reynolds, 2000; Nell, 2000)

4. A family therapist would run the risk of being baffled and professionally ineffective if he or she was not aware of the various ways that family structures and functions differ across cultures (Kagitcibasi, 1996).

The above may be simplistic and mundane examples of reasons in favor of cultural competency. However, it is not at all simple or easy to be competent in this domain. In one's own culture, one knows that people can be confusing, unpredictable, and hard to understand. If one adds the cultural, and often with it, the linguistic dimension, cultural competency can only be reached through much effort and experience. Competence of this type does not come "naturally."

Increasing interest in the training of culturally competent psychologists is evident in several quarters. For instance, a special issue of the *International Journal of Intercultural Relations* focused on this topic. Titled "The Training of Global Psychologists" and guest-edited by Mark Leach, this issue included several invited articles. In one of the articles, Lonner (1997) argued that there are three basic paths leading to increased cultural competence. The first is experiential, or simply "being there" (in a different culture) for significant periods of time. Anthropological field workers have called this *deep cultural immersion*, and it is perhaps the best way to learn, firsthand, the subtleties of a particular culture. The second path is what you are doing as you read this book: academic discourse. A great deal, obviously, has been written about most of the world's cultures. Through dedicated immersion in books and journals, and through discourse in different classes and discussions in colleges and universities, one can learn a great deal about other societies. The third way to learn about other cultures is through participating in formal culture-training techniques, an orientation that is briefly described below.

Both the second and the third of these paths to cultural competence are educational, one in the more classical educational mold and the other through training, or focused and goal-specific education. We turn, then, to some characteristics of the educational realm as it relates to competence.

EDUCATION, FORMAL AND INFORMAL, AND COMPETENCE

Implicit in the notion of competence is the ability to intelligently select one's behavior or course of action in response to the various opportunities and challenges of daily living, including managing social and work-focused relationships as well as conceptualizing and executing solutions to an array of human problems (Csikszentmihalyi & Sawyer, 1995; Sternberg, 1988a). Clearly, the diverse cultures of the world suggest that there are many ways to demonstrate social, emotional, intellectual, athletic, and occupational competence. For example, there are many ways to teach and coach soccer players from differing nations of the world. Yet athletes from Canada to Argentina or Russia to India use common skills and techniques to score goals and win matches. The game is basically the same, yet it is perceived, valued, and executed differently by athletes around the world. Multiple parallels exist for human endeavors in agricultural, artistic, educational, technological, and social domains.

Under severe or extremely challenging conditions, such as natural or social disasters and extremes of heat and cold, unusual levels of competence may be required for mere survival. If natural, economic, and social conditions are ideal, demonstrated competence may result in high levels of productivity and efficiency in the arts, sciences, and cooperative social interactions (Freud, 1962). However, human history is marked by cycles of peaks and valleys in the cultural ebb and flow of societies that thrived and subsequently fell into relative obscurity. Consider the paths of Aztec, Chinese, Egyptian, Greek, Incan, or Roman cultures over the past 2,000 years.

One's competence may also result in sufficient and perhaps even extraordinary adaptation or adjustment to new social–cultural challenges. The process of learning to be competent always occurs in a culturally prescribed context (Bruner, 1996). Much depends on the criteria and models put forward by the traditions and practices of the particular society with which one identifies. Therefore, the way one learns to act intelligently and competently, regardless of one's native abilities or talents, is guided by the cultural prompts and input that shape one's personal and social growth and development. In the early formation of the social and political organization of the British and French colonies that became the United States of America, formal and compulsory schooling for children was deemed essential to the collective well-being. Education was linked to the moral formation of responsible and productive (e.g., competent) citizens in a struggling and vulnerable democratic confederation.

In his text *How We Think*, John Dewey (1910) proposed that thinking is stimulated by the need to solve problems or to calm doubts and persistent questions. To become efficient at this process, one needs both an absence and a presence of knowledge and skills in adequate proportion that affords the motivation to persist toward discovering and using information and skills to solve problems, and thereby demonstrate competence. Thinking positively and consistently, Dewey said, requires the ability to determine the direction and momentum one's intelligence might take. Amassing a broad base of information about human and natural conditions, observing skilled problem solvers at work, and gaining experience as a problem solver, constitute the purpose of formal education, which enhances one's ability (or competence) to create and experience a meaningful life. The process of education is intended to pass along to the younger generation the valued knowledge and wisdom of those who have gone before them. In Dewey's words,

> were it not for this process by which the achievements of one generation form the stimuli that direct the activities of the next, the story of civilization would be writ in water, and each generation would have laboriously to make for itself, if it could, its way out of savagery. (Dewey, 1910, pp. 159–160)

However, if a person needs to solve problems that demand information and skills far greater than those he or she possesses, the motivation to act competently is diminished by feelings of frustration and helplessness. Thus, motivation includes a sense of hopefulness and social trust that members of the older generations, parents and grandparents, communicate to their children and grandchildren. Motivation to take action within one's social and physical environment requires a combination of analytical skills and emotional perceptions and intuition that supports the confidence that action will be useful and hopefully valuable to one's self and one's community members. When children in a society are young and inexperienced, there is a strong need and reliance on the feedback and reinforcement of elders to guide their naïve attempts to demonstrate their competence. Whether they are learning to feed themselves, walk across a room, or open a book, children need assistance and encouragement from adults. Cultural traditions and norms will dictate who provides this instruction and how to proceed in such crucial endeavors (Bruner, 1996). Simultaneously, no community or society is without cultural variance among its members due to patterns of in and out migration as well as adaptation to various aspects of environmental conditions. However, despite perceived differences, there are also clear areas of common ground that reinforce feelings and beliefs that all people have some shared cultural perspectives.

In Aronson's (2000) study of adolescent youths, those who possessed high levels of emotional intelligence—the ability to understand and empathetically respond to intra- and interpersonal relationships—experienced both positive mental health and positive school achievement. Furthermore, emotionally intelligent adolescents were able to control tendencies to behave impulsively and aggressively toward others. They learned through the experience of parental guidance and positive modeling that interpersonal relationships are enhanced through respectful, kindly interactions with others. This further contributes to the notion that cultural competence is deeply connected to recognizing the usefulness of self-control, delayed gratification, and cooperation with others. As a result of investigations into the effects of social environment at school on students' behavior, Aronson (2000) found that schools that nurture cooperative and harmonious social interactions also have higher rates of academic achievement than is the case for schools in which interpersonal conflict and competition are relatively unchecked. This strongly suggests that emotional and academic competence are mutually interactive and positively correlated. It also suggests that the social climate or culture of the school is malleable and takes shape according to the input of school and community leaders.

Social and educational psychologists observe that as children confront challenges on a daily basis, they integrate their experience and informational resources to expand their range and depth of competencies. With systematic and protracted inquiry, followed by careful reflection on critical aspects of the problems, solutions are proposed and implemented. It is important that Dewey (1910) observed that a thinking person is not pushed only by instinct or habit but chooses a course of action that is enlightened by expanded information and experience. Use of imagination and experimental inquiry, characteristics of scientific thinking, begin in early childhood and expand throughout life. Therefore, educators guide and support their students as they demonstrate readiness to advance into new areas of academic and social competence (Dewey, 1910).

Depending on one's cultural context, teachers may be certified and college educated, community sages, artists, craftsmen, farmers, scholars, or shamans. However, underlying the scientific approach to education and competence is Bandura's (1986) assessment that often unconsciously held belief systems, rather than logical analysis, frequently prompt human behavior. For example, when children must cope with grief and loss due to the death of loved ones, they are flooded with emotions that many adults could not manage very effectively. In the absence of answers or solutions to feelings of fear or dismay, they resort to beliefs that are conveyed through their cultural heritage and find the confidence and resolve to regain emotional and social stability.

Relating an individual's competencies to those of whole societies, Dewey noted that leaders of nations go to great pains to warn and advise each other of impending harm or danger that can be foretold on the basis of the recognition of economic and social indicators. By combining their observational abilities and powers of assessment, communities can effectively maintain the common good. Throughout human history, Socratic guidelines of common sense, reason, memory, and creativity have been applied to the solution of human problems (Saul, 1997). Endurance of these guidelines over time and across nations suggests there are universal characteristics of competent communities that have been integrated into formal education systems across cultures.

In contemporary technological societies, however, it has been observed that the well-being of many can be seriously compromised by the self-serving and manipulative behavior of a persuasive and powerful few. Lured by images of ever-increasing wealth, physical, and social power, the Socratic tenets may be rejected as irrelevant by those whom Saul (1997) referred to as *the unconscious civilization*. In his view, extraordinary achievements in some aspects of applied intelligence or problem solving (e.g., advances in medicine, communication systems, and manufacturing) have focused attention on selected areas and left others ignored (e.g. distribution of food to the famine stricken, or provision of basic education and health services for the suffering and illiterate). As a result, in the contemporary world, there is an illusion of holistic high-level functioning within some communities whereas others appear overshadowed by human deficiencies. This condition contributes to a dangerous and dehumanizing polarization of those who have an abundance of material goods and services and those who are on the brink of devastation.

Clearly, despite the collective wisdom of centuries of human effort, true competency has not been achieved. If one did nothing else in life, it would be possible to dedicate all conscious effort to searching for an adequate if not exact description of how intelligence and experience can be used to produce both individual and collective human competence (Gardner, 1982). With the development of Cartesian logic and scientific methods, the study of human thinking and behaving was singled out and transferred into the arena of experimental laboratories. Knowledge of human intellectual functioning has expanded beyond a structuralist approach, which seeks to discover specific rules of mental operations like language acquisition, response patterns to specific stimuli, and situational problem solving tactics; a broader approach now includes studies of emotions and creative abilities. In Gardner's (1982) view, and Walters and Gardner's (1986) view, the power of emotion and creativity was frequently excluded from psychological research in an effort to avoid unscientific content. As knowledge about intelligence and its effects on behavior has expanded, one can argue that an accurate definition of intelligence must include the diverse manifestations of human emotions and creativity (Boden, 1991).

The deep and complex interaction between human competence and culture is expressed in Sue and Sue's (1999) statement that culture includes all that people have learned to do, believe, value, and pass along through their history from generation to generation. Culture is so pervasive and all-encompassing that it shapes every part of life, from the kind of food and drink that is consumed to the way the death of community members is acknowledged and finalized in funeral rites and burial practices. In effect, culture is so dominant in life that it is the means by which one's reality is defined (Pedersen, Draguns, Lonner, & Trimble, 2002). The *Oxford English Dictionary* (2nd ed., 1989) includes in its definition of culture the notion of refinement of human faculties and manner of living. Culture is, at some levels, an intentional process of improving human life through concerted, pre-scribed interactions with the natural and the social environment. Therefore, one can conclude that competence, including the ability to adapt to changes while maintaining appropriate living conditions, is unquestionably cultur-ally determined.

Srivastava and Misra (1999) have examined how intelligence, as demon-strated through individual competence, is perceived and assessed within an Indian cultural context. Although aspects of intelligence such as social com-petence, logical thinking, and problem solving are valued in India, the most highly respected demonstrations of intelligence are behaviors that contribute to social harmony and community well-being. The collective definitions of intelligence in the ancient traditions of India include both mental processes like decision making as well as personal characteristics such as determination and open expression of feelings and opinions (Srivastava & Misra, 1999).

When a sample of 12 U.S. graduate students who participated in a semi-nar on the theories and research strategies of cross-cultural psychologists were asked if they were culturally competent, there was considerable variation in responses from "no" to "yes." Those who said they were not culturally com-petent felt very limited by their lack of experiences and associations with people from cultures other than their own. Others thought they were mov-ing toward cultural competence because they were open to new people and experiences and ready to learn. Those who said they were culturally compe-tent had in-depth experiences with cultural differences including extensive travel and growing up in dual culture families. Generally, all students stated that culturally competent people had both the respect for and ability and desire to learn about different cultures. It is by no means alarming that a few of the students did not evaluate themselves very highly on cultural compe-tence. People who have limitations in some areas of knowledge and experi-ences, and admit it, may be among the better candidates to make great im-provements. This small sample supports the conjecture, for the instructor in this class (one of the authors) considers these 12 students to be excellent candidates for a high level of cultural competence. The common denomina-tor across cultures seems to be this: a person is "intelligent" if he or she is socially aware, empathetic, and capable of interacting respectfully with oth-ers especially within the circles of family or kin. A statement from a reserva-tion-based Native American parent of six children from the Pacific North-west suggests her views about cultural competence:

> I always wanted my children to know that we have a creator who made all things here on earth and we have to recognize him and always give thanks for that which we are about to gather from the earth. Life is a hard struggle to make sure that your children have that understanding espe-cially with the way our society is today. (Billie Jo Bray, personal commu-nication, July, 2002)

One obvious indication of competence that she considers important is the willingness to express gratitude for the abundance of the earth's resources, be they camus root, bitterroot, or wild berries.

PERSPECTIVES ON CULTURAL COMPETENCE FROM THE LITERATURE IN CROSS-CULTURAL PSYCHOLOGY

Cross-cultural psychology, an orientation in psychology that we represent, is an organized and exciting way to look at the broader world (e.g., Berry et al, 1997; Matsumoto, 2001; Segall, Lonner, & Berry, 1998; Triandis et al. 1980). It has several aims. Although its main goal is to examine human behavior from a global perspective and thus contribute to the development of a universally valid behavioral science, one of its central desires is to enhance the development of culturally competent individuals. Indeed, one could argue that virtually all of psychology consists of a complex and multifaceted attempt to understand the sources of individual differences in thought and behavior of ourselves and others and to become increasingly competent to deal with them. That's a tall enough order in any one culture; to do so across the many hundreds if not thousands of cultures would require a promethean effort.

Psychologists, working in their broad, diffuse, and interesting discipline, have provided an enormous number of concepts, dimensions, and perspectives that help us understand what competence is and is not, both within and across cultures and ethnic groups (across cultures mainly by inference or extension because most of the major theories that have guided psychologists for years are generally silent about culture). Indeed, one could argue that the discipline of psychology is a search for deep understanding of all human beings. Some parts of the discipline are expressly committed to train and teach professionals to be culturally competent in various applied settings. For instance, the field of cross-cultural counseling (e.g., Pedersen, Draguns, Lonner, & Trimble, 2002; Sue & Sue, 1999) is totally devoted to enhancing the cultural competence of professional counselors. It is unequivocal that a culturally incompetent counselor is an incomplete counselor. It can also be said that a psychologist who does not understand and appreciate some of the major sources of variation across individuals who come from different cultures and speak different languages is an incomplete psychologist whose vision is obscured by culture-blindness and culture-boundness. Hence, in this section we summarize a number of dimensions, syndromes, and other ways to categorize people with a primary focus on culture.

First, however, consider some of the basic "big names" in the field of individual differences or personality. Nearly all theories of personality have had something to say about interpersonal competence, either directly or indirectly. Jung (1971), for instance, talked about the *transcendent function* and *individuation*, in both cases implying that an individual cannot be interpersonally competent until a certain level of psychic maturity and unity is reached. Carl Rogers (1951) said essentially the same thing in his theorizing about "unconditional positive regard." Abraham Maslow (1968), the founder of humanistic psychology, expressed similar views when he talked about "fully actualized" individuals. For instance, one of the characteristics of the actualized person is a natural willingness to accept people for who they are and never to degrade people or to deal with them in pejorative ways. Such individuals are also, according to Maslow (1968), unfailingly democratic. George Kelly (1955), in his psychology of personal constructs, discussed individuals who develop either a *tight* construct system (rule-governed, with a small number of tidy categories for all people) or a *loose* construct system (numerous and flexible ways to categorize individuals and accommodate them in creative ways). To Kelly, a culturally competent individual would be a "loose construer" and one who has a construct system that could easily accommodate other individuals. Sidney Jourard (1971) discussed the open and closed mind and all that this dichotomy entails or implies in terms of prejudice and other characteristics that may be involved in interpersonal competence. Erik Erikson (1950), in his theory based on epigenetic development of self, asserts that individuals may achieve a solid level of interpersonal competence when, in the last of his eight stages, they reach generativity as opposed to stagnation. Even perspectives on personality that are based on learning theory deal effectively with the learning of interpersonal competence. For instance, is it possible that Clifford's dislike of "those people," discussed at the beginning of this chapter, was largely based on a conditioned avoidance reaction or simple association learning as outlined many years ago by Ivan Pavlov? In the area of social learning, one of Albert Bandura's (1997) basic explanations for interpersonal incompetence is the extent to which inept individuals are merely reflecting the attitudes and behaviors they see on television and in environments in which the actions of models do not promote kindly, accommodating, and appropriate behavior. For Bandura (1986), to be effective and self-enhanced is to be interpersonally competent, a life-long process that is based on social modeling and reinforcement of behaviors that are socially valued by nurturing and dedicated members of society.

One wonders how orthodox Freudian theory would explain the presence or absence of interpersonal competence. One might expect such a rationale as an expansive super-ego or perhaps the ability to deflect negative thoughts and feelings through humor or artistic outlets (Freud, 1962). We are not aware of any particular Freudian perspective explaining exactly what cultural competence is, but we are confident that one could be found by searching the psychodynamic literature. However, Freud was concerned mainly with personal competence and the reduction of intrapsychic conflict. One could deduce, on the basis of some of his final writings, that Freud would identify excessive aggression as a primary obstacle to the development of intercultural competence. In fact, Freud hardly ventured out of his fairly clois-tered environment in Vienna. We cannot recall his ever mentioning doing psychoanalysis with anyone outside the fairly wealthy and well-educated European population. His well-known "armchair psychoanalysis" of the Trobriand Islanders, done largely by interested proxy members of his inner circle, did not benefit at all from his actual visitation to different and ex-otic places. However, in all fairness to Freud he was living in a decidedly insulated environment. It was the rare psychologist or psychoanalyst dur-ing the halcyon days of orthodox Freudianism who ventured beyond his or her borders. Jung is a striking example of an early icon who recognized the importance of travel to other places for the study of behavioral and cultural differences.

In the cross-cultural realm, numerous perspectives can be used as help-ful guides in understanding the nature of competence. A brief overview of several of these viewpoints will serve as an introduction to different ways to explain behavior that can be characterized as either competent or incompe-tent. For instance, the dichotomy of *subjective culture* versus *objective culture* (Triandis, 1972) has guided much research that is relevant in understanding intercultural competence. It is important to distinguish between these two concepts of culture. Objective culture consists of the "man-made" part of the environment. This would include such things as architecture (buildings), art and music, types of agriculture, manufacturing (e.g., farm tools), modes of transportation, and so on. Although people can, and do, have diverse reac-tions to everything that can be called objective culture, this does not have much to do with the concept of cultural competence. However, subjective culture (especially the understanding of it) has everything to do with compe-tence. Subjective culture includes such things as attitudes, beliefs, values, appropriate behaviors, rules of address, and status hierarchies. If an individual understands another's subjective culture, and acts accordingly within a strong and democratically just and moral framework, one could say that a high level of cultural competence has been reached. Subjective cultures are extraordi-narily complex and perhaps can never be truly mastered (except, of course, one's own; but one's own subjective culture is extraordinarily complex). Even lifelong members of a specific culture can be confused by various interactions in that culture. To the outsider, certain behaviors and practices will be to-tally baffling and many subtle aspects of interpersonal interaction will simply not be noticed. We may even assert a possible axiom here: A person will be interpersonally competent in another organized human group to the extent that he or she understands the subjective culture of the group in question and acts accordingly. To become competent to this degree may require ex-tensive involvement with specific cultures or assistance through various cul-ture-training techniques or programs (discussed later in this chapter) or both.

Another perspective that can help one understand individual varia-tions in interpersonal competence is Witkin's theory of psychological differentiation (Witkin & Berry, 1975; Witkin, Dyk, Faterson, Goodenough, & Karp, 1962). This theory posits a continuum bounded by field independence on one end and field dependence on the other. Field-independent individuals are generally viewed as relatively insensitive to interpersonal cues, having more interest in things and spatial relationships than in people. Field-dependent individuals, who have also been called field-sensitive, are hypothesized to be much more aware of interpersonal cues. This cognitive style perspective is somewhat dated. However, it is conceptually close to the more recent and heavily researched notion of individualism–collectivism. Often referred to as INDCOL, this perspective also embraces a continuum bounded by individualists (or idiocentric) people who are psychologically independent and relatively distant interpersonally (except in small groups, such as their family) and collectivists (or allocentric) individuals who are hypothesized to be much more interpersonally aware. In turn, the INDCOL perspective is conceptually similar to the idea of an independent as opposed to an interdependent sense of self (Markus & Kitayama, 1991). The essential point here is that theoretically, culture "programs" individuals to function more toward one end of the continuum than the other. Although these interrelated continua can potentially be helpful in understanding interpersonal competence, we caution readers to avoid sweeping generalizations. Thus, in some societies that are hypothesized to foster individualism and independence (e.g., the United States), one can fully expect to find many people who defy this simple dichotomy and become genuinely interpersonally competent. The same is true for cultures that may be described as collectivistic and interdependent (e.g., many Asian societies). One must remember that the culture is not the individual (and vice versa).

Detweiler's (1978) idea of category width contains another worthwhile view of a component of intercultural competence. As natural attributes of their cognitive capacities, individuals categorize colors, concepts, parts of speech, and many other things. They do so to add order to their world. Detweiler (1978) suggested that some people use wide and extensive categories in dealing with things and people (in our context especially people), whereas others use narrow category widths. Those using wide categories can make more fine-grained and specific decisions about others (e.g., idealists, pragmatists, realists), whereas those with narrow category widths tend to lump people into broad categories (e.g., Blacks, Whites, and Asians). This is related to Bieri's (1955) idea that some people are cognitively "simple" (not unintelligent in the classical sense, but simplistic in their use of categories), whereas others are cognitively complex. Those in the latter group can make many more distinctions and discriminations, quickly discerning differences between people during intercultural interactions.

Our understanding of cultural competence may be aided by the notion of openness to experience, or simply Openness, which is one of the factors in Five-Factor Model of personality (McCrae, Costa, del Pilar, Rolland, & Parker,

1998). In fact, researchers would have an explanatory chore on their hands if the Openness factor should be found not to correlate positively with the construct of cultural competence. A more recent dimensional or factorial way to look at individual differences in this regard is the concept of *social axioms*. Social axioms consist of general beliefs about how the world functions (Leung, 2002). Because they are probably related to thought and behavior across time, culture, and individuals, they can be thought of as tentative, or exploratory, universals. Researchers are currently investigating five social axioms: Fate Control, Reward for Application, Social Cynicism, Spirituality, and Social Flexibility. Although researchers have not yet compared the construct of intercultural competence with the social axioms, one can easily hypothesize that interculturally competent individuals should score low on Social Cynicism and high on both Social Flexibility and Spirituality. Given the tendency of creative cross-cultural researchers to examine plausible ways to understand relationships between culture and behavior, surely research on the relationships between social axioms and intercultural competence will be forthcoming.

TRAINING FOR CULTURAL COMPETENCE

That behavior is a function of the person and the situation is one of the fundamental truths of the social and behavioral sciences. It therefore follows that the more an individual knows about the intricacies of interpersonal interaction, the more understanding he or she will be of the unfolding situation and perhaps, therefore, the more competent he or she will be when engaged in such dynamics. In a sense, this is much like ongoing manifestations of aspects of attribution theory in social psychology. For example, the fundamental attribution error holds that humans tend to explain what happens to themselves as attributable to the situation (e.g., I failed the test because the room was noisy and the questions were poorly written) whereas what happens to others is often explained by the characteristics they are assumed to possess (e.g., they failed because they have poor reasoning ability or do not have much motivation). Much prejudice and bias can be immediately reduced, and much can be done toward making people more interpersonally competent, by taking steps to help them understand that attribution theory is a double-edged sword: the more one knows about "them" the less will one condemns them because of our own ignorance, and vice versa, of course.

The truism that behavior is a function of the person–situation interaction, and that this can reach heights of complexity when culture enters the equation, is the main reason behind the popularity of various culture-training programs. As Brislin (2000) explained, "the goals of cross-cultural training are to prepare for intercultural interactions so that they have a greater likelihood of meeting the four-part criteria of success" (p. 260)—with success defined essentially as a person having reached a level of interpersonal competence that results in solid outcomes for all concerned. The four criteria of success are (a) developing positive feelings about the development of intercultural relationships, (b) benefiting from reciprocation of these feelings from other members of other culture groups, (c) accomplishing specific tasks, and (d) experiencing minimal stress stemming from intercultural misunderstandings and difficulties.

There are several types of culture training techniques and programs (Landis & Bhagat, 1996). One of the most popular uses the "critical incident" technique (Cushner & Brislin, 1996). These incidents are short vignettes or mini-case studies that capture the essence of frequently encountered intercultural difficulties. The trainee reads each vignette and then tries to decide which of four or five plausible reasons is best to use to explain each of the difficulties. Hundreds of vignettes are available (the Cushner & Brislin book contains 100 incidents). They are spread across about 20 areas of potential common difficulties such as disconfirmed expectations, anxieties, role assignments, and everyday beliefs. Moreover, there are culture-specific as well as culture-general training techniques. In the former, the focus is on a specific culture, or a specific aspect of one culture (e.g., how to avoid problems in intercultural meetings with people from Japan, if the trainee is from the United States or another Western country). The former, obviously, is more broad-banded and is designed to encompass a large number of cultures in a sweeping manner or perhaps only on a single, common interpersonal topic such as "rules of address" and their variations around the world.

Although organized, systematic culture-training techniques seem to have been started during the early days of the U.S. Peace Corps (e.g., intensive training of individuals who were assigned for volunteer work in Swaziland), currently these methods are used primarily by large, multinational companies. A culturally competent individual will obviously be a better candidate to negotiate a large contract or to "seal a deal" than one who makes mistakes and blunders during the everyday business of negotiating and bargaining.

Kealey (1996), in a chapter discussing selecting individuals for employment in other countries or in companies with individuals from many cultures, provides a profile of the model cross-cultural collaborator. His three-part categorization includes the following:

Adaptation Skills
   Positive attitudes
   Flexibility
   Stress tolerance
   Patience
   Marital or family stability
   Emotional maturity
   Inner security

Cross-Cultural Skills
    Realism
    Tolerance
    Involvement in culture
    Political astuteness
    Cultural sensitivity

Partnership Skills
    Openness to others
    Professional commitment
    Perseverance
    Initiative
    Reliance building
    Self-confidence
    Problem solving

TYLER'S TRANSCULTURAL ETHNIC VALIDITY MODEL OF INTRACULTURAL COMPETENCE

In a major book dealing with psychosocial competence, Forrest Tyler (2001) presented details of what he has termed a *transcultural ethnic validity model* (TEVM). In his view, individual psychosocial competence must encompass an integrated understanding of individuals and their communities, ethnicities, and cultures. All individuals use their own self-directing skills as guides throughout life. How well one manages this, according to Tyler, is a product of what he calls individual psychosocial competence. It has several components, or factors, including (a) a sense of self-efficacy, (b) a sense of a self–world relationship involving optimism and trust or their opposites, (c) some level of active planfulness, and elements in our lives such as physical and psychological (d) supports and (e) threats.

An important part of Tyler's perspective is his two-part notion of *personal validity* and *ethnic validity*, both of which are to be understood in the context of our psychosocial heritage. In addition, it is an important part of his perspective to note that people's heritages consist of a hierarchical structure that differentiates culture-defining (CD) and non-culture-defining (NCD) roles, status, and memberships. As explained by Tyler,

> Before we can focus on the *individual psychosocial competence configuration* [his emphasis] that everyone forms, we need to identify and consider the underlying shared and unshared senses of reality that we use to organize our societies and our lives. . . . We must transcend the belief that any particular [conception of the world contained in nested frameworks] is the true view of reality if we are to gain a less ethnocentric basis for forming a comprehensive picture of our societies, our lives, and ourselves. (p. 118)

Further details are to be found in Tyler's richly textured and soundly argued book. Suffice to say, in this context a culturally competent individual has the ability to move freely between CD and NCD groups or roles by realizing that the ethnic validity of all individuals can be understood by "others" only by granting other groups the respect they deserve.

Respect is, in fact, at the core of cultural competency. Perhaps above anything else, all humans crave and want respect. By giving others the same genuine esteem and regard that one personally wants, and by acting on this respect in all interactions with others, one will have displayed a good deal of intercultural competence.

CONCLUSION

Like nearly everything else in psychology, the concept of cultural or intercultural competence is easy to grasp as a worthwhile human attribute. However, the exact nature of its component parts seems to be rather ephemeral and multifaceted. It is particularly important to try to understand why some people have a healthy degree of intercultural competence and others do not. Like our fictional Clifford and Ted, briefly depicted at the beginning of this chapter as stark contrasts in cultural competence, we currently seem unable to specify the exact path one needs to take on the way to becoming culturally competent. There are many helpful theories and perspectives that are useful in providing insight into the nature of this phenomenon. There is every indication that if a person truly wants to become more culturally competent, he or she will be at least moderately successful. Simply living and interacting with people who are different will help a great deal. Various training techniques may enhance the process. The literature on prejudice and stereotypes, on the other hand, strongly suggested that if an individual does not want to be culturally competent then he or she will likely remain insulated and isolated.

In this chapter we have attempted to summarize and often speculate about some of the ways that the concept of intercultural competence may be understood and examined. We hope that our modest effort has provided some insight into the topic, and that in the context of this book our views will find solid company among those who are trying to understand the nature of cultural and intercultural competence and enhance ways to improve this important human characteristic in a world that screams for more individuals who have what it takes to understand others and be effective in dealing with them in the various dimensions of human interaction.

REFERENCES

Aronson, E. (2000). *Nobody left to hate*. New York: Holt.

Bandura, A. (1986). *Social foundations of thought and action*. Englewood Cliffs, NJ: Prentice Hall.

Bandura, A. (1997): *Self-efficacy: The exercise of control*. New York: Freeman.

Berry, J. W., Poortinga, Y. H., Pandey, J., Dasen, P. R., Saraswathi, T. S., Segall, M. H., & Kagitcibasi, C. (Eds.). (1997). *Handbook of cross-cultural psychology* (2nd ed.). Boston: Allyn & Bacon.

Bieri, J. (1955). Cognitive complexity–simplicity and predictive behavior. *Journal of Abnormal and Social Psychology, 51*, 61–66.

Boden, M. A. (1991). *The creative mind: Myths and mechanisms*. New York: Basic Books.

Brislin, R. W. (2000). *Understanding culture's influence on behavior*. Fort Worth, TX: Harcourt Brace.

Bruner, J. (1996). *The culture of education*. Cambridge, MA: Harvard University Press.

Csikszentmihalyi, M., & Sawyer, K. (1995). Creative insight: The social dimension of a solitary moment. In R. J. Sternberg & J. E. Davidson (Eds.), *The nature of insight* (pp. 329–363). Cambridge, MA: MIT Press.

Cushner, K., & Brislin, R. W. (1996). *Intercultural interactions: A practical guide* (2nd ed.). Thousand Oaks, CA: Sage.

Detweiler, R. A. (1978). Culture, category width, and attributions: A model-building approach to the reasons of cultural effects. *Journal of Cross-Cultural Psychology, 9*, 259–284.

Dewey, J. (1910). *How we think*. Boston: Heath.

Dinges, N. G., & Baldwin, K. D. (1996). Intercultural competence: A research perspective. In D. Landis & R. Bhagat (Eds.), *Handbook of intercultural training* (2nd ed.) (pp. 106–123). Thousand Oaks, CA: Sage.

Erikson, E. H. (1950). *Childhood and society*. New York: Norton.

Fletcher-Janzen, E., Strickland, T. L., & Reynolds, C. R. (Eds.). (2000). *Handbook of cross-cultural neuropsychology*. New York: Kluwer Academic/Plenum Publishers.

Freud, S. (1962). *Civilization and its discontents*. New York: Norton.

Gardner, H. (1982). *Art, mind, and brain*. New York: Basic Books.

Gardner, H. (1993). *Multiple intelligences: The theory in practice*. New York: Basic Books.

Goleman, D. (1995). *Emotional intelligence*. New York: Bantam Books/Doubleday/Dell.

Jahoda, G. (2002). The shifting sands of "culture." In P. Boski, F. J. R. van de Vijver, & A. M. Chodynicka (Eds.), *New directions in cross-cultural psychology: Selected papers from the 15ᵗʰ International Congress of the International Congress of the International Association of Cross-Cultural Psychology* (pp. 91–106). Warsaw: Polish Psychological Association.

Jourard, S. M. (1971). *The transparent self*. New York: Van Nostrand Reinhold.

Jung, C. G. (1971). *Psychological types* (H. G. Baynes, Trans.; rev. R. F. C. Hull, Ed; Bollingen Series XX, Vol. 6). Princeton, NJ: Princeton University Press.

Kagitcibasi, C. (1996). *Family and human development across cultures: A view from the other side.* Hillsdale, NJ: Erlbaum.

Kealey, D. J. (1996). The challenge of international personnel selection. In D. Landis & R. S. Bhagat (Eds.), *Handbook of intercultural training* (2nd ed., pp. 81–105). Thousand Oaks, CA: Sage.

Kelly, G. W. (1955). *The psychology of personal constructs.* New York: Norton.

Koester, J., & Olebe, M. (1988). The Behavioral Assessment Scale for Intercultural Communication Effectiveness. *International Journal of Intercultural Relations, 12,* 233–246.

Kroeber, A. L., & Kluckhohn, C. (1952). *Culture: A critical review of concepts and definitions.* [Papers]. Peabody Museum of Archaeology and Ethnology: Cambridge, MA. Vol. 47, No. 1.

Landis, D., & Bhagat, R.S. (Eds.). (1996). *Handbook of intercultural training* (2nd ed.). Thousand Oaks, CA: Sage.

Leung, K., Bond, M., de Carrasquel, S. R., Munoz, C., Hernandez, M., et al. (2002). Social axioms: The search for universals dimensions of general beliefs about how the world functions. *Journal of Cross-Cultural Psychology, 33,* 286–302.

Lonner, W. J. (1997). Three paths leading to culturally competent psychological practitioners. *International Journal of Intercultural Relations, 21,* 195–212.

Lonner, W. J., & Adamopoulos, J. (1997). Culture as antecedent to behavior. In J. W. Berry, Y. H. Poortinga, & J. Pandey, et al. (Eds.), *Handbook of cross-cultural psychology* (Vol. 1, pp. 43–48). Boston: Allyn & Bacon.

Markus, H. R., & Kitayama, S. (1991). Culture and self: Implications for cognition, emotion, and motivation. *Psychological Review, 98,* 224–253.

Maslow, A. H. (1968). *Toward a psychology of being.* Princeton: Van Nostrand.

Matsumoto, D. (Ed.). (2001). *Handbook of culture and psychology.* New York: Oxford University Press.

McCrae, R. M., Costa, P. T., del Pilar, G. H., Rolland, J.-P., & Parker, W. D. (1998). Cross-cultural assessment and the five-factor model: The Revised NEO Personality Inventory. *Journal of Cross-Cultural Psychology, 29,* 171–188.

Nell, V. (2000). *Cross-cultural neurological assessment.* Mahwah, NJ: Erlbaum.

Oxford English Dictionary (2nd ed.). (1989). Oxford University Press: Cambridge, MA.

Pedersen, P. B., Draguns, J. G., Lonner, W. J., & Trimble, J. E. (Eds.). (2002). *Cross-cultural counseling.* Thousand Oaks, CA: Sage.

Rogers, C. R. (1951). *Client centered therapy: Its current practice, implications, and theory.* Boston: Houghton Mifflin.

Salovey, P., & Mayer, J. D. (1990). *Emotional intelligence: Imagination, cognition, and personality.* New York: Harper.

Saul, J. R. (1997). *The unconscious civilization.* New York: Free Press.

Segall, M. H., Lonner, W. J., & Berry, J.W. (1998). Cross-cultural psychology as a scholarly discipline: On the flowering of culture in behavioral research. *American Psychologist, 53,* 1101–1110.

Srivastava, A. K., & Misra, G. (1999). An Indian perspective on understanding intelligence. In W. J. Lonner, D. L. Dinnel, D. K. Forgays, & S. A. Hayes (Eds.), *Merging past, present, and future in cross-cultural psychology* (pp. 159–172).Lisse, The Netherlands: Swets & Zeitlinger.

Sternberg, R. J. (1985). *Beyond IQ: A triarchic theory of human intelligence*. New York: Cambridge University Press.

Sternberg, R. J. (1988a). Intelligence. In R. J. Sternberg & E. E. Smith (Eds.), *The psychology of thought* (pp. 267–308). New York: Cambridge University Press.

Sternberg, R. J. (1988b). A triarchic view of intelligence in cross-cultural perspective. In S. H. Irvine & J. W. Berry (Eds.), *Human abilities in cultural context* (pp. 60–85). Cambridge, England: Cambridge University Press.

Sue, D. W., & Sue, D. (1999). *Counseling the culturally different* (3rd ed). New York: Wiley.

Triandis, H. C. (1972). *The analysis of subjective culture*. New York: Wiley.

Triandis, H. C., Lambert, W., Berry, J. W., Lonner, W. J., Heron, A., Brislin, R. W., & Draguns, J. G. (Eds.). (1980). *Handbook of cross-cultural psychology* (Vols. 1–6). Boston: Allyn & Bacon.

Tyler, F. B. (2001). *Cultures, communities, competence, and change*. New York: Kluwer Academic/Plenum Publishers.

Walters, J., & Gardner, H. (1986). The crystallizing experience: Discovering an intellectual gift. In R. J. Sternberg & J. E. Davidson (Eds.), *Conceptions of giftedness* (pp. 411–455). London: Cambridge University Press.

Ward, C. (2001). The ABC's of acculturation. In D. Matsumoto (Ed.), *Handbook of culture and psychology* (pp. 411–445). New York: Oxford University Press.

Witkin, H. A., & Berry, J. W. (1975). Psychological differentiation in cross-cultural perspective. *Journal of Cross-Cultural Psychology, 6*, 4–82.

Witkin, H. A., Dyk, R. B., Faterson, H. F., Goodenough, D. R., & Karp, S. A. (1962). *Psychological differentiation*. New York: Wiley.

5

THE CULTURAL DEEP STRUCTURE OF PSYCHOLOGICAL THEORIES OF SOCIAL DEVELOPMENT

JOAN G. MILLER

Psychological theories of social development not only describe behavior but also include prescriptive assumptions about what constitutes more or less adequate or mature modes of psychological functioning. In this respect, they offer visions of social competence that complement those that are offered by psychological theories of intelligence. As is observed in the area of intelligence, individual differences on psychological measures of social development tend to be positively correlated and to predict real-life adaptive outcomes.

In the present chapter, I argue that theories of social development need to be seen as resembling theories of intelligence in being informed by shared conceptual premises that contribute to their intercorrelations with each other and to their predictive power. The case is made that the dominant psychological theories of social development are informed by problems for the self that are salient in the middle-class European American cultural setting in which psychology to date has largely developed. Thus, the correlations among different measures of social development result, in part, from the theories being based on a common conceptual definition of competence rather than exclusively from empirical relationships existing among them. Evidence is presented to suggest that this conceptual definition of competence does not adequately represent the beliefs and values of diverse cultural and socioeconomic subgroups and, as a result, leads to such groups, in cases, being appraised as showing less developed forms of competence than are displayed by middle-class European Americans. The conclusion is drawn regarding the need to broaden psychological definitions of social competence to tap the contrasting beliefs, values, and problems for the self that are salient in different cultural and subcultural communities, with such efforts contributing to the enhancement of basic psychological theory.

The chapter is organized into three sections. In the first section, I consider respects in which concerns with cultural insularity have been raised in the case of theories of intelligence—concerns that in many ways provide a model for the related issues that exist in the case of theories of social development. In the second section, I argue that, although it is not generally recognized, psychological theories of social development share a common culturally grounded conceptual structure related to balancing autonomy and relatedness. In turn, in the last section, I present evidence suggesting that this conceptual structure is conceptually inadequate to capture various outlooks on social development that are emphasized within diverse cultural and subcultural communities.

THE CULTURAL GROUNDING OF THEORIES OF INTELLIGENCE

Psychological theories of intelligence provide a useful example for illustrating respects in which theories may form closed systems, in which their explanatory force and predictive power derive, in part, from their grounding in conceptual assumptions that favor the perspective of particular cultural or subcultural populations. In contrast to the case of theories of social development, in which there has been little attention to the existence of a common culturally based deep structure as characterizing diverse frameworks, the problem of potential culturally bound views of intelligence has been subject to extensive debate. This debate centers on the issue of how to define intelligence and on how to interpret the associations observed between intelligence and everyday adaptation.

In terms of defining intelligence, it is widely accepted that intelligence involves an evaluative appraisal of experience. As Haslam and Baron (1994) observed, "intelligence clearly refers to abilities, properties of performance that can be evaluated along a continuum from better to worse" (p. 41). Intelligence furthermore is identified with adaptation, a stance seen in Pintner's early definition of intelligence as the ability "to adapt (one)self adequately to relatively new situations in life" (Pintner, 1921, p. 139). Recognizing that what is adaptive varies with the resources and values of different communities, culturally based approaches to intelligence accept that the content of intelligent behavior is necessarily culturally variable to a significant degree (e.g., Ceci, 1990; Charlesworth, 1976). However, the views of intelligence emphasized in the psychometric tradition of IQ testing, views that presently are the most influential both within the field and within the larger society, typically reject such a conclusion. Rather, they forward content-based definitions of intelligence that privilege the types of abstract abilities that appear on IQ tests. These abilities are seen as reflecting a capacity factor, g, that is assumed to underlie individual differences in performance not only on intelligence tests but also in everyday life.

Given these assumptions, the predictive power of measures of IQ or g become crucial as an index of the validity of conceptions of intelligence. As Eysenck has argued, ". . . we would feel disinclined to call something intelligence that did not correlate with external criteria, such as success at school and university, or in life or at work" (Eysenck, 1979, p. 78). However, as seen later in this chapter, although there is evidence that IQ predicts consequential adaptive outcomes, this does not settle the issue of the validity and cultural adequacy of conceptions of intelligence. Rather, the findings give rise to questions about the meaning of the observed associations between IQ and adaptive outcomes.

As support for the construct validity and cultural adequacy of existing conceptions of intelligence, theorists within the psychometric tradition point to findings indicating that intelligence tests show high interrelationship with each other and with valued outcomes. For example, it is found that if results of batteries of standard intelligence tests are factor analyzed, a first-principal component emerges that accounts for approximately 30% of the variance— a component believed to reflect the general intelligence factor, g (Ceci, 1990). Furthermore, IQ predicts more than merely academic success, such as higher grades in school, greater number of years of school completed, and higher standardized test scores. It also predicts a range of consequential life outcomes, including lower criminality, better mental health, lower marriage dissolution rates, and higher levels of occupational attainment (e.g., Hartigan & Wigdor, 1989; Hunt, 1995; Hunter, 1986). Theorists within the psychometric tradition interpret this type of evidence as reflecting the centrality of IQ in enabling individuals to adapt in flexible and effective ways with environmental demands. As Itzkoff (1989) concludes, "Persons with high g can retrain themselves to do many different tasks in one lifetime and often at a highly creative level" (p. 85).

Theorists identified with culturally based approaches to intelligence, in contrast, do not question the existence of this type of evidence nor dismiss it as inconsequential, but rather raise concerns about the extent to which the association between IQ and valued adaptive outcomes arises, at least in part, from a priori linkages in the ways in which intelligence is defined and measured and the behavioral indices of adaptive performance adopted as outcome criteria. It is noted that the items that were sampled on the first intelligence test, which was developed by Binet, and that resemble those found in most contemporary intelligence tests, were selected because they were observed to be successful in predicting school outcomes. This then introduces circularity into IQ measures if they are used to predict school performance or other related outcomes, because a criterion that was used initially in developing the tests is now being treated as evidence of the test's predictive power. In turn, the predictive power of psychometric definitions of intelligence is magnified as this definition of intelligence is adopted in assessing intelligence on a wide range of diagnostic tests used in schools and work settings. Thus, for example, contemporary United States admissions tests for college (SAT, ACT), graduate (GRE), and professional schools (LSAT, GMA, MCAT) all tap intellectual abilities in ways that closely resemble those used on IQ measures.

The circularity of associations between performance on IQ-type measures and everyday adaptive outcomes, in turn, is viewed as further heightened by the gatekeeping role of school performance and performance on intelligence test type measures on valued outcomes (Ceci, 1990). Society selects candidates for higher educational opportunities or career advancement, in part, on the basis of their having strong academic records and high test performance. As a consequence, it is only individuals with high achievement in school and on standardized intelligence test type measures who are admitted to elite positions in society. Once admitted to these positions, they tend to be accorded preferential treatment, in terms of having greater resources and opportunities for advancement, whereas individuals who score poorly tend to suffer disadvantages. As Sternberg points out, in thus providing individuals who score well on intelligence tests with societal advantages, while handicapping those who score poorly, the performance gap between high and low test performers is heightened and the tests themselves contribute to producing gaps in individuals' levels of achievement and societal outcomes:

> Low test scores set in motion a chain of events that can lead to poor later outcomes, independent of the abilities the tests measure. Once a child is labeled as stupid, his opportunities start to dry up. . . . Labels are not just descriptions of reality; they contribute toward shaping reality. (Sternberg, 1996, p. 23)

The observation then that individuals of middle- or upper-middle-class background tend to have higher IQ than individuals of working or lower class occupations becomes, in part, an artifact of the gatekeeping structure of societal institutions in only admitting individuals who score well on intelligence test type measures. In turn, evidence of better life outcomes, such as lower criminality or greater mental health and marital success, being linked to higher IQ, may also be seen to reflect, in part, the greater societal advantages enjoyed by individuals of middle class background. These are the groups who tend to perform at superior levels in school and to score higher on IQ-type indices and thus to be accorded more opportunities for advancement.

Perhaps the strongest type of argument for the limited predictive power of IQ measures, beyond performances that are correlated with school-type skills, however, is that IQ measures do not predict well performance in everyday contexts that draw on different types of abilities (Ceci, 1990; Laboratory of Comparative Human Cognition, 1983; Miller, 1997; Sternberg, 1996). Thus, for example, it has been shown that IQ is not related to competent performance in such everyday settings as betting at a racetrack, efficiently distributing goods within a factory, or budgeting expenses at the grocery store (Lave & Wenger, 1991; Schliemann, Carraher, & Ceci, 1997; Scribner, 1984). In such contexts, it is observed that quality of performance tends to be related to task-specific expertise that draws on a broader range of competencies than those tapped by traditional IQ measures and that is enhanced by experience or practice within the activity.

Evidence of this type has led critics to argue for the need to conceptually broaden conceptions of intelligence to tap a wider range of competencies. Such an argument is forwarded by Sternberg (1985, 1988), for example, in his triarchic theory of intelligence, a framework that portrays intelligence as encompassing not merely analytic skills but also synthetic or creative abilities as well as street smarts or practical intelligence. It also represents an insight that underlies the proposal by Gardner (1983, 1993) to expand conceptions of intelligence to encompass a variety of different types of skills, ranging from artistic to musical abilities. Finally, this type of conceptual argument has informed the growing interest among psychologists in examining lay conceptions of intelligence in an attempt to identify new dimensions of intelligence that, although they are not tapped in present definitions of IQ, are integral to everyday adaptation in different sociocultural settings (e.g., Grigorenko et al., 2001; Sternberg, Conway, Ketron, & Bernstein, 1981).

In sum, work on intelligence highlights the need to broaden contemporary definitions of intelligence to take into account intellectual competences that are considered important to everyday adaptation in different social and cultural settings but that are not represented in psychometric theories of intelligence or in intelligence test measures. This work also points to the biases that ensue from a failure to broaden definitions of intelligence. In particular, limitations in predictive power occur, as psychometric definitions of intelligence fail to relate to intelligent performance in everyday contexts that require different types of abilities than those that appear on IQ-type measures. Also, group bias arises as the narrow constructs tapped on IQ-type measures tend to be privileged by societal institutions, with only individuals or groups who display these types of abilities accorded societal advantages and individuals or groups who emphasize other types of abilities experiencing some disadvantage.

These types of problems that arise in the case of intelligence, however, are not unique to this domain but rather reflect a stance that I argue also exists in other work on competence. This type of stance more generally arises whenever a narrow definition of competence is treated as the normative criterion that is privileged in psychological theories and in society more generally. Once this stance has been adopted, multiple measures that are informed by this same construct will tend to be highly correlated with each other. Also, to the extent that societal structures are premised on the same values, significant correlations will be observed between everyday adaptive outcomes and these constructs. However, as observed in the case of theories of intelligence, this type of system also will tend to be severely limited in its power to predict adaptation in contexts that value different types of abilities. It will also tend to disadvantage individuals or groups who emphasize alternative forms of competence.

In the next section, I show that this same type of analysis can be applied in understanding the need for conceptual broadening of contemporary psychological theories of social development. Through comparison of respects in which theories of social development, like theories of intelligence, privilege narrow definitions of competence, insight can be gained into the extent that this issue of conceptual and cultural bias arises in the case of a wide range of social theories. It becomes equally clear that the same strategies being adopted to conceptually broaden theories of intelligence may also be relevant to conceptually broadening theories of social development.

THE CULTURAL GROUNDING OF THEORIES OF SOCIAL DEVELOPMENT

Like theories of intelligence, theories of social development center on explaining what constitutes more or less successful adaptation. However, whereas the criterion of adaptation in theories of intelligence tends to be formulated in a highly general way, such as the ability to adapt flexibly to environmental challenges, the criteria adopted in the case of theories of social development are content specific. Thus, for example, theories of parenting are concerned with explaining more or less successful parenting, whereas theories of motivation are concerned with explaining more or less adaptive motivation. Although acknowledging this content specificity, I argue here that on a somewhat implicit level, psychological theories of social development share a common deep conceptual structure that links them with each other. This shared conceptual structure functions in a way that, in many respects, resembles the construct of g in the case of intelligence. It contributes to the tendencies of the theories of social development to show strong intercorrelation as well as to have high predictive power, at the same time that it limits their explanatory force in accounting for modes of social development emphasized in diverse sociocultural settings.

The dominant contemporary psychological theories of social development may be seen to reflect problems for the self that are salient in the individualistic, middle-class, European American cultural context that has been adopted as the default standard for normative models of human development in psychology. These problems concern effecting a balance between autonomy and relatedness. As anthropologists have noted, the modern Western view of self that is prominent in middle-class European American culture includes not only an emphasis on autonomy but also a tension in relation to the collective (e.g., Farr, 1991; Taylor, 1989). Within such a view, agency comes to be identified with internal psychological characteristics and to be regarded as opposed to the demands of the social context.

> An analytic framework that equates "self/individual" with such things as spontaneity, genuine feeling, privacy, uniqueness, constancy, the "inner life" and then opposes those to mask, role, rule or context is a reflection of dichotomies that constitute the modern Western self. (Rosaldo, 1984, p. 146)

This type of cultural outlook gives rise to an ambivalence about social demands, with the collective regarded, on the one hand, as necessary for individual survival, while, on the other hand, as a constraint on individual autonomy. As Plath (1980) observed, "our cultural nightmare is that the individual throb of growth will be sucked dry in slavish social conformity. All life long, our central struggle is to defend the individual from the collective" (p. 216). In such a stance, it is assumed that adaptation requires a certain balancing of self that weighs responsiveness to the requirements of the social whole with individuality.

Just as the type of abstract abilities that comprise g are reflected in psychometric theories of intelligence, this type of cultural concern with effecting a balance between the self and the social whole is increasingly being reflected in general psychological conceptions of healthy human functioning. Thus, for example, Guisinger and Blatt (1994) have proposed that individuality and relatedness are both integral to personality development: ". . . we need to recognize that healthy personality development involves equal and complementary emphasis on individuality and relatedness for both men and women" (pp. 108–109). Likewise, Bakan (1966) argued for the importance of balancing concerns with self with human connection. As Spence (1985) commented in characterizing Bakan's position:

> In his book, *The Duality of Human Existence*, Bakan proposed two fundamental but antagonistic senses: A sense of self (or agency), manifested in self-assertiveness and self-protectiveness, and a sense of selflessness (or communion), the desire to become one with others. (p. 1290)

As she further observed, the developmental task according to Bakan is "to reconcile and balance these two contradictory senses." As a balance, the optimum stance is considered to be one that combines elements of each while avoiding extremes. On the one hand, an extreme stance is associated with too much self-assertiveness, a position that is insufficiently social, if not out of control. On the other hand, an extreme stance is also associated with too much connectedness, a position that is insufficiently autonomous and susceptible to excessive social control.

In the discussion below, I show that this vision about the need to balance autonomy with relatedness has come to have a major role in contemporary psychological theories of social development, forming the deep structure of a range of specific theories, in a way that parallels that of the construct of g, constituting the deep structure of psychometrically based theories of intelligence. Focus here centers on major contemporary psychological models of attachment, social motivation, parenting, and interpersonal morality. In each case, one sees that a significant part of the theoretical contribution and appeal of the model under consideration is its offer of a way to resolve this problem of integrating autonomy and relatedness. In defining individual differences or levels of developmental competence, each theory identifies less adaptive stances that give too much weight either to individual autonomy or to social relatedness and contrasts them with an optimum stance that embodies a balance between autonomy and relatedness.

Attachment

The model of attachment forwarded by Bowlby, Ainsworth, and their colleagues constitutes one of the most influential contemporary psychological theories of personality, social, and developmental psychology (Ainsworth, 1978; Bowlby, 1969–1980). Attachment is viewed as fundamental to all social relationships, with attachment behaviors implicated not only in the young child's formation of a bond with his or her primary caregiver but also in the mediation of other close relationships. The domain of attachment research has expanded from a consideration only of early parent–infant relationships to a consideration of the attachments that individuals form with their romantic partners, spouses, and other significant others (e.g., Fraley, 2002). The assumption is made of longitudinal stability in styles of attachment across the life span and of the centrality of attachment relationships to success in other areas of social life.

As formulated by Bowlby, attachment theory centers on the child's bond with his or her caregiver, with attachment behaviors being those that allow the infant to seek and maintain proximity to this figure. Attachment behaviors are considered to have evolutionary roots in the infant's initial state of dependency and inability to flee unaided from predators or other dangers. The attachment system exists alongside other behavioral subsystems within the developing infant, with the pull to remain attached to the caregiver set against other goals, such as exploration, that are also critical to survival. The infant and the caregiver coordinate their behavioral tendencies in such a way that proximity to the caregiver is assured under conditions of danger or threat, yet exploration of the environment is enabled and promoted to the maximum degree.

Related to issues of survival, attachment is a universal aspect of human experience and, in this sense, represents a cross-culturally robust phenomenon. In all viable human communities, attachment is achieved in a way that ensures human growth and adaptation. However, the thrust of psychological research on attachment centers on the quality of attachment and not merely on its presence. With the development of the Strange Situation assessment procedure (Ainsworth, 1978), and with the theoretical emphasis placed on clinical issues, psychological work on attachment has developed into a tripartite theory of individual differences that maps closely onto the adaptive problem for the self discussed earlier.[1]

The attachment model of individual differences posits a behavioral continuum characterized by less adaptive orientations at two opposing poles and an optimum adaptive orientation at its midpoint. The Group A or *anxious–avoidant* pattern of attachment forms one of the poles. Arising in the case of infants who have experienced rebuff or rejection in having their attachment needs met in a responsive way, this pattern of behavior is marked by defensive avoidance. In turn, the Group C or *anxious–resistant* pattern forms the other pole. This pattern arises in cases in which infants have experienced inappropriate or inconsistent responsiveness by the caregiver, leading them to develop a wariness of exploration. Finally, the Group B or *secure* pattern forms the midpoint of the continuum and constitutes the optimum stance. This pattern arises in cases in which infants have experienced consistent responsiveness from the caregiver, leading to the development of a representation of the caregiver as a secure base that allows exploration of the environment and affiliation with others.

This individual difference model of attachment, it may be seen, is framed in terms of the issue of balancing autonomy and relatedness discussed earlier. Specifically, the A pattern of attachment constitutes a stance that gives too much weight to autonomy at the expense of relatedness. As seen in the Strange Situation research procedure, the A type infant freely explores the lab in the absence of his or her caregiver, but embodies a deficit in connection, showing little or no distress at the caregiver's absence or affection toward the caregiver on his or her return to the lab. In turn, the C pattern of attachment reflects a stance that gives too much weight to relatedness at the expense of autonomy. As seen in the Strange Situation paradigm, the C type infant becomes overly distressed at his or her caregiver's absence, a level of distress that precludes him or her from being able to explore successfully in the

---

[1] A category of Group D or "disorganized/disorganized" attachment patterns was later added to this scheme to capture the experience of infants experiencing severe abuse or neglect.

caregiver's absence or to affiliate with others. Finally, the B pattern of secure attachment represents a stance that successfully bridges these two poles and that allows for both autonomy and relatedness. Secure in his or her representation of the caregiver, the B type infant remains emotionally connected with his or her caregiver, at the same time that he or she has the confidence to explore the environment.

Social Motivation

For many years, a gap existed in psychological theories of social motivation, in terms of accounting for the motivation that individuals experience in meeting social role expectations. The contribution of self-determination theory (e.g., Deci & Ryan, 1985, 1991) was in filling this theoretical gap by forwarding a model that made it possible to account for compliance with social expectations in a way that embodied agency.

Early theories of intrinsic motivation had assumed a strong sense of personal agency (e.g., deCharms, 1968; White, 1959). Individuals were seen as spontaneously motivated to undertake a range of behaviors, including mastery of the world, exploration, and activities involving fun and enjoyment. However, the activities encompassed by theories of intrinsic motivation were limited. Although they included behaviors involving affiliation and interpersonal responsiveness, they did not encompass the many types of behaviors that individuals are not spontaneously inclined to undertake. Thus, for example, theories of intrinsic motivation did not apply in cases in which individuals are undertaking behavior that is not intrinsically interesting but merely socially expected, such as the behavior of completing an uninteresting homework assignment. In turn, early behaviorist theories (e.g., Hull, 1943; Skinner, 1953) were able to account for why individuals undertake the latter type of behavior by reference to the structure of reinforcement contingencies existing in the environment. However, they entailed a passive view of the person and thus could not explain how individuals come to experience a sense of agency and personal satisfaction in complying with social requirements.

Through its focus on processes of internalization, self-determination theory offered a model that bridged these two extremes and that succeeded in explaining how one could experience oneself as agentic even in the context of meeting social expectations (Deci & Ryan, 1985, 1987, 1991). Self-determination theory assumes that individuals initially may be externally motivated to meet a social expectation because the behavior is socially required or because they will be sanctioned if they fail to perform it. However, gradually this expectation becomes internalized as the person makes it his or her own and comes subjectively to experience it as freely chosen. Once internalization has been achieved, the individual no longer experiences his or her behavior as motivated by social expectations but as based exclusively on his or her own subjective endorsement of it.

Self-determination theory speaks to the issue of balancing autonomy and relatedness in its views of motivation as forming a continuum of types. On one pole is intrinsic motivation, a form of motivation that explains autonomous behavior, but that may be considered, from the present perspective, to be insufficiently related, in that it does not account for compliance with social norms. On the other pole is external motivation, a form of motivation that emphasizes relatedness at the expense of autonomy, in portraying the individual as passively conforming to social norms. In this model, the optimum stance is identified as a middle position that integrates a perceived sense of choice with a commitment to meeting requirements of the social whole. In present terms, this represents a form of integration of autonomy and relatedness.

Parenting

One of the most influential contemporary psychological theories of parenting, the model of authoritarian parenting, developed by Baumrind, was responsive to historically shifting beliefs (Baumrind, 1966, 1971, 1996). An emphasis on the appropriateness of despotic rule by parents represented a widely held belief before the 20th century, with such an outlook evident in the writings of social theorists such as Rousseau, Hegel, and Mill. Children, it was assumed, need to be controlled by their elders and are incapable of self-determination. However, although providing control, this type of stance was emotionally harsh and domineering. It came to be challenged during the mid-20th century by perspectives that emphasize child permissiveness. Influenced by psychoanalytical views of the child's vulnerability, and spurred on by movements during the 1970s for extending greater rights to children, these latter approaches emphasized granting children maximum freedom of choice. However, they were subject to criticism themselves for failing to afford the child with needed guidance and protection.

The parenting model developed by Baumrind identifies an optimum midpoint between these two extremes. As Baumrind (1996) noted in describing the formation of her theory:

> The authoritative model . . . rejects both extremes of the authoritarian–permissive (or conservative–liberal) polarity, representing instead an integration of opposing unbalanced childrearing positions. At one extreme, child-centered permissiveness high on responsiveness and low on demandingness . . . at the opposite extreme, restrictive parent-centered authoritarianism . . . . Within the authoritative model, behavioral compliance and psychological autonomy are viewed not as mutually exclusive but rather as interdependent objectives: children are encouraged to respond habitually in pro-social ways and to reason autonomously. (p. 405)

Within the model of parenting developed by Baumrind, three contrasting styles of parenting are identified, reflecting these two opposing parenting philosophies and a stance that effects an integration of them. Overly harsh and restrictive styles of parenting are assumed to reflect an authoritarian style, whereas overly permissive and uninvolved styles of parenting are seen as reflecting a permissive style. The optimum stance of *authoritative* parenting constitutes a style that combines affective warmth and democratic decision making with provision of guidance and direction to the child.

The tripartite model of parenting developed by Baumrind may be seen to embody concerns with balancing autonomy and relatedness. Permissive styles of parenting, in affording the child inadequate guidance and not insuring the child's compliance with behavioral standards, promote the child's autonomy while embodying a deficit in relatedness. In turn, authoritarian styles of parenting, in being emotionally harsh and overcontrolling, embody an overemphasis on relatedness and an underemphasis on autonomy. Finally, the stance of authoritative parenting embodies the optimum approach in its balance of autonomy with relatedness, with the child encouraged to reason autonomously while being given active guidance in meeting societal standards.

Interpersonal Morality

In a final illustrative example, the morality of caring framework developed by Carol Gilligan represents the most influential contemporary theoretical model of interpersonal morality (Gilligan, 1977, 1982; Gilligan & Wiggins, 1988). Beyond its impact on the field of moral development, Gilligan's theory has stimulated the interest of feminist theorists as well as theorists of personality. The morality of caring model posits that individuals who have developed a morality of caring outlook feel a responsibility to care for needy individuals when they become aware of the others' needs and are able to help. This sense of moral responsibility is based on the individual having developed a connected view of self, in which they consider meeting the other's needs as integral to their self-identity. Although the morality of caring had originally been assumed to be gender-related, research has documented that it tends to be found among both men and women (Walker, 1984). The morality of caring orientation represents a freely given commitment that is compatible with individuality. The type of stance associated with this perspective is illustrated, for example, in the response of one of Gilligan's respondents who conveys her ideal image of a family as a setting in which "everyone is encouraged to become an individual and at the same time everybody helps others and receives help from them" (Gilligan, 1982, p. 54).

In terms of theories of moral judgment, Gilligan's model responded to theoretical gaps in the Kohlbergian model of moral development. Within the Kohlbergian framework, it had been assumed that the content of morality is limited to issues of justice and that responsibilities to family and friends constitute forms of social conventional reasoning (Kohlberg, 1969, 1971). The Kohlbergian framework thus emphasized individual autonomy, but only in the context of a morality of justice, and gave weight to interpersonal responsibilities but only in the context of a social conformist stance. Within Gilligan's model, in contrast, interpersonal responsiveness and caring are not only treated as fully moral, they are approached in ways that place greater emphasis on the individual's personal decision making than is the case in approaches based on role obligations.

In terms of the development of a morality of caring outlook, individuals are seen as first experiencing a phase in which their focus is on caring for themselves. This is followed, in turn, by a phase in which emphasis is placed on "caring for others," to the individual's "exclusion of herself," a stance that is overly selfless. Finally, a fully developed morality of caring stance is achieved during which the individual has resolved "the tension between selfishness and responsibility," giving concern both to the needs of self and to those of others (Gilligan, 1982, p. 74).

The morality of caring framework embodies an emphasis on balancing autonomy and relatedness in its views of the path and endpoint of development. To achieve a mature morality of caring outlook, the individual is seen as first passing through a developmental phase characterized by a selfish stance that reflects too much autonomy, followed by a selfless stance that reflects too much relatedness. The mature morality of caring position integrates autonomy with relatedness through combining caring for the self with caring for others.

Summary and Implications

In sum, it is evident that major contemporary theories of social development in the areas of attachment, social motivation, parenting, and interpersonal morality share a common deep structure that is responsive to problems in balancing autonomy with relatedness. This deep structure may be seen to function in a way that is similar to that observed in the case of the construct of g that underlies diverse theories of intelligence. The various theories of social development forward viewpoints in which the most adaptive form is portrayed as a balanced position that integrates the concerns with autonomy and relatedness. This structure maps onto the problem in achieving agency, identified by Bakan (1966), and resonates with various Western individualist cultural themes. In a similar way, the content definition of intelligence reflected in the construct of g privileges characteristics that are also highly valued in Western cultural settings, such as an emphasis on abstract analytical abilities and on response speed.

Paralleling the high intercorrelations observed among different IQ type measures, the diverse theories of social development also show positive correlation with each other. Thus, for example, it has been found that an authoritative style of parenting is associated with a self-determined motivational stance (e.g., Grolnick & Ryan, 1989; Grolnick, Deci, & Ryan, 1997) and is linked to the development of secure forms of attachment (e.g., Bretherton, Golby, & Cho, 1997; LaGuardia, Ryan, Couchman, & Deci, 2000; Leak & Cooney, 2001). Equally, just as high IQ predicts a range of positive adaptive outcomes, the optimum modes of social development identified are likewise related to similar types of positive consequences. For example, authoritarian styles of parenting, secure modes of attachment, and self-determined motivational orientations are associated with higher educational attainment, positive work performance, as well as positive health behaviors and effects, such as lower levels of alcohol use and depression (Baumrind, 1996; Grusec & Kuczynski, 1997). Of equal importance, as is also the case with IQ measures, positive adaptive outcomes in the area of social development are consistently linked to higher socioeconomic status.

TOWARD A CULTURAL BROADENING OF THEORIES OF SOCIAL DEVELOPMENT

In the following section, discussion focuses on cultural research that points to contrasting problems for the self as assuming a prominent role in everyday adaptation in diverse cultural contexts and that highlights the need to expand present theoretical models of social development to accommodate this variation. The purpose of this type of research resembles that being undertaken by cultural theorists in the area of intelligence who likewise are working to broaden the types of abilities taken into account in models of intelligence (e.g., Grigorenko et al., 2001; Schliemann et al., 1997). The evidence on social development considered here is from a range of cultural populations that each emphasize somewhat distinctive outlooks. Accordingly, it may be seen, the types of underlying problems for the self that appear salient also are somewhat distinctive from each other, even as they differ from the middle-class European American outlooks privileged in contemporary mainstream psychology.

Cultural Variation in Forms of Attachment

Cross-cultural research conducted by attachment researchers has uncovered what appears to be a universal preference for secure over insecure forms of attachment as well as has established links between attachment and desired adaptive endpoints (Crittenden & Clausen, 2000; Sagi, 1990; Waters & Cummings, 2000). However, increasingly cultural work that is sensitive to indigenous cultural categories is suggesting that attachment theory fails to capture certain dimensions of attachment that are salient in various collectivist cultural populations.

Evidence for the latter claim may be seen in research that explored the meanings that groups of mothers give to attachment behavior (Harwood, Miller, & Irizarry, 1995). Asked to describe the qualities that they would like their toddlers to emphasize as they grow older, European American mothers spontaneously mentioned themes involving balancing autonomy and relatedness, dimensions that are central to attachment theory. Such an emphasis may be seen, for example, in the sample responses by European American mothers given below:

> I'd like him to be independent and love us, but stand on his own.
> I want her to be independent, but yet, you know it's good to have other people around to be with and stuff. (Harwood et al., 1995, p. 89)

In contrast, in describing their images of an ideal child, Puerto Rican mothers spontaneously focused on the child developing such qualities as being calm, obedient, and respectfully attentive to the teaching of their elders. As seen in the descriptions given below by Puerto Rican mothers, emphasis within this community tends to be placed on the child coming to know what is expected in particular situations and behaving in appropriate ways to gain the respect of others:

> I would love it if they were . . . *respetuosos* (respectful) toward their elders as well as with people their own age, so that when they're adolescents and then adults, they know how to use particular aspects of their personality at the appropriate time, so that others will *respetan* them.
> *I would like for my son to be respetuoso, amable, obediente.* I would like him to be that way so that one does not have to have a hard time (dealing) with the boy. (Harwood et al., p. 98)

It is notable that when presented with experimental vignette situations that portrayed toddlers displaying the three forms of attachment tapped in the Strange Situation research paradigm, the European American mothers interpreted these situations in ways that are congruent with attachment theory. They spontaneously admired the B type baby for being secure, while criticizing the A type baby for emotional detachment, and the C type baby for excessive dependence. In contrast, the Puerto Rican mothers spontaneously applied contrasting criteria in appraising the hypothetical toddlers. Thus, for example, the A type toddler was criticized for what the Puerto Rican mothers interpreted to be an overly active and insufficiently calm mode of behavior, whereas the C type toddler was criticized for what was perceived as a willful and pampered stance. In turn, the B type toddler was praised for what the Puerto Rican mothers regarded as a stance that reflected respectful attentiveness and positive engagement in interpersonal relationships.

Such results imply that there are salient culturally variable dimensions of attachment that are not tapped by existing measuring instruments. Although the Puerto Rican mothers showed an overall preference for the B form of attachment, they attended to dimensions of behavior, namely proper demeanor and positive engagement with the environment, that are not captured in attachment theory.

Similar observations underlie calls to broaden definitions of attachment theory to encompass concerns with *amae* (an emotional experience that involves positive feelings of depending on another's benevolence) that are salient in Japanese cultural contexts (Rothbaum, Pott, Azuma, Miyake, & Weisz, 2000; Rothbaum, Weisz, Pott, Miyake, & Morelli, 2000; Takahashi, 1990). Thus, in contrast to the types of orientations emphasized in attachment theory, Japanese normative assumptions place greater value on the child's development of empathy as well as stress parental practices that reflect greater parental emotional involvement as compared with verbal involvement.

In sum, cultural research on attachment does not challenge the universality of the distinction between secure and insecure behavior but rather suggests that the dimension of security of attachment is not fully adequate to tap salient aspects of attachment that are emphasized in different cultural contexts. The concerns with empathy, interdependence, and indulgence of the other's needs that are salient in the stance of *amae* are notably not the same as the concerns with maintaining respect, tranquility, and compliance that are salient in the stance of proper relatedness emphasized by Puerto Rican mothers. However, in both instances, the salient dimensions being emphasized do not readily map onto the concerns with balancing autonomy and relatedness that inform contemporary attachment theory.

Cultural Variation in Social Motivation

Cross-cultural research that has used scales developed in the tradition of self-determination theory provides support for the claims of this model (Deci, Ryan, Gagne, Leone, Usunov, & Kornazheva, 2001). It has been demonstrated that if social expectations assume a controlling form, they are experienced as aversive and associated with negative motivational implications. However, research is also revealing that in many collectivist cultural populations, individuals do not tend to experience role-based social expectations as controlling. Thus, in such cases, acting to fulfill role obligations is not associated with the negative implications typically observed among European American populations and predicted by self-determination theory.

Providing evidence for this type of cross-cultural difference, Bontempo, Lobel, and Triandis (1990) found that compared with Americans, Brazilians reported that they would experience more enjoyment in being responsive to need-based role expectations (e.g., fulfilling a request by a family member for a loan). The results indicated that Brazilians fully internalize social norms of this type, whereas Americans tend to experience them as controlling. As Bontempo and his colleagues observe, "unlike their Brazilian counterparts who may derive a sense of satisfaction from acting dutifully, the more individualistic U.S. sample reports little satisfaction with this 'forced' behavior" (Bontempo et al., 1990, p. 207).

Similar types of trends were documented in a study that contrasted the outlooks on helping behaviors held by European American as compared with Hindu Indian adults (Miller & Bersoff, 1995). This latter work demonstrated that Hindu Indians not only consider it more desirable than do Americans to respond to the needs of family members in situations involving high cost, but also indicate that they would experience such behavior as more satisfying. The nature of this cross-cultural difference may be illustrated through a contrast of responses given in the case of a situation involving a wife providing extended care for her husband who was paralyzed in a motorcycle accident. Focusing on the dissatisfaction that she expected that the wife would experience, a U.S. participant portrayed the wife's duty to her husband as antithetical to her individual satisfaction: "She is acting out of obligation—not other reasons like love. She has a sense of duty, but little satisfaction for her own happiness" (Miller & Bersoff, 1995, p. 275). The U.S. respondent, it may be seen, is adopting an outlook that treats individual satisfaction and duty as antithetical elements, the same type of assumption informing self-determination theory and underlying the opposition between the poles of autonomy and relatedness that has been seen informing psychological theories of motivation. In contrast, in a prototypical response, an Indian informant associated duty with the fulfillment of role obligations: "She will have the satisfaction of having fulfilled her duty. She helped her husband during difficulty."

Related experimental research suggests that in many collectivist cultural populations duty does not reflect a form of internalization in which a sense of obligation disappears as a constraint is internalized but rather a form of internalization in which motivation is simultaneously experienced as endogenously and exogenously generated (Miller & Bersoff, 1994). In a between-participants manipulation, European American and Hindu Indian respondents made attributions about the motives of hypothetical agents who were portrayed as providing aid to a neighbor either in the context of prior reciprocity or in their absence. The attributions of Americans conformed to the predictions of self-determination theory, with greater liking for helping and satisfaction inferred to be present in the condition in which behavior was less normatively based than in the experimental condition. In contrast, Indians considered the agents equally endogenously motivated in both conditions. Such a trend suggested that they saw less of a tension between individual inclinations and social expectations than did Americans but rather instead viewed social expectations as compatible with individual satisfaction.

Experimental work by Iyengar and Lepper (1999) documents similar types of cross-cultural differences on a behavioral level. Consonant with the emphasis on freely chosen behavior predicted by self-determination theory, European American children were found to perform better and to display greater intrinsic motivation when they had selected an anagram task themselves as compared with when their mothers had selected it for them. In contrast, Asian American children performed better when complying with the wishes of their mothers.

Overall, the present findings point to the existence of a form of motivation not anticipated in self-determination theory. Self-determination theory posits that the tension between freely chosen behavior and normatively directed behavior (i.e., which in present terms is seen as mapping onto the deep structure of the tension between autonomy and relatedness) is resolved through a middle position in which social expectations have been internalized so that they are subjectively experienced as purely internal. However, the results observed among the present collectivist populations highlight the existence of a form of internalization in which behavior is experienced as simultaneously endogenously and exogenously motivated (i.e. as guided by external norms and as expressions of the self).

Cultural Variation in Parenting

Comparative research supports the claims of the Baumrind model that extremes of parenting behavior—that is, stances that are experienced as overly harsh and punitive or ones that are insufficiently involved—are associated with maladaptive child outcomes (Chen, Liu, Li, Cen, Chen, & Wang, 2000). However, work has also documented that the meanings accorded to and adaptive implications of parenting behaviors vary in different cultural communities, with such variation not fully accommodated by the categories of Baumrind's parenting model (e.g., Rudy & Grusec, 2001).

Research demonstrates, for example, that in the context of neighborhoods that are highly impoverished or dangerous, a style of parenting that is restrictive may be associated with positive adaptive outcomes. In such cases, close monitoring of the child's behavior serves to provide the child with needed supervision and support that is less necessary in more benign environmental contexts. It is notable that this work also suggests that the present definition of authoritarian parenting is not fully adequate to capture the nature of this normatively preferred form, because this directive form that is found in certain inner city communities, tends to be associated with perceived parental warmth rather than with perceived parental harshness, as is the case with authoritarian parenting.

Cross-cultural research has also demonstrated that unlike European American adolescents, Korean adolescents associate greater perceived parental warmth with greater perceived parental control (Rohner & Pettengill,

1985). Of equal importance, researchers have found that the controlling styles of parenting that tend to be emphasized within Chinese families are informed by an indigenous concept of training (*chiao shun*). Such an orientation combines an emphasis on standards of conduct and preserving the integrity of the family with affective concern and caring for the child. Not only is this directive form of parenting accorded positive rather than negative affective meanings within this community, but it is also associated with positive adaptive outcomes such as higher levels of educational achievement.

It is notable that cultural research also has suggested that within Swedish and Nordic cultural communities, the parenting practices represent a blend of forms that do not readily fit into one of the types in the Baumrind typology. Nordic parents make less use of physical punishments than their U.S. counterparts, but also less use of reasoning and more use of physical restraint (Baumrind, 1996).

In sum, there is evidence of a distinction made between adaptive and abusive or maladaptive parenting in all cultural populations. However, available research suggests that normatively acceptable modes of parenting are not fully captured by the Baumrind scheme, with its identification of an ideal midpoint that combines democratic decision making (autonomy) with effective social control (relatedness). Rather, the forms of parenting that are normative in different cultural communities appear responsive to contrasting ecological conditions as well as to contrasting cultural values, such as emphases on family harmony or on nonviolence, that do not readily gloss onto this continuum.

Cultural Variation in Interpersonal Morality

Concerns with caring have been observed to be central to morality universally (Snarey & Keljo, 1991). However, cross-cultural research also reveals the existence of cultural variation in forms of interpersonal morality and suggests that the voluntaristic approach to caring of Gilligan's model is culturally specific (Miller, 1994, 2001; Shimizu, 2001).

Rather than reflecting a concern with balancing responsibilities to self (autonomy) with responsibilities to others (relatedness), forms of interpersonal morality found in many collectivist cultural populations place greater emphasis on fulfillment of role-related responsibilities. In such traditions, role-related responsibilities tend to be approached as approximations of the nature of being or as a perceived natural law, rather than as a mere societal construction. For example, it has been found that moral outlooks emphasized within certain Chinese populations reflect the construct of *jen*, an outlook that merges ideas of fulfillment of duty and respect for authority with benevolence and love (Dien, 1982; Ma, 1997) and that within Japanese communities caring tends to be viewed as a communal responsibility, extending beyond individual cognitions and feelings (Shimizu, 2001). In turn, work within Hindu Indian communities has documented the centrality to interpersonal moral outlooks of the construct of *dharma*, a concept that denotes simultaneously inherent disposition, nature, code for conduct, and natural law (Miller, 1994; Vasudev, 1994; Vasudev & Hummel, 1987). In another example, studies conducted among Buddhist monks have highlighted the foundation of interpersonal moral commitments in that community on metaphysical cultural premises grounded in *dukha*, or a view of life as suffering and of negative karma as accumulating through transgressions (Huebner & Garrod, 1991, 1993). From such a perspective, there is assumed to be a moral imperative that is central to the self's spiritual advancement to act to eliminate the suffering of others and to overcome the effects of negative accumulated karma.

Cross-cultural research conducted among European American and Hindu Indian populations demonstrates that these contrasting moral outlooks give rise to cultural variation in the morality of caring. For example, Hindu Indians show a greater tendency to treat meeting the needs of family and friends as role-related duties, whereas European Americans show a greater tendency to treat them as matters for personal decision making (Miller & Bersoff, 1992; Miller, Bersoff, & Harwood, 1990). Furthermore, Hindu Indians are more prone than European Americans to consider it as morally required, rather than beyond the scope of morality, to give priority to the needs of family, friends, or other in-group members in the face of personal hardship or sacrifice (Miller & Bersoff, 1995). Also, whereas European Americans tend to judge that there is less responsibility to help a family member or friend with whom one does not have a close relationship, Hindu Indians tend to treat interpersonal responsibilities as independent of such nonmoral considerations (Miller & Bersoff, 1998).

Overall, the perspectives on interpersonal morality under consideration here do not embody the same type of cultural tension that it was argued informs Gilligan's morality of caring model. The collective tends generally to be conceptualized in less problematic terms, as a natural and omnipresent aspect of experience that is integral to self, rather than as a discretionary commitment to be balanced against the needs and desires of an autonomous individual.

IMPLICATIONS AND CONCLUSION

In sum, this chapter has shown that similar conceptual assumptions underlie contemporary mainstream psychological theories of social development. These assumptions concern achieving a balance between autonomy and relatedness in different spheres of social life. This deep conceptual structure is evident in the tendencies within the theories to identify problematic adaptive endpoints at opposing ends of an autonomy–relatedness continuum and to identify the optimum adaptive form at the midpoint of this continuum as a stance that achieves a balance between these two poles.

However, I have also presented evidence suggesting that approaches that are informed by this deep structure do not appear adequate to accommodate the somewhat contrasting perspectives in these areas emphasized in different sociocultural communities. Although contrasting themes are salient in different settings, certain common tendencies were observed. Thus, for example, there appears a broad theme related to responding appropriately to features of the social context. Such a stance was seen in the emphasis placed by Puerto Rican mothers on their children's display of both respect and affection toward their elders or in the emphasis placed on training among Chinese parents. Furthermore, this concern with social responsiveness tends to be regarded as a fulfillment of self as a social and spiritual being. Thus, as evident in the case of Hindu and Buddhist outlooks on morality, responsiveness to the needs of others is understood metaphysically as a vehicle for spiritual refinement, which represents an expression of the self even as it also represents a response to social requirements.

These multiple types of normatively based visions of social development do not appear readily to fit into a dichotomous formulation marked by a tension between the individual and the group. Rather, in distinct and variable ways, the various visions tend to reflect monistic outlooks, in which the fulfillment of social requirements and of self tends to be experienced as coterminous. Of equal importance, the perceived challenge is to cultivate the self through social relatedness rather than to preserve the self's autonomy while meeting the somewhat competing demands of the social order.

In terms of implications, the existence of a common deep structure in contemporary theories of social development suggests that such theories suffer from some of the same concerns with limited predictive range and circularity that have been raised in the case of theories of intelligence. It becomes expected on conceptual grounds alone that measures of social development based on the autonomy–relatedness framework will correlate with each other, just as measures of intelligence that are informed by a common psychometrically based conception of intelligence also tend to correlate with each other. Also, to the extent that an emphasis on balancing autonomy and relatedness reflects central values of the middle-class European American power structure that informs many societal institutions, such as schools and corporations, it will tend to be rewarded with positive evaluations and opportunities for advancement. In this respect, such a normative standard for competence becomes a gatekeeping mechanism similar in many respects to that observed in the case of IQ.

The present considerations more generally highlight the need to broaden present theories of social development and their associated measuring instruments to accommodate diverse cultural and subcultural outlooks, just as similar calls have been made to broaden the scope of abilities encompassed within theories of intelligence. The goal is not to expand the number of explanatory frameworks so that theories are formulated at a level of specificity that applies only to an isolated cultural or social group. Rather, it is to recognize that important variation in modes of adaptation exists that is not being taken into account in contemporary psychological theories and research methodologies (Miller, 2002). Such an expansion holds the promise of contributing to basic psychological theory, through its introduction of new theoretical constructs and process models of development.

It is important methodologically to recognize that our present assessment instruments lack sufficient cultural sensitivity and need to be made more culturally inclusive, just as intelligence tests likewise need to be adapted to tap the competencies of diverse cultural populations (Greenfield, 1997). It was observed, for example, that in several cases, theories of social development appeared to be supported when existing measuring instruments were administered in comparative cultural research. For instance, in the area of attachment, culturally based research that presented individuals with the three attachment categories from the Strange Situation paradigm has revealed a universal preference for secure over insecure forms of attachment (Harwood et al., 1995). Of equal importance, cross-cultural researchers using measuring instruments developed in the tradition of self-determination theory have documented a universal preference for identified over controlling motivational orientations (Deci et al., 2001).

However, in cases such as these, identifications are being observed that may be considered only best-guess glosses, as respondents are confronted with research questionnaires that typically do not tap the subtlety of the types of orientations emphasized in their respective communities. For example, the type of respectful and affectionate child valued by Puerto Rican mothers does not closely match the type of secure and independent child that is considered most adaptive within the Strange Situation research paradigm. However, the positive connotations accorded to this child fit the secure category of attachment much more closely than they do either of the two less adaptive patterns that are presented as alternatives in the Strange Situation research paradigm. Likewise, the endogenous view of duty that is entailed in social motivation among Hindu Indian populations tends to be linked with satisfaction even as it is also regarded as based on duty. It is likely then that a Hindu Indian respondent would find that this type of outlook fits most closely the identified orientation on scales in the tradition of self-determination theory, given the positive affective connotations of the items that comprise the identified orientation on such scales and the predominately negative affective connotations of the items that comprise the external orientation. However, although Hindu Indians might thus show results on self-determination measures that are identical to those shown by Americans, this response commonality would obscure important cultural variation that exists in Hindu Indian as compared with European American outlooks. A similar conclusion, it may be noted, follows from cultural work in the area of intelligence. This work has documented that frequently only a partial overlap exists between the operational definitions of intelligence on IQ tests and the ways that intelligence is defined in local cultural communities. Although IQ tests then may appear to have universal validity, they are not sufficiently sensitive to tap these local salient outlooks on intelligence.

In conclusion, it must be recognized that in all cultural populations, distinctions are made between behaviors that are considered to be more or less adaptive and that, at the extremes, considerable cross-cultural agreement exists concerning what constitutes extremely maladaptive forms of social and intellectual development. However, beyond this commonality there tends to be more openness in pathways of normal human development than is taken into account in contemporary psychological theories. Just as there are multiple culturally variable criteria of what constitutes intelligence, there are multiple culturally variable criteria of what constitutes competent social development. Psychological theories of social development and of intelligence must be broadened to accommodate this variation, with the recognition that the normative endpoints of human development are multiple and cannot be captured by the values and practices of any single group.

REFERENCES

Ainsworth, M. D. (1978). *Patterns of attachment: A psychological study of the strange situation*. Hillsdale, NJ: Erlbaum.

Bakan, D. (1966). *The duality of human existence*. Chicago: Rand McNally.

Baumrind, D. (1966). Effects of authoritative parental control on child behavior. *Child Development, 37*, 887–907.

Baumrind, D. (1971). Current patterns of parental authority. *Developmental Psychology Monographs, 4*(1, Part 2).

Baumrind, D. (1996). The discipline controversy revisited. *Family Relations: Journal of Applied Family & Child Studies, 45*, 405–414.

Bontempo, R., Lobel, S., & Triandis, H. (1990). Compliance and value internalization in Brazil and the U.S. *Journal of Cross-Cultural Psychology, 21*, 200–213.

Bowlby, J. (1969–1980). *Attachment and loss*. New York: Basic Books.

Bretherton, I., Golby, B., & Cho, E. (1997). Attachment and the transmission of values. In J. E. Grusec & L. Kuczynski (Eds.), *Parenting and children's internalization of values: A handbook of contemporary theory* (pp. 103–134). New York: Wiley.

Ceci, S. J. (1990). *On intelligence . . . more or less*. Englewood Cliff, NJ: Prentice Hall.

Charlesworth, W. (1976). Human intelligence as adaptation: An ecological approach. In L. Resnick (Ed.), *The nature of intelligence*. Hillsdale, NJ: Erlbaum.

Chen, X., Liu, M., Li, B., Cen, G., Chen, H., & Wang, L. (2000). Maternal authoritative and authoritarian attitudes and mother–child interactions and relationships in urban China. *International Journal of Behavioral Development, 24*(1), 119–126.

Crittenden, P. M., & Claussen, A. H. (2000). *The organization of attachment relationships: Maturation, culture, and context*. New York: Cambridge University Press.

deCharms, R. (1968). *Personal causation: The internal affective determinants of behavior*. New York: Academic Press.

Deci, E. L., & Ryan, R. M. (1985). *Intrinsic motivation and self-determination in human behavior*. New York: Plenum Press.

Deci, E. L., & Ryan, R. M. (1987). The support of autonomy and the control of behavior. *Journal of Personality and Social Psychology, 53*, 1024–1037.

Deci, E. L., & Ryan, R. M. (1991). A motivational approach to self: Integration in personality. In R. Dienstbier (Ed.), *Nebraska Symposium on Motivation: Vol. 38. Perspectives on motivation* (pp. 237–288). Lincoln: University of Nebraska Press.

Deci, E. L., Ryan, R. M., Gagne, M., Leone, D. R., Usunov, J., & Kornazheva, B. P. (2001). Need satisfaction, motivation, and well-being in the work organizations of a former Eastern Block country. *Personality and Social Psychology Bulletin, 27*, 930–942.

Dien, D. S.-F. (1982). A Chinese perspective on Kohlberg's theory of moral development. *Developmental Review, 2*, 331–341.

Eysenck, H. (1979). *A model for intelligence*. New York: Springer-Verlag.

Farr, R. M. (1991). Individualism as a collective representation. In V. Aebisher, J. P. Deconchy, & M. Lipiansky (Eds.), *Ideologies et representations sociales*. Cousset (Fribourg), Switzerland: Delval.

Fraley, R. C. (2002). Attachment stability from infancy to adulthood: Meta-analysis and dynamic modeling of developmental mechanisms. *Personality and Social Psychology Review, 6*(2), 123–151.

Gardner, H. (1983). *Frames of mind: The theory of multiple intelligences*. New York: Basic Books.

Gardner, H. (1993). *Multiple intelligence: The theory in practice*. New York: Basic Books.

Gilligan, C. (1977). In a different voice: Women's conceptions of self and of morality. *Harvard Educational Review, 47*, 481–517.

Gilligan, C. (1982). *In a different voice: Psychological theory and women's development*. Cambridge, MA: Harvard University Press.

Gilligan, C., & Wiggins, G. (1988). The origins of morality in early childhood relationships. In C. Gilligan, J. Ward, & J. Taylor (Eds.), *Mapping the moral domain: A contribution of women's thinking to psychological theory and education* (pp. 111–138). Cambridge, MA: Harvard University Press.

Greenfield, P. M. (1997). You can't take it with you: Why ability assessments don't cross cultures. *American Psychologist, 52*, 1115–1124.

Grigorenko, E., Geissler, P. W., Prince, R., Okatacha, F., Nokes, C., Kenny, D. A., et al. (2001). The organisation of Luo conceptions of intelligence: A study of implicit theories in a Kenyan village. *International Journal of Behavioral Development, 25*, 367–378.

Grolnick, W. S., Deci, E. L., & Ryan, R. M. (1997). Internalization within the family: The self-determination theory perspective. In J. E. Grusec & L. Kuczynski

(Eds.), *Handbook of parenting and the transmission of values* (pp. 135–161). New York: Wiley.

Grolnick, W. W., & Ryan, R. M. (1989). Parent styles associated with children's self-regulation and competence in school. *Journal of Educational Psychology, 81,* 143–154.

Grusec, J. E., & Kuczynski, L. (Eds.). (1997). *Parenting and children's internalization of values: A handbook of contemporary theory.* New York: Wiley.

Guisinger, S., & Blatt, S. J. (1994). Individuality and relatedness: Evolution of a fundamental debate. *American Psychologist, 49,* 104–111.

Hartigan, J. A., & Wigdor, A. K. (Eds.). (1989). *Fairness in employment testing: Validity, generality, minority issues, and the General Aptitude Test Battery.* Washington, DC: National Academy Press.

Harwood, R. L., Miller, J. G., & Irizarry, N. L. (1995). *Culture and attachment: Perceptions of the child in context.* New York: Guilford Press.

Haslam, N., & Baron, J. (1994). Intelligence, personality, and prudence. In R. J. Sternberg & P. Ruzgis (Eds.), *Personality and intelligence* (pp. 32–58). New York: Cambridge University Press.

Huebner, A., & Garrod, A. C. (1991). Moral reasoning in a Karmic world. *Human Development, 34,* 341–352.

Huebner, A. M., & Garrod, A. C. (1993). Moral reasoning among Tibetan Monks: A study of Buddhist adolescents and young adults in Nepal. *Journal of Cross-Cultural Psychology, 24*(2), 167–185.

Hull, C. L. (1943). *Principles of behavior: An introduction to behavior theory.* New York: Appleton-Century-Crofts.

Hunt, E. (1995). *Will we be smart enough: Cognitive changes in the coming workforce.* New York: Russell Sage Foundation.

Hunter, J. E. (1986). Cognitive ability, cognitive aptitudes, job knowledge, and job performance. *Journal of Vocational Behavior, 29,* 340–362.

Itzkoff, S. W. (1989). *The making of the civilized mind.* New York: Peter Longmans.

Iyengar, S. S., & Lepper, M. R. (1999). Rethinking the value of choice: A cultural perspective on intrinsic motivation. *Journal of Personality and Social Psychology, 76,* 349–366.

Kohlberg, L. (1969). Stage and sequence: The cognitive-developmental approach to socialization. In D. A. Goslin (Ed.), *Handbook of socialization theory* (pp. 347–380). Chicago: Rand McNally.

Kohlberg, L. (1971). From is to ought: How to commit the naturalistic fallacy and get away with it in the study of moral development. In T. Mischel (Ed.), *Cognitive development and epistemology* (pp. 151–236). New York: Academic Press.

Laboratory of Comparative Human Cognition. (1983). Culture and cognitive development. In W. Kessen & P. H. Mussen (Eds.), *Handbook of child psychology: History, theory and method* (pp. 295–356). New York: Wiley.

LaGuardia, J. G., Ryan, R. M., Couchman, C. E., & Deci, E. L. (2000). Within-person variation in security of attachment: A self-determination theory perspective on attachment, need fulfillment, and well-being. *Journal of Personality and Social Psychology, 79,* 367–384.

Lave, J., & Wenger, E. (1991). *Situated learning: Legitimate peripheral participation.* Cambridge, England: Cambridge University Press.

Leak, G. K., & Cooney, R. R. (2001). Self-determination, attachment styles, and well-being in adult romantic relationships. *Representative Research in Social Psychology, 25,* 55–62.

Ma, H. K. (1997). The affective and cognitive aspects of moral development: A Chinese perspective. In H. Kao & D. Sinha (Eds.), *Asian perspectives on psychology* (pp. 93–109). Thousand Oaks, CA: Sage.

Miller, J. G. (1994). Cultural diversity in the morality of caring: Individually oriented versus duty-based interpersonal moral codes. *Cross-Cultural Research, 28*(1), 3–39.

Miller, J. G. (1997). A cultural-psychology perspective on intelligence. In R. J. Sternberg & E. L. Grigorenko (Eds.), *Intelligence, heredity, and environment* (pp. 269–302). New York: Cambridge University Press.

Miller, J. G. (2001). Culture and moral development. In D. Matsumoto (Ed.), *The handbook of culture and psychology* (pp. 151–169). New York: Oxford University Press.

Miller, J. G. (2002). Bringing culture to basic psychological theory—Beyond individualism and collectivism: Comment on Oyserman et al. (2002). *Psychological Bulletin, 128,* 97–109.

Miller, J. G., & Bersoff, D. M. (1992). Culture and moral judgment: How are conflicts between justice and interpersonal responsibilities resolved? *Journal of Personality and Social Psychology, 62,* 541–554.

Miller, J. G., & Bersoff, D. M. (1994). Cultural influences on the moral status of reciprocity and the discounting of endogenous motivation. *Personality and Social Psychology Bulletin, 20,* 592–602.

Miller, J. G., & Bersoff, D. M. (1995). Development in the context of everyday family relationships: Culture, interpersonal morality, and adaptation. In M. Killen & D. Hart (Eds.), *Morality in everyday life: Developmental perspectives* (pp. 259–282). New York: Cambridge University Press.

Miller, J. G., & Bersoff, D. M. (1998). The role of liking in perceptions of the moral responsibility to help: A cultural perspective. *Journal of Experimental Social Psychology, 34,* 443–469.

Miller, J. G., Bersoff, D. M., & Harwood, R. L. (1990). Perceptions of social responsibilities in India and in the United States: Moral imperatives or personal decisions? *Journal of Personality and Social Psychology, 58,* 33–47.

Pintner, R. (1921). Contribution to "Intelligence and its Measurement: A Symposium." *Journal of Educational Psychology, 12,* 139–143.

Plath, D. W. (1980). *Long engagements: Maturity in modern Japan.* Stanford, CA: Stanford University Press.

Rohner, R. P. & Pettengill, S. M. (1985). Perceived parental acceptance–rejection and parental control among Korean adolescents. *Child Development, 52,* 524–528.

Rosaldo, M. A. (1984). Toward an anthropology of self and feeling. In R. A. Shweder & R. A. LeVine (Eds.), *Culture theory: Essays on mind, self, and emotion* (pp. 137–157). New York: Cambridge University Press.

Rothbaum, F., Pott, M., Azuma, H., Miyake, K., & Weisz, J. (2000). The development of close relationships in Japan and the United States: Paths of symbiotic harmony and generative tension. *Child Development, 71*, 1121–1142.

Rothbaum, F., Weisz, J., Pott, M., Miyake, K., & Morelli, G. (2000). Attachment and culture: Security in the United States and Japan. *American Psychologist, 55*, 1093–1104.

Rudy, D., & Grusec, J. E. (2001). Correlates of authoritarian parenting in individualist and collectivist cultures and implications for understanding the transmission of values. *Journal of Cross-Cultural Psychology, 32*, 202–212.

Sagi, A. (1990). Attachment theory and research from a cross-cultural perspective. *Human Development, 33*, 10–22.

Schliemann, A. D., Carraher, D. W., & Ceci, S. J. (1997). Everyday cognition. In *Handbook of cross-cultural psychology: Vol. 2. Basic processes and human development* (2nd ed., pp. 177–216). Needham Heights, MA: Allyn & Bacon.

Scribner, S. (1984). Studying working intelligence. In B. Rogoff & J. Lave (Eds.), *Everyday cognition: Its development in social context* (pp. 9–40). Cambridge, MA: Harvard University Press.

Shimizu, H. (2001). Japanese adolescent boys' senses of empathy (*omoiyari*) and Carol Gilligan's perspectives on the morality of care: A phenomenological approach. *Culture and Psychology, 7*, 453–475.

Skinner, B. F. (1953). *Science and human behavior*. New York: Macmillan.

Snarey, J., & Keljo, K. (1991). In a Gemeinschaft voice: The cross-cultural expansion of moral development theory. In *Handbook of moral behavior and development: Vol. 1. Theory* (pp. 395–424). Hillsdale, NJ: Erlbaum.

Spence, J. T. (1985). Achievement American style: The rewards and costs of individualism. *American Psychologist, 40*, 1285–1295.

Sternberg, R. J. (1985). *Beyond IQ: A triarchic theory of human intelligence*. New York: Cambridge University Press.

Sternberg, R. J. (1988). *The triarchic mind: A new theory of human intelligence*. New York: Viking Press.

Sternberg, R. J. (1996). *Successful intelligence: How practical and creative intelligence determine success in life*. New York: Simon & Schuster.

Sternberg, R. J., Conway, B. E., Ketron, J. L., & Bernstein, M. (1981). People's conceptions of intelligence. *Journal of Personality and Social Psychology, 41*, 37–55.

Takahashi, K. (1990). Are the key assumptions of the "strange situation" procedure universal? A view from Japanese research. *Human Development, 33*, 23–30.

Taylor, C. (1989). *Sources of the self: The making of the modern identity*. Cambridge, MA: Harvard University Press.

Vasudev, J. (1994). *Ahimsa*, justice, and the unity of life: Postconventional morality from an Indian perspective. In M. E. Miller (Ed.), *Transcendence and mature* thought in adulthood: The further reaches of adult development (pp. 237–255). Lanham, MD: Rowman & Littlefield.

Vasudev, J., & Hummel, R. C. (1987). Moral stage sequence and principled reasoning in an Indian sample. *Human Development, 30*(2), 105–118.

Walker, L. J. (1984). Sex differences in the development of moral reasoning: A critical review. *Child Development, 55*, 677–691.

Waters, E., & Cummings, E. M. (2000). A secure base from which to explore close relationships. *Child Development, 71*(1), 164–172.

White, R. W. (1959). Motivation reconsidered: The concept of competence. *Psychological Review, 66*, 297–333.

6

CULTURE AND COGNITION: PERFORMANCE DIFFERENCES AND INVARIANT STRUCTURES

YPE H. POORTINGA AND FONS J. R. VAN DE VIJVER

Cross-cultural differences in score distributions of cognitive tasks are often substantial. Such findings are of practical significance; high scores on intelligence tests reflect skills or competencies that tend to be an asset for educational and economic advancement, at least in urban industrial settings. The present chapter focuses on the challenge these results offer for theoretical analysis. In our view the relationship between culture and cognition is a fascinating field of study. However, research often yields differences that are difficult to interpret. Do differences in Raven scores (Raven, 1938) obtained with children from different countries reflect differences in reasoning, as we are often inclined to conclude? And what is the role of educational differences? Do children learn to reason better in school or does their everyday environment make them more familiar with the abstract figures and tasks of the Raven? In our view these questions are too infrequently dealt with. We question the wisdom of uncritically interpreting observed differences as reflecting differences in the traits the tests are supposed to measure, without examining the validity of the interpretation. In particular, if participants come from rather dissimilar cultures it is very easy to find (replicable) significant differences in cognitive test scores. True progress in the field is contingent on our ability to go beyond the mere observed scores and to identify the elements of cultural contexts that are the basis of the observed differences.

We begin with a brief historical overview. In cognition, as in other areas of cross-cultural psychology, research has often started with strong claims about essential differences in functioning that subsequently are redressed in more carefully controlled studies. In the second section we mention evidence, largely obtained with psychometric tests, pointing to structural similarities in cognition across cultural populations. In the third section we present some recent quasiexperimental studies that seem to narrow the gap between observed differences in cognitive behavior and hypothetical traits. In the final section we discuss our own interpretation of the current state of knowledge. Except in the first section, we draw heavily on research conducted by our own group.

SOME HISTORY: GREAT DIVIDES AND BEYOND

A cursory overview of the history of empirical cross-cultural research as it has developed over the past century makes clear that with a new topic of research substantial differences in psychological functioning tend to be reported initially. Subsequently, more precise examination tends to lead to more modest views on cross-cultural variation and a more careful description of context factors that play a role (Poortinga, 2003). For example, on the acuity of hearing Bruner concluded in 1908: "The one fact standing out most prominently as a result of [my] measurements is the clearly evident superiority of Whites over all other races, both in the keenness and in the range of hearing sense" (p. 111). In personality research there is the well-known view of Benedict (1932) of culture as the personality of a society "thrown large upon the screen, given gigantic proportions and a long time span" (p. 24), which brought her to typify entire societies with a single stark characteristic, like "Apollonian" or "Dionysian." In the 1990s social cross-cultural psychology has become a domain of significant cross-cultural differences with the dimension of individualism–collectivism (Triandis, 1989) or independence–interdependence (Markus & Kitayama, 1991) as the flagship. With criticisms emerging (Fijneman et al., 1996; Kagitcibasi, 1997; Matsumoto, 1999) it may be speculated that a more differentiated view and a tuning down of value dimensions as broad explanatory frames will be only a matter of time.

The field of cognition provides a similar picture. Initially large differences in cognitive functioning were claimed also by authors who, like Wundt (1913), argued that his view did "not at all imply that within the narrower sphere that constitutes his world, the intelligence of primitive man is inferior to that of cultural man" (p. 113). However, even at such a broad level the notion of universality was not shared by all. Lévy-Bruhl (1922) considered non-Western thought processes to be "pre-logical," representing a worldview in which individual cognitive functions were based in mythical and religious beliefs shared as "collective representations" by the members of a society. Segall, Dasen, Berry, and Poortinga (1999) have referred to such ideas as "great divide" theories. These split the world according to some major category, like race (Rushton, 1995) or literacy (Luria, 1971, 1976) and explain a host of differences on cognitive tasks in terms of such a monolithic antecedent factor. Mechanisms that bring about these differences are usually presumed rather than empirically studied.

A shift from broad generalizations in terms of entire stages of cognitive development to more specific culturally relevant activities can be found in cross-cultural research on Piagetian stages of cognitive development. Early empirical studies, reviewed by Dasen (1972), showed average differences of several years for the onset of concrete operational thinking in illiterate groups as compared with Western data. The stage of formal thinking as assessed in this tradition might not be reached at all by typical members of such groups. Dasen (1975; see also Segall et al., 1999) suggested that a distinction was needed between actual performance and cognitive competence. With various samples of children who did not show spontaneous evidence of operational thinking it was demonstrated that a small amount of training was sufficient to elicit this mode of thinking, also on tasks that had not been included in the training. In addition, large differences in the onset of operational thinking with the well-known conservation tasks became suspect as pointing to method artifacts (e.g., Irvine, 1978). Piagetian cross-cultural research by no means implies that cognitive performance is immune to cultural context. According to Dasen, ecological variables do have an influence in the sense that (spontaneous) operational thinking on conservation tasks occurs somewhat earlier in domains that are prevalent in the environment. For example, among hunter-gatherers conservation of space occurs relatively early, whereas among agriculturalists this is the case for conservation of quantity, weight, and volume. Extensive research on what Piaget called the stage of formal thinking comes from another tradition to which we turn now.

A clear illustration of how findings of initially large cross-cultural differences in cognition have been redressed over time can be found in the sociocultural tradition started by Vygotsky and Luria. In line with Marxist thinking, Vygotsky (1978) believed that typically human psychological functions are culturally mediated. They are first present in a society and only thereafter can be transmitted to the individual in the process of individual development. This process of cultural mediation was not limited to *what* one learns in a given context, but thought to determine *how* one functions cognitively. Luria (1971, 1976) interpreted his research in Central Asia on syllogistic reasoning in this way. He found that illiterate farmers did not make logical deductions when presented with simple syllogisms, but that a few years of schooling had a substantial impact on the performance. Luria concluded that formal education led to the development of a mental faculty for abstract thinking. However, subsequent research with think-aloud methods by Scribner (1979) showed that illiterate respondents do not contravene the rules of Aristotelian logic. They are inclined to introduce prior experiential knowledge, rather than using only the information provided in the premises of syllogisms presented by the interviewer. Still, Scribner maintained that such an "empiric" mode of answering, in contrast to the "theoretic" mode of formal reasoning, reflected more general processes of understanding. This point of view was also emphasized by Tulviste (1991), who sees the theoretic mode of thinking as qualitatively new; it is learned at school and only afterwards applied to everyday life.

Although continuing to accept the principle of cultural mediation, Cole (1992, 1996) has argued against broad and sweeping cultural differences in cognition. Scribner and Cole (1981) conducted a landmark study among the Vai in Liberia. They made use of the rather exceptional circumstances that in Vai society one finds illiteracy as well as various forms of literacy, namely (a) literacy in Vai, a local syllabic script that is transmitted to some on an individual basis and used for bookkeeping and exchange of messages; (b) literacy in Arabic, learned by those who attend Quran school, with an emphasis on learning the Quran by heart; and (c) literacy in English, the language of instruction of the national education system. Specific cognitive requirements of Vai and Arabic (Quran) literacy could be shown to have some effect on performance with tasks that matched such requirements. However, major differences in performance levels on a wider range of ability tests like those in intelligence batteries were found between, on the one hand, illiterates, Vai literates, and Quran literates and, on the other hand, literates with Western-style school education. Thus, pervasive differences in cognitive performance were not a matter of a great divide in functioning between literates and illiterates, but rather of Western-style school curricula that presumably teach the cognitive algorithms found in intelligence tests.

Cognition has been linked repeatedly to language. The position of Whorf (1956) that one's language is intrinsic to the kinds of ideas and thoughts that one can form has been widely dismissed (Hunt & Agnoli, 1991), and even less encompassing suggestions about substantial effects of language on thinking could not be sustained. Perhaps the clearest example concerns the conditional mode in a statement such as, "If I could read French, I could read Voltaire." To speakers of English it is evident that the speaker cannot read French. Bloom (1981) pointed out that no counterfactual marker of this kind exists in Chinese languages and in his view the differences in linguistic form "may well be highly responsible for important differences in the way English speakers, as opposed to Chinese speakers, categorize and operate cognitively with the world" (p. 29). Initial support was found by Bloom with stories in which counterfactual information was embedded, but others could not replicate this (Au, 1983; Liu, 1985). Moreover, Vorster and Schuring (1989), making use of the fact that in Sepedi (Northern Sotho) there are two levels of counterfactuality, showed that with stronger counterfactuality in the grammar of a story Sepedi children made more use of these cues than with the weaker form of counterfactuality. The differences in reactions to two grammatical versions of the same story would seem to indicate that, not a general mode of thinking, but the way in which counterfactuality is formulated in a specific instance, is the crucial factor (cf. Berry, Poortinga, Segall, & Dasen, 2002).

Peng and Nisbett (1999) have suggested a new "great divide." They distinguish between *differentiation in thinking* (i.e., comparison of opposites and the selection of one as the correct position) and *dialectical thinking* (i.e., seeking reconciliation between opposites). Chinese students showed relatively more preference for dialectical solutions if confronted with logically contradictory information. Students from the United States were more inclined to polarize conflicting perspectives and to choose one alternative as correct. Peng and Nisbett believe that "dialectical versus nondialectical reasoning will turn out to be only one of a set of interrelated cognitive differences between Asians and Westerners" (p. 750). It is probably too early to pass a more definite judgment on this conclusion, but we like to note that it has not remained unchallenged (Chan, 2000; Ho, 2000).

ORGANIZATION OF COGNITIVE FACTORS

The most widely used instruments in cognitive cross-cultural psychology are intelligence tests. In the psychometric tradition, more than elsewhere in cross-cultural psychology, there have been explicit attempts to distinguish between differences in the traits or processes that are the target of investigation, and nontarget related differences in performance that are due to cultural bias or inequivalence of assessment methods. In this section we first introduce the notion of different levels of equivalence. Then we mention some findings that quite unequivocally point to cross-cultural invariance in the organization of cognitive behavior. Unfortunately these findings are mainly limited to literate societies.

Equivalence

Inequivalence refers to the unequal representativeness across cultural groups of a measure for a domain of behavior or a hypothetical trait; inequivalent scores cannot be directly compared across cultures. The equivalence of scores can be threatened because of systematic differences in traits (e.g., formal logical reasoning could be absent in some cultures), because the measurement procedure fails to address in themselves equal traits (e.g., syllogistic reasoning problems as presented do not elicit formal logical reasoning), and because of incidental difficulties with specific items or stimuli (e.g., an item has an ambivalent meaning if translated). Strictly speaking, any form of comparison implies that a common standard or scale exists for entities to be compared. One cannot compare the weight of one object with the height of another object; the measurements are not equivalent. Comparison of differences in terms of quantities of weight additionally implies that units of measurement are the same, and that there is a common anchor point (often the zero point of the scale). These distinctions can be illustrated with reference to measurements of temperature. Direct comparison of temperature readings of objects leads to anomalous findings if some measurements were made on a Celsius scale and others on a Fahrenheit scale, or even if both a Celsius and a Kelvin scale were used. The various levels of scale identity illustrated with these examples are referred to as levels of comparability or levels of equivalence. Three such levels have been distinguished by Van de Vijver and Leung (1997a, 1997b):

1. Structural or functional equivalence: A test measures the same trait (or set of traits) cross-culturally, but not necessarily on the same quantitative scale (cf. Celsius and Fahrenheit scales).
2. Metric or measurement unit equivalence: Measurement units of the scales are the same in all cultures, but there is no common scale anchor (origin). A difference between two scores has then the same meaning, independent of the culture in which it was found (cf. Celsius and Kelvin scales).
3. Scale equivalence or full-score comparability: Scores of a given value have in all respects the same meaning cross-culturally and can be interpreted in the same way (cf. Celsius and Celsius).

The relevance of the distinctions lies in a range of statistically testable conditions that presumably are satisfied by equivalent scores, but not by inequivalent or culturally biased scores. Structural equivalence is mainly examined by means of multivariate analyses such as exploratory factor analysis. Statistical procedures are available to estimate the degree of factorial similarity in datasets collected in different societies, for example, by means of a congruence coefficient usually called *Tucker's phi* (Tucker, 1951). If factor structures of the items in an instrument are similar across cultures, this is an indication that the same traits are measured; if the factor structures show substantial differences, meaningful comparison is ruled out. Measurement unit equivalence can be examined by means of analysis of covariance structures (usually confirmatory factor analysis) or by means of comparison of patterns of test scores obtained from repeated measurements (Van de Vijver, Daal, & van Zonneveld, 1986). A necessary (but not sufficient) condition for full-score equivalence is the absence of item bias (or differential item functioning) that can be checked with analysis of variance or item response theory (Holland & Wainer, 1993; Van de Vijver & Leung, 1997a, 1997b).

Evidence for Equivalence

Substantial information on equivalence is available from the translation and transfer of intelligence batteries that lend themselves to factor analysis. A recent example can be found in a cross-cultural comparison of 12 standardization studies of the Wechsler Intelligence Scale for Children–III (WISC–III; Wechsler, 1991), including Canada ($n = 1,100$); Germany, Austria, and German-speaking Switzerland ($n = 1,570$); France and French-speaking Belgium ($n = 1,120$); Greece ($n = 956$); Japan ($n = 1,125$); Lithuania ($n = 452$); The Netherlands and Dutch-speaking Belgium ($n = 1,229$); Slovenia ($n = 1,080$); South Korea ($n - 2,231$); Sweden ($n = 1,036$); Taiwan ($n = 1,100$); and the United States ($n = 2,200$) (Georgas, Van de Vijver, Weiss, & Saklofske, 2003). Different factor solutions have been proposed in the literature (from one up to four). When all data were pooled (correcting for differences in sample sizes and country differences in mean scores of the subtests), clear evidence was found for the presence of the factors reported in the literature. For example, the four-factor solution showed the commonly reported factors: Verbal Comprehension (with high loadings of Vocabulary, Comprehension, Similarities, and Information), Processing Speed (with Coding and Symbol Search), Perceptual Organization (with Object Assembly, Block Design, Picture Completion, and Picture Arrangement), and Freedom from Distractibility (Digit Span and Arithmetic). The stabilities of the one-, two-, three-, and four-factor solutions were compared by making pairwise comparisons of the factor solutions obtained in the countries. The evidence for structural equivalence was impressive. The one-, two-, and three-factor solutions showed excellent agreement, whereas the agreement of the fourth factor was high in most (but not all) country comparisons.

A more focused study investigated the equivalence of inductive reasoning tasks with school pupils in Zambia, Turkey, and the Netherlands (Van de Vijver, 2002). There were four age groups (grades 5–8; in Zambia grades 6–9). The test battery consisted of eight tests, four with figures and four with letters as stimuli. For each stimulus mode there was a test of inductive reasoning, as well as three tests that assess one of the component skills of inductive reasoning derived from Sternberg's (1977) work, namely, rule classification, rule generating, and rule testing. All tasks were designed with item-generating rules for various facets and levels of difficulty within facets. This allowed for a systematic analysis of the facets and levels as components of the difficulty of items.

For analysis of equivalence, the relative difficulty of an item was taken as the sum of the difficulties of the facet levels used in its construction. These level difficulties were estimated by means of a logistic linear model (Fischer, 1995) in each of the three cultural samples. The correlations between these estimates and the Rasch item difficulties varied between .76 and .95 for the eight tasks in the three groups, with the lower values (in The Netherlands) probably due to ceiling effects. These high correlations indicate that the item-generating rules adequately predicted item-level difficulties in each cultural group and that these item-level difficulties showed the same patterning of easy and difficult items across the samples. In our view, this finding provides powerful evidence that there was correspondence among the three cultural samples in the determinants of item difficulty and that the tasks could be taken as structurally equivalent. The high cross-cultural agreement of the item difficulty argues strongly for the basic identity of inductive reasoning processes in the populations included in this study.

Van de Vijver (2002) then proceeded to test for metric equivalence by estimating whether the various components had the same difficulty across samples. Although there was a good deal of correspondence across the three countries, significant differences in relevant statistical tests showed that conditions for metric equivalence were not fully met by the data. This held even more strongly for the condition of full-score equivalence. Hence, the analysis showed that the substantial differences in scores that existed among the three cultural samples should not be interpreted at face value in terms of inductive reasoning.

The studies mentioned so far in this section involved literate samples. There is no lack of studies of intelligence batteries with populations without formal education, but most of them are less recent. Already in 1979 Irvine could collect 91 factor analyses based on studies in non-Western countries, many of them with illiterate testees in Africa. He found numerous, in his view compelling, similarities in factor labels, but also a tendency for more educated samples to reflect a larger number of factors. The latter finding suggested an increase in cognitive complexity with school education that also has been proposed by other authors (Kendall, Verster, & Von Mollendorf, 1988). Until today the equivalence of multifactorial batteries has not been analyzed in any systematic way for literate versus illiterate or schooled versus nonschooled populations. As a consequence, the hypothesis that the cognitive structure increases with schooling still requires firm empirical testing. Such tests are difficult to carry out because literate and illiterate samples tend to differ in many respects (such as schooling), and effects of method-related factors such as test-wiseness are often difficult to rule out. We need cross-cultural research with batteries of tests based on types of tasks more prevalent in hunting-gathering and traditional agricultural societies. The adaptation and administration of instruments for various abilities, including reasoning tests, would be feasible though difficult, as demonstrated, for example, by Reuning and Wortley (1973) for Bushmen in the Kalahari desert and by Berry and colleagues (1986) for Pygmies in central Africa. In this way more definite answers on universalities in the organization of cognitive factors could be investigated with psychometric tests, but the effort that would be required for a systematic exploration at a global scale seems quite forbidding.

In summary, the picture that emerges from the literature about the structural equivalence of cognitive tasks is fairly unambiguous: many cognitive tests show a good structural equivalence, in particular among schooled groups. Metric and full-score equivalence have been addressed less frequently. However, the results obtained so far are not very encouraging. We often do not fully understand the nature of the cross-cultural differences in cognitive test performance that we observe. The somewhat naive assumption that cross-cultural score differences found with an IQ test must reflect differences in intelligence, which is still widely held, is an impediment to progress in the field. The patterning of cross-cultural differences in scores is a major challenge. We turn to this topic in the next section.

Patterns of Differences and Similarities in Score Levels

In a meta-analysis of 345 cross-national studies with cognitive tests published between 1973 and 1994 Van de Vijver (1997) found an effect size of .71. Most frequently used were (various versions of) the WISC (Wechsler, 1991), Raven's Matrices (Raven, 1938), the Kaufman Assessment Battery for Children (Kaufman & Kaufman, 1983), the Stanford–Binet Intelligence Scale (Thorndike, Hagen, & Sattler, 1986), and the Wechsler Adult Intelligence Scale (WAIS; Wechsler, 1997). All of these batteries have been developed in the United States, with one exception (Raven) that originated in Great Britain. Effect size was defined as the absolute difference between two sample means divided by the pooled standard deviation. A complex of economic affluence variables (gross national product [GNP], expenditure on education, individualism) showed a positive relationship with differences in cognitive test scores. The role of country-level variables was also addressed in the cross-cultural study of the WISC–III, briefly described in the previous section (Georgas et al., 2003). Country means were compared in a multivariate analysis of variance, with country as independent variable and subtest performance as the dependent variables (the subtest scores were the raw scores for closely translated subtests and ability estimates based on item response theory for adapted subtests). The average proportion of variance accounted for by country across the 12 subtests was .03. Subtest scores were then combined into a single overall score, which was transformed to the well-known IQ scale. The average IQ per country varied from 95.9 to 103.2. Although the differences were rather small, these averages could be related to country-level variables. It was found that a set of mainly economical indicators, labeled *affluence*, showed a correlation of .49 with full-scale IQ, while both verbal and performance IQ correlated .43 (although in the expected direction, these correlations were not significant because of the small number of countries involved). An index that combined various education-related indicators at country level, such as per capita expenditure on education and percentage enrollment in tertiary education, showed a significant correlation of .68 with the full-scale IQ; the index correlated .55 with verbal IQ and .63 with performance IQ. These correlations confirm that in particular educational variables have an impact on observed cross-cultural score differences.

We have presented the correlation of IQ with affluence-related and education-related variables for both a meta-analysis and a more controlled cross-cultural comparison of intelligence test scores. However, such a correlation does not yet show us the underlying mechanisms. Why are IQ and GNP correlated? Because little is known about quantitative aspects of equivalence, it is far from clear whether cross-cultural variations in performance levels reflect quantitative differences in some underlying cognitive or even biological factor (e.g., children in more affluent countries have a richer diet), or are due to noncognitive factors, like the extent to which school curricula differ from the United States where, after all, most of the tests originated (e.g., familiarity with tasks).

For practical purposes, intelligence test batteries can be considered as samples of knowledge and competencies relevant in urban industrial societies. In support of such an interpretation we can refer to research by Drenth and colleagues who developed intelligence batteries to be used for educational selection in low-income countries (Bali, Drenth, Van der Flier, & Young, 1984; Drenth, Van der Flier, & Omari, 1983). In such countries there is often a large variation in school quality. An important rationale was to tap a broad range of mental abilities so that pupils with a poor school background but good educational potential could be better identified. However, studies in countries like Kenya, Tanzania, Uganda, Indonesia, and Surinam by and large showed that the incremental predictive value of these intelligence tests for educational criteria was small. In other words, school curriculum and the content of intelligence batteries appeared to be strongly related, a set of findings consonant with those of Scribner and Cole (1981) referred to before.

Absence of information about quantitative aspects of equivalence imposes limitations on inferences that can be validly derived from differences in test scores. However, this does not mean that such differences have not been further explored. In particular, through inclusion in a study design of variables that are likely to have explanatory value for expected cross-cultural differences (including those due to inequivalence), the range of plausible alternatives of interpretation can be narrowed down (Poortinga & Van de Vijver, 1987).

This rationale was followed in a study of Spearman's hypothesis (Helms-Lorenz, Van de Vijver, & Poortinga, 2003). The hypothesis, as formulated by Jensen (1985), predicts larger score differences between African Americans and European Americans that are more pure measures of g (Spearman's general intelligence factor). A test of higher cognitive complexity tends to have a higher g-saturation, usually expressed by its loading on the first factor of the intercorrelation matrix of a battery of tests. Support for Spearman's hypothesis has been derived from a number of studies (Jensen, 1998). It has also been used in interpreting ethnic differences in cognitive test scores in the Netherlands (Te Nijenhuis & Van der Flier, 1997). Helms-Lorenz and colleagues questioned the equivalence of g loadings as an index of (inborn) intellectual capacity. They argued that these loadings are likely to tap additional factors such as cultural practices, cognitive algorithms learned at school, and especially knowledge of the (Dutch) language of the test designer. Twelve tests were administered to 6 to 12-year-old Dutch school children, including a sample of autochthonous descent and a sample of second-generation Turkish migrants. Structural equivalence could be demonstrated. The migrants showed on average a lower score than the autochthonous sample. The nature of the difference was further explored. Ratings were obtained per test on complexity level (Carroll, 1993; Fischer, 1980), verbal loading and cultural loading (rated by advanced psychology students). Two factors were extracted from these ratings. The first labeled *aggregate g* showed high loadings for complexity and Jensen's measure of g; the second called *aggregate c* (c for culture) had high loadings for verbal loading and cultural loading. Culturally more entrenched tests (i.e., tests with a high loading on the c factor) showed a positive correlation with the difference in scores between the two ethnic samples, whereas the g factor showed a negative correlation. This indicates that, contrary to Spearman's hypothesis, performance differences did not increase with g-saturation; rather intergroup performance differences were better predicted by c than by g. It was concluded that familiarity with the Dutch language and culture was an important source of intergroup differences.

PURSUING CROSS-CULTURAL VARIATIONS AGAINST A BACKGROUND OF INVARIANCE

There are two strategies to move forward. The first is to identify cognitive tasks in the behavior repertoire of a specific group and to analyze the cognitive demands and problem-solving strategies. This ethnographic approach is followed in the tradition of everyday cognition (Schliemann, Carraher, & Ceci, 1997). Fascinating phenomena have been described including, for example, counting among the Oksapmin, who have a number system based on parts of the body (Saxe, 1981, 1982), and a similar system among the Yupno (Wassmann & Dasen, 1994a, 1994b). Perhaps the most extensively studied activity is weaving (e.g., Childs & Greenfield, 1980; Rogoff & Gauvain, 1984; Tanon, 1994). Studies of everyday cognition have generally shown limited transfer and generalization of learning from one class of situations (domain) to another, including from school to nonschool situations (Segall et al., 1999). Despite the often interesting accounts of striking cognitive behavior in this literature, the relevance of the everyday cognition tradition for our present purposes is limited because the tradition does not aim at explaining cross-cultural differences.

This points to a second strategy, namely, attempting to design studies in such a way that problems of interpretation of cross-cultural differences are minimized. From the perspective of an equivalence framework, this implies attempting to establish standards of comparison that are equivalent (if possible, in a quantitative as well as in a quantitative sense) and to manipulate tasks in a more or less controlled fashion so that cross-cultural differences can be interpreted against a background of invariance. We describe three recent projects that pursue this strategy.

Invariant and Variable Aspects of Memory

A common distinction in memory research is between structural features (e.g., short-term memory store, rate of forgetting) and control processes (Atkinson & Shiffrin, 1968). Control processes, like rehearsal, help in the encoding and retrieval of information. It seems well established that the structural features are universally similar, and that cross-cultural differences are a matter of control processes (e.g., Wagner, 1974, 1981). This background knowledge was used in three studies of memory development in samples of Libyan school children at two grade levels (grades 2 and 4) with corresponding samples of Dutch children (Shebani, 2001; Shebani, Van de Vijver, & Poortinga, 2003). The three studies of the project use different strategies to increase the interpretability of cross-cultural differences.

The first study examined memory span and reading speed. We used a theoretical framework that allows for an account of cross-cultural differences in precise quantitative terms. The study was based on a specific model of working memory for auditory information, called the phonological loop hypothesis (Baddeley, 1997). The model specifies two components, namely, a store that can retain information for approximately 1.5 to 2.0 seconds before decay sets in, and rehearsal processes that help to maintain stored information as well as to recode verbal information presented visually. It follows that memory span should be a function not only of the number of stimuli presented in a task but also of their duration. In numerous studies this has also been found to be the case in a cross-cultural context in which differences in memory span, especially for digits, have been found to be correlated with reading time (e.g., Naveh-Benjamin & Ayres, 1986; Stigler, Lee, & Stevenson, 1986). Shebani and colleagues could show that quite substantial differences in memory span between the Libyan and Dutch samples became small and nonsignificant for digits as well as for other words, after correction for differences in reading speed. Thus, in this study the cross-cultural differences in memory span could be fully explained in terms of some explicit characteristic, namely, word length in the two languages.

The second study addressed the question of whether training in rehearsal could help to improve memory span; this study attempts to increase the interpretability of cross-cultural score differences by comparing gains after training across the two countries. Rehearsal is a memorizing strategy that tends to become more efficient with age over the middle years of primary school but is often not spontaneously used in illiterate groups (Cole, Gay, Glick, & Sharp, 1971). Both samples that received training as well as control samples in Libya and the Netherlands showed higher posttest scores, but the gains for the children in the experimental condition were higher than for those in the control group. Statistically significant but small interactions of culture with experimental condition (training vs. no training) and measurement occasion (pretest–posttest) could not be accounted for. Also, there was a small overall difference between the two countries that could only be ascribed tentatively to small age differences between the samples. All in all, some effects of culture remained unexplained, but they were minor and would not lead to different recommendations, for example, for the possible introduction of classroom training in rehearsal strategy.

The third study by Shebani and colleagues (2003) used psychometric procedures (i.e., the statistical study of structural and metric equivalence) to enhance the interpretability of cross-cultural differences. The study dealt with metamemory. This is an encompassing concept for which a variety of assessment methods have been developed that tend to show low intercorrelations as well as low correlations with scores on memory tasks. Metamemory–memory relationships are complex and may involve multiple aspects of memory, suggesting that metamemory is more a collection of specific procedures and competencies than a more or less unitary ability (Flavell & Wellman, 1977; Schneider & Pressley, 1997). Cross-cultural studies of metamemory are rare (e.g., Schneider, Körkel, & Weinert, 1987) and limited to Western countries. Shebani and colleagues administered four measures adapted from a metamemory battery described by Belmont and Borkowski (1988). With one minor exception, all mean scores were higher for the older samples, but the four tasks showed low and even negative intercorrelations in both Libya and The Netherlands, and correlations of metamemory scores with indices of school performance were also poor. This is in line with previous findings. Moreover, two of the tasks did not meet psychometric conditions for structural equivalence, thereby preempting an analysis of metric equivalence. This may be due to cultural bias affecting structural equivalence in these tasks, but such a result is also compatible with metamemory being a loose assembly of procedures and skills that correspond poorly across cultures. In this third study, the meaning of the findings in Libya was hardly informed by those in The Netherlands (or vice versa), pointing to limits of culture-comparative analysis in explaining cross-cultural differences in performance.

Context Effects in Logical Reasoning

A major strategy used in this project to enhance the interpretability of cross-cultural performance differences was a careful selection of stimulus materials (using a pilot study to establish the cultural appropriateness of these materials). Assuming cross-cultural invariance of Aristotelian logic across cultural populations, Willemsen (2001) investigated context effects on logical reasoning in Zambia and The Netherlands with ten kinds of reasoning schemes, like conditional rules and syllogisms. To develop an equivalent instrument a domain of behavior was needed that showed important overlaps between the two societies, but to allow for effects of differential context this overlap should not be complete. The domain selected was that of expectations of mothers about the development of children, more specifically the age at which children acquire certain knowledge and competencies (Willemsen & Van de Vijver, 1997). Logical reasoning items were developed that covered four possibilities: an item could be empirically correct in both countries, in either of the two countries, or in none. For example, the expected age of eating without help had a mean of 2 years 6 months in Zambia and a mean of 1 year 9 months in The Netherlands. Hence, contextual knowledge would differ for a logical problem in which the premises refer to a child of 2 years old.

A large proportion of the mothers in both countries answered most of the logical reasoning items correctly. Rules that determined task difficulty appeared to be common; for example, items based on premises that contained grossly incorrect (counterfactual) information proved to be more difficult in both samples (which supported the structural equivalence of the measures). A more subtle manipulation using the previously established age differences between the two societies did not have any noticeable impact on the results of either sample. A further manipulation that involved embedding the reasoning scheme in a prose passage made the reasoning tasks easier in both samples. Cross-cultural differences were mainly found for items with negations in the premises. Overall, such differences were rather minor and they were further reduced by half when corrected for differences in number of years of education. Willemsen (2001) concluded:

> If pragmatic knowledge is available about the domain of logical reasoning, the basic structure of the reasoning process may be rather universal. Differences in responses on logical reasoning tests may be more due to differences in knowledge, associations, expectations, and beliefs with regard to the application of the reasoning than to a differential availability of reasoning schemes. (p. 83)

Cross-Cultural Differences in Information Processing

The third project to be mentioned here attempted to maximize the interpretation of cross-cultural performance differences by manipulation of an aspect of a cognitive task thought to be at the basis of score differences.

Speed of information processing has been postulated as a major factor in intelligence, and as a potentially valid index of group differences (e.g., Eysenck, 1987, 1988; Jensen, 1982). In the simplest reaction time task, with a single clear stimulus to which the participant has to react as fast as possible, mean or modal response times have an approximately equal distribution in all cultural samples that have been investigated (Jensen, 1982, 1985; Poortinga 1971). As soon as a task consists of more than one stimulus and one response, cross-cultural differences in mean reaction time begin to emerge (Jensen, 1985; Verster, 1983). For example, in experiments with four colored lights that were all very clearly distinguishable and similarly with a set of four sounds, Poortinga (1971) found differences between samples of African and European students in South Africa who did not show such differences on a simple reaction time task. At the same time, patterns of differences remain similar if task parameters are changed. For example, Sonke (2001) found that patterns of reaction times of three samples—namely, South Africans with at most a few years of schooling, South African students, and Dutch students—were similar to those found previously, including differences in performance levels even on cognitively simple tasks. This makes it plausible that cross-cultural differences have to be explained in a way that leaves the cross-cultural identity of cognitive processing unaffected. Improvement of performance with training makes it likely that prior exposure and experience play a role (e.g., Poortinga, 1985; Posner, 1985). This implies that familiarity with various aspects of the task is an important factor; familiarity can pertain to the stimuli, the task (i.e., the operations or transformations needed to connect a stimulus to a response), and the execution of the response.

Sonke, Poortinga, and De Kuijer (1999) administered three fairly simple tasks with geometric stimuli to samples of Dutch students and recently arrived Iranian refugees in The Netherlands. The pattern of results was as reported in previous investigations; the reactions of the Dutch students on average were faster, and the differences in performance between the two samples increased with the complexity of the tasks. Three days of training on the tasks led to greater improvements for the more complex task, but on all tasks changes were similar for both samples, indicating that cross-cultural differences were stable at least over a relatively short period of training. In this study, a fourth task was administered with Arabic letters as stimuli that, except for stimulus content, closely matched one of the tasks with geometric stimuli. However, the levels of scores for the two groups were reversed for the Arabic-letters task, with the Iranian sample clearly performing better than the Dutch. In our opinion these results provide a persuasive argument that equal familiarity across cultural populations should not be assumed even for simple tasks. At the same time they make understandable why full-score equivalence in the assessment of cognitive traits is practically out of reach for cross-cultural psychologists.

CAPTURING RELATIONSHIPS BETWEEN CULTURE AND COGNITION

There does not seem to be much disagreement among contemporary researchers that there is a basic invariance in cognitive functioning. For example, Cole (1996, 2002) argued that culture builds on universal "skeletal principles," and Shweder, Goodnow, Hatano, LeVine, Markus, and Miller (1998) assumed a common mind underlying different cultural mentalities. Such a common architecture is reflected in cross-culturally invariant features such as Baddeley's phonological loop, effects of stimulus familiarity, and common reasoning schemes. The three projects described in the previous section (on memory, logical reasoning, and reaction times) have in common that they start from elementary tasks for which cross-cultural differences are minimal or can be fully explained in terms of a common underlying model.

Analyses of equivalence have begun to extend the evidence on invariance to complex tasks, while at the same time demonstrating the limitations on inferences based on differences in score levels. Thus, the same task aspects that made inductive reasoning items difficult in Zambia made them difficult in Turkey and in The Netherlands. The most ample results on structural equivalence derive from factor analyses of cognitive test batteries. Observed similarities in factor structures we see as important evidence that distinctions largely made in American psychology also apply elsewhere. Invariance of factor structures is a common finding, also for values (Schwartz, 1992) and in personality research (McCrae & Allik, 2002). In the latter field quite different models and instruments all appear to lead to this finding of invariance (Paunonen & Ashton, 1998). Thus, the theories and models from which factor structures are derived may be rather tentative (Poortinga, Van de Vijver, & Van Hemert, 2002); they may provide a distorted or incomplete picture and perhaps leave out more culture-specific aspects of psychological functioning. However, the fact that we find invariant factor structures in domains as diverse as personality, values, and intelligence is difficult to understand unless the factors are based on behavior samples from a common underlying universe. In the end findings of structural equivalence can be said to contribute to the empirical validation of notions of invariance and allow us to better demarcate what is common and what is specific across cultures in human cognition.

Structural equivalence as evidence of a common cognitive architecture implies that cross-cultural differences can be explained in terms of the common dimensions that define a structure. At the same time, it does not allow an interpretation of quantitative differences in score levels. Analyses of quantitative aspects of equivalence cannot be of much help here. First of all, they have not received much attention from culture-comparative researchers, who are still inclined to interpret differences at face value even when agreeing that there is no such a thing as a "culture-free" or "culture-fair" test. Moreover, such analyses are difficult to carry out. They require (quasi-)manipulation of relevant conditions, as demonstrated in the study by Sonke and colleagues (1999). Unfortunately, such manipulation is difficult to realize in research on effects of long-lasting cultural factors like economic affluence, socialization, or formal education.

There is a paradoxical relationship in cross-cultural psychology between replicability and interpretability of findings. Performance differences, for example, between two cultural populations with different school education, are often easy to predict but difficult to explain, except in very general terms. This difficulty can be illustrated by the exchangeability of concepts. In many instances quite different notions like affluence, level of education, socialization style, ethnicity, and westernization, or for that matter familiarity and cultural experiences, can be used to "explain" the same variance. The paradox becomes even more manifest if the question is asked precisely what aspect of affluence, education, and so forth can best account for the difference on a given task. If a culture is conceptualized as a psychological system, this amounts to asking which element or aspect of the system is associated with the performance difference. In psychometric parlance, the question is how an explanatory factor for an observed difference can be operationalized.

In our view the paradox is a consequence of the difficulty of distinguishing between broad and inclusive culture behavior relationships and co-occurrence of large numbers of situation-specific, nontransferable relationships. The consistency of performance differences does not only fit an explanation in terms of consistent cognitive differences: An accumulation of specific algorithms and items of knowledge in the course of schooling leads to the same consistency in observed differences. Because transfer and generalization of knowledge are a questionable and controversial issue in psychology (e.g., Detterman, 1994), it seems to us that the main research task ahead is the identification of specific explanatory factors to account for cross-cultural differences. Admittedly, for more complex cognitive tasks (i.e., tasks with a stronger relationship with general intelligence in Carroll's [1993] scheme), it is difficult to identify reasons for differences, and descriptive interpretative approaches may be more useful for the exploration of the relationship between culture and cognition (Berry et al., 2002). For example, at present we have no idea how to interpret the scattered differences in metamemory found by Shebani and colleagues (2003). Rather than evoking more fuzzy concepts indicating that there must be "something" in Libyan culture, as compared with Dutch culture, we would argue that psychologists should accept the limitations of their endeavors (Poortinga, 1997).

There are two issues reflected in our arguments. The first is the rejection of broad and inclusive explanations of differences in test performances. The second is the need for precise operationalization of explanatory factors. For example, the notion of cultural mediation as used by Cole (1996) tends to be nonspecific in terms of precise operationalization of antecedent factors. The two issues converge in studies as reported in the previous section. Differences in memory span could be explained in terms of the word length in the languages concerned; differences in logical reasoning to an important extent could be attributed to a specific feature, namely negation, in the formulation of items; differences in speed of information processing reflected familiarity with the stimuli and stimulus–response connections that need no explanatory principles beyond classical learning theory. There appears to be a common thread in our findings namely, that often rather concrete and precise conditions in the environment can be used to reach an understanding, pre-empting the need for fuzzier or more inclusive variables.

CONCLUSIONS

A cautionary attitude toward broad differences in cognition as a function of cultural context implies the need for research from which both cross-cultural invariance and cultural variation can emerge. At first sight, broad cognitive factors may seem plausible to explain cross-cultural differences in performance because such differences tend to correlate over a range of tasks. Whoever postulates a new "great divide" theory from the perspective of one's own culture is likely to come up with initial supporting evidence. In this chapter we have provided evidence for cross-cultural invariance of the structural organization of cognition at least for schooled populations on the basis of analyses of structural equivalence in the most common kind of data— namely, scores on ability tests. We added evidence from studies in which elementary cognitive tasks were explored that allow interpretation of differences in terms of rather concrete explanatory variables (like word length and stimulus familiarity). For further validation more data are needed, particularly from illiterate societies. However, as it stands now our findings suggest that cross-cultural research may have focused too much on differences at the neglect of what is culturally common in human cognition. Historically, we build on work of predecessors, many of who were quite willing to make sweeping statements about cross-cultural differences in all kinds of psychological domains on a narrow empirical basis. This spirit still lingers on; cross-cultural differences are still being taken for granted too often, even in the cognitive domain. It is important to realize that carefully designed studies of cognitive processes and outcomes that attempt to control for alternative interpretations frequently report only small performance differences. A frame of mind in which we try to explore or explain cross-cultural differences against a background of similarities in all relevant basic processes appears to be a productive research strategy.

REFERENCES

Atkinson, R. C., & Shiffrin, R. M. (1968). Human memory: A proposed system and its control processes. In K. W. Spence & J. T. Spence (Eds.), *The psychology of learning and motivation* (Vol. 2, pp. 89–105). New York: Academic Press.

Au, T. K. (1983). Chinese and English counterfactuals: The Sapir–Whorf hypothesis revisited. *Cognition, 15,* 155–187.

Baddeley, A. (1997). *Human memory: Theory and practice* (Rev. ed.). Mahwah, NJ: Erlbaum.

Bali, S. K., Drenth, P. J. D., Van der Flier, H., & Young, W. C. E. (1984). *Contribution of aptitude tests to the prediction of school performance in Kenya: A longitudinal study.* Lisse, The Netherlands: Swets & Zeitlinger.

Belmont, J. M., & Borkowski, J. G. (1988). A group-administered test of children's metamemory. *Bulletin of the Psychonomic Society, 26,* 206–208.

Benedict, R. (1932). Configurations of culture in North America. *American Anthropologist, 34,* 1–27.

Berry, J. W., Poortinga, Y. H., Segall, M. H., & Dasen, P. R. (2002). *Cross-cultural psychology: Research and applications* (2nd ed.). Cambridge, England: Cambridge University Press.

Berry, J. W., Van de Koppel, J. M. H., Sénéchal, C., Annis, R. C., Bahuchet, S., Cavalli-Sforza, L. L., & Witkin, H. A. (1986). *On the edge of the forest: Cultural adaptation and cognitive development in Central Africa.* Lisse, The Netherlands: Swets & Zeitlinger.

Bloom, A. (1981). *The linguistic shaping of thought: A study in the impact of language on thinking in China and the West.* Hillsdale, NJ: Erlbaum.

Bruner, F. G. (1908). The hearing of primitive peoples. *Archives of Psychology, Columbia Contributions to Philosophy and Psychology, 23*(3), 1–113.

Carroll, J. B. (1993). *Human cognitive abilities: A survey of factor-analytic studies.* Cambridge, England: Cambridge University Press.

Chan, S. F. (2000). Formal logic and dialectical thinking are not incongruent. *American Psychologist, 55,* 1063–1064.

Childs, C. P., & Greenfield, P. M. (1980). Informal modes of learning. The case of Zinacanteco weaving. In N. Warren (Ed.), *Studies in cross-cultural psychology* (Vol. 2, pp. 269–316). London: Academic Press.

Cole, M. (1992). Context, modularity and the cultural constitution of development. In L. Winegar & J. Valsiner (Eds.), *Children's' development within social contexts* (Vol. 2, pp. 5–31). Hillsdale, NJ: Erlbaum.

Cole, M. (1996). *Cultural psychology: A once and future discipline.* Cambridge, MA: Belknap.

Cole, M. (2002). Culture and development. In H. Keller, Y. H. Poortinga, & A. Schölmerich (Eds.), *Between biology and culture: Perspectives on ontogenetic development* (pp. 303–319). Cambridge, England: Cambridge University Press.

Cole, M., Gay, J., Glick, J., & Sharp, D. W. (1971). *The cultural context of learning and thinking*. London: Basic Books.

Dasen, P. R. (1972). Cross-cultural Piagetian research: A summary. *Journal of Cross-Cultural Psychology, 7*, 75–85.

Dasen, P. R. (1975). Concrete operational development in three cultures. *Journal of Cross-Cultural Psychology, 6*, 156–172.

Detterman, D. K. (1994). The case for the prosecution: Transfer as an epiphenomenon. In D. K. Detterman & R. J. Sternberg (Eds.), *Transfer on trial: Intelligence, cognition and instruction* (pp. 1–24). Norwood, NJ: Ablex.

Drenth, P. J. D., Van der Flier, H., & Omari, I. M. (1983). Educational selection in Tanzania. *Evaluation in Education, 7*, 93–217.

Eysenck, H. J. (1987). Speed of information processing, reaction time, and the theory of intelligence. In P. A. Vernon (Ed.), *Speed of information-processing and intelligence* (pp. 21–68). Norwood, NJ: Ablex.

Eysenck, H. J. (1988). The biological basis of intelligence. In S. H. Irvine & J. W. Berry (Eds.), *Human abilities in cultural context* (pp. 70–104). New York: Cambridge University Press.

Fijneman, Y., Willemsen, M., & Poortinga, Y. H. (with Erelcin, F. G., Georgas, J., Hui, H. C., Leung, K., & Malpass, R. S.). (1996). Individualism–collectivism: An empirical study of a conceptual issue. *Journal of Cross-Cultural Psychology, 27*, 381–402.

Fischer, G. H. (1995). The linear logistic test model. In G. H. Fischer & I. W. Molenaar (Eds.), *Rasch models: Foundations, recent developments and applications* (pp. 131–180). New York: Springer.

Fischer, K. W. (1980). A theory of cognitive development: The control and construction of hierarchies of skills. *Psychological Review, 87*, 477–531.

Flavell, J. H., & Wellman, H. M. (1977). Metamemory. In R. V. Kail, Jr., & J. W. Hagen (Eds.), *Perspectives on the development of memory and cognition* (pp. 3–33). Hillsdale, NJ: Erlbaum.

Georgas, J., Van de Vijver, F. J. R., Weiss, L., & Saklofske, D. (2003). A cross-cultural analysis of the WISC–III. In J. Georgas, L. Weiss, F. J. R. Van de Vijver, & D. Saklofske (Eds.), *Cultures and children's intelligence: A cross-cultural analysis of the WISC–III* (pp. 278–313). New York: Academic Press.

Helms-Lorenz, M., Van de Vijver, F. J. R., & Poortinga, Y. H. (2003). Cross-cultural differences in cognitive performance and Spearman's hypothesis. *Intelligence, 31*, 9–29.

Ho, D. Y. F. (2000). Dialectical thinking: Neither Eastern nor Western. *American Psychologist, 55*, 1064–1065.

Holland, P. W., & Wainer, H. (Eds.). (1993). *Differential item functioning*. Hillsdale, NJ: Erlbaum.

Hunt, E., & Agnoli, F. (1991). The Whorfian hypothesis: A cognitive psychology perspective. *Psychological Review, 98*, 377–389.

Irvine, J. T. (1978). Wolof "magic thinking": Culture and conservation revisited. *Journal of Cross-Cultural Psychology, 9*, 300–310.

Irvine, S. H. (1979). The place of factor analysis in cross-cultural methodology, and its contribution to cognitive theory. In L. Eckensberger, W. Lonner, & Y. H. Poortinga (Eds.), *Cross-cultural contributions to psychology* (pp. 300–341). Lisse, The Netherlands: Swets & Zeitlinger.

Jensen, A. R. (1982). Reaction time and psychometric *g*. In H. J. Eysenck (Ed.), *A model for intelligence* (pp. 93–132). Berlin: Springer.

Jensen, A. R. (1985). The nature of Black–White difference on various psychometric tests: Spearman's hypothesis. *Behavioral and Brain Sciences, 8*, 193–263.

Jensen, A. R. (1998). *The g factor: The science of mental ability*. Westport, CT: Praeger.

Kagitcibasi, C. (1997). Individualism and collectivism. In J. W. Berry, M. H. Segall, & C. Kagitcibasi (Eds.), *Handbook of cross-cultural psychology: Vol. 3. Social behavior and applications* (pp. 1–49). Boston: Allyn & Bacon.

Kaufman, A. S., & Kaufman, N. L. (1983). *Kaufman assessment battery for children*. Circle Pines, MN: American Guidance Service.

Kendall, I. M., Verster, M. A., & Von Mollendorf, J. W. (1988). Test performance of Blacks in Southern Africa. In S. H. Irvine & J. W. Berry (Eds.), *Human abilities in cultural context* (pp. 340–357). New York: Cambridge University Press.

Lévy-Bruhl, L. (1922). *Mentalité primitive* [Primitive mentality]. Paris: Alcan.

Liu, L. A. (1985). Reasoning counterfactually in Chinese: Are there any obstacles? *Cognition, 21*, 239–270.

Luria, A. R. (1971). Towards the problem of the historical nature of psychological processes. *International Journal of Psychology, 6*, 259–272.

Luria, A. R. (1976). *Cognitive development: Its cultural and social foundations*. Cambridge, MA: Harvard University Press.

Markus, H. R., & Kitayama, S. (1991). Culture and the self: Implications for cognition, emotion and motivation. *Psychological Review, 98*, 244–253.

Matsumoto, D. (1999). Culture and self: An empirical assessment of Markus and Kitayama's theory of independent and interdependent self-construals. *Asian Journal of Social Psychology, 2*, 289–310.

McCrae, R. R., & Allik, J. (Eds.). (2002). *The Five-Factor Model across cultures*. New York: Kluwer Academic.

Naveh-Benjamin, M., & Ayres, T. J. (1986). Digit span, reading rate, and linguistic relativity. *Quarterly Journal of Experimental Psychology, 38*(A), 739–751.

Paunonen, S. V., & Ashton, M. C. (1998). The structured assessment of personality across cultures. *Journal of Cross-Cultural Psychology, 29*, 150–170.

Peng, K., & Nisbett, R. (1999). Culture, dialectics and reasoning about contradiction. *American Psychologist, 54*, 741–754.

Poortinga, Y. H. (1971). Cross-cultural comparison of maximum performance tests: Some methodological aspects and some experiments [Monograph]. *Psychologia Africana* (Suppl. 6).

Poortinga, Y. H. (1985). Empirical evidence of bias in choice reaction time experiments. *The Behavioral and Brain Sciences, 8*, 236–237.

Poortinga, Y. H. (1997). Towards convergence? In J. W. Berry, Y. H. Poortinga, & J. Pandey (Eds.), *Handbook of cross-cultural psychology: Vol. 1. Theory and method* (pp. 347–387). Boston: Allyn & Bacon.

Poortinga, Y. H. (2003). Coherence of culture and generalizability of data: Two questionable assumptions in cross-cultural psychology. In J. Berman & J. Berman (Eds.), *Proceedings of the 49th Nebraska Symposium on Motivation*. Lincoln, NE: University of Nebraska Press.

Poortinga, Y. H., & Van de Vijver, F. J. R. (1987). Explaining cross-cultural differences: Bias analysis and beyond. *Journal of Cross-Cultural Psychology, 18*, 259–282.

Poortinga, Y. H., Van de Vijver, F. J. R., & Van Hemert, D. A. (2002). Cross-cultural equivalence of the Big Five: A tentative interpretation of the evidence. In R. R. McCrae & J. Allik (Eds.), *The Five-Factor Model across cultures* (pp. 271–293). New York: Kluwer Academic.

Posner, M. I. (1985). Chronometric measures of g. *Behavioral and Brain Sciences, 8*, 237–238.

Raven, J. C. (1938). *Progressive matrices: A perceptual test of intelligence, 1938 individual form*. London: Lewis.

Reuning, H., & Wortley, W. (1973). Psychological studies of the Bushmen [Monograph]. *Psychologia Africana* (Suppl. 7).

Rogoff, B., & Gauvain, M. (1984). The cognitive consequences of specific experiences, weaving versus schooling among the Navajo. *Journal of Cross-Cultural Psychology, 15*, 453–475.

Rushton, P. (1995). *Race, evolution and behavior*. New Brunswick, NJ: Transaction Publishers.

Saxe, G. B. (1981). Body parts as numerals: A developmental analysis of numeration among remote Oksapmin village populations in Papua New Guinea. *Child Development, 52*, 306–316.

Saxe, G. B. (1982). Developing forms of arithmetical thought among the Oksapmin of Papua New Guinea. *Child Developmental Psychology, 18*, 583–594.

Schliemann, A., Carraher, D., & Ceci, S. (1997). Everyday cognition. In J. W. Berry, P. R. Dasen, & T. S. Saraswathi (Eds.), *Handbook of cross-cultural psychology: Vol. 2. Basic processes and human development* (2nd ed., pp. 177–216). Boston: Allyn & Bacon.

Schneider, W., Körkel, J., & Weinert, F. E. (1987). The effects of intelligence, self-concept and attributional style on metamemory and memory behavior. *International Journal of Behavioral Development, 10*, 281–299.

Schneider, W., & Pressley, M. (1997). *Memory development between two and twenty* (2nd ed.). Mahwah, NJ: Erlbaum.

Schwartz, S. H. (1992). Universals in the content and structure of values: Theoretical advances and empirical tests in 20 countries. In M. Zanna (Ed.), *Advances in experimental social psychology* (Vol. 25, pp. 1–65). Orlando, FL: Academic Press.

Scribner, S. (1979). Modes of thinking and ways of speaking: Culture and logic reconsidered. In R. O. Freedle (Ed.), *New directions in discourse processing* (pp. 223–243). Norwood, NJ: Ablex.

Scribner, S., & Cole, M. (1981). *The psychology of literacy.* Cambridge, MA: Harvard University Press.

Segall, M. H., Dasen, P. R., Berry, J. W., & Poortinga, Y. H. (1999). *Human behavior in global perspective: An introduction to cross-cultural psychology* (2nd ed.). Boston: Allyn & Bacon.

Shebani, M. F. A. (2001). *Memory development of Libyan and Dutch children.* Unpublished doctoral dissertation, Tilburg University, Tilburg, The Netherlands.

Shebani, M. F. A., Van de Vijver, F. J. R., & Poortinga, Y. H. (2003). *Aspects of memory development in Libyan and Dutch children.* Manuscript submitted for publication.

Shweder, R. A., Goodnow, J., Hatano, G., LeVine, R. A., Markus, H., & Miller, P. (1998). The cultural psychology of development: One mind, many mentalities. In W. Damon (Series Ed.) & R. M. Lerner (Vol. Ed.), *Handbook of child psychology: Vol. 1. Theoretical models of human development* (5th ed., pp. 865–923). New York: Wiley.

Sonke, C. J. (2001). *Cross-cultural differences on simple cognitive tasks: A psychophysiological investigation.* Unpublished doctoral dissertation, Tilburg University, Tilburg, The Netherlands.

Sonke, C. J., Poortinga, Y. H., & De Kuijer, J. H. J. (1999). Cross-cultural differences on cognitive task performance: The influence of stimulus familiarity. In W. J. Lonner, D. L. Dinnel, D. K. Forgays, & S. A. Hayes (Eds.), *Merging past, present, and future in cross-cultural psychology* (pp. 146–158). Lisse, The Netherlands: Swets & Zeitlinger.

Sternberg, R. J. (1977). *Intelligence, information processing, and analogical reasoning: The componential analysis of human abilities.* New York: Wiley.

Stigler, J. W., Lee, S. W., & Stevenson, H. W. (1986). Digit memory span in Chinese and English: Evidence for a temporary limited store. *Cognition, 23,* 1–20.

Tanon, F. (1994). A cultural view on planning: The case of weaving in Ivory Coast. *Cross-Cultural Psychology Monographs, 4.*

Te Nijenhuis, J., & Van der Flier, H. (1997). Comparability of GATB scores for immigrants and majority group members: Some Dutch findings. *Journal of Applied Psychology, 82,* 675–687.

Thorndike, R. L., Hagen, E. P., & Sattler, J. M. (1986). *Technical manual: Stanford-Binet Intelligence Scale: Fourth Edition.* Chicago: Riverside Publishing.

Triandis, H. C. (1989). The self and social behavior in differing cultural contexts. *Psychological Review, 96,* 506–520.

Tucker, L. R. (1951). *A method for synthesis of factor analytic studies* (Personnel Research Section Report No. 984). Washington, DC: Department of the Army.

Tulviste, P. (1991). *The cultural-historical development of verbal thinking.* New York: Nova Science Publishers.

Van de Vijver, F. J. R. (1997). Meta-analysis of cross-cultural comparisons of cognitive test performance. *Journal of Cross-Cultural Psychology, 28,* 678–709.

Van de Vijver, F. J. R. (2002). Inductive reasoning in Zambia, Turkey, and The Netherlands: Establishing cross-cultural equivalence. *Intelligence, 30,* 313–351.

Van de Vijver, F. J. R., Daal, M., & van Zonneveld, R. (1986). The trainability of abstract reasoning: A cross-cultural comparison. *International Journal of Psychology, 21,* 589–615.

Van de Vijver, F. J. R., & Leung, K. (1997a). Methods and data analysis of comparative research. In J. W. Berry, Y. H. Poortinga, & J. Pandey (Eds.), *Handbook of cross-cultural psychology: Vol 1. Theory and method* (pp. 257–300). Boston: Allyn & Bacon.

Van de Vijver, F. J. R., & Leung, K. (1997b). *Methods and data analysis for cross-cultural research.* Newbury Park, CA: Sage.

Verster, J. M. (1983). The structure, organization and correlates of cognitive speed and accuracy: A cross-cultural study using computerized tests. In S. H. Irvine & J. W. Berry (Eds.), *Human assessment and cultural factors* (pp. 275–292). New York: Plenum Press.

Vorster, J., & Schuring, G. (1989). Language and thought: Developmental perspectives on counterfactual conditionals. *South African Journal of Psychology, 19,* 34–38.

Vygotsky, L. S. (1978). *Mind in society: The development of higher psychological processes.* Cambridge, MA: Harvard University Press.

Wagner, D. A. (1974). The development of short-term and incidental memory: A cross-cultural study. *Child Development, 45,* 389–396.

Wagner, D. A. (1981). Culture and memory development. In H. C. Triandis & A. Heron (Eds.), *Handbook of cross-cultural psychology: Developmental psychology* (Vol. 4, pp. 178–232). Boston, MA: Allyn & Bacon.

Wassmann, J., & Dasen, P. R. (1994a). Yupno number system and counting. *Journal of Cross-Cultural Psychology, 25,* 78–94.

Wassmann, J., & Dasen, P. R. (1994b). "Hot" and "cold": Classification and sorting among the Yupno of Papua New Guinea. *International Journal of Psychology, 29,* 19–38.

Wechsler, D. (1991). *Wechsler Intelligence Scale for Children—Third Edition.* San Antonio, TX: The Psychological Corporation.

Wechsler, D. (1997). *Wechsler Adult Intelligence Scale—Third Edition.* San Antonio, TX: The Psychological Corporation.

Willemsen, M. M. E. (2001). *Logical reasoning and culture.* Unpublished doctoral dissertation, Tilburg University, Tilburg, The Netherlands.

Willemsen, M. M. E., & Van de Vijver, F. J. R. (1997). Developmental expectations of Dutch, Turkish-Dutch, and Zambian mothers: Towards an explanation of cross-cultural differences. *International Journal of Behavioral Development, 21,* 837–854.

Whorf, B. L. (1956). *Language, thought and reality.* Cambridge, MA: MIT Press.

Wundt, W. (1913). *Elemente der Völkerpsychologie* [Elements of the psychology of people] (2nd ed.). Leipzig, Germany: Alfred Kroner Verlag.

7

THE CULTURAL PRACTICE OF INTELLIGENCE TESTING: PROBLEMS OF INTERNATIONAL EXPORT

ROBERT SERPELL AND BRENDA PITTS HAYNES

Competence is defined by a culturally constituted system of representation. Its presence or absence in a given individual is construed in emergent ways through interpersonal interactions, which in turn are informed by a system of meanings shared among the coparticipants and their various audiences (Jenkins, 1998; Serpell, 2001). The cultural practice of intelligence testing falls within this framework as an institutionalized network of recurrent activities, scripts, artifacts, roles, and social functions. In this chapter we seek to situate the technology of intelligence testing within the system of meaning that informs professional practices and guarantees their sociocultural legitimacy. Many of the assumptions underpinning the legitimacy of the practice in American society are much less widely shared in contemporary African societies. As a result, we argue that the process of institutionalizing intelligence testing in Africa threatens to distort important aspects of

An earlier version of this chapter was presented in a symposium on "Cultural Approaches to Intellectual and Social Competencies" (R. J. Sternberg, Chair) at the 13th Annual Convention of the American Psychological Society, Toronto, Canada, June 15, 2001.

education in dysfunctional ways rather than enhancing its precision and efficiency.

INTELLIGENCE TESTING AS A CULTURAL PRACTICE

Culture is often perceived by American psychologists as something other people have, in other societies, "while we have human nature" (Schwartz, 1992, p. 329). This "blind spot in American psychology" (Serpell & Boykin, 1994, p. 385) may make the notion of intelligence testing as a cultural practice appear somewhat fanciful to Americans. For testing is part of the water in which they swim, the air they breathe, the taken-for-granted and therefore imperceptible texture of their ordinary life. Yet it may be productive to consider intelligence testing as being just as deeply embedded in the American way of life as other, more obviously cultural, ritualized practices such as the celebration of holy communion in the Christian church or the swearing in of the President of the United States.

A practice, according to Scribner and Cole (1981) is "a recurrent, goal-directed sequence of activities using a particular technology and particular systems of knowledge" (p. 236). Recurrent activities in the case of intelligence testing include presenting a prestructured task in a standard format to an individual in relative social isolation; providing the respondent with explicit instructions; recording her or his responses in terms of a set of discrete, precoded alternatives; assigning numerical scores to those categorical responses; and calculating a derived score relative to a set of norms established by pretesting a standardization sample of respondents on the task. The technology deployed in this activity context includes a test kit with an accompanying administration manual, a set of scoring protocols, and norms and guidelines for the interpretation of individual scores. The system of knowledge informing the practice includes the methodological field of psychometrics (with its paradigm of standardization, norm-referenced scoring, and research procedures for establishing reliability and validity) as well as the professional tradition of assessment (including principles of rapport-building, constrained prompting, and reporting on the results of testing to various technical, professional, and lay audiences). Figure 7.1 summarizes these constituent elements of the practice of intelligence testing in comparison with elements of the cultural practice of literacy.

The functions of this practice within the larger social system have been described repeatedly in textbooks designed to facilitate the training of specialists (e.g., Anastasi, 1988; Kaufman, 1979; Sattler, 1988). Like the biomedical practice of testing body temperature, blood pressure, and so forth, intelligence testing purports to provide an objective description of the individual in terms of numerical ratings on highly specific dimensions whose range of variation in the general population is known. Taken together, these

	Literacy		Psychological Assessment	
Reading	Writing		Intelligence testing	Interviewing

Goals

Literacy	Psychological Assessment
Problem solving Entertainment Relevant Information retrieval	Educational needs assessment Psychiatric diagnosis Documentation of current level of cognitive functioning

Sequence of activities

Literacy	Psychological Assessment
documentary resource selection survey of document content text ovorviow reading passage for meaning encoding/recording/memorizing relevant information	test selection arrangements for testing orientation of testee test administration interpreting/reporting/acting on test data

Technology & associated artifacts

Literacy		Psychological Assessment	

Script
Printing
Electronic IP
	tests
	pens
	PCs
		norms
		assessment
		  procedures
		  (e.g., rapport building, constrained
		  prompting, etc.)
			manuals
			kits
			scoring protocols

Systems of knowledqe

Literacy	Psychological Assessment
Orthography Grammar Narrative genres & structures Documentation & information retrieval systems	psychological theory psychometrics validity, reliability criteria standardization

Figure 7.1. A comparison of two cultural practices.

various ratings make up a profile of the individual that can be used to inform (a) the identification of problems (including diagnosis of pathological conditions), (b) the design of ameliorative interventions (including instruction), and (c) the predictive estimation of the individual's prospects for successful performance in various educational and occupational settings. Each of these applications has been incorporated within the standard practices of a particular professional cadre known respectively as clinical psychologists, school or educational psychologists, and industrial or occupational psychologists. The stability and predictability of the activity structure of intelligence testing is maintained through a combination of professional standard setting and monitoring, training, and legislation. The guild of professional psychologists serves on the one hand to maintain a degree of public accountability, and on the other to protect the interests of its specialist members against external pressures.

In American society, the professionalization of psychological assessment has acquired a layer of rigidity beyond the emphasis on regulation. As

Devlieger (1998, p. 68) notes, the explicit textual specification of individual program plans for persons with intellectual or other disabilities reflects a distinctive strand of American culture: the special significance attached to texts, as evidenced in the American Constitution, the Declaration of Independence, the Christian Bible, and the law. Paradoxically, this preoccupation with adherence to regulations as laid out in authoritative texts sometimes leads to a distortion of the very social purposes for which they were designed. Thus Harry and her colleagues (1995) have shown how the accountability of professionals to the families of children with special educational needs, although nominally guaranteed by the consultative process designated as an admission review and dismissal committee (ARD) meeting, often ends up with the imposition of a program plan that the family members perceived as having been presented to them for blindly compliant ratification. This perception arises largely because the plan is expressed in terms that are too technically specialized for lay parents to understand. In societies in which literacy is much less widely distributed in the general population than in the United States (a characteristic shared among all African nations), the dangers of such distortion, masked behind the principle of adherence to regulations, are even greater.

Like many other Western technological inventions (such as the printing press, the sewing machine, the bicycle, and the tractor), the intelligence test (popularly known as the IQ test) has been widely exported around the world. Like tractors (see Dumont, 1966), intelligence tests bring with them both ostensible utility and hidden implications that may or may not be valuable to the society into which they are imported. Our purpose in this chapter is to explore some of the latent characteristics of intelligence testing as applied to the domain of education in Africa. Why would an African society want to consider importing the Western cultural practice of intelligence testing? One line of reasoning might invoke scientific considerations. We turn to these in the next section.

CONNECTIONS BETWEEN SCIENTIFIC RESEARCH AND THE PRACTICE OF TESTING

A number of commentators (e.g., Gardner & Clarke, 1992) have noted the paradoxical fragmentation of Western psychology in the mid-20th century into three largely independent strands with potential relevance to the understanding of intelligence: the field of basic cognitive processes such as memory, perception, and reasoning (largely addressed by the methods of experimental psychology); the field of cognitive development (dominated by Piaget's theory of genetic epistemology); and the field of mental testing (dominated by the statistical techniques of psychometrics). Important steps were taken in the later decades of the century to build bridges between these subdisciplines, giving rise to the emergence of an information-processing perspective on cognitive development that builds on Piaget's developmental insights and incorporates the experimental analysis of cognitive processes (Siegler, 1983), an information-processing perspective on intelligence that applies the experimental analysis of cognitive processes to the design of mental tests (Sternberg, 1984), and even some attempts to incorporate Piagetian constructs into the design of a standardized intelligence test (Eliot, 1983).

Nevertheless the distinctive, separate preoccupations of the three traditions tend to weaken their claims within one another's respective primary constituencies. Thus the task force charged by the American Psychological Association with providing an authoritative review of contemporary scientific knowledge about intelligence (Neisser et al., 1996) noted that many well-established theoretical perspectives in intelligence are underrepresented in or completely ignored by the major contemporary tests of intelligence. The task force concluded that

> the psychometric approach is the oldest and best established, but others also have much to contribute . . . (and) we should be open to the possibility that our understanding of intelligence in the future will be rather different from what it is today. (p. 80)

However, at about the same moment in history, an influential group of psychometrically oriented American psychologists (Gottfredson et al., 1994), abandoned all such caution and pronounced, as a matter of established fact, that

> intelligence is a very general capability. . . . It is not merely book learning, a narrow academic skill, or test-taking smarts. Rather, it reflects a broader and deeper capability for comprehending our surroundings . . . [and] intelligence, so defined, can be measured, and intelligence tests measure it well. (p. 13)

This type of unreserved confidence is, of course, much more attractive to the nonexpert consumers of a technology on offer for export. If they "read the small print," consumers will be reminded by the proponents of standardized tests that the tenets of the technology stipulate that standardization be conducted on an appropriate normative population, as a precondition of individual scores being interpretable. But what constitutes an appropriate normative population turns out to be a subtle and contestable topic to which no easy, technically grounded answers are available.

Figure 7.2 presents a series of methodological steps adopted by Hibist Astatke (2000) for systematically testing the applicability of a Western scientific theory to a practical social problem in Ethiopian society: namely, preventing adolescents from engaging in HIV-hazardous behaviors (Astatke & Serpell, 2000, p. 368). This methodological strategy, arguably, has some generality and is applicable in principle to the appraisal of how best to apply

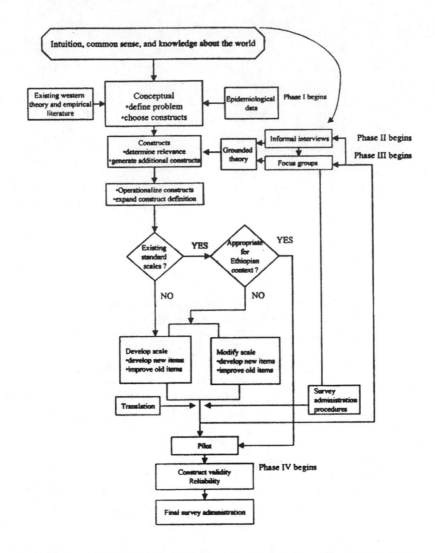

Figure 7.2. Process model of the development and administration of AIDS risk behavior review. From "Testing the Application of a Western Scientific Theory of AIDS Risk Behavior Among Adolescents in Ethiopia," by H. Astatke and R. Serpell, 2000, *Journal of Pediatric Psychology, 25,* p. 367. Copyright 2000 by Oxford University Press. Reprinted with permission.

psychology to various educational problems in a given African society. Note, however, that most applied research on cognitive factors relevant to performance in educational and industrial settings in Africa starts around the middle of the conceptualization process: Do relevant standard scales exist? Are they appropriate to this context? The more radical, prior questions of how to define the problem, and what constructs are perceived as relevant in the host society, are skipped.

The question of how the relationship is conceptualized between intelligence and other dimensions of human behavior has been examined in some depth by studies in several indigenous African cultures (Bissiliat, Laya, Pierre, & Pidoux, 1967; Dasen et al., 1985; Grigorenko et al., 2001; Kingsley, 1985; Mukamurama, 1985; Serpell, 1977, 1993; Super, 1983; Whyte, 1998). Across a wide spectrum of African societies, it appears that there are strong grounds for questioning the separation of cognitive alacrity from social responsibility that has tended to inform most Western scientific conceptions of intelligence. In traditional African cultures a person who is cognitively quick but lacks social responsibility is not generally regarded as intelligent. Indeed, even in Connecticut, in the United States, a sizable sample of middle-class, lay respondents placed greater emphasis on social dimensions of behavior in their conceptions of an ideally intelligent person than did a sample of expert American researchers on intelligence (Sternberg, Conway, Ketron, & Bernstein, 1981). But these public opinions carry little or no weight in the development of standardized intelligence tests, which consistently focus on cognitive alacrity to the virtual exclusion of social responsibility.

One reason for this state of affairs is the narrow focus of research on the design and standardization of mental tests in general and intelligence tests in particular. To fully understand the topic of intelligence and its assessment, researchers need not only to draw on the specialized techniques of psychometrics, theories of information processing, and ontogenesis but also to reach out beyond the traditional confines of psychology into the other social sciences to reflect on the whole nature of education, including its economic and political parameters. Indeed the concept of intelligence also needs to be situated in relation to studies of society and history, and of language and culture. In short, the scientific study of intelligence lies at the intersection of many disciplines. Yet, it is rare to see more than a few words devoted to such matters in the manuals of any of the widely marketed intelligence tests. Instead, the package is primarily organized in terms of its standardization, reliability, and external validity. Apart from laying out the procedures for administration and scoring of the test, the manual documents the population sample to whom it was administered in arriving at "norms" with reference to which an individual's test scores are interpreted as evidence of relatively low or high intelligence, the reliability with which scores can be attached to the performance of an individual, and the degree to which those scores are predictive of performance on other indicators (such as educational achievement or occupational success). On the surface, this account of a test appears to be unpretentious pragmatism. Like a tractor, or a sewing machine, the test is presented as a tool carefully designed to perform a well-defined type of task. But, by leaving unstated the epistemological, economic, and political premises on which the technology rests, the technical description of intelligence tests may be somewhat deceptive. In the next section, we analyze the social theory that informs the context in which formal psychological testing has been imported to African societies.

HUMAN RESOURCE MANAGEMENT IN THE ECONOMICS OF "DEVELOPMENT"

The context of educational testing in Africa at the beginning of the 21st century is dominated by the twin themes of economic scarcity and equity. Education is construed in economic development planning as a way of adding value to the resource of manpower. Management of this resource for national development is facilitated by deploying its units (individuals) in such a way that they are allocated to the occupational tasks for which they are best qualified. Testing is thus understood as a means to the end of optimizing the fit between individuals and their economic occupations by matching the demands of a job to the skills and interests of candidates.

Without including the factor of scarcity, this model might appear entirely functional—a matter of putting square pegs in square holes. However, in reality very little of the variance in job performance can be predicted from aptitude test scores because (a) humans are extremely adaptable and (b) the distribution of job opportunities is largely driven by competition for jobs on the basis of how well they are paid. The theme of equity enters the picture as a way of rationalizing (in terms of economic efficiency) which of the many candidates for a job will be accorded the extrinsic rewards attached to it. Theoretically, the collective interests of society will be better served if access to well-paid jobs is determined more by individual aptitude than by social privilege. The scale of public educational provision is calibrated in development plans to generate a sufficient pool of manpower with each type of qualification to meet the demand projected for it in the national economy. Because so-called higher-level, specialized qualifications are construed as needed in smaller numbers than the more general basic education necessary for all forms of civic participation, a pyramidal structure of educational provision is established, with fewer and fewer opportunities as candidates progress upwards.

The extractive recruitment model of education (illustrated in Figure 7.3) purports to select, at each stage of the narrowing staircase of educational opportunity, those individuals best qualified to proceed. Within this functional framework, a set of implicit values can be detected that inform the design of educational tests. The external validity of a test is judged by how well it identifies the most deserving candidates for selection in a competition for scarce opportunities. The ideology behind such competition is known as meritocracy. Those who win the competition are accorded the prestige of success, and those who lose are branded with the stigma of failure (Serpell, 1993). The motivation nurtured by this ideology is notoriously selfish, yet

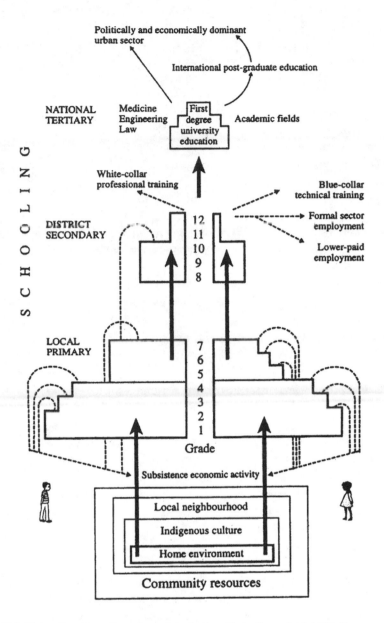

Figure 7.3. Extractive recruitment model of education. Copyright 1999 From *Education, Cultures, and Economics: Dilemmas for Development* (p. 116) by F. Leach & A. Little (Eds.). Reproduced by permission of Routledge/Taylor & Francis Books, Inc.

often lauded in American public discourse as "rugged individualism" (Boykin, 1983; Spence, 1985).

Educational selection in African public education systems is only sometimes based on intelligence-type aptitude tests. More often it is based on attainment tests. According to Kellaghan and Greaney (1992), Zambia was the only one among the eight African countries they studied to have made extensive use of aptitude tests over the previous 20 years; the others had all relied on achievement tests. The policy of including general aptitude tests in the battery used for the national secondary school selection examination at Grade 7 was elaborated in Zambia in the 1960s and 1970s on the grounds that these were relatively less biased in favor of students enrolled in urban primary schools over those in rural schools (Heron, 1971), and that they were more strongly predictive of performance at the next tier of national educational selection in Grade 10 (Sharma, 1974). They were thus construed as being more sociopolitically impartial and more genuinely indicative of academic potential than achievement tests in the various subject content areas. Stating the case more crudely, general aptitude tests were interpreted as more valid indices of students' underlying intelligence, relative to the quality of their learning opportunities, than measures of subject knowledge and understanding.

Nevertheless, it should be recognized that the various standardized intelligence tests used in studies of Zambian school pupils over the period in question consistently discriminated in favor of urban over rural pupils and in favor of boys over girls (Heron, 1971; Irvine, 1969). The criticism that such findings were indicative of inappropriate, exogenous cultural bias was dismissed by Vernon (1967) and by Durojaiye (1984) on the grounds that politicians and other representatives of the African people had deliberately, and wisely, opted for a Western-style education as an instrument of national modernization, through which the human capital of the economy would be transformed to address the challenges of the modern state. Thus, they argued, aptitude for that type of education is an appropriate criterion for selecting those to be accorded opportunities for further education, and ultimately for appointment to positions of national responsibility. A contrary argument, presented elsewhere (Serpell, 1977, 1984, 2000), is that the use of such indices to "validate" tests of intelligence in Africa has condemned the field to a circular logic that amounts to little more than the notoriously sterile dictum that intelligence is what intelligence tests measure.

As Little (2000) has observed, one of the consequences of so-called globalization in the world economy has been the commoditization of educational qualifications. Individuals in Africa no longer confine their educational and occupational aspirations within the framework of the national economy into which they were born. They include among their range of occupational choices opportunities in the wider, global economy for which the scale of extrinsic rewards reflect not only the social hierarchy of their own society but also the uneven distribution of material wealth across the world's nations. Note that, in this scheme of things, a job as a retail sales assistant or as a nontechnical service provider in an affluent MIC (more industrialized country) may prove to be more lucrative than a highly specialized, professional job in an economically embattled LIC (less industrialized country). Thus the whole technocratic rationale of educational qualification that underpins the design and external validation of psychological testing is placed at risk for redundancy and ridicule. Educational qualifications have become recognized as commodities with a market value, and we are witnessing a growing proliferation of educational programs offered to international students by MIC institutions seeking to cash in on the global market potential of certificates (Little, 2000). Associated with this trend is the danger that the value of certificates on this commodity market may be grounded less in the content of the educational programs whose completion they nominally certify than in the prestige associated with their institutional underwriters and the credentialist access they afford to lucrative occupations.

TESTING AS A SOURCE OF SYSTEMATIC DISTORTION IN PUBLIC EDUCATION

Within the extractive recruitment model of schooling described above, the technocratic formulation of psychological testing as an efficient means of achieving equity has a number of unfortunate consequences. It legitimizes elitism in terms of education as a source of "enlightenment," buttressing the notion that the privileges attached to educational credentials are rightfully deserved by those who achieve them. It defines those excluded from further education as personal failures. Moreover, by invoking extraction as an index of success, this application of standardized testing tends indirectly to devalue the home community and its culture (Serpell, 1993).

Furthermore, the cultural content and form of most of the intellectual tests currently in use in Africa mediate a sociocultural bias in the allocation of educational opportunity. In African societies, children from more affluent, urban homes, whose parents have mastered the language and culture of public affairs, consistently score higher than their less privileged peers on Western-type tests of cognitive ability. This finding has been a focus of numerous studies, and a variety of explanations for it have been advanced. Some authors such as Vernon (1969) have attributed the higher scores to enhanced intelligence due to privileged environmental stimulation inspired by Western cultural influences. Others have suggested that Western cultural influence gives rise to a more analytical cognitive style (Berry, 1976; Dawson, 1967), or to a more visual sensotype (Wober, 1967). Yet another approach has been to identify specific perceptual skills and cognitive operations fostered by particular cultural practices (Serpell, 1979). In relation to the cultural practice of intelligence testing analyzed above, for instance, it appears likely that children of elite families in Africa receive as part of their home socialization a facilitative orientation not only to the conventions of two-dimensional line drawings and diagrams (Serpell & Deregowski, 1980), and of adhering to arbitrary, task-related rules, but also to such features of the testing paradigm as face-to-face interaction with a friendly, but unfamiliar adult in relative social isolation (Harkness & Super, 1977) and such interactional routines as displaying competence in response to "known-answer" questions, striving energetically to excel at a factitious task, and making strategic use of supportive, task-related verbal prompts. Yet such children may be less competent than many of their less privileged peers in the use of indigenous languages, or in pattern reproduction in the medium of clay or wire. Tests designed to avoid such cultural biases need to draw on more generally distributed opportunities for the development of cognitive and social skills (e.g., Kathuria & Serpell, 1998; Serpell, 1989).

An additional dimension of the systematic distortion introduced into education by current testing practices is the so-called backwash of assessment criteria into pedagogical practices and student motivation. Teachers in African schools and the students under their guidance focus their studies on those particular skills and forms of knowledge that are emphasized in the public examinations used to select candidates for further educational opportunity. But, like intelligence tests, the public examinations used for selection and certification in African school systems tend to be esoteric in content: "life outside of school seldom features in examination questions" (Kellaghan & Greaney, 1992). Thus teachers are indirectly encouraged to teach intellectual skills that are divorced from students' experience of the real world, fostering the alienating idea that education is primarily about a set of specialized activities that only go on in schools.

ALTERNATIVE VISIONS FOR THE FUTURE OF PSYCHOEDUCATIONAL ASSESSMENT IN AFRICA

Two contrasting views of the way forward have been expressed in the literature. One favors incremental incorporation of established Western testing practices into the texture of public life, whereas the other advocates reformulation of the social functions of psychological assessment and programmatic development of a testing technology to serve those functions.

An incrementalist perspective was articulated by Owen (1998) in an authoritative overview on "the role of psychological tests in education in South Africa." Favoring the continued application of psychometric validity criteria, he writes:

> By emphasizing and promoting a common core of educational objectives and identifying the referent culture as the school culture, psychoeducational testing and assessment in South Africa can be cross-cultural. Consequently, common measuring instruments, based primarily on a Eurocentric approach, can be used with the various groups. (p. 84)

It is significant that in the same paragraph, Owen advances two explicit economic justifications for this proposal: affordability, and participation in the global economy—"Otherwise [i.e., if a common set of instruments is not used], different measuring instruments and assessment techniques must be developed for each cultural group—which is not only impractical but also economically unaffordable" (pp. 84–85). Owen further states that

> Whatever the attitudes and views of the education authorities may be, if South Africa wants to continue in its role as a significant player on international markets, the educational objectives set for the country cannot be vastly different from those of our trading partners. (p. 84)

Owen (1998) invokes an American analysis by Valencia and Lopez (1992) to support his advocacy of "the school culture" as a shared frame of reference for assessment. But conspicuously absent from this analysis is any reference to the most salient difference between the ethnodemographic profiles of the United States and South Africa. Valencia and Lopez (1992) derived their proposal to focus on school culture from an argument presented in a landmark American court case brought against the Chicago school system in 1980, alleging cultural bias in the use of tests to determine eligibility of students for special education placement. It was agreed in that case between the plaintiffs and the defense "that ability tests, school grades and achievement tests were all part of the same culture and . . . that school children in Chicago were not being trained for life in . . . Greece, China, Tasmania, or (in Judge Grady's final comparison) 'another planet'" (Elliott, 1987, p. 198).

Now some of us would take issue with the conclusion that this justifies maintenance of the status quo, arguing that cultural change in the American school curriculum is essential to accommodate productively the contributions of its increasingly diverse population (Serpell, 2000). Others, however, contest this on (a) the pragmatic grounds that cultural diversity itself makes for difficulties in extrapolating implications for coherent curriculum development; on (b) the contestable sociological grounds that voluntary migration implies at least a modicum of approval of the culture of the host society; or on (c) the more conservative grounds that the cultural canon of mainstream America deserves to retain an enduring, privileged significance within the nation's cultural heritage.

But, in the case of South Africa, it is widely understood that the majority of the population were until recently, forcibly subjugated by adherents of an alien culture who systematically stigmatized every element of the indigenous culture as "primitive," "immoral," and devoid of sophistication or relevance to the modern world. Moreover, explicit repudiation of that hostile propaganda was a conspicuous element of the rationale advanced by the movement for political change that culminated in the emancipatory, new dispensation enshrined in the new constitution of South Africa in 1992. How ironic, that in the context of that new dispensation, a publication by the national Human Resources Research Council (Owen, 1998) should appear arguing that the culture of the former oppressor group should be the defining criterion of what is important in the nation's educational system. Ironic, but hardly surprising, given the exclusionary ideology that characterized South African psychology from 1948 to 1988 (Seedat, 1998).

In contrast with Owen's incrementalist perspective, Mpofu and Nyanungo (1998) advance compelling arguments for a fundamental shift of emphasis in the practices of educational and psychological testing in Zimbabwean schools. First, they point out that a number of questionable assumptions accord spurious legitimacy to the use of imported tests for classification and placement decisions, even with middle-to-upper-class African children rated as fluent in English and in drawing inferences from scores on achievement tests standardized in other school systems. Hardly any of the tests in use for assessment in Zimbabwe have been subjected to any systematic restandardization on the local population. The designation of an individual child as above or below normal on a given scale is thus implicitly grounded in the untested assumption that what was found to be normal for a child in the population sampled for the test's original standardization in Britain or the United States would also be normal for a child growing up in this particular segment of Zimbabwean society. Yet many relevant factors set these two reference populations apart, including patterns of language use, officially prescribed age of initial enrollment in school, range and type of preschool provision, basic school curricula, and so forth.

Furthermore, Mpofu and Nyanungo (1998) contend that the professional training of Zimbabwean psychologists, modeled on Western standards "may compromise their responsiveness to the unique demands of psychoeducational testing in an African culture" (p. 74). Similar concerns were expressed by Brownell, de Jager, and Madlala (1987), who conducted a survey of a small sample of school psychologists serving in Black schools in South Africa, and noted that at that juncture in the history of the nation, all of the professional training offered at South African universities had "a distinctly Western and first-world character" (p. 38). Their respondents, although expressing general satisfaction with the Western-oriented training they had received, also noted as problematic that they had been afforded little opportunity while in training to learn how to deal with actual problems that occur within Black education, and that all of the theory to which they had been exposed was derived from practices in cultures other than that of the Black South African population they were now committed to serve.

Likewise, Mpofu and Nyanungo (1998) contend that a major impediment to the development of indigenous psychological tests in Zimbabwe is "the low level of adoption of African epistemology by education and psychology departments in Africa and internationally" (p. 79). Drawing on Azuma's (1984) insightful account of the history of psychology in Japan, these authors conclude that psychology in Africa is presently in a passing phase of development characterized by translation and modeling, and that a truly appropriate psychology for the region must await sustained efforts by African psychologists to indigenize the discipline.

Meanwhile, they note that the practice of "the school guidance and counseling program in the country is geared toward life-style adjustment counseling in areas such as self-awareness, relating to others, health-related habits and study skills" (p. 82), more than toward career counseling, which has little if any relevance to the career paths open to young Zimbabweans in current economic conditions.

In light of their analysis, Mpofu and Nyanungo (1998) suggest that "authentic" testing strategies, such as Curriculum Based Assessment, and Portfolio Assessment, offer several distinctive benefits relative to the use of standardized, Western-type tests, including affordability and ecological validity. Moreover, they "can be taught to teachers at little cost" (p. 88), and they "bring both the process and result of testing to the direct users of the products of testing: teachers, pupils, and parents" (p. 88).

It is not without significance that extended accounts of the status and prospects of psychological testing in Africa are only available for Zimbabwe and South Africa. Their uniquely bifurcated heritage as nations must be counted as something of a mixed blessing in this regard. The peculiar racial and cultural makeup of Zimbabwean and South African society has a number of important implications for how to situate the research of both Owen and Mpofu and his colleagues in the broader context of the African region at the end of the 20th century. On the one hand, the presence in these countries of a European-origin segment of the national population that is both demographically significant and culturally prestigious is arguably responsible for the relatively high profile maintenance of exogenous professional practices of applied psychology in both states. Sociocultural institutions mediate this connection at several levels. The curriculum and medium of instruction of public education are informed by a process of "one-way integration," in which the indigenous African population has been accorded access to schools formerly reserved (in the racially segregated system established by colonial authorities) exclusively for students of European descent (known as "Whites"). The underlying premise feeding public perceptions is that the language and curriculum of the education reserved for "Whites" was inherently more beneficial and empowering than the indigenous African languages and curriculum content. Likewise a one-way integrative process is under way in the manning of industry, with indigenous Africans increasingly gaining access to positions of responsibility formerly reserved for "Whites." To maintain the profitable links of industry with their international trading partners, this transition is commonly accompanied by a mentoring process in which experienced "Whites" explain their administrative practices and train their apprenticed successors in faithful adherence to them. Continuity is further entrenched by the fact that many aspects of professional practices in psychology, as in engineering and medicine, are institutionalized in the law. Mpofu, Zindi, Oakland, and Peresuh (1997) found that Zimbabwe and South Africa were unique among the countries they surveyed in Eastern and Southern Africa in this respect. Moreover, tightly linked with these legally enforced professional practices, the credentials required to qualify as a psychologist are only accorded by institutions dominated by senior members of the guild who see to it that the new generation are trained in accordance with the Western tradition. For instance, Sattler's (1988) classic American textbook was closely followed in the training offered to educational psychologists at the University of Zimbabwe in the early 1990s.

On the other hand, the continuing visibility in both nations of advantage in educational achievement by their White citizens and a Black elite with conspicuously Western cultural orientation serves as an irritating reminder of the fact that something is amiss, and that unevenly distributed access to exogenous cultural capital is part of the explanation.

In many of the contexts to which we have been privy over the past two decades, when the African continent was surveyed with a view to selecting a subregional focus for so-called development efforts, South Africa and neighboring Zimbabwe have been identified as relatively modern, developed, and hence in a sense privileged candidates for international investment. Yet in terms of critically analyzing the applicability of imported, exogenous technology to local conditions, and seeking systematically to adapt or transform it, they may be more appropriately described as relatively backward, old-fashioned, or underdeveloped. During the first half of the 20th century, it was widely assumed among colonial politicians, administrators, and commercial entrepreneurs in Africa that technology designed, elaborated, and tested in the industrialized societies of the West would be directly applicable in other cultural settings. This assumption has since been thoroughly undermined by several developments:

- the ascendancy of East Asian industry, and the collapse of McClelland's need for achievement (nAch) theory of international differences in economic development (cf. Spence, 1985)
- repeated demonstration by cross-cultural psychology of unsuspected limitations in the methods and theories of Western psychology (Berry, Dasen, & Saraswathi, 1997; Triandis, 1980)
- documentation by both African and Western social scientists of the degree to which the educational practices introduced by Western administrators were informed by considerations of political oppression and economic exploitation rather than the benevolent, progressivist rhetoric under which they were publicly promoted (Ball, 1983; Mazrui, 1986; Snelson, 1974; Tignor, 1976)

- analysis of the enduring myths of cultural superiority that permeate the writings of 19th-century Western commentators on Africa and other cultural regions and those of contemporary Western social scientists (Jahoda, 1993; Said, 1978)
- alternative, strength-based cultural perspectives on human development in non-Western societies (e. g., Doi, 1971; Enriquez, 1994; Nsamenang, 1992; Sinha, 1997).

The need to adopt a more contextually relativistic approach to the validation of psychology is widely understood in the psychology and education departments of most African universities and has informed their teaching of psychology to undergraduates since the 1980s. Yet, in South Africa, even in the post-emancipation era, the enduring professionalism of a formerly unabashedly Western testing industry feeds the publication of injunctions from the gatekeepers of Western cultural hegemony "not to reinvent the wheel" (Shuttleworth-Jordan, 1996) and to beware of setting "a lower standard for one group than another" (Owen, 1998, p. 77). The expression of these views in universalistic terms attempts to legitimize the preservation of a guild in which Western ideas and practices will continue to hold a privileged position in societies in which they have more often been deployed for the exclusionary functions of competitive recruitment than for the nurturant functions of guided participation.

RECOMMENDED DIRECTIONS FOR AFRICAN PSYCHOEDUCATIONAL ASSESSMENT

At the conclusion of their analysis of literacy as a cultural practice, Scribner and Cole (1981) noted that the range of functions in which each of the particular literacies they examined had come to empower depended on both technological and social constraints. In this chapter we have argued that likewise the future prospects of the cultural practice of intelligence testing can best be understood not only attending to its technological features (e. g., by adjusting test design to match local patterns of developmental opportunity, and collecting local norms) but also by situating these within the social, economic, and political context in which it came into being historically and those in which it currently operates.

One overarching principle that could, in our view, channel the development of psychological assessment in African societies in this period of history in a more socially productive and less culturally invasive direction is to prioritize the guidance function of assessment over the selection function: The growth curve is more important than the bell curve (Serpell, 1996).

The extractive recruitment model of basic education tends to prioritize as the central function of psychological assessment systematic exclusion rather than guided participation. The contrast between these two functional orientations for the practice of testing is starkly highlighted by Mpofu and Nyanungo's (1998) observation that during the colonial era the use of tests in Rhodesia (now Zimbabwe) was "designed to minimize rather than facilitate Black children's access to and benefit from education" (p. 73). Although the pernicious element of racism was attenuated by the achievement of political independence, inequities in the distribution of educational opportunity have persisted in African societies, with children of impoverished communities on the margins of the industrially driven economy, and girls (who were marginalized as a group within the system of public education inherited from the colonial administration) performing systematically less well on psychological tests and public examinations, and therefore surviving in fewer numbers the drastic selection filters of the narrowing staircase. Thus the continued use of imported tests for educational selection, even if tempered with some local adaptation, is fraught with dangers of cultural hegemony.

However, the following functions of assessment do not raise the problems addressed in this paper with the same intensity:

- identifying the strengths and needs of an individual within a differentiated profile of competencies;
- tracking the impact of supportive interventions on an individual's progressive mastery of specified target skills; and
- monitoring development within an individual's own trajectory.

These applications of psychological assessment are all well recognized in the Western world (e. g., American Association on Mental Retardation, 2002) and could be deployed by educational or school psychologists in African societies as resources for the refinement of educational practices, as indeed they already have been in modest ways in the delivery of services to children with various types of disability (Serpell, Mariga, & Harvey, 1993).

REFERENCES

American Association on Mental Retardation. (2002). *Mental retardation: The new definition*. Washington, DC: Author.

Anastasi, A. (1988). *Psychological testing* (6th ed.). New York: Macmillan.

Astatke, H. (2000). *HIV-hazardous behaviors among adolescents in Nazareth, Ethiopia*. Unpublished doctoral dissertation, University of Maryland Baltimore County.

Astatke, H., & Serpell, R. (2000). Testing the application of a Western scientific theory of AIDS risk behavior among adolescents in Ethiopia. *Journal of Pediatric Psychology, 25*(6), 367–379.

Azuma, H. (1984). Psychology in a non-Western country. *International Journal of Psychology, 19,* 45–55.

Ball, S. J. (1983). Imperialism, social control, and the colonial curriculum in Africa. *Journal of Curriculum Studies, 15,* 237–263.

Berry, J. W. (1976). *Human ecology and cognitive style: Comparative studies in cultural and psychological adaptation.* New York: Wiley.

Berry, J. W., Dasen, P. R., & Saraswathi, T. S. (1997). *Handbook of cross-cultural psychology: Vol. 2. Basic processes and human development.* Boston: Allyn & Bacon.

Bissiliat, J., Laya, D., Pierre, E., & Pidoux, C. (1967). La notion de lakkal dans la culture Djerma-Songhai [The concept of lakkal in Djerma-Songhai culture]. *Psychopathologie Africaine, 3,* 207–264.

Boykin, A. W. (1983). The academic performance of Afro-American children. In J. Spence (Ed.), *Achievement and achievement motives* (pp. 322–369). San Francisco: Freeman.

Brownell, A. J. J., de Jager, A. C., & Madlala, C. F. M. (1987). Applying first-world psychological models and techniques in a third-world context. *School Psychology International, 8,* 34–47.

Dasen, P. R., Barthelemy, D., Kan, E., Kouame, K., Daouda, K. K., Adjei, K. K., & Assande, N. (1985). N'glouele, l'intelligence chez les Baoule. *Archives de Psychologie, 53,* 295–324.

Dawson, J. L. (1967). Cultural and psychological influence upon spatial-perceptual processes in West Africa: Part 1. *International Journal of Psychology, 2,* 115–128.

Devlieger, P. J. (1998). (In)competence in America in comparative perspective. In R. Jenkins (Ed.), *Questions of competence: Culture, classification and intellectual disability* (pp. 54–75). Cambridge, England: Cambridge University Press.

Doi, T. (1971). *The anatomy of dependence.* New York: Kodansha International.

Dumont, R. (1966). *False start in Africa* (P. N. Ott, Trans.; originally *L'Afrique noire est mal partie*). New York: Praeger Publishers.

Durojaiye, M. O. (1984). The impact of psychological testing on educational and personnel selection in Africa. *International Journal of Psychology, 19,* 135–144.

Eliot, C. D. (1983). *British Ability Scales.* Slough, England: NFER/Nelson.

Elliott, R. (1987). *Litigating intelligence: IQ tests, special education, and social science in the courtroom.* Dover, MA: Auburn House.

Enriquez, V. G. (1994). *Pagbabangong-Dangal: Indigenous psychology and cultural empowerment.* Quezon City, Philippines: Akademya ng Sikolohiya at Kulturang Pilipino.

Gardner, M. K., & Clarke, E. (1992). The psychometric perspective on intellectual development in childhood and adolescence. In R. J. Sternberg & C. Berg (Eds.), *Intellectual development* (pp. 16–43). Cambridge, England: Cambridge University Press.

Gottfredson, L. S., et al. (1994, December 13). Mainstream science on intelligence. *The Wall Street Journal,* p. A18.

Grigorenko, E., Geissler, P., Prince, R., Okatcha, F., Nokes, C., Kenny, D., et al. (2001). The organization of Luo conceptions of intelligence: A study of implicit theories in a Kenyan village. *International Journal of Behavioral Development, 25*(4), 367–378.

Harkness, S., & Super, C. M. (1977). Why African children are so hard to test. In L. L. Adler (Ed.), *Annals of the New York Academy of Sciences: Vol. 285. Issues in cross-cultural research* (pp. 326–331). New York: New York Academy of Sciences.

Harry, B., Allen, N., & McLaughlin, M. (1995). Communication versus compliance: African-American parents' involvement in special education. *Exceptional Children, 61*, 364–377.

Heron, A. (1971). Concrete operations, "g" and achievement in Zambian children. *Journal of Cross-Cultural Psychology, 2*(4), 325–336.

Irvine, S. H. (1969). Factor analysis of African abilities and attainments: Constructs across cultures. *Psychological Bulletin, 71*, 20–32.

Jahoda, G. (1993). *Crossroads between culture and mind: Continuities and change in theories of human nature.* Cambridge, MA: Harvard University Press.

Jenkins, R. (Ed.). (1998). *Questions of competence.* Cambridge, England: Cambridge University Press.

Kathuria, R., & Serpell, R. (1998). Standardization of the Panga Munthu Test: A nonverbal cognitive test developed in Zambia. *Journal of Negro Education, 67*, 228–241.

Kaufman, A. S. (1979). *Intelligent testing with the WISC-R.* New York: Wiley.

Kellaghan, T., & Greaney, V. (1992). *Using examinations to improve education: A study in fourteen African countries* (World Bank Technical Paper No. 165, Africa Technical Department Series). Washington, DC: World Bank.

Kingsley, P. R. (1985). Rural Zambian values and attitudes concerning cognitive competence. In I. R. Lagunes & Y. H. Poortinga (Eds.), *From a different perspective: Studies of behavior across cultures* (pp. 281–303). Lisse, The Netherlands: Swets & Zeitlinger.

Little, A. (2000). Globalisation, qualifications and livelihoods: Towards a research agenda. *Assessment in Education, 7*, 299–312.

Mazrui, A. (1986). *The Africans: a triple heritage.* Boston: Little, Brown.

Mpofu, E., & Nyanungo, K. R. L. (1998). Educational and psychological testing in Zimbabwean schools: Past, present and future. *European Journal of Psychological Assessment, 14*, 71–90.

Mpofu, E., Zindi, F., Oakland, T., & Peresuh, M. (1997). School psychology practices in East and Southern Africa: Special educators' perspectives. *Journal of Special Education, 31*, 387–402.

Mukamurama, D. (1985). La notion d'intelligence: Ubwenge dans la culture rwandaise: Essai d'une definition emique de l'intelligence dans sa conception intra-culturelle. Fribourg, Switzerland: Memoire de license.

Neisser, U., Boodoo, G., Bouchard, T. J., Boykin, A. W., Brody, N., Ceci, S. J., et al. (1996). Intelligence: Knowns and unknowns. *American Psychologist, 51*, 77–101.

Nsamenang, A. B. (1992). *Human development in cultural context: A third world perspective*. Newbury Park, CA: Sage.

Owen, K. (1998). *The role of psychological tests in education in South Africa: Issues, controversies and benefits*. Pretoria, South Africa: Human Resources Research Council. (ERIC Document Reproduction Service No. ED423483).

Sattler, J. M. (1988). *Assessment of children* (3rd ed.). San Diego, CA: Sattler.

Said, E. (1978). *Orientalism*. New York: Pantheon Books.

Schwartz, T. (1992). Anthropology and psychology: An unrequited relationship. In T. Schwartz, G. White, & C. Lutz (Eds.), *New directions in psychological anthropology* (pp. 324–349). New York: Cambridge University Press.

Scribner, S., & Cole, M. (1981). *The psychology of literacy*. Cambridge, MA: Harvard University Press.

Seedat, M. (1998). A characterisation of South African psychology (1948–1988): The impact of exclusionary ideology. *South African Journal of Psychology, 28,* 74–85.

Serpell, R. (1977). Estimates of intelligence in a rural community of eastern Zambia. In F. M. Okatcha (Ed.), *Modern psychology and cultural adaptation* (pp. 179–216). Nairobi, Kenya: Swahili Language Consultants and Publishers.

Serpell, R. (1979). How specific are perceptual skills? A cross-cultural study of pattern reproduction. *British Journal of Psychology, 70,* 365–380.

Serpell, R. (1984). Commentary: the impact of psychology on Third World development. *International Journal of Psychology, 19,* 179–192.

Serpell, R. (1989). Psychological assessment as a guide to early intervention: Reflections on the Zambian context of intellectual disability. In R. Serpell, D. Nabuzoka, & F. Lesi (Eds.), *Early intervention, developmental disability and mental handicap in Africa*. Lusaka: University of Zambia/UNICEF.

Serpell, R. (1993). *The significance of schooling: Life-journeys in an African society*. Cambridge, England: Cambridge University Press.

Serpell, R. (1996, August). Educational alternatives to schooling in Zambia. In R. Serpell & B. Nsamenang (Cochairs), *Basic education for the modern world: Alternatives to Western cultural hegemony*. Symposium conducted at the XVIth Biennial Congress of the International Society for the Study of Behavioural Development, Quebec, Canada. (ERIC Document Reproduction Service No. 416980.htm)

Serpell, R. (1999). Local accountability to rural communities: A challenge for educational planning in Africa. In F. Leach & A. Little (Eds.), *Education, cultures and economics: Dilemmas for development* (pp. 107–135). New York: Garland.

Serpell, R. (2000). Intelligence and culture. In R. J. Sternberg (Ed.), *The handbook of intelligence* (pp. 549–577). Cambridge, England: Cambridge University Press.

Serpell, R. (2001). Cultural dimensions of literacy promotion and schooling. In L. Verhoeven & C. Snow (Eds.), *Literacy and motivation* (pp. 243–273). Mahwah, NJ: Erlbaum.

Serpell, R., & Boykin, A. W. (1994). Cultural dimensions of cognition: A multiplex, dynamic system of constraints and possibilities. In R. J. Sternberg (Ed.), *Handbook of perception and cognition: Vol. 12. Thinking and problem-solving* (pp. 369–408). San Diego, CA: Academic Press.

Serpell, R., & Deregowski, J. B. (1980). The skill of pictorial perception: An interpretation of cross-cultural evidence. *International Journal of Psychology, 15,* 145–180.

Serpell, R., Mariga, L., & Harvey, K. (1993). Mental retardation in African countries: Conceptualization, services, and research. *International Review of Research in Mental Retardation, 19,* 1–39.

Sharma, R. (1974). The grade seven composite examination: A critique. *Psychological Service Reports, 2.* (Available from Ministry of Education, Lusaka, Zambia)

Shuttleworth-Jordan, A. B. (1996). On not reinventing the wheel: A clinical perspective on culturally relevant test usage in South Africa. *South African Journal of Psychology, 26,* 96–103.

Siegler, R. (1983). Information processing approaches to development. In P. H. Mussen (Series Ed.) and W. Kessen (Vol. Ed.), *Handbook of Child Psychology: Vol. 1. History, theory, and methods* (4th ed., pp. 129–211). New York: Wiley.

Sinha, D. (1997). Indigenizing psychologies. In J. W. Berry, Y. H. Poortinga, & J. Pandey, (Eds.), *Handbook of cross-cultural psychology: Vol. 1. Theory and methods* (pp. 129–169). Needham Heights, MA: Allyn & Bacon.

Snelson, P. D. (1974). *Educational development in Zambia: 1883–1945.* Lusaka, Zambia: National Educational Company of Zambia.

Spence, J. (1985). Achievement American style: The rewards and costs of individualism. *American Psychologist, 40,* 1285–1295.

Sternberg, R. J. (1984). Towards a triarchic theory of human intelligence. *Behavioral and Brain Sciences, 7,* 269–315.

Sternberg, R. J., Conway, B., Ketron, J., & Bernstein, M. (1981). People's conceptions of intelligence. *Journal of Personality and Social Psychology, 4,* 37–55.

Super, C. M. (1983). Cultural variation in the meaning and uses of children's intelligence. In J. B. Deregowski, S. Dzurawiecz, & R. C. Annis (Eds.), *Expiscations in cross-cultural psychology* (pp. 199–212). Lisse, The Netherlands: Swets & Zeitlinger.

Tignor, R. L. (1976). *The colonial transformation of Kenya.* Princeton, NJ: Princeton University Press.

Triandis, H. (Ed.). (1980). *Handbook of cross-cultural psychology.* Boston: Allyn & Bacon.

Valencia, R. R., & Lopez, R. (1992). Assessment of racial and ethnic minority students: Problems and prospects. In M. Zeidner & R. Most (Eds.), *Psychological testing: An inside view* (pp. 399–439). Palo Alto, CA: Consulting Psychologists Press.

Vernon, P. (1967). Abilities and educational attainments in an East African environment. *Journal of Special Education, 1,* 335–345.

Vernon, P. (1969). *Intelligence and cultural environment*. London: Methuen.

Whyte, S. R. (1998). Slow cookers and madmen: Competence of heart and head in rural Uganda. In R. Jenkins (Ed.), *Questions of competence: Culture, classification and intellectual disability* (pp. 153–175). Cambridge, England. Cambridge University Press.

Wober, M. (1967). Adapting Witkin's field independence theory to accommodate new information from Africa. *British Journal of Psychology, 58,* 29–38.

8

INTELLECTUAL, ATTITUDINAL, AND INTERPERSONAL ASPECTS OF COMPETENCE IN THE UNITED STATES AND JAPAN

LAUREN J. SHAPIRO AND HIROSHI AZUMA

In contemporary industrialized societies around the world, the core of competence is considered to be the intelligence to solve problems, achieve valued goals, and manage situations in the outside world. Yet competence involves more than just brainpower. It can be seen as a set of knowledge, skills, and attitudes that support success in some real-world task. Although cognitive factors are a highly salient aspect of effectively getting things done, other personal qualities contribute to real-world success as well. Furthermore, because real-world tasks and ideas about success are culture-bound, competence will be differently conceived in different cultures. Japan is one society in which the idea of competence conspicuously incorporates the realm of the heart. Although this chapter cannot touch on all aspects of Japanese competence, it will discuss a variety of ways in which interpersonal and attitudinal dimensions are brought to the fore across the life span, using the United States as a point of comparison.

THE JAPANESE CONCEPT OF COMPETENCE

Prompted by American research on folk concepts of intelligence (Sternberg, Conway, Ketron, & Bernstein, 1981), Azuma and Kashiwagi (1987) conducted a study on the concept of intelligence in Japan. Participants were asked to think about someone whom they knew personally and saw as highly intelligent, and to describe the characteristics of the person that led them to judge that person as intelligent. Descriptors were obtained and categorized, and from each category the clearest, most frequent descriptors were selected to create a list of 67 descriptors. This list included concepts commonly associated with intelligence, along with interpersonal qualities like getting along well with people, knowing one's place, being modest, being a good listener, excelling in penetrating people's feelings, being sympathetic, and so on. Next, a new group of participants was asked to think about a highly intelligent person whom they knew well and to rate on a three-point scale how well each of the 67 descriptors fit that person. Finally, each participant was asked to repeat the task with a second intelligent person to check reliability. The main study included 332 male and 300 female college students, as well as 132 mothers of students.

The descriptors that participants rated most highly aligned closely with what would be expected based on the American data collected by Sternberg and colleagues. Namely, intellectual concerns were emphasized by all three groups. Speed of thinking and ability to grasp the gist of a topic received the highest ratings, and most other high-ranked items addressed memory, judgment, or school performance. Factor analysis, however, revealed another aspect: Of five factors obtained, two emphasized interpersonal qualities. The first interpersonal factor was characterized by sociability, humor, and leadership and corresponds roughly to the Social Competence factor that the Sternberg group obtained with American participants. This factor accounted for 47%, or almost half, of the variance in Japanese responses, whereas in the U.S. study it had been only the third factor of a three-factor solution. The second interpersonal factor was Receptive Social Competence, which accounted for 17% of the total variance in Japanese responses and was characterized by items like sympathy, social modesty, and the ability to take other people's perspective. The remaining three factors were Problem Solving, Originality, and Reading/Writing. Combined, these latter three factors accounted for only 36%, or substantially less than half, of the total variance. In short, whereas intellectual factors like problem solving and verbal ability were the dominant aspects of an ideally intelligent person in the United States, interpersonal factors accounted for 64% of total variance in Japan. The emergence of Receptive Social Competence as a separate factor is particularly noteworthy.

The above comparison must remain somewhat tentative, because the method and item pool used in Japan differed somewhat from those used by the Sternberg group in the United States. However, a cross-cultural study that did use a standard paradigm (Oe, Allard, & Fujinaga, 1989) produced similar findings. In this investigation, 338 French Canadian, 107 English-speaking Canadian, and 348 Japanese college students rated how well each of the 67 descriptors fit an intelligent person whom they knew. Responses were analyzed by correspondence analysis, and nine clusters of items were identified. Once again, items representing intellectual abilities were endorsed highly across all three groups. Yet at the same time, the Japanese endorsed items representing receptive social competence more highly than did either of the Canadian groups. A study that compared Americans and Japanese directly (Azuma, Kashiwagi, & Ohno, 1990) led to parallel results. Interpersonal qualities therefore appear to make up one important aspect of the Japanese concept of competence.

A second notable aspect of the Japanese competence relates to the regulation of one's own internal attitude. Weisz and others (Weisz, Rothbaum, & Blackburn, 1984) have drawn a distinction between primary control and secondary control, with the former being control of the outside world and the latter being control of one's own internal state. They argued, quite perceptively, that whereas Americans tend to value primary control, Japanese traditionally have given substantial weight to secondary control, which Americans frequently overlook. It is not that Japanese do not value having control over their environment. Indeed, if a Japanese person were asked whether they personally would prefer to have primary control or secondary control, assuming that both were equally feasible, the answer most likely would favor the former. Yet if the question were reframed to ask about social desirability, then the latter would gain ground. Although a discrepancy between personal preference and societal prescriptions also would exist for Americans, the difference would almost certainly be much more pronounced in Japan.

We have defined competence in terms of characteristics that support success. Because Japanese society tends to value secondary control more than Americans do, the meaning of success should differ somewhat across these two countries. More specifically, achieving control over one's own inner state should more often qualify as success among Japanese, whereas the American view of success should be more limited to achieving control over external circumstances. In fact, there is good reason to believe that this is the case.

One source of support for this idea comes from an analysis of Japanese versus Western story structure. Hayao Kawai, a Jungian clinical psychologist, has compared Japanese folk tales with European folk tales and legends (Kawai, 1982). Among other observations, he pointed out that Japanese stories tend to lack the hero figure typical of Western stories. The hero in a Western story usually is a protagonist who achieves or aspires to achieve some end goal, maintaining a clear direction while striving to push through various incidents, difficulties, and barriers. In such stories, the protagonists aspire to control the external situations in which they find themselves.

A Japanese story also will have a protagonist, but very often one who does not aspire to change anything. The tales that Kawai quotes tend to be stories about fitting into situations, rather than overcoming them. Typically, Japanese protagonists do something in routine everyday life that triggers the situation to start rolling, either for good or for bad. Then changes successively occur, accompanied by appropriate emotional responses and personal efforts to make the best of the situation. This sequence typically ends without the protagonist exercising any purposeful control over the chain of events. Indeed, Americans and Europeans often are left with the impression that these stories lack a climax or conclusion because success or failure in striving to achieve a conquest does not constitute the central theme.

Data offering additional support for this asymmetry in ideas of success comes from a study conducted by Mashima and the present authors (Mashima, 1998; Mashima, Shapiro, & Azuma, 1998). We asked American and Japanese college students to write about tasks that they had carried out with conscious effort in the previous few months. One finding of this study was that only 29% of Japanese described success or failure in terms of achieving some effortful end goal, versus 70% of Americans. Instead, most Japanese described the internal process of exerting effort, without mentioning whether any final outcome had ever been attained. Similarly, other research (e.g., Stevenson & Stigler, 1992) has found that Japanese attribute academic success or failure to effort more readily than Americans do. Because success in Japan does appear to include the ability to regulate one's own inner state, the Japanese concept of competence can be said to incorporate the idea of maintaining an appropriate attitude toward the task at hand. Thus, although intellectual dimensions of competence loom large in both Japan and the United States, Japanese tend to be more sensitive to the role of attitudinal and interpersonal qualities.

THE ACQUISITION OF COMPETENCE

The different amount of weight placed on nonintellectual aspects of competence in Japan and the United States leads to divergent assumptions about how best to help novices increase their competence, with implications for the structuring of real-world educational contexts in both countries. Specifically, Japanese tend to place greater emphasis on the concurrent development of socioemotional characteristics, whereas Americans tend to focus attention on the timely acquisition of new content.

Acquiring Competence in Japan

There is a widely held assumption among Japanese that learning will be most effective in the long run if skills and knowledge are acquired gradually, in the course of participating in relevant activities. By this view, if learners stick with an activity for the long haul, relevant skills will become more and more automatic, eventually leading to mastery. Learning is believed to proceed best within an emotionally close master–apprentice-style relationship, with both parties participating wholeheartedly in the educational process. Ideally, it begins with *minarai kikan*, a period of learning through watching during which the expert draws the novice onto the right path by modeling what is appropriate, while the novice actively emulates the expert. Although this relationship-focused approach requires more time and persistence than direct instruction, many Japanese favor it because it gives learners the psychological space to develop their own personal understandings, which is believed to produce an internal attitude of deep, sincere commitment to the correct way of doing things. At the same time, this approach also is thought to instill other desirable attitudinal qualities like discipline, persistence, and self-reflection, alongside intellectual content.

This model of the learning process is put into practice across a range of Japanese settings (Hori, 1994). Carpentry training, for instance, traditionally commenced with an extended period during which the apprentice was assigned menial tasks and was taught nothing about carpentry. When formal training finally began, however, the novice was expected already to have acquired a great deal of relevant knowledge. The training of modern sushi chefs follows in this pattern as well. Similarly, *Rinzai* Zen monks are expected to become competent in all aspects of monastery life without being taught. They are meant to arrive at spiritual understandings through spontaneous insight during meditation, and, even if assigned to communal roles like cook, they are expected to gain competence solely through practice and other monks' complaints. Understanding gained through instruction is viewed as comparatively superficial.

This educational approach also extends beyond vocational domains. For example, the Kumon method, a widely used supplemental system for studying mathematics in Japan, also emphasizes spontaneous insight and learning-through-doing (Russell, 1994). Learners are assigned numerous repetitive worksheets and are expected to discover their own strategies for solving the problems in the course of completing them. The role of the teacher is not to instruct, but rather to assign worksheets at an appropriate pace while motivating students by acknowledging incremental advancement. Otherwise, teachers try to avoid "interfering with" students' learning. In the same vein, the Suzuki method for studying music incorporates emulation and huge amounts of practice (Peak, 1986). Students begin by incorporating music into the mother–child relationship, listening repeatedly to tape recordings and observing other students' lessons together with their mothers. Finally, their own lessons begin in a group setting in which students are meant to observe one another to pick up relevant points. It is expected that simple passages will be repeated until they have become automatic. The developer of the Suzuki method maintains that its primary goal is to enhance character by instilling diligence and persistence. Such pacing also is typical of traditional extracurricular activities like calligraphy and abacus training.

In sum, one prominent Japanese model of acquiring competence places observation, emulation, and an extended period of learning-through-doing at the heart of the educational process. Although explicit instruction may be recognized as an efficient way to convey content, it frequently is eschewed in favor of this more time-consuming, relationship-focused approach, which is believed to produce deeper levels of learning while also instilling a good mind-set toward relevant tasks. In Japan, the acquisition of competence is treated not as a purely intellectual enterprise, but rather as a process that should incorporate attitudinal and interpersonal components as well.

Acquiring Competence in the United States

Like Japanese, Americans also recognize that learning can occur in the absence of explicit instruction. The ongoing furor over children's exposure to television violence (Bushman & Anderson, 2001), for example, illustrates how seriously observational learning is taken in the United States. Yet whereas Japanese frequently view observation-sans-instruction as the ideal path to competence, Americans tend to feel more comfortable placing their faith in the power of direct explanation, seeing it as a more efficient and reliable way to acquire new information. Rather than waiting for emulation and active engagement to run their course, Americans are more likely to favor getting right down to business in a way that promotes rapid advancement. Although attitudinal qualities and socioemotional bonds are seen as important, their development is considered tangential to the acquisition of competence per se.

When the Suzuki and Kumon methods were brought from Japan to the United States, for instance, it was necessary to modify them in ways that would accommodate American assumptions about teaching and learning (Peak, 1986; Russell, 1994). In general, American parents and students are oriented toward accomplishing the functional task at hand rather than character-building. Indeed, Kumon centers have suffered from comparatively high dropout rates in the United States because of a tendency for Americans to focus on short-term objectives like raising a grade. Americans also have tended to measure progress by rate of advancement through new material, rather than quality of performance. For example, whereas Japanese Suzuki parents were comfortable with learners imitating a model and practicing simple material to perfection, American parents wanted them to be taught to read music and assigned more advanced pieces as soon as they were capable of giving them a try. Some American Kumon parents even found repetition so superfluous that they assumed its only purpose was to collect extra tuition. In addition, many Suzuki parents in the United States also were impatient with the group-learning format, believing that one-on-one instruction was key to children's success and relatively little was gained by having learners observe each other. These two case studies of cross-cultural transfer illustrate the way in which many Americans tend to favor explicit teaching and prompt presentation of new content. Although emulation may be seen as important, it typically is not considered the ideal path to acquiring competence.

COMPETENT CHILD REARING

One important domain in which assumptions about the acquisition of competence play out in everyday life is child rearing. Americans and Japanese share the belief that mothers should scaffold children's growth toward competence by helping them learn to function effectively in the world. Indeed, in both Japan and the United States, being a competent mother is bound up with raising a competent child.

Being a Competent Japanese Mother

Just as many Japanese tend to believe that learners will achieve a deeper, more sincere level of understanding by being given the space to gain personal insight, so many Japanese consider desirable developmental outcomes to be more likely if young children are allowed to converge with societal standards on their own. Japanese child-care experts have advised parents for centuries to avoid direct teaching until children already had absorbed basic knowledge. Instead, parents should provide children first with an opportunity to observe and then with an opportunity to imitate a task in its entirety once they seemed ready. Corrections were to be avoided early on because improvement would come with practice, and when feedback was offered it should focus not on behavior, but on the child's attitude (Hara & Wagatsuma, 1974; Kojima, 1986). The 13th-century *noh* master Zeami, for instance, maintained that children raised in families of *noh* theater players should not be encouraged to learn the art until they began to imitate spontaneously, and even then parents should avoid evaluative comments (Azuma, 1986).

In children's early years, Japanese parents therefore tend to be oriented primarily toward instilling the socioemotional prerequisites of competence rather than knowledge or skills as such. In particular, Japanese mothers tend to focus on cultivating interpersonal receptivity and an engaged, devoted attitude in the child. Such a mind-set is viewed as the foundation of later learning in that it encourages children to open up to the thinking of others, thereby enhancing their educability. To that end, mothers try to behave like a close ally or playmate, minimizing status differences by downplaying their authority. For instance, Japanese mothers are more likely than Americans to give in when children persist in resisting their efforts (Conroy, Hess, Azuma, & Kashiwagi, 1980). At the same time, Japanese mothers do their best to maximize shared empathy by creating a warm, stimulating interpersonal environment. Moreover, even Japanese preschool and elementary school teachers share this relationship-focused approach (Holloway, 2000; Lewis, 1995). It is assumed that once children become open to the thinking of other people, rudimentary competence will blossom naturally and incrementally. Indeed, when children do show signs of developmental progress, their accomplishments are viewed not merely as an indication of personal ability, but also as evidence that they have begun to become responsive to the socializing milieu (White & LeVine, 1986).

Many of the qualities that Japanese parents desire most in children are those that indicate a willingness to open up to others in this way. First and foremost, parents want children to be *ningen-rashii* (human being-like), a quality that entails the ability to maintain smooth relationships with other people (White & LeVine, 1986). More specifically, parents want their children to be empathetic, cooperative, and open, while also being self-controlled and self-reflective (Hess, Kashiwagi, Azuma, Price, & Dickson, 1980; White, 1987). One oft-mentioned quality of an *ii ko* (good child) is being *sunao*, which means pleasantly receptive to adult input and easy to get along with, but which is frequently translated as "obedient." Another desired quality is *oriko*, which also tends to be translated as "obedient," but literally means "smart," implying that the child is intelligent enough to know how to listen (White & LeVine, 1986). In one study, for instance, learning sympathy, empathy, and concern for others was listed by 80% of Japanese as a top reason for a society to have preschools, versus only 39% of Americans (Tobin, Wu, & Davidson, 1989). In an opinion survey in which 500 Japanese and 500 American mothers were asked to rank-order 13 potentially desirable qualities of children (Sorifu, 1981), for instance, 38% of Japanese mothers placed "following instructions" among the top three, as opposed to only 10% of American mothers. Having a patient, diligent attitude also was included by 32% of Japanese, versus only 20% of Americans.

A "competent" mainstream Japanese mother therefore encourages interpersonal awareness. For instance, Japanese mothers have been found to actively promote empathy and helpfulness by orienting their preschool children to the thoughts and needs of other people (Clancy, 1986). When urging children to do something, Japanese mothers also are more likely than Americans to draw children's attention toward consequences and other people's feelings (Conroy et al., 1980). Similarly, during relaxed play Japanese mothers are more likely to engage infants in social routines, such as exchanging greetings and physically passing objects back and forth (Fernald & Morikawa, 1993). Japanese mothers also have been found to spend more time than Americans highlighting interpersonal aspects of a dyadic problem-solving task, such as shared experiences and emotions; indeed, Japanese mothers spent comparatively little time focusing on solving the problem itself (Azuma, Kashiwagi, & Hess, 1981).

At the same time, mainstream Japanese mothers also tend to downplay explicit instruction. Japanese parents generally are less willing than Americans to take up the role of teacher, feeling that the best way for them to help their young children is to show an interest in their activities and keep them healthy (Stevenson & Stigler, 1992). As early as infancy, Japanese mothers are less likely than Americans to label objects during free play (Fernald & Morikawa, 1993). Later on, they also are relatively unlikely to teach young children linguistic symbols, numbers, and shapes. For instance, Japanese parents make fewer attempts than Americans to teach four-year-olds to read. Indeed, many Japanese parents report making no attempts at all and expecting children to learn to read *shizen-ni*, naturally (Hess & Azuma, 1991). Strikingly, most Japanese children nevertheless acquire these skills before starting school, already outperforming Americans by the first grade (Stevenson & Stigler, 1992). Japanese mothers also were found to provide relatively little direct instruction in a block-sorting task, instead producing speech that focused on engaging children and orienting their attention. They emphasized attitude, urging children to take a careful, deliberate approach to the problem, to examine it more closely and consider it more carefully. The task tended to be framed as an engaging game rather than a quiz, with mothers rarely stating the correct answer. Japanese mothers seemed comparatively less concerned than Americans with getting children to learn the underlying abstract concepts, and more concerned with having them physically engage in the task (Azuma et al., 1981). In summary, Japanese child rearing in the early years focuses primarily on instilling the socioemotional characteristics that are considered to be the bedrock of later competence. Indeed, the Japanese Ministry of Education itself has stated officially that preschooling should focus not on academic preparation, but on helping children establish proper relationships and good personal habits and attitudes (Peak, 1992).

Being a Competent American Mother

Because Americans tend to have somewhat different assumptions about the nature of competence and how it should be acquired, an alternate approach to child rearing is prevalent in the United States. In the same way that Americans generally prefer for learners to advance quickly through new material, so American parents tend to feel that the sooner children start to act more like little adults, the better (Fujita & Sano, 1988). Independent behaviors like first sitting up on one's own and taking one's first step alone popularly are viewed as important developmental accomplishments, and it is not uncommon for American parents to shame older children into self-sufficiency in achieving everyday tasks through expressions like, "You can do that by yourself now—you're a big girl!" (White, 1987). Indeed, independent functioning seems to be treated as a goal for which children are meant to strive, and although developmental readiness may be a limiting factor, it is best that children accomplish what they are capable of in a timely way.

Many of the characteristics that American parents value in young children reflect such a willingness to stand on their own two feet. In the survey described earlier (Sorifu, 1981), 42% of American mothers included independence and leadership among their three most desired qualities of children, versus only 24% of Japanese. Americans also desire that children be verbally assertive (e.g., asking for explanations when in doubt) and that they take the initiative in playing with peers. Furthermore, American mothers expect children to demonstrate these qualities at an earlier age than Japanese mothers do (Hess et al., 1980; White & LeVine, 1986).

As in other learning contexts, Americans tend to believe that the best way to facilitate prompt development is to provide children with clear explanations and direct instruction. The underlying assumption seems to be that children's acquisition of knowledge and skills is contingent on the amount of explicit teaching they receive. This approach casts the parent in the role of teacher and the young child in the role of student, with a clear distinction in status and competence between the two. The child is meant to assimilate new information, whereas the parent is meant to impart it and monitor the child's progress. Because of this emphasis on information transfer, there typically is heavy reliance on dialogue and verbal exchange.

A "competent" mainstream American mother therefore uses language to provide children with direct instruction from an early age. In particular, many American parents focus on teaching children academic and verbal skills. In fact, half of American parents believe that the best way to help their kindergartners is by fostering academic activities, and more than half believe that providing an academic head start is a top reason for a society to have preschools. Among Japanese, by contrast, the corresponding rates were only 2% and less than 1%, respectively (Stevenson & Stigler, 1992; Tobin, Wu, & Davidson, 1989). In line with this belief, 91% of Americans report reading to their preschoolers, versus only 68% of Japanese mothers. Similarly, 90% of American mothers report teaching numbers and linguistic symbols to their kindergartners at home, whereas the corresponding rates in Japan were 36% and under 33%, respectively (Stevenson & Stigler, 1992). Indeed, in one study, most American parents could describe more than two methods that they used to teach reading to their four-year-olds, such as using alphabet blocks to spell words (Azuma, 1994). And in the block-sorting task mentioned earlier (Azuma et al., 1981), Americans tended to provide children with step-by-step verbal instructions for sorting the blocks, framing the task as a quiz, and offering suggestions aimed at helping them arrive promptly at the right answer. American mothers also were more likely than Japanese to request a verbal statement from the child indicating that a concept had been grasped. Indeed, even in infancy, American mothers tend to provide labels for objects relatively more frequently and consistently than Japanese mothers do (Fernald & Morikawa, 1993). Overall, then, American child rearing in the early years emphasizes children's timely acquisition of new information and ability to accomplish tasks independently.

In sum, Japanese and American assumptions about competence and its acquisition lead to somewhat divergent patterns of child rearing. In Japan, mothers are likely to eschew direct teaching in the early years, focusing instead on instilling the interpersonal awareness and actively engaged attitude that are considered to underlie later learning. In the United States, by contrast, mothers are more likely to get right down to the business of teaching children verbal skills and intellectual content through dialogue and direct instruction.

Maternal Competence in Dyadic Interaction

A fine-grained analysis of the speech produced by four American and four Japanese mothers during free play with their three-year-olds (two boys and two girls from each culture, matched on various demographic measures, each with a mean age of three years three months) explored how these divergent views of maternal competence play out in the daily lives of young children (Shapiro, Ho, & Fernald, 2001). Mother–child dyads in the San Francisco and Kyoto areas were visited at home and videotaped playing freely with semistandardized sets of tea party toys and supermarket toys. Coding focused on maternal directives, defined as maternal speech intended to influence a child's verbal or physical behavior. Although the results from this small sample cannot be taken as definitive, these data provide a revealing window into the way in which maternal assumptions about early learning enter into children's everyday experience.

The noted American emphasis on information exchange between two distinct parties manifested itself during free play as a tendency for American mothers to request information from children more frequently than did Japanese mothers. Although both Americans and Japanese requested similar amounts of information during tea party play, with about 20% of maternal directives consisting of questions, Americans diverged significantly from this baseline up to a rate of 40% during supermarket play, whereas Japanese remained at around 20% $F(1, 6) = 10.22, p < .02$. At the same time, the American tendency toward encouraging academic and verbal skills in the early years was manifest as a tendency for American mothers to orient children's attention toward intellectual tasks like remembering, counting, evaluating, or processing new information. Across both kinds of play, 68% of American directives consisted of cognition-focused utterances like "What goes in a smoothie?" or "What's this?" whereas only 44% of Japanese directives focused on intellectual concerns, $F(1, 6) = 9.72, p < .05$. Moreover, across both kinds of play, 84% of American directives were aimed at getting children to either think about something or say something; only 16% prompted them to carry out some physical action.

Conversely, the noted Japanese emphasis on active engagement manifested itself across both kinds of play as a tendency for Japanese mothers to produce more directives prompting children to physically carry out some physical action, such as "Do you want to go shopping?" or "Eggs are fragile, so put them on top." This highly significant cross-cultural contrast, $F(1, 6) = 15.32$, $p < .01$, reflects the fact that Japanese mothers were much more balanced than Americans in the kind of child behavior that they targeted, producing a roughly 50–50 ratio of intellectual to physical directives. In addition, the Japanese preference for encouraging interpersonal awareness in the early years seemed to be manifest in a tendency for Japanese mothers to produce more directives that oriented children's attention toward interpersonal concerns like moral standards, social scripts, and social conventions. Among Japanese, 30% of directives were of this type, such as "She's thirsty, too" or "You should cut your cake with a fork like this," whereas among Americans, only 17% of directives included any focus on social concerns. However, this trend did not achieve significance.

This set of findings on mother–child interaction provides a snapshot of several ways in which assumptions about teaching and learning tend to be made concrete in the patterns of American and Japanese children's everyday experience. However, within-culture variation exists in both countries as well, particularly across different socioeconomic groups. The patterns described here are best representative of American and Japanese parents in cosmopolitan areas who are fairly well-educated and at least comfortably middle class. Yet despite the presence of intracultural variability, these general tendencies have been linked to the rearing of competent children in the United States and Japan.

COMPETENCE IN THE EARLY YEARS

American and Japanese parents agree that once children reach school age, scholastic performance is an important competence. Indeed, many see success in school as children's main real-world task. To the extent that mothers' competence in early child rearing can be measured by their children's subsequent scholastic performance, mothers who align with the culturally preferred pattern during the preschool years can in a sense be seen as more successful.

In Japan, where mainstream parents tend to encourage an engaged, diligent attitude in young children, Japanese four-year-olds already show more of this quality than Americans (Hess & Azuma, 1991). In a task in which preschoolers were instructed to draw a circle as slowly as possible, for instance, Japanese took an average of 16.5 seconds, whereas Americans took only 11.5 seconds. Similarly, in a task in which preschoolers were asked to choose the figure that corresponded to a model from among several distractors, Japanese took an average of 76.5 seconds to make their first choice, whereas Americans took only 57.5 seconds, and Japanese also made significantly fewer errors. Analogous results were found in a cross-modal matching task. Furthermore, demonstrating this kind of patient, diligent attitude in preschool was found to predict later scholastic competence among Japanese children ($r = .56$), although not among Americans.

The interpersonal receptivity cultivated by mainstream Japanese mothers in the early years also was found to pay off later in terms of academic competence. In both Japan and the United States, a variety of variables that related to maternal interaction style at preschool age correlated with school readiness at age 5 to 6. In Japan, however, many of these variables continued to affect school performance as strongly or more strongly six to seven years later, even after the effects of school readiness had been partialled out (Azuma, 1994). In particular, Japanese mothers' sensitivity and responsiveness to their children, assessed across a variety of tasks, correlated with fourth- to sixth-grade scores in Japanese language, math, science, and social studies, with rs ranging from .25 to .40. They also correlated with gym class grades, suggesting an attitudinal rather than intellectual mediator. Among Americans, in contrast, no correlations emerged for maternal interaction style at either age 5 to 6 or age 11 to 12.

Even more strikingly, Japanese mothers' aspirations for their preschoolers' ultimate educational attainment (e.g., attending graduate school), showed a partial correlation of .42 with children's school performance at age 11 to 12 (along with a correlation of .33 at age 5 to 6), whereas among Americans, mothers' aspirations related directly to scholastic competence only at age 5 to 6 ($r = .54$). The enduring influence of the mother–preschooler relationship in Japan as compared with the United States suggests that the early socioemotional bond cultivated by Japanese mothers comes to permeate children's academic outlook, affecting their later work habits for the better. In fact, making mother happy was found to be one of Japanese fifth graders' top reasons for doing well on exams.

In the United States, where mainstream parents tend to encourage independence and initiative in young children, preschoolers' independence and originality in an unstructured task has been linked to their scholastic competence at age 11 to 12 ($r = .39$). Mainstream American mothers also tend to favor explicit teaching, and mothers' clarity of instruction in the block-sorting task was in fact found to correlate with children's later academic achievement. Neither of these relationships was obtained in Japan, however (Hess & Azuma, 1991).

Indeed, somewhat counterintuitively from an American point of view, the degree of importance that Japanese mothers assigned to direct teaching actually correlated negatively with children's grades in fourth grade math, science, social studies, and Japanese language (with *r*s ranging from –.26 to –.30). Similarly, the extent to which they labeled objects in the block-sorting task and in a picture-naming task correlated negatively with children's Japanese language scores in fourth grade ($r = -.46$). Instead, what correlated positively with later math, science, and social studies scores was the importance that Japanese mothers assigned to children's social skills (with *r*s ranging from .30 to .34). These findings probably are confounded with effects of socioeconomic status, because many lower-income Japanese families view explicit teaching as a pathway to upward mobility for their children. Nevertheless, these results indicate that the positive association between direct teaching and early learning frequently taken for granted by Americans does not necessarily obtain in all cultural contexts.

Thus, whereas Americans mothers' efforts to encourage independence and explicitly teach intellectual content constitutes a successful strategy for rearing scholastically competent children in the United States, Japanese mothers' avoidance of explicit teaching and encouragement of desirable interpersonal and attitudinal qualities offers an alternate, equally successful path to academic competence in Japan.

COMPETENCE ACROSS THE LIFE SPAN

The intellectual, interpersonal, and attitudinal qualities that American and Japanese mothers encourage in young children continue to be central aspects of competence across all stages of life. As part of a larger cross-cultural project, Karasawa and Azuma studied characteristics of the ideal self in Americans and Japanese of various ages. In individually tailored home interviews, participants were shown the list of twenty positive personal characteristics displayed in Exhibit 8.1 and were asked, "What sort of person would you like to be? Looking at this list, choose as many as you like."

After participants had made their choices, they were further asked, "Out of all you have circled, select the three you think are most important." Each item ranked among the top three received two points, and all other selected items received one point. In total, 1,562 Americans in the Detroit area and 1,842 Japanese in the Yokohama area participated. Participants were aged 9 through 92, roughly balanced by gender. (Data from participants under age 12 are not included here due to a different method of data collection.)

In the first selection, Americans showed a strong tendency to choose more items than did Japanese. Hence, most items received more average points from Americans than from Japanese at almost every age level. Exceptions were items 12, 16, and 19, which were favored more heavily by Japanese, leading to point averages that were about equal across cultures. As a result of this baseline difference in item scores in the United States and Japan, subsequent data analyses relied on intracultural rank-ordering of items.

EXHIBIT 8.1
Twenty Desirable Personal Characteristics

1. Someone who follows rules.
2. Someone who is good at sports.
3. Someone who is gentle and kind.
4. Someone who is good at studying.
5. Someone who is popular.
6. Someone who is good at music and arts.
7. Someone who is doing his or her job well.
8. Someone who fights against social injustice.
9. Someone who is never afraid to say what he or she thinks right.
10. Someone who is physically attractive.
11. Someone who is respected by society.
12. Someone who understands people's feelings, who is empathetic.
13. Someone who is self-reliant.
14. Someone who looks after others.
15. Someone who thinks deeply about things.
16. Someone who is a cheerful person.
17. Someone who is smart.
18. Someone who is trustworthy.
19. Someone who is a warm-hearted person.
20. Someone who is working for the good of the world.

Among participants aged 13 to 18, Americans gave the highest ratings to items 17, 18, 7, 4, and 13 (in that order), whereas Japanese gave the highest ratings to items 3, 18, 12, 5 and 19. Americans in this age range gave the lowest ratings to items 16, 12, 6, 8, and 14, whereas the lowest-ranked Japanese items were 8, 13, 15, 20, and 1. One of the top-ranked items among Japanese, being empathetic, was among the bottom five for Americans, whereas one of the top-ranked items for Americans, being self-reliant, was among the bottom five for Japanese. The only item to make the top five in both cultures was being trustworthy, perhaps because this characteristic includes both a performance aspect and a relationship aspect.

Table 8.1 presents the top five choices for participants above age 18 in both countries. The intracultural consistency across the adult age groups is striking, indicating that the findings are robust. Such stability suggests that the personal qualities individuals desire for themselves are reflective of a set of characteristics that the larger society values in its members more generally. Every adult age group in both countries chose items 18 and 3, showing that Americans and Japanese resemble one another in certain regards. However, the consistent prevalence of items 7, 9, and 13 in the United States versus that of items 12, 16, and 19 in Japan points to cross-cultural divergence as well. Overall, in line with noted asymmetries in the idea of competence, Americans tended to favor items related to independence and accomplishing tasks, whereas Japanese tended to favor items related to interpersonal warmth.

There is some indication that interpersonal qualities may become an even more important aspect of Japanese competence in the later stages of

TABLE 8.1
Top Five Important Personality Attributes Selected by
Americans and Japanese Participants, by Age Group

	United States				Japan			
Rank	19–30	30–50	51–65	65+	19–30	31–50	51–65	65+
1.	18	18	18	18	12	12	18	3
2.	7	7	3	3	18	18	3	18
3.	13	3	7	7	3	19	19	19
4.	9	13	13	13	19	3	16	12
5.	3	9	9	9	16	16	13	1

life. Karasawa and Azuma (1992) studied how descriptors of intelligent people fluctuated by age in Japan, asking participants to rate how well 23 descriptors fit a particular intelligent person. Five factors emerged in a factor analysis, including a Receptive Social Competence factor characterized by sympathy, kindness, and modesty. This was the second most important factor among participants aged 51 to 65, and rose to become the most important factor among participants aged 66 to 92. This increase in importance may reflect the fact that one of the roles elderly people are expected to take on in Japan is that of maintaining interpersonal harmony.

Although Japanese do show a strikingly consistent tendency to emphasize interpersonal qualities across the life span, this stability does not necessarily entail within-culture uniformity. A separate analysis of the Japanese rank-order data that compared men to women (Kojima & Azuma, 1991) found that although interpersonal warmth was emphasized by both genders, subtle variation was evident as well. Among Japanese women, the top four items related to empathy and emotional warmth at all age levels. Among Japanese men, however, the top item was the more task-oriented quality of trustworthiness, which women ranked only fifth. These results suggest that Japanese participants' rankings incorporated role expectations that are gender-bound. Table 8.2 displays the top five choices for Japanese participants, by gender. (Age categories are slightly different from those above because this analysis was carried out prior to the creation of a standard age categorization scheme.) Considered together, these Japanese and American data underscore the fact that within-culture variability and cross-cultural similarity can coexist peacefully alongside cross-culture divergence in the understanding of competence.

CONCLUSION

This chapter has addressed several important aspects of competence in Japan, using the United States as a point of comparison. We have shown

TABLE 8.2
Top Five Important Personality Attributes Selected by Japanese Participants, by Gender and Age Group

Rank	Females				Males			
	19–30	30–50	51–65	65+	19–30	31–50	51–65	65+
1.	12	12	12	12	12	18	18	18
2.	16	19	19	3	18	12	7	19
3.	3	16	16	19	3	19	12	12
4.	19	3	3	16	19	16	19	3
5.	18	18	18	18	16	7	16	16

that Japanese, like Americans, treat intellectual qualities as being central to the meaning of competence. Among Japanese, however, interpersonal and attitudinal qualities are given substantial weight as well. In both countries, beliefs about the nature of competence lead to culture-specific assumptions about the ideal way for teaching and learning to proceed, and these assumptions are made concrete across a range of culturally patterned educational settings, including parent–child interaction. Raising a child in accordance with the culturally preferred pattern of one's society appears to promote later scholastic competence in both Japanese and American children, and the competence-related characteristics that parents encourage in children early-on continue to be valued across the entire life span. Overall, although Japanese and American ideas about competence do bear some similarity to one another and within-group variability also exists, juxtaposing the assumptions and practices of these two cultures highlights the fact that achieving success in many real-world tasks depends not only on the mind, but on the heart as well.

REFERENCES

Azuma, H. (1986). Why study child development in Japan? In H. Stevenson, H. Azuma, & K. Hakuta (Eds.), *Child development and education in Japan* (pp. 3–12). New York: Freeman.

Azuma, H. (1994). Two modes of cognitive socialization in Japan and the United States. In P. M. Greenfield & R. R. Cocking (Eds.), *Cross-cultural roots of minority child development* (275–284). Hillsdale, NJ: Erlbaum.

Azuma, H., & Kashiwagi, K. (1987). Descriptors of an intelligent person: A Japanese study. *Japanese Psychological Research, 29,* 17–26.

Azuma, H., Kashiwagi, K., & Hess, R. D. (1981). *Hahaoya no taido koudo to kodomo no chiteki hattatsu* [The influence of the mother's attitude and behavior upon the child's intellectual development]. Tokyo: University of Tokyo Press.

Azuma, H., Kashiwagi, K., & Ohno, H. (1990). A Japan–U. S. comparison of the relationships between behavior characteristics and judgment of intelligence (an interim report). *Human Development Research: Center of Developmental Education and Research Annual Report, 6,* 47–62.

Bushman, B. J., & Anderson, C. A. (2001). Media violence and the American public: Scientific facts versus media misinformation. *American Psychologist, 56,* 477–489.

Clancy, P. M. (1986). The acquisition of communicative style in Japanese. In B. B. Schieffelin & E. Ochs (Eds.), *Language socialization across cultures* (pp. 213–250). New York: Cambridge University Press.

Conroy, M., Hess, R. D., Azuma, H., & Kashiwagi, K. (1980). Maternal strategies for regulating children's behavior: Japanese and American families. *Journal of Cross-Cultural Psychology, 11,* 153–172.

Fernald, A., & Morikawa, H. (1993). Common themes and cultural variations in Japanese and American mothers' speech to infants. *Child Development, 64,* 637–656.

Fujita, M., & Sano, T. (1988). Children in American and Japanese day-care centers: Ethnography and reflective cross-cultural interviewing. In H. T. Trueba & C. Delgado-Gaitan (Eds.), *School and society: Learning content through culture* (pp. 73–97). New York: Praeger Publishers.

Hara, H., & Wagatsuma, H. (1974). *Shitsuke* [Socializing discipline]. Tokyo: Kobundo.

Hess, R. D., & Azuma, H. (1991). Cultural support for schooling: Contrasts between Japan and the United States. *Educational Researcher, 20,* 2–8.

Hess, R. D., Kashiwagi, K., Azuma, H., Price, G. G., & Dickson, W. P. (1980). Maternal expectations for mastery of developmental tasks in Japan and the United States. *International Journal of Psychology, 15,* 259–271.

Holloway, S. (2000). *Contested childhood: Diversity and change in Japanese preschools.* Routledge.

Hori, G. V. S. (1994). Teaching and learning in the Rinzai Zen monastery. *Journal of Japanese Studies, 20,* 5–34.

Karasawa, M., & Azuma, H. (1992). The life course development of the concept of an "intelligent person." *Human Development Research: Center of Developmental Education and Research Annual Report, 8,* 155–161.

Kawai, H. (1982). *Mukashibanashi to nihonnjinn no kokoro* [Folk tales and the Japanese mind]. Tokyo: Iwanami Shoten.

Kojima, H. (1986). Child rearing concepts as a belief–value system of the society and the individual. In H. Stevenson, H. Azuma, & K. Hakuta (Eds.), *Child development and education in Japan* (pp. 39–54). New York: Freeman.

Kojima, A., & Azuma, H. (1991). Life-course development of the ideal self: Japanese subjects. *Human Development Research: Center of Developmental Education and Research Annual Report, 7,* 105–114.

Lewis, C. C. (1995). *Educating hearts and minds.* New York: Cambridge University Press.

Mashima, M. (1998). *Daigakusei no mokuhyo kozo to shorai tembo* [The goal structure and future perspective of college students: A U.S.–Japan comparison]. Unpublished doctoral dissertation, Shirayuri College, Tokyo.

Mashima, M., Shapiro, L., & Azuma, H. (1998). Sakubun kadai ni yoru mokuhyou kouzou to shourai tenbou ni kansuru kenkyu: "Mokuteki wo motte doryoku shita koto" no nichibei hikaku (chuukan houkoku) [Research on goal structure and future time perspective in an essay task: A U.S.–Japan comparison of "conscious goal-directed efforts" (an interim report)]. *Human Development Research, Journal of the Center of Developmental Education and Research, 13*, 106–118.

Oe, M., Allard, J., & Fujinaga, T. (1989). A cross-cultural study of the concept of "intelligent person:" IV. French and English Canadian and Japanese concepts. *Human Development Research: Center of Developmental Education and Research Annual Report, 5*, 223–242.

Peak, L. (1986). The Suzuki Method of music instruction. In M. White & S. Pollak (Eds.), *The cultural transition: Human experience and social transformation in the third world and Japan* (pp. 345–368). Boston: Routledge & Kegan Paul.

Peak, L. (1992). *Learning to go to school in Japan.* Berkeley: University of California Press.

Russell, N. U. (1994). The Kumon approach to teaching and learning. *Journal of Japanese Studies, 20*, 87–110.

Shapiro, L. J., Ho, K., & Fernald, A. (2001). Mother-child interaction and the creation of a culturally distinct environment: An American–Japanese comparison. Unpublished manuscript, Stanford University, Stanford, California.

Sorifu [Prime Minister's Office]. (1981). *Children and mothers of Japan.* Tokyo: Bureau of Printing of the Ministry of Finance.

Sternberg, R. J., Conway, B. E., Ketron, J. L., & Bernstein, M. (1981). People's conceptions of intelligence. *Journal of Personality and Social Psychology, 41*, 37–55.

Stevenson, H. W., & Stigler, J. W. (1992). *The learning gap: Why our schools are failing and what we can learn from Japanese and Chinese education.* New York: Simon & Schuster.

Tobin, J. J., Wu, D. Y. H., & Davidson, D. H. (1989). *Preschool in three cultures: Japan, China, and the United States.* New Haven, CT: Yale University Press.

Weisz, J. R., Rothbaum, F. M., & Blackburn, T. C. (1984). Standing out and standing in: Psychology of control in America and Japan. *American Psychologist, 39*, 955–969.

White, M. I. (1987). *The Japanese educational challenge: A commitment to children.* New York: Free Press.

White, M. I., & LeVine, R. A. (1986). What is an Ii Ko? In H. Stevenson, H. Azuma, & K. Hakuta (Eds.), *Child development and education in Japan* (pp. 55–62). New York: Freeman.

9

WHY CULTURAL PSYCHOLOGY IS NECESSARY AND NOT JUST NICE: THE EXAMPLE OF THE STUDY OF INTELLIGENCE

ROBERT J. STERNBERG AND ELENA L. GRIGORENKO

It is possible to live in a microworld without having much or any sense of what is going on in the macroworld at large. For example, for most of human history, diverse aggregations of people lived together but in splendid isolation from one another. Not only were they unaware of the similarities and differences among them but they were also not even aware that each other existed. In today's world, of course, such splendid isolation is impossible, at least in the developed world. Yet psychologists in the developed world often do research as though they were living in an isolated microworld with little or no contact with the other microworlds that together constitute the macroworld. Drawing universal conclusions from research in just one country, and often just a single culture within that country, constitutes such

Preparation of this book was supported by Grant REC-9979843 from the National Science Foundation and by a government grant under the Javits Act Program (Grant No. R206R000001) as administered by the Office of Educational Research and Improvement, U.S. Department of Education. Grantees undertaking such projects are encouraged to express freely their professional judgment. This article, therefore, does not necessarily represent the positions or the policies of any of the funding agencies.

isolation. This research continues despite pervasive evidence that people in different cultures think and act differently (e.g., Greenfield, 1997; Laboratory of Comparative Human Cognition, 1982; Nisbett, in press; Serpell, 2000). Consider, for example, expert conceptions of intelligence in the United States.

TWO SYMPOSIA ON AMERICAN EXPERT CONCEPTIONS OF INTELLIGENCE

Probably the most well-known study of American experts' definitions of intelligence was one done by the editors of the *Journal of Educational Psychology* ("Intelligence and its measurement," 1921). Contributors to the symposium were asked to address two issues: (a) what they conceived intelligence to be and how it best could be measured by group tests, and (b) what the most crucial next steps would be in research. Fourteen experts gave their views on the nature of intelligence, with paraphrased definitions such as the following:

- the power of good responses from the point of view of truth or facts (E. L. Thorndike);
- the ability to carry on abstract thinking (L. M. Terman);
- sensory capacity, capacity for perceptual recognition, quickness, range or flexibility of association, facility and imagination, span of attention, quickness or alertness in response (F. N. Freeman);
- having learned or ability to learn to adjust oneself to the environment (S. S. Colvin);
- the ability to adapt oneself adequately to relatively new situations in life (R. Pintner);
- the capacity for knowledge and knowledge possessed (B. A. C. Henmon);
- a biological mechanism by which the effects of a complexity of stimuli are brought together and given a somewhat unified effect in behavior (J. Peterson);
- the capacity to inhibit an instinctive adjustment, the capacity to redefine the inhibited instinctive adjustment in the light of imaginally experienced trial and error, and the capacity to realize the modified instinctive adjustment in overt behavior to the advantage of the individual as a social animal (L. L. Thurstone);
- the capacity to acquire capacity (H. Woodrow);
- the capacity to learn or to profit by experience (W. F. Dearborn); and
- sensation, perception, association, memory, imagination, discrimination, judgment, and reasoning (N. E. Haggerty).

Other contributors to the symposium did not provide clear definitions of intelligence but rather concentrated on how to test it. B. Ruml refused to present a definition of intelligence, arguing that not enough was known about the concept. S. L. Pressey described himself as uninterested in the question, although he became well known for his tests of intelligence.

Of course, there have been many definitions of intelligence since those represented in the journal symposium, and an essay even has been written on the nature of definitions of intelligence (Miles, 1957). One well-known set of definitions, also American, was published in 1986 explicitly as a follow-up to the 1921 symposium (Sternberg & Detterman, 1986).

Sternberg and Berg (1986) attempted a comparison of the views of the experts in 1986 (including P. Baltes, J. Baron, J. Berry, A. Brown, J. Campione, E. Butterfield, J. Carroll, J. P. Das, D. Detterman, W. Estes, H. Eysenck, H. Gardner, R. Glaser, J. Goodnow, J. Horn, L. Humphreys, E. Hunt, A. Jensen, J. Pellegrino, R. Schank, R. Snow, R. Sternberg, and E. Zigler) with those of the experts in 1921. They reached three general conclusions.

First, there was at least some general agreement across the two symposia regarding the nature of intelligence. When attributes were listed for frequency of mention in the two symposia, the correlation was .50, indicating moderate overlap. Attributes such as adaptation to the environment, basic mental processes, higher-order thinking (e.g., reasoning, problem solving, and decision making) were prominent in both symposia.

Second, central themes occurred in both symposia. One theme was the one versus the many: Is intelligence one thing or is it multiple things? How broadly should intelligence be defined? What should be the respective roles of biological versus behavioral attributes in seeking an understanding of intelligence?

Third, despite the similarities in views over the 65 years, some salient differences could also be found. Metacognition—conceived of as both knowledge about and control of cognition—played a prominent role in the 1986 symposium but virtually no role at all in the 1921 symposium. The later symposium also placed a greater emphasis on the role of knowledge and the interaction of mental processes with this knowledge.

LAY IMPLICIT THEORIES OF INTELLIGENCE AROUND THE WORLD

In some cases, Western notions about intelligence are not shared by other cultures. For example, at the mental level, the Western emphasis on speed of mental processing (Sternberg, Conway, Ketron, & Bernstein, 1981) is not shared in many cultures. Other cultures may even be suspicious of the quality of work that is done very quickly. Indeed, other cultures emphasize depth rather than speed of processing. They are not alone: Some prominent

Western theorists have pointed out the importance of depth of processing for full command of material (e.g., Craik & Lockhart, 1972).

Yang and Sternberg (1997a) have reviewed Chinese philosophical conceptions of intelligence. The Confucian perspective emphasizes the characteristic of benevolence and of doing what is right. As in the Western notion, the intelligent person spends a great deal of effort in learning, enjoys learning, and persists in lifelong learning with a great deal of enthusiasm. The Taoist tradition, in contrast, emphasizes the importance of humility, freedom from conventional standards of judgment, and full knowledge of oneself as well as of external conditions.

The difference between Eastern and Western conceptions of intelligence may persist even in the present day. Yang and Sternberg (1997b) studied contemporary Taiwanese Chinese conceptions of intelligence and found five factors underlying these conceptions: (a) a general cognitive factor, much like the g factor in conventional Western tests; (b) interpersonal intelligence; (c) intrapersonal intelligence; (d) intellectual self-assertion; and (d) intellectual self-effacement. In a related study but with different results, Chen (1994) found three factors underlying Chinese conceptualizations of intelligence: nonverbal reasoning ability, verbal reasoning ability, and rote memory. The difference may be due to different subpopulations of Chinese, differences in methodology, or differences in when the studies were done.

The factors uncovered in both studies differ substantially from those identified in U.S. people's conceptions of intelligence by Sternberg, Conway, Ketron, and Bernstein (1981)—which include (a) practical problem solving, (b) verbal ability, and (c) social competence—although in both cases, people's implicit theories of intelligence seem to go quite far beyond what conventional psychometric intelligence tests measure. Of course, comparing the Chen (1994) to the Sternberg and colleagues (1981) study simultaneously varies both language and culture.

Chen and Chen (1988) varied only language. They explicitly compared the concepts of intelligence of Chinese graduates from Chinese-language versus English-language schools in Hong Kong. They found that both groups considered nonverbal reasoning skills as the most relevant skill for measuring intelligence. Verbal reasoning and social skills came next, and then numerical skill. Memory was seen as least important. The Chinese-language-schooled group, however, tended to rate verbal skills as less important than did the English-language-schooled group. Moreover, in an earlier study, Chen, Braithwaite, and Huang (1982) found that Chinese students viewed memory for facts as important for intelligence, whereas Australian students viewed these skills as of only trivial importance.

Das (1994), also reviewing Eastern notions of intelligence, has suggested that in Buddhist and Hindu philosophies, intelligence involves waking up, noticing, recognizing, understanding, and comprehending, but also includes such things as determination, mental effort, and even feelings and opinions in addition to more intellectual elements.

Differences among cultures in conceptions of intelligence have been recognized for some time. Gill and Keats (1980) noted that Australian University students value academic skills and the ability to adapt to new events as critical to intelligence, whereas Malay students value practical skills, as well as speed and creativity. Dasen (1984) found that Malay students emphasize both social and cognitive attributes in their conceptions of intelligence.

The differences between East and West may be due to differences in the kinds of skills valued by the two kinds of cultures (Srivastava & Misra, 1996). Western cultures and their schools emphasize what might be called "technological intelligence" (Mundy-Castle, 1974), and so things like artificial intelligence and so-called smart bombs are viewed, in some sense, as intelligent or smart.

Western schooling also emphasizes other things (Srivastava & Misra, 1996), such as generalization or going beyond the information given (Connolly & Bruner, 1974; Goodnow, 1976), speed (Sternberg, 1985), minimal moves to a solution (Newell & Simon, 1972), and creative thinking (Goodnow, 1976). Moreover, silence is interpreted as a lack of knowledge (Irvine, 1978). In contrast, the Wolof tribe in Africa views people of higher social class and distinction as speaking less (Irvine, 1978). This difference between the Wolof and Western notions suggests the usefulness of looking at African notions of intelligence as a possible contrast to U.S. notions.

Studies in Africa in fact provide yet another window on the substantial differences. Ruzgis and Grigorenko (1994) have argued that, in Africa, conceptions of intelligence revolve largely around skills that help to facilitate and maintain harmonious and stable intergroup relations; intragroup relations are probably equally important and at times more important. For example, Serpell (1974, 1982, 1996) found that Chewa adults in Zambia emphasize social responsibilities, cooperativeness, and obedience as important to intelligence; intelligent children are expected to be respectful of adults. Kenyan parents also emphasize responsible participation in family and social life as important aspects of intelligence (Super & Harkness, 1982, 1986, 1993). In Zimbabwe, the word for intelligence, *ngware*, actually means to be prudent and cautious, particularly in social relationships. Among the Baoule, service to the family and community and politeness toward and respect for elders are seen as key to intelligence (Dasen, 1984).

Similar emphasis on social aspects of intelligence has been found as well among two other African groups, the Songhay of Mali and the Samia of Kenya (Putnam & Kilbride, 1980). The Yoruba, another African tribe, emphasize the importance of depth—of listening rather than just talking—to intelligence, and of being able to see all aspects of an issue and of being able to place the issue in its proper overall context (Durojaiye, 1993).

The emphasis on the social aspects of intelligence is not limited to African cultures. Notions of intelligence in many Asian cultures also emphasize the social aspect of intelligence more than does the conventional Western or IQ-based definition (Azuma & Kashiwagi, 1987; Lutz, 1985; Poole, 1985; White, 1985).

It should be noted that neither African nor Asian notions emphasize exclusively social notions of intelligence. These conceptions of intelligence much more emphasize social skills than do conventional conceptions of intelligence in the United States, at the same time that they recognize the importance of cognitive aspects of intelligence. In a study of Kenyan conceptions of intelligence (Grigorenko et al., 2001), it was found that there are four distinct terms constituting conceptions of intelligence among rural Kenyans—*rieko* (knowledge and skills), *luoro* (respect), *winjo* (comprehension of how to handle real-life problems), *paro* (initiative)—with only the first directly referring to knowledge-based skills (including but not limited to the academic).

It is important to realize, again, that there is no one overall conception of intelligence in the United States. Indeed, Okagaki and Sternberg (1993) found that different ethnic groups in San Jose, California, had rather different conceptions of what it means to be intelligent. For example, Latino parents of schoolchildren tended to emphasize the importance of social-competence skills in their conceptions of intelligence, whereas Asian parents tended rather heavily to emphasize the importance of cognitive skills. Anglo parents also more heavily emphasized cognitive skills. Teachers, representing the dominant culture, gave more emphasis to cognitive- than social-competence skills. The rank order of children of various groups' performance (including subgroups within the Latino and Asian groups) could be perfectly predicted by the extent to which their parents shared the teachers' conception of intelligence. In other words, teachers tended to reward those children who were socialized into a view of intelligence that happened to correspond to the teachers' own. Yet, as we shall argue later, social aspects of intelligence, broadly defined, may be as important as or even more important than cognitive aspects of intelligence in later life. Some, however, prefer to study intelligence not in its social aspect, but in its cognitive one.

EXPLICIT THEORETICAL INVESTIGATIONS OF INTELLIGENCE AROUND THE WORLD

Many times, investigations of intelligence conducted in settings outside the developed world can yield a picture of intelligence that is quite at variance with the picture one would obtain from studies conducted only in the developed world. In a study in Usenge, Kenya, near the town of Kisumu, Sternberg and his colleagues were interested in school-age children's ability to adapt to their indigenous environment. They devised a test of practical intelligence for adaptation to the environment (see Sternberg & Grigorenko,

1997; Sternberg, Nokes, et al., 2001). The test of practical intelligence measured children's informal tacit knowledge for natural herbal medicines that the villagers believe can be used to fight various types of infections. Children in the villages use their knowledge of these medicines an average of once a week in medicating themselves and others. Thus, tests of how to use these medicines constitute effective measures of one aspect of practical intelligence as defined by the villagers as well as their life circumstances in their environmental contexts. Middle-class Westerners might find it quite a challenge to thrive or even survive in these contexts, or, for that matter, in the contexts of urban ghettos often not distant from their comfortable homes.

The researchers measured the Kenyan children's ability to identify the medicines, where they come from, what they are used for, and how they are dosed. On the basis of work the researchers had done elsewhere, they expected that scores on this test would not correlate with scores on conventional tests of intelligence. To test this hypothesis, they also administered to the 85 children a measure of fluid or abstract-reasoning-based abilities, as well as a vocabulary scale, which was a measure of crystallized or formal-knowledge-based abilities. In addition, they gave the children a comparable test of vocabulary in their own Dholuo language. The Dholuo language is spoken in the home, English in the schools.

The researchers did indeed find no correlation between the test of indigenous tacit knowledge and scores on the fluid-ability tests. But to their surprise, they found statistically significant correlations of the tacit-knowledge tests with the tests of crystallized abilities. The correlations, however, were *negative*. In other words, the higher the children scored on the test of tacit knowledge, the lower they scored, on average, on the tests of crystallized abilities. This surprising result can be interpreted in various ways, but based on the ethnographic observations of the anthropologists on the team, Geissler and Prince, the researchers concluded that a plausible scenario takes into account the expectations of families for their children.

Many children drop out of school before graduation, for financial or other reasons, and many families in the village do not particularly value formal Western schooling. There is no reason they should, as the children of many families will for the most part spend their lives farming or engaged in other occupations that make little or no use of Western schooling. These families emphasize teaching their children the indigenous informal knowledge that will lead to successful adaptation in the environments in which they will live. Children who spend their time learning the indigenous practical knowledge of the community generally do not invest themselves heavily in doing well in school, whereas children who do well in school generally do not invest themselves as heavily in learning the indigenous knowledge— hence the negative correlations.

The Kenya study suggests that the identification of a general factor of human intelligence may tell us more about how abilities interact with patterns of schooling and especially Western patterns of schooling than it does about the structure of human abilities. In Western schooling, children typically study a variety of subject matters from an early age and thus develop skills in a variety of skill areas. This kind of schooling prepares the children to take a test of intelligence, which typically measures skills in a variety of areas. Often intelligence tests measure skills that children were expected to acquire a few years before taking the intelligence test. But as Rogoff (1990) and others have noted, this pattern of schooling is not universal and has not even been common for much of the history of humankind. Throughout history and in many places still, schooling, especially for boys, takes the form of apprenticeships in which children learn a craft from an early age. They learn what they will need to know to succeed in a trade, but not a lot more. They are not simultaneously engaged in tasks that require the development of the particular blend of skills measured by conventional intelligence tests. Hence it is less likely that one would observe a general factor in their scores, much as the investigators discovered in Kenya. Some years back, Vernon (1971) pointed out that the axes of a factor analysis do not necessarily reveal a latent structure of the mind but rather represent a convenient way of characterizing the organization of mental abilities. Vernon believed that there was no one right orientation of axes, and indeed, mathematically, an infinite number of orientations of axes can be fit to any solution in an exploratory factor analysis. Vernon's point seems perhaps to have been forgotten or at least ignored by later theorists.

We have found related although certainly not identical results in a study we have done among Yup'ik Eskimo children in southwestern Alaska (Grigorenko et al., 2002). We assessed the importance of academic and practical intelligence in rural and urban Alaskan communities. A total of 261 children were rated for practical skills by adults or peers in the study: 69 in 9th grade, 69 in 10th grade, 45 in 11th grade, and 37 in 12th grade. Of these children, 145 were girls and 116 were boys, and they were from seven different communities, six rural and one relatively urban. We measured academic intelligence with conventional measures of fluid and crystallized intelligence. We measured practical intelligence with a test of tacit knowledge as acquired in rural Alaskan Yup'ik communities. The urban children generally outperformed the rural children on a measure of crystallized intelligence, but the rural children generally outperformed the urban children on the measure of Yup'ik tacit knowledge. The test of tacit knowledge was superior to the tests of academic intelligence in predicting practical skills of the rural children (for whom the test was created), but not of the urban ones.

The test of practical intelligence developed for use in Kenya, as well as some of the other practically based tests described in this book, may seem more like tests of achievement or of developing expertise (see Ericsson, 1996; Howe, Davidson, & Sloboda, 1998) than of intelligence. But it can be argued that intelligence is itself a form of developing expertise and that there is no clear-cut distinction between the two constructs (Sternberg, 1998, 1999).

Indeed, all measures of intelligence, one might argue, measure a form of developing expertise.

An example of how tests of intelligence measure developing expertise rather than some fixed quantity emanates from work we have done with colleagues in Tanzania. One study (see Sternberg & Grigorenko, 1997, 2002; Sternberg, Grigorenko, et al., 2002) points out the risks of giving tests, scoring them, and interpreting the results as measures of some latent intellectual ability or abilities. The investigators administered to 358 school children between the ages of 11 and 13 years near Bagamoyo, Tanzania, tests including a form-board classification test, a linear syllogisms test, and a Twenty Questions Test, which measure the kinds of skills required on conventional tests of intelligence. Of course, the investigators obtained scores that they could analyze and evaluate, ranking the children in terms of their supposed general or other abilities. However, they administered the tests dynamically rather than statically (Brown & Ferrara, 1985; Budoff, 1968; Day, Engelhardt, Maxwell, & Bolig, 1997; Feuerstein, 1979; Grigorenko & Sternberg, 1998; Guthke, 1993; Haywood & Tzuriel, 1992; Lidz, 1987, 1991; Tzuriel, 1995; Vygotsky, 1978). Dynamic testing is like conventional static testing in that individuals are tested and inferences about their abilities made. But dynamic tests differ in that children are given some kind of feedback to help them improve their scores. Vygotsky (1978) suggested that the children's ability to profit from such guided instruction during the testing session could serve as a measure of children's zone of proximal development, or the difference between their developed abilities and their latent capacities. In other words, testing and instruction are treated as being of one piece rather than as being distinct processes. This integration makes sense in terms of traditional definitions of intelligence as the ability to learn ("Intelligence and its measurement," 1921; Sternberg & Detterman, 1986). What a dynamic test does is directly measure processes of learning in the context of testing rather than measuring these processes indirectly as the product of past learning. Such measurement is especially important if not all children have had equal opportunities to learn in the past.

In the assessments, children were first given the ability tests. Then they were given a brief period of instruction in which they were able to learn skills that would potentially enable them to improve their scores. Then they were tested again. Because the instruction for each test lasted only about 5 to 10 minutes, one would not expect dramatic gains. Yet, on average, the gains were statistically significant. More important, scores on the pretest showed only weak although significnt correlations with scores on the posttest. These correlations, at about the .3 level, suggested that if tests are administered statically to children in developing countries, they may be rather unstable and easily subject to influences of training. The reason could be that the children are not accustomed to taking Western-style tests, and so profit quickly even from small amounts of instruction as to what is expected from them. Of course, the more important question is not whether the scores changed or even correlated with each other, but rather how they correlated with other cognitive measures. In other words, which test was a better predictor of transfer to other cognitive performance, the pretest score or the posttest score? The investigators found the posttest score to be the better predictor.

In interpreting results, whether from developed or developing cultures, it is always important to take into account the physical health of the participants one is testing. In a study we did in Jamaica (Sternberg, Powell, McGrane, & McGregor, 1997), we found that Jamaican school children who experienced parasitic illnesses (for the most part, whipworm or Ascaris) did more poorly on higher-level cognitive tests (such as of working memory and reasoning) than did children who did not experience these illnesses, even after controlling for socioeconomic status. Why might such a physical illness cause a deficit in higher-level cognitive skills?

Ceci (1996) has shown that increased levels of schooling are associated with higher IQ. Why would there by such a relation? Presumably, in part, because schooling helps children develop the kinds of skills that are measured by IQ tests, and that are important in turn for survival in school. Children with whipworm-induced illnesses and related illnesses are less able to profit from school than are children without these illnesses. Every day they go to school, they are likely to be experiencing symptoms such as listlessness, stomachache, and difficulties in concentrating. These symptoms reduce the extent to which they are able to profit from instruction and in turn reduce their ultimate performance on higher-level cognitive tests.

Crystallized-ability tests, such as tests of vocabulary and general information, certainly measure developing and already-developed knowledge bases. Available data suggest that fluid-ability tests, such as tests of abstract reasoning, measure developing and developed expertise even more strongly than do crystallized-ability tests. Probably the best evidence for this claim is that fluid-ability tests have shown much greater increases in scores over the past several generations than have crystallized-ability tests (Flynn, 1984, 1987, 1998; Neisser, 1998). The relatively brief period of time during which these increases have occurred (about 9 points of IQ per generation) suggests an environmental rather than a genetic cause of the increases. And the substantially greater increase for fluid than for crystallized tests suggests that fluid tests, like all other tests, actually measure an expertise acquired through interactions with the environment. This is not to say that genes do not influence intelligence: Almost certainly they do (Bouchard, 1997; Plomin, 1997; Scarr, 1997). Rather, the point is that the environment always mediates their influence and tests of intelligence measure gene–environment interaction effects. The measurement of intelligence is by assessment of various forms of developing expertise.

The forms of developing expertise that are viewed as practically or otherwise intelligent may differ from one society to another or from one sector of a given society to another. For example, procedural knowledge about natural herbal medicines, on the one hand, or Western medicines, on the other, may be critical to survival in one society, and irrelevant to survival in another (e.g., in which one or the other type of medicine is not available). Whereas what constitutes components of intelligence is universal, the content that constitutes the application of these components to adaptation to and shaping and selection of environments is culturally and even subculturally variable. But practical aspects of intelligence are important everywhere, as shown in a study we conducted in Russia.

In this study (Grigorenko & Sternberg, 2001), we tested 511 Russian school children (ranging in age from 8–17 years) as well as 490 mothers and 328 fathers of these children. We used entirely distinct measures of analytical, creative, and practical intelligence. Consider, for example, the tests used for adults. Similar tests were used for children.

We measured fluid analytical intelligence by two subtests of a test of nonverbal intelligence. The Test of g: Culture Fair, Level II (Cattell & Cattell, 1973) is a test of fluid intelligence designed to reduce, as much as possible, the influence of verbal comprehension, culture, and educational level, although no test eliminates such influences. In the first subtest, Series, we presented individuals with an incomplete, progressive series of figures. The participants' task was to select, from among the choices provided, the answer that best continued the series. In the Matrices subtest, the task was to complete the matrix presented at the left of each row.

The test of crystallized intelligence was adapted from existing traditional tests of analogies and synonyms and antonyms used in Russia. We used adaptations of Russian rather than American tests because the vocabulary used in Russia differs from that used in the United States. The first part of the test included 20 verbal analogies (KR20 = 0.83). An example is *circle–ball = square–?* (a) *quadrangular*, (b) *figure*, (c) *rectangular*, (d) *solid*, (e) *cube*. The second part included 30 pairs of words and the participants' task was to specify whether the words in the pair were synonyms or antonyms (KR20 = 0.74). Examples are *latent–hidden*, and *systematic–chaotic*.

The measure of creative intelligence also comprised two parts. The first part asked the participants to describe the world through the eyes of insects. The second part asked participants to describe who might live and what might happen on a planet called Priumliava. No additional information on the nature of the planet was specified. Each part of the test was scored in three different ways to yield three different scores. The first score was for originality (novelty); the second was for the amount of development in the plot (quality); and the third was for creative use of prior knowledge in these relatively novel kinds of tasks (sophistication). The mean inter-story reliabilities were .69, .75, and .75 for the three respective scores, all of which were statistically significant at the $p < .001$ level.

The measure of practical intelligence was self-report and also comprised two parts. We designed the first part as a 20-item, self-report instrument, assessing practical skills in the social domain (e.g., effective and successful communication with other people), in the family domain (e.g., how to fix household items, how to run the family budget), and in the domain of effective resolution of sudden problems (e.g., organizing something that has become chaotic). For the subscales, internal consistency estimates varied from 0.50 to 0.77. In this study, only the total practical intelligence self-report scale was used (Cronbach's alpha =.71). The second part had four vignettes, based on themes that appeared in popular Russian magazines in the context of discussion of adaptive skills in the current society. The four themes were, respectively, how to maintain the value of one's savings, what to do if one makes a purchase and discovers that the item one has purchased is broken, how to locate medical assistance in a time of need, and how to manage a salary bonus one has received for outstanding work. Each vignette was accompanied by five choices and participants had to select the best one. Obviously, there is no one right answer in this type of situation. Hence we used the most frequently chosen response as the keyed answer. To the extent that this response was suboptimal, this suboptimality would work against the researchers in subsequent analyses relating scores on this test to other predictor and criterion measures.

In this study, exploratory principal-component analysis for both children and adults yielded very similar factor structures. Both varimax and oblimin rotations yielded clear-cut analytical, creative, and practical factors for the tests. Thus, with a sample of a different nationality (Russian), a different set of tests and a different method of analysis (exploratory rather than confirmatory analysis) again supported the theory of successful intelligence.

In this same study, the analytical, creative, and practical tests the investigators employed were used to predict mental and physical health among the Russian adults. Mental health was measured by widely used paper-and-pencil tests of depression and anxiety, and physical health was measured by self-report. The best predictor of mental and physical health was the practical intelligence measure. Analytical intelligence came second and creative intelligence came third. All three contributed to prediction, however. Thus, the researchers again concluded that a theory of intelligence encompassing all three elements provides better prediction of success in life than does a theory comprising just the analytical element.

CONCLUSION

We have argued in this chapter that doing research in microworlds can tell you a lot—about those microworlds. It does not tell you much about the macroworld of which the various microworlds are a part. People from developed countries, and especially Western ones, can show and have shown a certain kind of arrogance in assuming that concepts (such as implicit theories of intelligence) or results (such as of studies based on explicit theories of intelligence) obtained in one culture—usually their culture—apply anywhere. In all likelihood, they do not. Or at least, it cannot be assumed they do until this assumption is tested.

Many of the results we have described here are at variance with results typically obtained in Western countries. Other investigators, as well, have obtained results that differ dramatically from those obtained in the developed West. We believe, therefore, that cultural investigations of psychological constructs, such as intelligence, are not just nice, but also necessary.

REFERENCES

Azuma, H., & Kashiwagi, K. (1987). Descriptions for an intelligent person: A Japanese study. *Japanese Psychological Research, 29,* 17–26.

Bouchard, T. J., Jr. (1997). IQ similarity in twins reared apart: Findings and responses to critics. In R. J. Sternberg & E. L. Grigorenko (Eds.), *Intelligence, heredity, and environment* (pp. 126–160). New York: Cambridge University Press.

Brown, A. L., & Ferrara, R. A. (1985). Diagnosing zones of proximal development. In J. V. Wertsch (Ed.), *Culture, communication, and cognition: Vygotskian perspectives* (pp. 273–305). New York: Cambridge University Press.

Budoff, M. (1968). Learning potential as a supplementary assessment procedure. In J. Hellmuth (Ed.), *Learning disorders* (Vol. 3, pp. 295–343). Seattle, WA: Special Child.

Cattell, R. B., & Cattell, H. E. P. (1973). *Measuring intelligence with the Culture Fair Tests.* Champaign, IL: Institute for Personality and Ability Testing.

Ceci, S. J. (1996). *On intelligence . . . more or less* (Expanded ed.). Cambridge, MA: Harvard University Press.

Chen, M. J. (1994). Chinese and Australian concepts of intelligence. *Psychology and Developing Societies, 6,* 101–117.

Chen, M. J., Braithwaite, V., & Huang, J. T. (1982). Attributes of intelligent behaviour: Perceived relevance and difficulty by Australian and Chinese students. *Journal of Cross-Cultural Psychology, 13,* 139–156.

Chen, M. J., & Chen, H. C. (1988). Concepts of intelligence: A comparison of Chinese graduates from Chinese and English schools in Hong Kong. *International Journal of Psychology, 223,* 471–487.

Connolly, H., & Bruner, J. (1974). Competence: Its nature and nurture. In K. Connolly & J. Bruner (Eds.), *The growth of competence* (pp. 3–10). New York: Academic Press.

Craik, F. I. M., & Lockhart, R. S. (1972). Levels of processing: A framework for memory research. *Journal of Verbal Learning and Verbal Behavior, 11,* 671–684.

Das, J. P. (1994). Eastern views of intelligence. In R. J. Sternberg (Ed.), *Encyclopedia of human intelligence* (Vol. 1, pp. 387–391). New York: Macmillan.

Dasen, P. (1984). The cross-cultural study of intelligence: Piaget and the Baoule. *International Journal of Psychology, 19,* 407–434.

Day, J. D., Engelhardt, J. L., Maxwell, S. E., & Bolig, E. E. (1997). Comparison of static and dynamic assessment procedures and their relation to independent performance. *Journal of Educational Psychology, 89,* 358–368.

Durojaiye, M. O. A. (1993). Indigenous psychology in Africa. In U. Kim & J. W. Berry (Eds.), *Indigenous psychologies: Research and experience in cultural context* (pp. 211–220). Newbury Park, CA: Sage.

Ericsson, K. A. (Ed.). (1996). *The road to excellence.* Mahwah, NJ: Erlbaum.

Feuerstein, R. (1979). *The dynamic assessment of retarded performers: The learning potential assessment device theory, instruments, and techniques.* Baltimore, MD: University Park Press.

Flynn, J. R. (1984). The mean IQ of Americans: Massive gains 1932 to 1978. *Psychological Bulletin, 95,* 29–51.

Flynn, J. R. (1987). Massive IQ gains in 14 nations. *Psychological Bulletin, 101,* 171–191.

Flynn, J. R. (1998). WAIS-III and WISC-III gains in the United States from 1972 to 1995: How to compensate for obsolete norms. *Perceptual and Motor Skills, 86,* 1231–1239.

Gill, R., & Keats, D. M. (1980). Elements of intellectual competence: Judgments by Australian and Malay university students. *Journal of Cross-Cultural Psychology, 11,* 233–243.

Goodnow, J. J. (1976). The nature of intelligent behavior: Questions raised by cross-cultural studies. In L. Resnick (Ed.), *The nature of intelligence* (pp. 169–188). Hillsdale, NJ: Erlbaum.

Greenfield, P. M. (1997). You can't take it with you: Why abilities assessments don't cross cultures. *American Psychologist, 52,* 1115–1124.

Grigorenko, E. L., Geissler, P. W., Prince, R., Okatcha, F., Nokes, C., Kenny, D. A., et al. (2001). The organisation of Luo conceptions of intelligence: A study of implicit theories in a Kenyan village. *International Journal of Behavioral Development, 25*(4), 367–378.

Grigorenko, E. L., Meier, E., Lipka, J., Mohatt, G., Yanez, E., & Sternberg, R. J. (2002). *The relationship between academic and practical intelligence: A case study of the tacit knowledge of Native American Yup'ik people in Alaska.* Manuscript submitted for publication.

Grigorenko, E. L., & Sternberg, R. J. (1998). Dynamic testing. *Psychological Bulletin, 124,* 75–111.

Grigorenko, E. L., & Sternberg, R. J. (2001). Analytical, creative, and practical intelligence as predictors of self-reported adaptive functioning: A case study in Russia. *Intelligence, 29,* 57–73.

Guthke, J. (1993). Current trends in theories and assessment of intelligence. In J. H. M. Hamers, K. Sijtsma, & A. J. J. M. Ruijssenaars (Eds.), *Learning potential assessment* (pp. 13–20). Amsterdam: Swets & Zeitlinger.

Haywood, H. C., &. Tzuriel, D. (Eds.). (1992). *Interactive assessment.* New York: Springer-Verlag.

Howe, M. J., Davidson, J. W., & Sloboda, J. A. (1998). Innate talents: Reality or myth? *Behavioral and Brain Sciences, 21,* 399–442.

Intelligence and its measurement: A symposium. (1921). *Journal of Educational Psychology, 12,* 123–147, 195–216, 271–275.

Irvine, J. T. (1978). "Wolof magical thinking": Culture and conservation revisited. *Journal of Cross-Cultural Psychology, 9,* 300–310.

Laboratory of Comparative Human Cognition. (1982). Culture and intelligence. In R. J. Sternberg (Ed.), *Handbook of human intelligence* (pp. 642–719). New York: Cambridge University Press.

Lidz, C. S. (Ed.). (1987). *Dynamic assessment.* New York: Guilford Press.

Lidz, C. S. (1991). *Practitioner's guide to dynamic assessment.* New York: Guilford Press.

Lutz, C. (1985). Ethnopsychology compared to what? Explaining behaviour and consciousness among the Ifaluk. In G. M. White & J. Kirkpatrick (Eds.), *Person, self, and experience: Exploring Pacific ethnopsychologies* (pp. 35–79). Berkeley: University of California Press.

Miles, T. R. (1957). On defining intelligence. *British Journal of Educational Psychology, 27,* 153–165.

Mundy-Castle, A. C. (1974). Social and technological intelligence in Western or Nonwestern cultures. *Universitas, 4,* 46–52.

Neisser, U. (Ed.). (1998). *The rising curve.* Washington, DC: American Psychological Association.

Newell, A., & Simon, H. A. (1972). *Human problem solving.* Englewood Cliffs, NJ: Prentice-Hall.

Nisbett, R. E. (in press). *The geography of thought: Why we think the way we do.* New York: Free Press.

Okagaki, L., & Sternberg, R. J. (1993). Parental beliefs and children's school performance. *Child Development, 64*(1), 36–56.

Plomin, R. (1997). Identifying genes for cognitive abilities and disabilities. In R. J. Sternberg & E. L. Grigorenko (Eds.), *Intelligence, heredity, and environment* (pp. 89–104). New York: Cambridge University Press.

Poole, F. J. P. (1985). Coming into social being: Cultural images of infants in Bimin-Kuskusmin folk psychology. In G. M. White & J. Kirkpatrick (Eds.), *Person, self, and experience: Exploring Pacific ethnopsychologies* (pp. 183–244). Berkeley: University of California Press.

Putnam, D. B., & Kilbride, P. L. (1980). *A relativistic understanding of social intelligence among the Songhay of Mali and Smaia of Kenya.* Paper presented at the meeting of the Society for Cross-Cultural Research, Philadelphia.

Rogoff, B. (1990). *Apprenticeship in thinking: Cognitive development in social context.* New York: Oxford University Press.

Ruzgis, P. M., & Grigorenko, E. L. (1994). Cultural meaning systems, intelligence and personality. In R. J. Sternberg & P. Ruzgis (Eds.), *Personality and intelligence* (pp. 248–270). New York: Cambridge University Press.

Scarr, S. (1997). Behavior-genetic and socialization theories of intelligence: Truce and reconciliation. In R. J. Sternberg & E. L. Grigorenko (Eds.), *Intelligence, heredity and environment* (pp. 3–41). New York: Cambridge University Press.

Serpell, R. (1974). Aspects of intelligence in a developing country. *African Social Research, 17*, 576–596.

Serpell, R. (1982). Measures of perception, skills, and intelligence. In W. W. Hartup (Ed.), *Review of child development research* (Vol. 6, pp. 392–440). Chicago: University of Chicago Press.

Serpell, R. (1996). Cultural models of childhood in indigenous socialization and formal schooling in Zambia. In C. P. Hwang & M. E. Lamb (Eds.), *Images of childhood* (pp. 129–142). Mahwah, NJ: Erlbaum.

Serpell, R. (2000). Intelligence and culture. In R. J. Sternberg (Ed.), *Handbook of intelligence* (pp. 549–580). New York: Cambridge University Press.

Srivastava, A. K., & Misra, G. (1996). Changing perspectives on understanding intelligence: An appraisal. *Indian Psychological Abstracts and Review, 3*, 1–34.

Sternberg, R. J. (1985). *Beyond IQ: A triarchic theory of human intelligence.* New York: Cambridge University Press.

Sternberg, R. J. (1998). Abilities are forms of developing expertise. *Educational Researcher, 27*, 11–20.

Sternberg, R. J. (Ed.). (1999). *Handbook of creativity.* New York: Cambridge University Press.

Sternberg, R. J., & Berg, C. A. (1986). Quantitative integration: Definitions of intelligence: A comparison of the 1921 and 1986 symposia. In R. J. Sternberg & D. K. Detterman (Eds.), *What is intelligence? Contemporary viewpoints on its nature and definition* (pp. 155–162). Norwood, NJ: Ablex Publishing.

Sternberg, R. J., Conway, B. E., Ketron, J. L., & Bernstein, M. (1981). People's conceptions of intelligence. *Journal of Personality and Social Psychology, 41*, 37–55.

Sternberg, R. J., & Detterman, D. K. (1986). *What is intelligence?* Norwood, NJ: Ablex Publishing.

Sternberg, R. J., & Grigorenko, E. L. (1997, Fall). The cognitive costs of physical and mental ill health: Applying the psychology of the developed world to the problems of the developing world. *Eye on Psi Chi, 2*(1), 20–27.

Sternberg, R. J., & Grigorenko, E. L. (2002). Just because we "know" it's true doesn't mean it's really true: A case study in Kenya. *Psychological Science Agenda, 15*(2), 8–10.

Sternberg, R. J., Grigorenko, E. L., Ngrosho, D., Tantufuye, E., Mbise, A., Nokes, C., et al. (2002). Assessing intellectual potential in rural Tanzanian school children. *Intelligence, 30*, 141–162.

Sternberg, R. J., Nokes, K., Geissler, P. W., Prince, R., Okatcha, F., Bundy, D. A., & Grigorenko, E. L. (2001). The relationship between academic and practical intelligence: A case study in Kenya. *Intelligence, 29*, 401–418.

Sternberg, R. J., Powell, C., McGrane, P. A., & McGregor, S. (1997). Effects of a parasitic infection on cognitive functioning. *Journal of Experimental Psychology: Applied, 3*, 67–76.

Super, C. M., & Harkness, S. (1982). The development of affect in infancy and early childhood. In D. Wagnet & H. Stevenson (Eds.), *Cultural perspectives on child development* (pp. 1–19). San Francisco: Freeman.

Super, C. M., & Harkness, S. (1986). The developmental niche: A conceptualization at the interface of child and culture. *International Journal of Behavioral Development, 9*, 545–569.

Super, C. M., & Harkness, S. (1993). The developmental niche: A conceptualization at the interface of child and culture. In R. A. Pierce & M. A. Black (Eds.), *Life-span development: A diversity reader* (pp. 61–77). Dubuque, IA: Kendall/Hunt.

Tzuriel, D. (1995). *Dynamic-interactive assessment: The legacy of L. S. Vygotsky and current developments.* Unpublished manuscript.

Vernon, P. E. (1971). *The structure of human abilities.* London: Methuen.

Vygotsky, L. S. (1978). *Mind in society: The development of higher psychological processes.* Cambridge, MA: Harvard University Press.

White, G. M. (1985). Premises and purposes in a Solomon Islands ethnopsychology. In G. M. White & J. Kirkpatrick (Eds.), *Person, self, and experience: Exploring Pacific ethnopsychologies* (pp. 328–366). Berkeley: University of California Press.

Yang, S., & Sternberg, R. J. (1997a). Conceptions of intelligence in ancient Chinese philosophy. *Journal of Theoretical and Philosophical Psychology, 17*(2), 101–119.

Yang, S., & Sternberg, R. J. (1997b). Taiwanese Chinese people's conceptions of intelligence. *Intelligence, 25*(1), 21–36.

10

CULTURALLY SITUATED COGNITIVE COMPETENCE: A FUNCTIONAL FRAMEWORK

QI WANG, STEPHEN J. CECI, WENDY M. WILLIAMS,
AND KIMBERLY A. KOPKO

In traditional cognitive theory, competence is linked to solving problems or evaluating theories within particular task situations (See Ceci, 1996, for a critique of the approach). The bulk of this work has been acontextual, focusing on mental processes in vivo, disconnected from the settings in which the processes are generally acquired and deployed. In such research, the subject is viewed as a solitary actor who possesses a fixed computational processor, and the role, if any, of culturally updated, continuously revised processing is downplayed.

In this chapter we put forward an account of culture's role in cognitive development that we believe is comprehensive enough to handle the relevant empirical findings across cultures, and yet specific enough to provide an account of individual differences within a given culture. In our formulation, we posit the dynamic interplay of four factors that shape competence: cultural artifacts, cognitive domains, interpersonal contexts, and individual schemata. We discuss more about the empirical support for each of these factors later.

225

In the past two decades, researchers have increasingly emphasized the adaptive quality of cognitive competence and its development, and the elicitative role of sociocultural settings in which such competence is deployed. For many researchers, concepts such as cultural self-construal describe not only how information is processed, but also how it is organized, retained, and used in memory and problem solving. In his seminal treatise on the social construction of remembering, Bartlett (1932) argued that "[s]ocial organization gives a persistent framework into which all detailed recall must fit, and it very powerfully influences both the manner and the matter of recall" (p. 296).

Taking a cue from Bartlett and others, modern researchers have embedded context and social rules into their models of cognitive development. Thus, Gardner (1984) viewed individuals' cognitive competencies as "skills and modes of thinking requisite for assuming various roles in the technological and economic spheres of their society" (p. 258); Masten and Coatsworth (1995) viewed competencies as "a pattern of effective performance in the environment, evaluated from the perspective of development in ecological and cultural context" (p. 724). And Sternberg's (2002) concept of "successful intelligence" regards intelligence as the ability to achieve success in life, emphasizing the pragmatic nature of cognitive competence and how it develops as a result of adaptation of an individual's abilities to the sociocultural environments in which he or she resides.

An emphasis on the adaptability of cognitive competence poses the challenge to rethink the definition and evaluation of cognitive competence in culturally sensitive ways. Many theorists have pointed out cultural variations in conceptions of ability and competence and emphasized the importance of using ability tests that reflect values within a particular society (Berry, 1976, 1980; Cole, 1996; Goodnow, 2000; Goody, 2001; Sternberg, 2002; Sternberg & Grigorenko, 2001). For example, Berry (1993) proposed a concept of "indigenous cognition" in which variations in cognitive competence reflect adaptations to variations in cultural and ecological contexts and therefore are valuable developments in their own right. Sternberg and Grigorenko (2000) further criticized the traditional "theme-park psychology" that relies on research findings from easy-to-study populations, tasks, and contexts to generate theories of human cognition and to direct educational policy. It is thus crucial to take into account contextual diversity when identifying and measuring competencies and skills individuals develop for a successful and responsible life in each society.

To fully understand culturally situated cognitive competence, however, an important question remains: How does the cultural adaptability of cognitive competence take place? In other words, what are the mechanisms by which sociocultural factors shape the development of cognitive competence? Recent studies in anthropology, social psychology, cultural psychology, and cross-cultural psychology, as well as other related disciplines, have accumulated evidence of the culture-specific nature of human cognition. People in different cultures have been shown to possess different cognitive competencies unique to their living environments (e.g., Ceci & Roazzi, 1994; Han, Leichtman, & Wang, 1998; Kearins, 1981; Nisbett, Peng, Choi, & Norenzayan, 2001). Thus, there is a need to develop a theoretical framework built on existing cognitive and sociocultural theories to synthesize the burgeoning empirical findings pertinent to the development of cognitive competence in cultural contexts. Such a framework should be both sensitive to the empirical findings, while simultaneously being able to predict and explain empirical findings in such a manner that is specific and falsifiable.

Elsewhere, we have conceptualized culture as "the system and the process of symbolic mediation—a mode of configuration" (Wang & Brockmeier, 2002, p. 45). Such symbolic mediation manifests itself in social institutions as well as in the actions, thoughts, emotions, beliefs, and moral values of individuals, thereby regulating both intrapersonal and interpersonal psychological functions (Bruner, 1990; D'Andrade, 1992; Valsiner, 2000; Vygotsky, 1978). In this chapter, we will explore the various ways in which culture permeates thinking, and examine how sociocultural factors operate as mechanisms for transforming the "universal mind" into many culturally adaptive mentalities (Shweder, Goodnow, Hatano, LeVine, Markus, & Miller, 1998). We suggest that there are no such things as invariant, core competencies universal to every human child. Instead, cognitive competence is relative to specific cultures, to the particular cognitive spheres or domains valued in a culture, to the social and physical contexts in which the child participates in organized activities, and to the cultural and societal demands as perceived by the child him- or herself.

We here propose a functional framework to examine cognitive competence as a result of the impact of cultural artifacts (e.g., tools, language), cognitive domains, interpersonal contexts, and individual schemata. We highlight the cultural functionality and adaptability of cognitive competence and argue that the development of any cognitive competence is a result of the dynamic interplay among the four aspects of cultural influences in creating competent members of each human society (See Figure 10.1 for a schematic illustration of this view). In elaborating this framework, we draw on existing theories and empirical findings from anthropology and psychology. Our goal here is not exhaustive but illustrative: By examining some extant theories and data we envision this framework as an initial step toward a grand synthesis that requires the participation and collaboration of theorists and researchers from diverse disciplines. Importantly, we hope that the framework we put forward here goes beyond those that have been the object of criticisms by commentators for lack of specification of the "ill-defined outside world" (Oyama, 1998, p. 11).

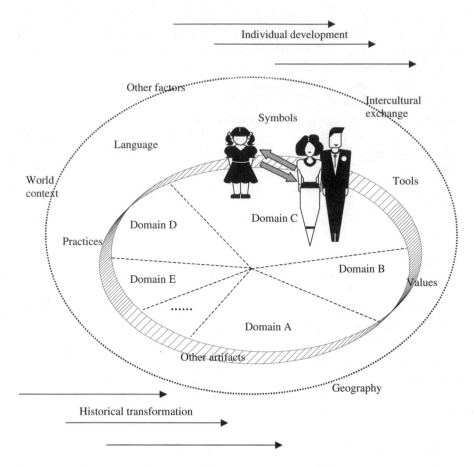

Figure 10.1. The dynamic system of culturally situated cognitive competence.

COMPETENCE AND CULTURALLY CONSTRUCTED ARTIFACTS

Culturally constructed artifacts constitute human life and influence human action through their roles as symbols, tools, and beliefs. For example, the most mundane forms of signs and symbols are such things as street signs, telephone dials, price tags, clocks, product labels, recipes, and patterns for dressmaking (Heath, 1983). In addition, cultural artifacts comprise material tools and forms of technology such as computers, cell phones, and electronic day planners, as well as symbolic systems like language, numeracy, and other representational systems such as proverbs, metaphors, and folk models of thinking that are familiar to individuals in a given culture (D'Andrade, 1987; Lakoff & Johnson, 1980; White, 1987). Finally, cultural artifacts include shared values, beliefs, and practices, as well as the material and symbolic orders of the overarching cultural system (including law, education, religion, philosophy, literature and the arts). As we show below, these tools, symbols, and beliefs affect cognitive competence by enhancing, mediating, and transforming the forms of thinking and communication available to members of a particular cultural community.

We concur with some contemporary researchers who view cognition not as a private matter confined to the individual's mind or brain, but rather, conceive of thinking (including reasoning, problem solving, memory, or self-representation) as a sociocultural practice carried out through the shared system of cultural artifacts (e.g., Ceci, 1996; Holland & Quinn, 1987; Resnick, Levine, & Teasley, 1991; Sternberg, 2002; Wang & Brockmeier, 2002; Wertsch, 1991). Thus, an important aspect of cognitive growth is children's learning to use cultural tools and signs that mediate both higher mental functions and the practical goals of daily life (Gauvain, 2001; Rogoff, 1990; Vygotsky, 1978). By actively engaging in everyday activities, regardless of whether this means using computers or abacuses or counting one's fingers, children gradually incorporate culturally constructed artifacts into their own repertoire of thinking and further develop culture-specific cognitive competencies. In this way, cultural artifacts indeed become inherent parts of human cognition.

Vygotsky (1978) argued that *tools of intellectual adaptation* are available in each culture to help children develop adaptive thinking and problem-solving strategies. Children's interactions with real tools, such as computers, provide tangible objects that facilitate learning. From symbolic tools, like language, children learn a means of communicating, expressing ideas, thinking critically, and transmitting and receiving the intellectual wealth of the society. For Vygotsky, such interactions take place at two different levels: the *institutional* and the *interpersonal* levels of social contexts. At the institutional level, cultural history provides organizations and tools useful to cognitive activity through institutions such as schools. Institutional interaction gives children broad behavioral and societal norms to guide their lives. The interpersonal level has a more direct influence on the child's mental functioning: More capable members of the culture, such as adults and older peers, guide the child, providing knowledge and support necessary for the child's intellectual growth. Through the organization of these interactional experiences embedded in a cultural backdrop, children's mental development occurs.

Although agreeing with the important mediating role played by societal institutions and more competent partners, we suggest that the effects of cultural artifacts may be more pervasive and less organized. They are, in fact, the way individuals live their lives and the mode used to perform even the most rudimentary forms of "cognitive tasks" like thinking, speaking, and counting. This view of the overarching impact of cultural artifacts coincides with the anthropological concept, the *immediacy of culture*. Super and Harkness (1999) discussed in depth the paramount importance of this concept in psychological research. They posited that the immediacy of culture "not only better reflects the phenomenological experience of daily life but also brings the cultural environment into reach for the empirical scientist" (p. 282).

Cross-linguistic studies provide perhaps the most convincing evidence for the inherence of cultural artifacts, including language, in human cognition. For example, Elgin (2000) compared the sentence "I was riding a horse" in English and its closest translation in Navajo, "The horse and I were moving about." Whereas the English version illustrates a subject–object relation between the rider and the ridee, the Navajo version expresses an equal relationship between two parties engaging in a joint endeavor. Although we do not go so far as to argue for a radical version of linguistic determinism (Sapir, 1964/1941; Whorf, 1956), we suggest that the different ways of formulating object relations in languages can influence how people perceive and process the information conveyed, which further shapes their cognition. As recent behavioral data indicate, language-specific linguistic features directly affect thought about such domains as classification, color perception, spatial categories, and conceptions of time (Boroditsky, 2001; Choi, McDonough, Bowerman, & Mandler, 1999; Gathercole & Min, 1997; Martinez & Shatz, 1996; Roberson, Davies, & Davidoff, 2000).

Another example comes from the number-naming systems in English and Chinese. Compared with English, Chinese language has a more systematic number-naming system. After the first ten digits, which need to be memorized as in English, the Chinese system follows a base-ten logic such that 11 is named "ten one," and 12 named "ten two," and so on. The two languages then become similar after 20, both using the base-ten logic. K. Miller and colleagues (Miller, Smith, Zhu, & Zhang, 1995) found that by age 4, Chinese children began to show an advantage in counting over U.S. children. This advantage became even larger at age 5, with only 48% of the U.S. children but 74% of the Chinese in their samples being able to count to 20. Notably, children in the two cultures did not differ in other aspects of mathematical competence such as to count small sets or to solve simple numerical problems, which rules out the explanation of innate difference in intelligence. Other studies have shown that the English number-naming system presents obstacles to children's early use of carrying, borrowing, and addition strategies (e.g., Fuson & Kwon, 1992; Siegler, 1987), and by the time of school entry Chinese children are able to use more sophisticated strategies than their U.S. peers (Geary, Fan, & Bow-Thomas, 1992). Divergent educational systems and upbringings in the two cultures further magnify the early difference in counting skills associated with different number-naming systems of languages, which leads to greater mathematical competence in Chinese than in U.S. schoolchildren and young adults (Geary, Bow-Thomas, Liu, & Siegler, 1996; Geary, Salthouse, Chen, & Fan, 1996; Stevenson & Lee, 1990; Stigler & Perry, 1990). Thus, cultural artifacts do not always facilitate cognitive growth but sometimes hinder it.

These examples tell us that cultural tools, beliefs, symbols, and other artifacts are not always located in a macro context (Bronfenbrenner & Morris, 1998) or at a distal level (Vygotsky, 1978). Their effects on cognitive development do not necessarily depend on the "go-betweens" of schools, parents, and other socialization agents, whose scaffolding, although effective, can be constrained by the characteristics of particular artifacts. Undoubtedly, societal institutions and more competent members of the culture are important mediators of many "higher-level" social–cultural–historical forces. Nevertheless, children are often directly exposed to these forces and influenced by them through simple imitation or implicit learning, which sometimes can be even more powerful than formal instructions in behavior and cognition (e.g., Chiu, Morris, Hong, & Menon, 2000; Nosek, Banaji, & Greenwald, 2002; Ross, 1989). Such cultural learning is functional for individuals' adaptation to their environment as it makes the acquisition of cultural heritage more pervasive. Cultural artifacts function in every moment, place, and aspect of human life. They define developmental pathways, provide opportunities and constraints for cognitive growth, and make direct and immediate impact on children's cognitive competence along culturally desired lines.

COMPETENCE AND CULTURALLY DEFINED DOMAINS

Humans' dynamic cultural environments define specific cognitive *domains* that, in turn, make demands on children's intellectual growth. Cognitive psychologists define domains as sets of representations sustaining specific areas of knowledge. Thus, they are likely to be specific to culture (Gardner, 1984; Mistry & Rogoff, 1985). Even for those domains that seem to exist universally and carry the same labels across cultures, such as math, arts, and literature, the representations of knowledge can be based on drastically different cultural artifacts and modes of thinking. To some extent, then, these domains do not refer to the same cognitive spheres from one culture to another.

Although cognitive theorists place a great emphasis on the domain specificity of cognitive development (Ceci, 1996), domain has been cast in terms of semantic representations that have rarely been viewed in the context of culture. Gardner (1984) proposed a preliminary framework that divides culture into a number of discrete domains, broadly characterized as the realms of the physical world (natural objects, living matter), the world of man-made artifacts (tools, art works, language), and the social world (people in one's immediate and distal contexts). He argued that although these realms can be found in every human culture, marked cultural variations exist in the ways in which they are defined and evaluated and in the forms of knowledge associated with each. For example, Western culture has traditionally valued greatly explicit knowledge about the physical world, with the educational system focusing on physical and natural sciences. In contrast, in cultures like Japan or India, explicit knowledge about the social world is valued much more and is the source of far more energy or effort than is knowledge about the physical world, especially if the latter is cast in a scientific form.

Hence, the manner in which cognitive domains are defined, constituted, and valued in a particular culture has profound consequences on the development of competence. On the other hand, the three realms or general domains of cognition outlined by Gardner (1984) are in fact inseparable aspects of culture and human life. For example, there is not a purely physical world without any man-made artifacts, and people create and use these artifacts. Thus, it is an oversimplification to divide the universe of knowledge into these overlapping domains and then contrast different cultures regarding how much value is placed on each. This approach can easily lead to pitfalls such as viewing Asian and other non-Western societies as less advanced in their science and technology than the West, because their cultures do not value as much the explicit knowledge of the physical world.

We suggest that cognitive domains specific to each culture be defined and analyzed in a more fine-grained and sensitive manner by really "putting culture in the middle" of the analysis (Cole, 1996). One way to achieve this goal is to look from the bottom up. Instead of judging whether a culture values a particular domain, we can consider the function and adaptability of domain-specific competencies in assisting individuals to perform effectively in their culture. As empirical findings have shown, cognitive domains arise in response to the demands of the physical and social environments in which children grow up, and the domains in turn facilitate the development of relevant cognitive competencies. For example, Australian aboriginal children of the desert regions develop extraordinary visual spatial memory (Kearins, 1981); the unschooled young street vendors in Brazil are capable of solving complicated math problems in their head (Carraher, Carraher, & Schliemann, 1985; Ceci & Roazzi, 1994); and New Zealand Maori adults remember their childhood from a much earlier age (32.6 months) than do Europeans (42.9 months) and Asians (57.8 months) because of their cultural emphasis on the past and oral tradition (MacDonald, Uesiliana, & Hayne, 2000). In each case, and many others like them, the physical and social challenges confronting individuals demand different skills, which become honed to different levels of expertise. Although one can never definitively rule out the possibility that in some of these examples there are inborn differences in potentials (e.g., for spatial memory), there is no evidence that this is so, and there is in fact every suspicion that the cultures facilitate some cognitive attainments while rendering others difficult or even impossible. For example, even in studies that have shown significant differences in the content of recollections from one culture to another, there appear to be no objective differences in the underlying memory capacities of the groups (Han, Leichtman, & Wang, 1998).

The converse of this point is that cultural change may be rapid, making it hard to explain how cultural legacies persist in producing cognitive differences (Caporael, 2001). However, within an individual's lifetime there may be physical and social challenges that shape peculiar cognitive profiles that may not exist in that same culture a generation later. A dramatic example of this phenomenon is the massive change in IQ performance over a few generations in many nations (e.g., Flynn, 1998). For example, if IQ norms were held constant, IQ scores would have risen for the past 70 years at an almost constant rate, and the results would be truly astounding. As Flynn stated, "[I]t would be difficult to defend any estimate that the mean IQ of Britons in 1892 was above 60. Therefore, at a minimum, 84% had an IQ below 75" (p. 20).

Moreover, the existence, importance, and meaning of particular cognitive domains can be further linked to a culture's intellectual history and how it conceives of the goal of intellectual growth. In Chinese culture there is a long tradition originating from Confucian teachings that emphasizes a life-long pursuit of self-perfection that encourages individuals to improve intellectually through continuous active learning and practice. Those who commit themselves to this process are regarded as *Jun-zi*, or moral persons (Tu, 1979). Learning is therefore no longer a merely academic matter or personal enjoyment, but carries important moral purposes for the Chinese and is often referred to as the "great learning" to differentiate from the purely academic learning of school subjects (Li, 2001). Consonant with this cultural belief, learning-related cognitive domains in Chinese culture seem to bear different meanings than those in the West. To use art as an example: Art for the Chinese entails aesthetic beauty and moral goodness, an effective means of achieving self-perfection and therefore becoming a *Jun-zi*. As a result, in China art learning and education each focus on basic skills, control, precision, and performance that, unlike in the West where art is valued as a form of active self-expression and determination, precede any encouragement of creativity (Gardner, 1989). It is a striking example of how cultures differ in the way they foster and shape cognitions.

Thus, cognitive domains are deeply rooted in the physical, social, and intellectual milieu of the culture. The existence of particular domains, and the importance and intrinsic meanings they entail, are in service of individuals' participation in culturally organized activities in their societies. The functions of individual competencies in particular cognitive domains elucidate how and why these domains develop and become embellished in a given culture. They provide insight into questions about how individuals identify, evaluate, test, and further facilitate their own cognitive growth in these important spheres of cultural knowledge.

COMPETENCE AND CULTURALLY EMBEDDED CONTEXTS

Compared with the first two cultural mechanisms for the development of cognitive competence, the importance of interpersonal contexts has been greatly emphasized by developmental, cognitive, and cultural psychologists (e.g., Bronfenbrenner, 1979; Cole, 1996; Gardner, 1984; Gauvain, 2001; Rogoff, 1990; Vygotsky, 1978). Children interact with more competent members of their society and gradually acquire techniques, literacy, cultural beliefs and customs, religious doctrines, and other culturally valued knowledge and skills that enable them to later become competent members themselves. And this process occurs regardless of whether through formal instruction at school or informal learning during play. This is perhaps the most important channel through which culture deliberately imparts cultural knowledge from one generation to the next to ensure its continuity.

Vygotsky's (1978) sociocultural theory of human development gives a systematic account of the process and mechanism involved in the face-to-face interactions between the child and more capable partners. He contends that development takes place when the child internalizes culturally valued skills, knowledge, and concepts into his or her own mental framework, a process that is initiated between the child and the partner (e.g., parents, teachers, older siblings) and leads to higher mental functions in the child. Children thus acquire *tools of intellectual adaptation* through their interactions with more competent members of the society, within *a zone of proximal development*, and eventually learn to use cultural tools, signs, and artifacts to guide their thinking and action. Rogoff (1990) elaborated on this early theoretical framework, regarding adult-guided participation as a forum of "apprenticeships in thinking" that "provide the beginner with access to both overt aspects of the skill and the more hidden inner processes of thought" (p. 40). Rogoff and other contemporary theorists (Gauvain, 2001; Goodnow, 2000; Rogoff; 1998; Valsiner, 2000) further maintain that children are more than just passive participants in these interactions with adults. Rather, they actively make use of opportunities presented to them and try out newly acquired skills, strategies, and cognitive tools. In addition, during joint activities, adults often adjust their levels of guidance contingent on a child's independent contribution to the task. Through this scaffolding process, children learn to eventually perform the task without help.

Extending these theories, we propose here that the effects of face-to-face interactions on cognitive competence can be further understood from a functional perspective that focuses on the culture-specific characteristics of interpersonal contexts, such as the persons involved, the dynamic relations among them, the purpose of the interaction, and the immediate and long-term outcomes of it. We believe that cognitive competence and its development are specific to particular contexts and subject to situational constraints that, in turn, reflect and further constitute the meaning system of the culture (Light & Butterworth, 1993). Thus, the form or style of interactions used by adults within particular contexts is consonant with the community's socialization goal of facilitating the development of culturally functional qualities in the child. Eventually, children acquire specific and general understanding of the meaning and utility of their culture's material and symbolic tools (physical devices, maps, plans) involved in problem solving, and, more importantly, they learn from more competent partners culturally adaptive ways of thinking (Gauvain, 2001; Goodnow, 2000; Rogoff, 1990, 1998; Valsiner, 2000).

Cross-cultural data help to illustrate our point. Consider language socialization as an example. Traditionally, academic studies on family linguistic interactions have focused on the outcomes of vocabulary skills and IQ in children while paying little, if any, attention to possible differences in the functional purpose of such interactions across cultures (see Small, 2001, for a critique of this approach). The amount of time mothers spend with children and the quantity of their utterances directed toward children are considered crucial for language and cognitive development (Hart & Risley, 1995). However, parents in other cultures may not see helping children develop linguistic skills as the paramount goal of child rearing. In a longitudinal study, Levine and colleagues (LeVine et al., 1994) observed Gusii and Bostonian mother–infant interactions over a period of 27 months. Strikingly, Bostonian mothers communicated with their infants twice as much as Gusii mothers, who were less verbally responsive to their children's vocalizations and rarely attempted to elicit a vocal response from or carry on a sustained verbal exchange with their young children. Strikingly, Gusii mothers would call an articulate child "a talker," which was considered a criticism rather than a compliment in their culture.

It appears that Gusii mothers, unlike their American counterparts, are not preoccupied with engaging in language interactions with their children to teach them words, phrases, or sentences. Instead, they often limit their utterances to "commands and warnings" to the child. The Gusii believe that children learn language through their social environment and therefore do not require much deliberate teaching. As LeVine and colleagues (1994) described, "[n]ormal social interaction in domestic settings is verbally restrained, with a slow conversational pace, a strong reliance on conventional routines and indirect speech, and a tendency to put responsibility for comprehension on the hearer rather than the speaker" (p. 216). Thus, the interaction style used by Gusii mothers is instrumental in reinforcing safety and compliance in their children, whereas that of American mothers is intended to facilitate their children's linguistic and cognitive competence. The different maternal interaction styles further reflect divergent cultural beliefs about language learning and teaching.

Some researchers (e.g., Miller & Hoogstra, 1992; Nelson, 1996; Ochs, 1993) further claim that language discourse helps children construct the system of interpretations, gain knowledge about self and others, and apprehend cultural meanings. Studies on family narrative interactions in different cultures have yielded fruitful results (e.g., Miller, Fung, & Mintz, 1996; Miller, Wiley, Fung, & Liang, 1997; Mullen & Yi, 1995; Wang, Leichtman, & Davies, 2000). For example, in a recent study, Wang (2001a) asked European American and Chinese mothers to discuss with their 3-year-olds at home four recent events in which they both participated and during which the child experienced happiness, sadness, fear, or anger. American mothers tended to use an "emotion-explaining" style, talking frequently about the situational causes of feeling states and providing elaborate explanations as to why and how an emotional reaction occurred. In contrast, Chinese mothers often used an "emotion-criticizing" style, in which they initiated little discussion with their children about the antecedents of emotions and often gave moral judgments about the incorrectness of children's (negative) emotional experience or behavior. Wang argued that the American mother–child conversations facilitate the development of children's emotional understanding, consistent with the socialization goal in their culture that regards emotion as a valuable means of self-expression and individuality. In contrast, the Chinese mother–child conversations put social constraints on children's emotions and commit children to behavioral standards rather than helping them develop emotion knowledge. This conversational style echoes the Chinese cultural emphasis on psychological discipline, and the view of emotion as potentially disruptive to social relations (Bond, 1991; Hsu, 1953; Kitayama & Markus, 1994). Intriguingly, children at age 3 seemed to have already internalized their mothers' styles in discussing the shared emotional past. Wang (2001a) found that American children themselves talked frequently about the causes of emotions whereas Chinese children often gave spontaneous comments on social rules and discipline.

These different styles of family discourse about emotion may have long-term consequences on children's emotion knowledge. To test this hypothesis, Wang (2003) had 154 European American and Chinese children interviewed individually at school. Children were presented 20 short stories with a protagonist of their age, gender, and ethnicity, and were asked to identify the feeling states of the protagonist by choosing among faces showing happy, sad, scared, or angry emotions. Children's mothers and a second group of adults read the same stories and judged the protagonist's emotions in the same fashion. On the basis of the proportion of concordant judgments between children and adults in each culture, findings showed that American children had a better grasp of emotion knowledge and made more rapid progress in such knowledge than did their Chinese peers.

Together, these cross-cultural data indicate that family discourse, in particular, and adult–child interaction, in general, serve different functions across cultures. The frequency, style, and content of the interactions are shaped by cultural beliefs about the particular topic of focus (e.g., language, emotional understanding), by parents' own beliefs about the topic and their child-rearing goals, by the dynamic relation between parents (or other socialization agents) and children (e.g., hierarchical or equal), and by the active role played by children themselves in developing valuable qualities specific to their cultures. These findings point to the importance of taking into account the functional characteristics of culturally embedded interpersonal contexts when we evaluate their effects on children's cognitive growth.

COMPETENCE AND THE CULTURALLY FRAMED MIND

The last cultural mechanism we propose here is the culturally framed mind. We refer to the cognitive models, schemata, or mental frames that are functional in a culture and operational in its individuals. Culture provides its individuals with meaningful scripts or ways of organizing knowledge about themselves and the world around them, which in turn have powerful effects on the way people sample, process, and retain information from the environment. We analyze this mechanism at two different levels: the cultural level (i.e., the formation and development of different modes of cognition across cultures) and the individual level (i.e., the roles of individuals who come to conform to or refuse the culturally predominant ways of thinking). Examining the culturally framed mind is therefore critical for our understanding of both individual and cultural diversities in cognitive functioning.

Cross-cultural studies have identified marked differences in cognitive characteristics between Western and Asian peoples (See Fiske, Kitayama, Markus, & Nisbett, 1998 for a review). Westerners tend to base their thinking and reasoning on the internal attributes of a person or object. They often analyze individual components in isolation and succession, decontextualize a behavior from its environment, and make dispositional judgments. In contrast, Asians tend to embed their thinking and reasoning in a situational context. They often focus on relations between objects or events, and ascribe the antecedent of a behavior to the interaction between a person or an object and the environment. These different orientations in thinking are evident in studies of self-knowledge (Cousins, 1989; Rhee, Uleman, Lee, & Roman, 1995; Trafimow, Triandis, & Goto, 1991), descriptions of other people (Shweder & Bourne, 1984), memory (Wang & Leichtman, 2000), and causal attribution and reasoning (Morris, Nisbett, & Peng, 1995). They have been identified even among children. For example, in a study requiring school-age children to group two out of three objects together and to state the reason for their choices, Chiu (1972) found that American children used a predominantly inferential and analytic style of categorization and reasoning, identifying object similarities based on inferred characteristics of the stimuli (e.g., "these are things to cut") or on manifest objective attributes (e.g., "they both are holding a gun"). In contrast, Chinese children tended to use a relational-contextual style of reasoning and to identify similarities on the basis of functional or thematic interdependence among the elements in a grouping (e.g., "the mother takes care of the baby"). Such differences have implications for cognitive assessments, in as much as the major IQ tests reward taxonomic sorting (e.g., both made of metal) over thematic sorting.

Nisbett and colleagues (Ji, Peng, & Nisbett, 2000; Nisbett, Peng, Choi, & Norenzayan, 2001) characterized the mode of thinking among Asians as holistic and dialectical, whereas that of Westerners is seen as analytic and logical. They argued that the cultural differences in the most "basic" cognitive processes stem from a long history of markedly different social systems between the East and the West. Developmental psychologists (e.g., Chiu, 1972; Wang & Leichtman, 2000) have emphasized the effects of early socialization on the formation of different cognitive styles. In Western cultures that value and encourage independence, autonomy, and spontaneity, children become attuned to the components of objects and the extended attributes through their active exploration of the environment. In contrast, in Asian cultures that emphasize discipline and mutual dependence, children learn early to see the world as a network of relationships and to try to find their right place in their immediate social environment. This leads to a tendency to perceive objects in the environment in terms of mutual dependence or relationships. Notably, and as we have already discussed, there exist marked differences in ways of thinking within Asian and Western cultures (e.g., Conway, Wang, Hanyu, & Haque, 2002; Nakamura, 1964; Wang, Leichtman, & White, 1998), which tend to be understudied and merit more research.

Cultural self-construal, a representational model of the self that integrates the framework of the culture and pervasively affects cognitive and other psychological processes, has attracted a great deal of research interests in the past decades. Markus and Kitayama (1991) claim that "[t]hese (cultural) construals of self and other are conceptualized as part of a repertoire of self-relevant schemata used to evaluate, organize, and regulate one's experience and action" (p. 229). Empirical data from psychology and anthropology have shown that many Western cultures, particularly North American culture, emphasize self-expression, individual uniqueness, and personal sufficiency. Individuals tend to develop an independently oriented self-construal that is conceived of as well-bounded, distinct, and separate from others or social context. In contrast, in many cultures such as East Asia, group solidarity, interpersonal harmony, and personal humility are highly valued. Individuals tend to develop an interdependently oriented self-construal and view themselves as connected to others within a relational network. The different cultural self-construals have important consequences on cognitive functioning such as attention, problem solving, causal attribution, social judgment, and creativity (for reviews, see Fiske et al., 1998; Kagitcibasi, 1996; Markus & Kitayama, 1991; Triandis, 1989).

Cultural models of cognition, including cultural self-construal, describe not only how information is perceived and processed, but also how it is organized, retained, and eventually recollected. As we noted in the introduction, Bartlett (1932) claimed that remembering is a constructive process in which both the manner and the matter of recall are predominantly determined by sociocultural influences. One particularly interesting area of current cross-cultural research concerns what Merlin Donald (1991) terms "episodic competence." Studies examining memories of episodic events, especially those related to personal experiences (i.e., autobiographical memory) in both children and adults have revealed intriguing cultural differences. Autobiographical memories of European American adults tend to be lengthy, detailed, emotionally elaborate, focusing on one's own roles, predilections, and opinions. In contrast, memories of Asians (Koreans and Chinese) are often brief and centered on collective activities, significant others, and daily routines. Compared with their Korean and Chinese peers, American preschoolers also tend to provide more elaborate, more specific, and more self-focused autobiographical accounts (Han, Leichtman, & Wang, 1998; Mullen, 1994; Wang, 2001b, in press; Wang & Leichtman, 2000).

From a functional perspective, personal memories of discrete, one-moment-in-time events with specific details and elaboration and with the individual cast as the central character (e.g., "the time I won the spelling bee competition") are particularly important for people with an independent self-construal. Such memories help to differentiate the self from others and thereby reaffirm the self as an autonomous entity. In contrast, memories of "scripted" events with a salient social orientation (e.g., "family dinners") are important for people with an interdependent self-construal, because these memories help to engage individuals in ongoing relationships and thereby reinforce the self as a relational entity (Wang, 2001b, in press). Thus, cultural construal of the self appears to play not just a role in the formation of culture-specific genres of autobiographical memory, but the determining role. The extent to which the meaning of selfhood in a given culture is tied to the unique attributes of the individual, versus being a result of the dominant social stratification, and the extent to which an individual focuses on his own versus others' thoughts, feelings, and personal roles in an event, are likely to affect the content, structure, and accessibility of memory for that event over the long term (Mullen, 1994; Pillemer, 1998; Röttger-Rössler, 1993; Wang, 2001b; Wang et al., 1998).

The effects of cultural self-construal tend to be selective on particular memory processes, however. For example, Conway and colleagues (2002) observed highly similar life span memory retrieval curves in their Japan, Bangladesh, England, China, and U.S. samples: The offset of childhood amnesia and the reminiscence bump were the same across cultures—although the U.S. sample showed a greater number of childhood memories than any other group. However, content analysis of memory descriptions found that memories from the Asian groups reflected an interdependent self focus, whereas the memory content of the Western groups showed an independent self focus, a pattern of findings consistent with other recent cross-cultural studies of memory content. Other research has also shown that although preschoolers in U.S. and Asian cultures remembered markedly different memory information from life events as well as from fictional stories, objective memory performance was equally accurate across cultures (Han et al., 1998; Wang & Leichtman, 2000). These differential cultural effects on the content, accessibility, and life span distribution of autobiographical memory suggest a complex relation among the self, memory, and culture.

Cognitive models or schemata promoted by a culture may not affect every individual in that culture to the same extent or in the same fashion. After all, it is through specific individual minds and within particular situational and task contexts that culture-specific modes of thought come into play. Thus, there exist at the individual level, individual-to-individual, context-to-context, and situation-to-situation variations in ways of thinking. Some variations may be deviant from the predominant cognitive models in a culture, but nevertheless their existence may be functional for the individual in performing cognitive tasks within particular contexts or situations. Indeed, variations can entail flexibility in cognitive functioning that may be particularly adaptive in fast-changing modern societies.

Individual differences in their internalization and application of culturally promoted cognitive models are less emphasized in cultural studies that mostly focus on between-group differences. Two theoretical approaches, however, require special attention here. The first is developed by cognitive anthropologists. For example, D'Andrade (1992) argued that individuals do not act mechanically according to cultural expectations. Instead, they acquire culturally formed models or cognitive schemas through early personal–social experiences, and these models or schemas, in turn, influence their cognition, motivation, and action unwittingly. To some extent, "different individuals internalize different parts of the same culture in different ways" (D'Andrade, 1992, p. 41). Other theorists have emphasized that children are active agents in participating in specific activities, interacting with specific individuals, and selecting specific means for solving problems (Rogoff, 1998; Shweder et al., 1998; Valsiner, 2000). Individuals thus create their own experiences in the developmental niche they share with others in their culture. The individualized enculturational processes give rise to both commonality and diversity among individuals within a single culture. The interaction between individual agency and cultural belief system further contributes both to the transformation of the culture and to the development of the individual.

The second theoretical framework is developed by social psychologists whose methodology has been influenced by cognitive research (Hong, Morris, Chiu, & Benet-Martinez, 2000; Libby & Eibach, 2002; Ross, Xun, & Wilson, 2002; Trafimow et al., 1991). For example, Hong, Chiu and colleagues (2000) suggest that individuals may develop different, and sometimes contrasting, cultural mental frames due to the growing globalization and intercultural exchanges in the modern era. The activation of and shifting between these mental frames are subject to specific situational requirements put forth by particular psychosocial orientations, such as autonomy versus interconnectedness. As a result, individuals use cultural knowledge to serve their motivational and epistemic in addition to cognitive needs specific to contexts or situations.[1]

Consistent with this theoretical claim, research has shown that, depending on particular contexts, situations, or incidental cues, some cultural beliefs may become more accessible to some individuals than others, which in turn differentially shape individuals' reasoning, attribution, and even self-perception (Chiu et al., 2000; Hong et al., 2000; Ross et al., 2002; Trafimow et al., 1991). In a recent study, Ross and colleagues (2002) examined the cultural frame adopted by bilingual Chinese-born Canadians in reporting self-related information. These researchers found that compared with participants who completed the tasks in English, those assigned to the Chinese-language group reported more self-descriptions of group memberships and social relations, had lower self-esteem scores, and showed more agreement with Chinese values such as "Modesty leads to success, pride leads to failure." It appears that self-knowledge varied as a function of the relative accessibility of different cultural beliefs induced by language.

Thus, cultural effects on cognitive competence are ultimately achieved and expressed by the culturally framed mind of individuals who may vary in other relevant experiences. A culture's centuries of religious, philosophical, and political traditions and its preferences in child-rearing practices lead to particular modes of cognition that are functional for most of its individuals in solving problems and making judgments in everyday life. On the other hand, individuals play an active role in selecting, modifying, and disputing one cognitive model or another from the "public pool" they share with other members of the culture. Some individuals may even adopt models that contradict their culture's value system but are functional in particular situations or for solving particular problems. It is through the dynamic interplay between culture and individuals that human cognition eventually comes into shape.

A FUNCTIONAL FRAMEWORK OF COGNITIVE COMPETENCE: CONCLUSION

The foregoing analysis suggests that models of competence crafted on the basis of data collected without respect to cultural context are unable to account for the dramatic differences observed—even between individuals with no underlying capacity differences. To recap our argument, individuals carry out everyday cognitive activities in which culturally constructed arti-

---

[1]"Although individuals may differ in what mechanisms they apply to a given task or situation, the potential set of mental mechanisms underlying intelligence is claimed to be the same across all individuals, social classes, and cultural groups." (Sternberg, 1986, pp. 23–24).

facts operate as both the mediating tools and the objects of action. Through formal and informal instructions as well as implicit learning, individuals gradually internalize their culture's artifacts into their own thinking and behavior. A culture's intellectual history and social and geographical environments define and further give meaning and importance to particular cognitive domains, some of which may be unique to this culture. Individuals develop competencies in these domains that are functional in terms of their adaptation to the social and intellectual lives in their society. Interpersonal contexts are embedded in the larger cultural milieu and serve culture-specific functions. Children acquire culturally promoted values, skills, and ways of thinking through actively interacting with more competent members of their society in culturally favored fashions. And finally, individuals selectively adopt existing cognitive models of their culture to interpret meanings, solve problems, and understand themselves. We presented both theoretical and empirical support for the view that the culturally framed mind enables the coexistence of individual diversity and shared values in the modes of thinking and communication within each society.

The functional framework we outlined here focuses on the adaptability of cognitive competence and its development in the cultural context. Culture is not viewed as a static whole existing metaphysically far away from the developing child and straitjacketing all members into the identical modes of cognizing. Instead, culture operates as a dynamic system and process of overarching influences that have both direct and mediated impact on cognitive growth. This framework further emphasizes a bottom-up approach to understanding the cultural specificity of cognitive competence. Rather than considering whether a culture values particular cognitive domains, particular styles of adult–child interaction, or particular ways of thinking, we ask what kinds of skills, qualities, and competencies individuals in this culture need to develop to function effectively in their daily lives. This approach, in turn, can help us identify culture-specific domains, interaction patterns, and cognitive models. In addition, our framework construes both group and individual differences in cognitive functioning, emphasizing the active roles played by individuals in constructing, selecting, and adopting values, skills, and folk theories available to them.

Furthermore, a functional perspective to cognitive competence has important implications for ability testing and evaluation. This framework does not view cognitive competence as a set of fixed components operating in varied sociocultural contexts. Instead, cognitive competence is conceived of as emerging from and further situated within culture-specific contexts as a result of individuals' adaptation to particular demands imposed by such contexts. Competence and context are thus an integrated construct in our theorization as well as a proper unit of analysis. Testing and evaluation of cognitive competence should therefore not only reflect values within a particular society, but also consider the interrelatedness between cognitive functioning and specific contextual constraints.

In conclusion, the four aspects of cultural influences—cultural artifacts, cognitive domains, interpersonal contexts, and individual schemata—are not seen as located at different levels or layers in the child's developmental context (Bronfenbrenner & Morris, 1998) or viewed as isolable subsystems of the child's developmental niche (Super & Harkness, 1994). Instead, we envision them as embodied in each other and permeating every aspect of the child's daily life. It is through their dynamic interactions that the cultural adaptability of cognitive competence takes place, as reflected in the child's increasingly effective participation in his or her community of practice, in changes in the relationships between the child and significant others, and in the child's gradual assuming of an individual identity sanctioned by his or her culture.

REFERENCES

Bartlett, F. C. (1932). *Remembering: A study in experimental and social psychology.* Cambridge, England: Cambridge University Press.

Berry, J. (1976). *Human ecology and cognitive style.* New York: Wiley.

Berry, J. (1980). Cultural universality of any theory of human intelligence remains an open question. *Behavioral and Brain Sciences, 3,* 584–585.

Berry, J. W. (1993). An ecological approach to understanding cognition across cultures. In A. Jeanette (Ed.), *Advances in psychology: Vol. 103. Cognition and culture: A cross-cultural approach to cognitive psychology* (pp. 361–375). Amsterdam: Elsevier.

Bond, M. H. (1991). *Beyond the Chinese face.* Hong Kong: Oxford University Press.

Boroditsky, L. (2001). Does language shape thought? Mandarin and English speakers' conceptions of time. *Cognitive Psychology, 43,* 1–22.

Bronfenbrenner, U. (1979). *The ecology of human development.* Cambridge, MA: Harvard University Press.

Bronfenbrenner, U., & Ceci, S. J. (1994). Nature–nurture reconceptualized in developmental perspective: A bioecological model. *Psychological Review, 101,* 568–586.

Bronfenbrenner, U., & Morris, P. A. (1998). The ecology of developmental processes. In W. Damon (Series Ed.) & R. M. Lerner (Vol. Ed.), *Handbook of child psychology: Vol. 1. Theoretical models of human development* (5th ed., pp. 993–1028). New York: Wiley.

Bruner, J. (1990). *Acts of meaning.* Cambridge, MA: Harvard University Press.

Caporael, L. (2001). Evolutionary psychology: Toward a unifying theory and hybrid science. *Annual Review of Psychology, 52,* 607–628.

Carraher, T. N., Carraher, D., & Schliemann, A. D. (1985). Mathematics in the streets and in the schools. *British Journal of Developmental Psychology, 3*, 21–29.

Ceci, S. J. (1996). *On intelligence: A bioecological treatise on intellectual development.* Cambridge, MA: Harvard University Press.

Ceci, S. J., & Roazzi, A. (1994). The effects of context on cognition: Postcards from Brazil. In R. J. Sternberg & R. K. Wagner (Eds.), *Mind in context: Interactionist perspectives on human intelligence* (pp. 74–101). New York: Cambridge University Press.

Chiu, C. Y., Morris, M. W., Hong, Y. Y., & Menon, T. (2000). Motivated cultural cognition: The impact of implicit cultural theories on dispositional attribution varies as a function of need for closure. *Journal of Personality and Social Psychology, 78*, 247–259.

Chiu, L. H. (1972). A cross-cultural comparison of cognitive styles in Chinese and American children. *International Journal of Psychology, 7*, 235–242.

Choi, S., McDonough, L., Bowerman, M., & Mandler, J. M. (1999). Early sensitivity to language-specific spatial categories in English and Korean. *Cognitive Development, 14*, 241–268.

Cole, M. (1996). *Cultural psychology.* Cambridge, MA: Harvard University Press.

Conway, M., Wang, Q., Hanyu, K., & Haque, S. (2002). *A cross-cultural investigation of autobiographical memory: On the universality and cultural variation of the "reminiscence bump."* Manuscript submitted for publication.

Cousins, S. D. (1989). Culture and self-perception in Japan and the United States. *Journal of Personality and Social Psychology, 56*, 124–131.

D'Andrade, R. G. (1987). A folk model of the mind. In D. Holland & N. Quinn (Eds.), *Cultural models in language and thought* (pp. 112–148). New York: Cambridge University Press.

D'Andrade, R. G. (1992). Schemas and motivation. In R. G. D'Andrade & C. Strauss (Eds.), *Human motives and cultural models* (pp. 23–44). New York: Cambridge University Press.

Donald, M. (1991). *Origins of the modern mind: Three stages in the evolution of culture and cognition.* Cambridge, MA: Harvard University Press.

Elgin, S. H. (2000). *The language imperative.* Cambridge, MA: Perseus Books.

Fiske, A. P., Kitayama, S., Markus, H. R., & Nisbett, R. E. (1998). The cultural matrix of social psychology. In D. T. Gilbert, S. T. Fiske, & G. Lindzey (Eds.), *The handbook of social psychology* (4th ed., Vol. 4, pp. 915–981). Boston: McGraw-Hill.

Flynn, J. R. (1998). The schools: IQ tests, labels, and the word "intelligence". In J. S. Carlson, J. Kingma, & W. Tomic (Eds.), *Advances in cognition and educational practice: Vol. 5. Conceptual issues in research on intelligence* (pp. 13–42). London: JAI Press.

Fuson, K. C., & Kwon, Y. (1992). Effects of the system of number words and other cultural tools on children's addition and subtraction. In J. Bideaud & C. Meljac (Eds.), *Pathways to number: Children's developing numerical abilities* (pp. 127–149). Hillsdale, NJ: Erlbaum.

Gardner, H. (1984). The development of competence in culturally defined domains: A preliminary framework. In R. Shweder & R. Levine (Eds.), *Culture theory: Essays on mind, self, and emotion* (pp. 257–275). Cambridge, England: Cambridge University Press.

Gardner, H. (1989). *To open minds.* New York: Basic Books.

Gathercole, V. C. M., & Min, H. (1997). Word meaning biases or language-specific effects? Evidence from English, Spanish and Korean. *First Language, 17,* 31–56.

Gauvain, M. (2001). Cultural tools, social interaction and the development of thinking. *Human Development, 44,* 126–143.

Geary, D. C., Bow-Thomas, C. C., Liu, F., & Siegler, R. S. (1996). Development of arithmetic competencies in Chinese and American children: Influence of age, language, and schooling. *Child Development, 67,* 2022–2044.

Geary, D. C., Fan, L., & Bow-Thomas, C. C. (1992). Numerical cognition: Locus of ability differences comparing children from China and the United States. *Psychological Science, 3,* 180–185.

Geary, D. C., Salthouse, T. A., Chen, G.-P., & Fan, L. (1996). Are East Asian versus American differences in arithmetical ability a recent phenomenon? *Developmental Psychology, 32,* 254–262.

Goodnow, J. J. (2000). Combing analyses of culture and cognition: Essay review of mind, culture, and activity. *Human Development, 43,* 115–125.

Goody, J. (2001). Competencies and education: Contextual diversity. In D. S. Rychen & L. H. Salganik (Eds.), *Defining and selecting key competencies* (pp. 175–189). Kirkland, WA: Hogrefe & Huber Publishers.

Han, J. J., Leichtman, M. D., & Wang, Q. (1998). Autobiographical memory in Korean, Chinese, and American children. *Developmental Psychology, 34,* 701–713.

Hart, B., & Risley, T. R. (1995). *Meaningful differences in the everyday experience of young American children.* Baltimore: Brookes Publishing.

Heath, S. B. (1983). *Ways with words: Language, life, and work in communities and classrooms.* New York: Cambridge University Press.

Holland, D., & Quinn, N. (Eds.). (1987). *Cultural models in language and thought.* New York: Cambridge University Press.

Hong, Y.-Y., Morris, M. W., Chiu, C.-Y., & Benet-Martinez, V. (2000). Multicultural minds: A dynamic constructivist approach to culture and cognition. *American Psychologist, 55,* 709–720.

Hsu, F. L. K. (1953). *Americans and Chinese: Two ways of life.* New York: Henry Schuman.

Ji, L., Peng, K., & Nisbett, R. E. (2000). Culture, control, and perception of relationships in the environment. *Journal of Personality and Social Psychology, 78,* 943–955.

Kagitcibasi, C. (1996). *Family and human development across cultures: A view from the other side.* Hillsdale, NJ: Erlbaum.

Kearins, J. M. (1981). Visual spatial memory in Australian aboriginal children of the desert regions. *Cognitive Psychology, 13,* 434–460.

Kitayama, S., & Markus, H. R. (Eds.). (1994). *Emotion and culture: Empirical studies of mutual influence*. Washington, DC: American Psychological Association.

Lakoff, G., & Johnson, M. (1980). *Metaphors we live by*. Chicago: University of Chicago Press.

LeVine, R. A., Dixon, S., LeVine, S., Richman, A., Leiderman, P. H., Keefer, C. H., & Brazelton, T. B. (1994). *Child care and culture: Lessons from Africa*. New York: Cambridge University Press.

Li, J. (2001). Chinese conceptualization of learning. *Ethos, 29*, 111–137.

Libby, L. K., & Eibach, R. P. (2002). Looking back in time: Self-concept change affects visual perspective in autobiographical memory. *Journal of Personality and Social Psychology, 82*, 167–179.

Light, P., & Butterworth, G. (Eds.). (1993). *Context and cognition: Ways of learning and knowing*. Hillsdale, NJ: Erlbaum.

MacDonald, S., Uesiliana, K., & Hayne, H. (2000). Cross-cultural and gender differences in childhood amnesia. *Memory, 8*, 365–376.

Markus, H. R., & Kitayama, S. (1991). Culture and the self: Implications for cognition, emotion, and motivation. *Psychological Review, 98*, 224–253.

Martinez, I. M. & Shatz, M. (1996). Linguistic influences on categorization in preschool children: A crosslinguistic study. *Journal of Child Language, 23*, 529–545.

Masten, A., & Coatsworth, D. (1995). Competence, resilience, and psychopathology. In D. Cicchetti & D. J. Cohen (Eds.), *Developmental psychopathology: Vol. 2. Risk, disorder, and adaptation* (pp. 715–752). New York: Wiley.

Miller, K. F., Smith, C. M., Zhu, J., & Zhang, H. (1995). Preschool origins of cross-national differences in mathematical competence: The role of number-naming systems. *Psychological Science, 6*, 56–60.

Miller, P. J., Fung, H., & Mintz, J. (1996). Self-construction through narrative practices: A Chinese and American comparison of early socialization. *Ethos, 24*, 237–280.

Miller, P. J., & Hoogstra, L. (1992). Language as tool in the socialization and apprehension of cultural meanings. In T. Schwartz, G. M. White, & C. A. Lutz (Eds.), *New directions in psychological anthropology* (Vol. 3, pp. 83–101). New York: Cambridge University Press.

Miller, P. J., Wiley, A. R., Fung, H., & Liang, C. H. (1997). Personal storytelling as a medium of socialization in Chinese and American families. *Child Development, 68*, 557–568.

Mistry, J., & Rogoff, B. (1985). A cultural perspective on the development of talent. In F. D. Horowitz & M. O'Brien (Eds.), *The gifted and talented: Developmental perspectives* (pp. 125–144). Washington, DC: American Psychological Association.

Morris, M. W., Nisbett, R. E., & Peng, K. (1995). Causal attribution across domains and cultures. In D. Sperber, D. Premack, & A. J. Premack (Eds.), *Causal cognition: A multidisciplinary debate* (pp. 577–612). Oxford, England: Clarendon Press.

Mullen, M. K. (1994). Earliest recollections of childhood: A demographic analysis. *Cognition, 52*(1), 55–79.

Mullen, M. K., & Yi, S. (1995). The cultural context of talk about the past: Implications for the development of autobiographical memory. *Cognitive Development, 10*, 407–419.

Nakamura, H. (1964). *Ways of thinking of Eastern peoples: India–China–Tibet–Japan.* Honolulu, HI: East-West Center Press.

Nelson, K. (1996). *Language in cognitive development: The emergence of the mediated mind.* New York: Cambridge University Press.

Nisbett, R. E., Peng, K., Choi, I., & Norenzayan, A. (2001). Culture and systems of thought: Holistic versus analytic cognition. *Psychological Review, 108*, 291–310.

Nosek, B. A., Banaji, M. R., & Greenwald, A. G. (2002). Math = male, me = female, therefore math not = me. *Journal of Personality and Social Psychology, 83*, 44–59.

Ochs, E. (1993). Constructing social identity: A language socialization perspective. *Research on Language and Social Interaction, 26*, 287–306.

Oyama, S. (1998). Locating development, locating developmental systems. In E. K. Scholnick, K. Nelson, S. A. Gelman, & P. H. Miller (Eds.), *Conceptual development: Piaget's legacy* (pp. 2–26). Hillsdale, NJ: Erlbaum.

Pillemer, D. B. (1998). *Momentous events, vivid memories.* Cambridge, MA: Harvard University Press.

Resnick, L. B., Levine, J. M., & Teasley, S. D. (Eds.). (1991). *Perspectives on socially shared cognition.* Washington, DC: American Psychological Association.

Rhee, E., Uleman, J. S., Lee, H. K., & Roman, R. J. (1995). Spontaneous self-descriptions and ethnic identities in individualistic and collectivistic cultures. *Journal of Personality and Social Psychology, 69*, 142–152.

Roberson, D., Davies, I., & Davidoff, J. (2000). Color categories are not universal: Replications and new evidence from a stone-age culture. *Journal of Experimental Psychology: General, 129*, 369–398.

Rogoff, B. (1990). *Apprenticeship in thinking: Cognitive development in social context.* New York: Oxford University Press.

Rogoff, B. (1998). Cognition as a collaborative process. In W. Damon (Series Ed.) & D. Kuhn & R. S. Siegler (Vol. Ed.), *Handbook of child psychology: Vol. 2. Cognition, perception, and language* (5th ed.). New York: Wiley.

Ross, M. (1989). Relation of implicit theories to the construction of personal histories. *Psychological Review, 96*, 341–357.

Ross, M., Xun, E., & Wilson, A. E. (2002). Language and the bicultural self. *Personality and Social Psychology Bulletin, 28*, 1040–1050.

Röttger-Rössler, B. (1993). Autobiography in question: On self-presentation and life description in an Indonesian society. *Anthropos, 88*, 365–373.

Sapir, E. (1964). *Culture, language, and personality.* Berkeley: University of California Press. (Original work published in 1941)

Shweder, R. A., & Bourne, E. J. (1984). Does the concept of the person vary cross-culturally? In R. A. Shweder & R. A. LeVine (Eds.), *Culture theory: Essays on mind, self, and emotion* (pp. 158–199). New York: Cambridge University Press.

Shweder, R. A., Goodnow, J., Hatano, G., LeVine, R. A., Markus, H., & Miller, P. (1998). The cultural psychology of development: One mind, many mentalities. In W. Damon (Series Ed.) & R. M. Lerner (Vol. Ed.), *Handbook of child psychology: Vol. 1. Theoretical models of human development* (5th ed., pp. 865–937). New York: Wiley.

Siegler, R. S. (1987). The perils of averaging data over strategies: An example from children's addition. *Journal of Experimental Psychology: General, 116,* 250–264.

Small, M. F. (2001). *Kids: How biology and culture shape the way we raise our children.* New York: Doubleday.

Sternberg, R. J. (1986). *Intelligence applied: Understanding and increasing your intellectual skills.* Orlando, FL: Harcourt Brace Jovanovich.

Sternberg, R. J. (2002). Intelligence is not just inside the head: The theory of successful intelligence. In J. Aronson (Ed.), *Improving academic achievement: Impact of psychological factors on education* (pp. 227–244). San Diego, CA: Academic Press.

Sternberg, R. J., & Grigorenko, E. L. (2000). Theme-park psychology: A case study regarding human intelligence and its implications for education. *Educational Psychology Review, 12,* 247–268.

Sternberg, R. J., & Grigorenko, E. L. (2001). Ability testing across cultures. In L. A. Suzuki, J. G. Ponterotto, & P. J. Meller (Eds.), *Handbook of multicultural assessment: Clinical, psychological, and educational applications* (2nd ed., pp. 335–358). San Francisco, CA: Jossey-Bass.

Stevenson, H. W., & Lee, S. Y. (1990). Context of achievement. *Monographs of the Society for Research in Child Development, 55* (Serial No. 221).

Stigler, J. W., & Perry, M. (1990). Mathematics learning in Japanese, Chinese, and American classrooms. In J. W. Stigler, R. A. Shweder, & G. Herdt (Eds.), *Cultural psychology* (pp. 328–353). New York: Cambridge University Press.

Super, C. M., & Harkness, S. (1994). The developmental niche. In W. J. Lonner & R. Malpass (Eds.), *Psychology and culture* (pp. 95–99). Boston: Allyn & Bacon.

Super, C. M., & Harkness, S. (1999). The environment as culture in developmental research. In S. L. Friedman & T. D. Wachs (Eds.), *Measuring environment across the life span* (pp. 279–323). Washington, DC: American Psychological Association.

Trafimow, D., Triandis, H. C., & Goto, S. G. (1991). Some tests of the distinction between the private and the collective self. *Journal of Personality and Social Psychology, 60,* 649–655.

Triandis, H. C. (1989). The self and social behavior in differing cultural contexts. *Psychological Review, 96,* 506–520.

Tu, W. M. (1979). *Humanity and self-cultivation: Essays in Confucian thought.* Berkeley, CA: Asian Humanities Press.

Valsiner, J. (2000). *Culture and human development.* Newbury Park, CA: Sage.

Vygotsky, L. (1978). *Mind in society.* Cambridge, MA: Harvard University Press.

Wang, Q. (2001a). "Did you have fun?": American and Chinese mother–child conversations about shared emotional experiences. *Cognitive Development, 16,* 693–715.

Wang, Q. (2001b). Cultural effects on adults' earliest childhood recollection and self-description: Implications for the relation between memory and the self. *Journal of Personality and Social Psychology, 81,* 220–233.

Wang, Q. (2003). Emotion situation knowledge in American and Chinese preschool children and adults. *Cognition & Emotion, 17,* 725–746.

Wang, Q. (in press). The emergence of cultural self-construct: Autobiographical memory and self-description in American and Chinese children.

Wang, Q., & Brockmeier, J. (2002). Autobiographical remembering as cultural practice: Understanding the interplay between memory, self and culture. *Culture & Psychology, 8,* 45–64.

Wang, Q., & Leichtman, M. D. (2000). Same beginnings, different stories: A comparison of American and Chinese children's narratives. *Child Development, 71,* 1329–1346.

Wang, Q., Leichtman, M. D., & Davies, K. (2000). Sharing memories and telling stories: American and Chinese mothers and their 3-year-olds. *Memory, 8,* 159 177.

Wang, Q., Leichtman, M. D., & White, S. H. (1998). Childhood memory and self-description in young Chinese adults: The impact of growing up an only child. *Cognition, 69,* 75–105.

Wertsch, J. V. (1991). *Voices of the mind: A sociocultural approach to mediated action.* Cambridge: Harvard University Press.

White, G. M. (1987). Proverbs and cultural models: An American psychology of problem solving. In D. Holland & N. Quinn (Eds.), *Cultural models in language and thought* (pp. 151–172). New York: Cambridge University Press.

Whorf, B., & Carroll, J. B. (Ed.). (1956). *Language, thought and reality: Selected writings of Benjamin Lee Whorf.* Cambridge, MA: MIT Press.

11

ETHNOEPISTEMOLOGIES AT HOME AND AT SCHOOL

ISABEL ZAMBRANO AND PATRICIA GREENFIELD

Both intelligence and knowledge acquisition represent core human competencies. Yet they do not mean the same thing around the world. There is
by now a rich tradition of theory and data on cultural conceptions of intelli-

Earlier versions of this chapter appeared as a paper with the same title by Isabel Zambrano and in a paper
called "Cultural Context and Developmental Theory: Evidence from the Maya of Mexico"; both were
presented at the symposium *Cultural Context and Developmental Theory* organized by Patricia Greenfield
at the 29th Annual Symposium of the Jean Piaget Society for the Study of Knowledge and Development, Mexico City, June, 1999. Isabel Zambrano is currently supported by an NSF Minority Postdoctoral
Fellowship. The research in Mitontik was supported by the National Science Foundation (a Minority
Graduate Fellowship and a Dissertation Improvement Fellowship), the Harvard Foundation (Mexico en
Harvard Fund), the Tinker Foundation, the Harvard Department of Anthropology, the Harvard Insti-
tute for International Development, and the Harvard Graduate School of the Arts and Sciences (a
Harvard Prize Fellowship).

The authors would like to thank Steven Lopez, Principal Investigator of the Fogarty Minority Interna-
tional Research Training Grant for his support, as well as El Colegio de la Frontera Sur in San Cristobal
de las Casas, who hosted and made their facilities available to us in the summer of 1997. The research in
Zinacantán in the 1990s was also made possible by grants from the Spencer Foundation, the National
Geographic Society, the Wenner-Gren Foundation, the University of California—Los Angeles (UCLA)
Latin American Studies Center, UCLA Center for the Study of Women, and the UCLA Academic
Senate. The research in Zinancantán in 1969 and 1970 was made possible by the Harvard Chiapas
Project, the Harvard Center for Cognitive Studies, National Science Foundation, Harvard Center for
Cognitive Studies, and the Milton Fund. We would also like to thank our friends in Mitontik and
Nabenchauk, who patiently made our understanding of *na'* and *know* possible.

gence (Dasen, 1984; Gill & Keats, 1980; Grigorenko et al., 2001; Nsamenang, 1992; Serpell, 1993; Super, 1983; Wober, 1974). This body of work, stemming from the field of cultural psychology, makes it clear that our Western presuppositions about the nature of intelligence are not the only ones. However, most researchers, like most lay people, would probably be surprised to learn that there are alternative conceptions of a closely related set of notions: knowledge and knowing. Because these concepts are central to the fields of cognitive psychology and cognitive development, they are particularly interesting to explore from the perspective of cross-cultural variability.

Why is our chapter titled "Ethnoepistemologies at Home and at School?" The term *epistemology* comes from the discipline of philosophy and refers to an explicit, formal theory of knowledge. *Ethnoepistemology*, the key word in our title, refers to the thesis of this chapter: Different ethnic groups have their own implicit, informal theories of knowledge and that these ethnotheories form the assumptions on which the explicit formal theories are based.

As an example of variability in the conception of knowledge, we contrast the Tzotzil Mayan term *na'* (know) with the English word *know*. Although *na'* clearly glosses as "know" (Laughlin, 1975) and even overlaps with it, its core meanings are surprisingly different. *Na'* is much more demanding in key respects, such as in its reference to practice. However, in a world in which different cultures have been in close contact—through involuntary processes such as conquest, voluntary processes such as immigration, and systemic processes such as economic globalization—different ethnoepistemologies can also come into contact. And this is exactly what has happened to *na'* and *know* in the Tzotzil-speaking community of Mitontik. *Na'*, as we shall show, epitomizes indigenous values concerning knowledge, whereas *know* is highly valued in the school, an institution that has been imposed on Mayan communities from outside.

Know and *na'* allow us to explore the cultural nature of knowledge and knowing and the intellectual and social competencies they index. These competencies consist of cultural forms of intelligence, which in turn presuppose cultural forms of knowing. Contrasting forms of knowledge have important implications for developmental theory as well as for cognitive psychology. We therefore move from cultural conceptions of intelligence to cultural conceptions of knowledge, and, from there, to implications for developmental and cognitive psychology. Although cultures differ in their emphasis on the two kinds of knowledge indexed by *know* and *na'*, we end by discussing how both forms of knowledge exist side by side in a single culture.

CULTURAL CONCEPTIONS OF INTELLIGENCE

In developmental psychology, the classical theory of intelligence is that of Piaget. Understanding the basis for Western scientific thought was Piaget's most fundamental theoretical concern (Piaget, 1977). Under Inhelder's leadership, Piaget investigated the development of scientific thought (chemistry and physics) in a set of experimental studies (Inhelder & Piaget, 1958). This body of theory and research implies the importance of scientific intelligence as a developmental goal (Greenfield, 1974). Clearly, scientific intelligence involves the acquisition of scientific knowledge; hence the close connections between theories of intelligence and theories of knowledge.

Although Piaget considered his theory to be universal, it has turned out to rest on an ethnotheory, a culture-specific concept of intelligence. We know this because its assumptions are not shared around the world. Indeed, in sharp contrast to the value of scientific intelligence, social intelligence has been found to be the predominant ideal in Africa and Asia (e.g., Dasen, 1984; Gill & Keats, 1980; Grigorenko et al., 2001; Serpell, 1993; Super, 1983; Wober, 1974). For example, the central feature of the Baoulé concept of intelligence is willingness to help others (Dasen, 1984). This quality of intelligence privileges social understanding, a quite different form of knowledge than that privileged by scientific intelligence. As we will see with *know* and *na'*, in Africa, competing ethnotheories of intelligence may be operative at home and at school, the latter being of European origin (Dasen, 1984).

Whereas the most comprehensive theory of development in Europe is Piaget's theory of cognitive development, the most comprehensive theory of development in Cameroon, West Africa, is that of Nsamenang, who outlines stages of development in terms of social roles (Nsamenang, 1992). In general, African cultures not only emphasize social intelligence, but also see the role of technical skills as a means to social ends (Dasen, 1984).

As we have seen, particular conceptions of intelligence privilege particular conceptions of knowledge. In this chapter, we focus on two different conceptions of knowledge, one indexed by the Tzotzil Mayan word *na'*, the other indexed by the English word *know*. As we will show, in San Miguel Mitontik, the Tzotzil word *na'*, meaning to know, has a more person-centered meaning, compared with the English word *know* (Zambrano, 1999). Whereas to "know" in English always involves the mind, *na'* often involves the heart and soul. (According to Li [2002], a similar concept of "heart and mind for wanting to learn" is found in China.) Whereas "knowing" connotes factual knowledge, theoretical understanding, or know-how, *na'* also connotes knowledge of practice that is habitual and characteristic of a given person; it is very much akin to character. The former type of knowledge is more important in a culture valuing the individual's possession of credentialed knowledge. The latter is more important in a culture placing a greater value on social character. Both coexist in San Miguel Mitontik; however, *na'* a Tzotzil word, originates in the indigenous Maya culture and is traditionally valued at home. *Know* (or *saber* in Spanish) originates in the school, imposed on Mayan communities by the Spanish-speaking Mexican state, the institutional inheritance of the Spanish conquest.

METHODOLOGY

Isabel Zambrano, an anthropologist, identified the revealing contrast between *na'* and *know* during 10 years of ethnographic and historical research in the Tzotzil-speaking highland Maya community of San Miguel Mitontik. (The people often refer to themselves as Migueleros, and the short name of the community is simply Mitontik.) In this chapter, we combine Zambrano's insights about *na'* in Mitontik with findings from Patricia Greenfield's long-term (begun in 1969) field research in Zinacantán; Greenfield is a cultural and developmental psychologist. In addition to Zambrano and Greenfield's work, further examples are taken from Eber and Rosenbaum's (1998) studies of Chenalhó and Chamula, also in highland Chiapas, from Maynard and De Leon's studies in Zinacantán, and from Gaskin's research among the Yucatec Maya. But, although most of our examples come from a few rural Maya communities in north central Chiapas (see Figure 11.1), the epistemological findings have implications for other Maya communities and other non-Maya face-to-face (local) contexts.

In her ethnography, Zambrano (1999) acted as a participant–observer in Mitontik and the nearby city of San Cristobal de las Casas, recording observations of everyday life into her field notes, while getting to know the language, the ideas, the lifeways, and the people of the community. Her experiences, recorded in field notes, furnished examples of *know* and *na'*. Ethnography is a core methodological concept from anthropology; its individualized and contextualized nature contrasts sharply with the methodology of cross-cultural psychology, in which standardized procedures, such as IQ tests, are typically administered across multiple cultural settings (Greenfield, 1997). Zambrano also used historical data from official government archives to find out about the history of schooling, relevant to changing conceptions of the nature of knowledge.

Greenfield and colleagues (Greenfield, 1999, in press; Greenfield, Maynard, & Childs, in press) took her methods from cultural psychology, a field that amalgamates psychology and anthropology. Indeed, this chapter is in itself an interdisciplinary endeavor, authored by an anthropologist and a psychologist and combining methodology and concepts from the two disciplines. As is normative in cultural psychology, Greenfield's procedures were derived from and adapted to Zinacantec culture and then standardized within the community. They were not meant to "travel" abroad. Most pertinent to the topic of this chapter, she made videotapes of girls at various stages of learning to weave, a culturally valued form of knowledge.

Gaskins (1999) and Maynard's (1999, 2002) studies followed in this tradition of cultural psychology, while Eber (Eber & Rosenbaum, 1998) worked in the anthropological tradition of Zambrano. De Leon (1999) is a linguistic anthropologist, who, like Greenfield, uses video as a record-keeping tool, but, in the anthropological tradition, does not try to standard-

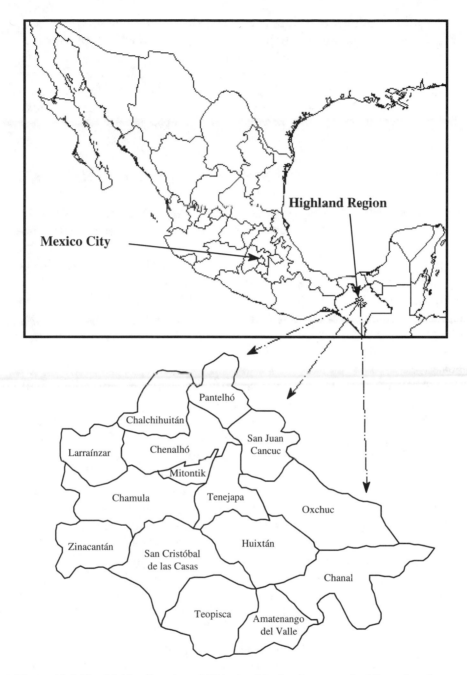

Figure 11.1. The highland region of Chiapas, Mexico (gray section) in national context.

ize the situations that she videotapes. To capture naturally occurring inter-action among a few interactants takes precedence over the achievement of comparability across large numbers of participants. Because the most significant feature of culture for a cultural or linguistic anthropologist is the process of constructing meaning and because language is the human tool par excellence for doing this, what people say—that is, their spontaneous interpretations of their own experience—is a prime data source in these fields (e.g., Duranti, 1997). We begin with some ethnographic examples from Zambrano's extensive fieldwork in Mitontik. From spontaneous talk in defined contexts emerges a cultural interpretation of knowing and knowledge.

AN INTRODUCTION TO *NA'*: DO YOU KNOW THE DRINKING OF SODA?

Zambrano was first introduced to the special nature of *na'*-type knowledge when some Mitontik friends extended her their special brand of hospitality by asking "*Mi xana' yuch'el rasqu?*" Instead of directly asking "Would you like something to drink?" her Miguelero friends posed a question that, literally translated, means "Do you know the drinking of soda?" (*rasqu*, from *refresco*, the regional Spanish word for soda pop). This question may be particularly posed to foreign guests as an inquiry as to whether people from another land are used to (or are in the habit of) drinking this particular type of beverage.

Although these invitations to have a soda were important and usually hard-won marks of acceptance and friendship, they left Zambrano wondering, "Why does this simple offer of a soda require a reference to knowledge?" and "What form of knowledge would that be?" Even with this first encounter, it seemed clear to Zambrano that the *na'* form of knowledge had *practice*, especially habitual practice, as one of its core meanings.

A second example of the use of *na'* occurred during a Mitontik graduation dinner. A delightful one-and-a-half-year-old girl smiled and made friendly gestures toward Zambrano—then a stranger to her—throughout the meal. The child's behavior was striking because most infants and toddlers in Mitontik, as in other highland Maya communities, are extremely wary of people from outside of their household. Leonor, the student whose graduation was being celebrated, noted the interaction and remarked, in Spanish, "*No sabe tener miedo*" —literally, "The child doesn't *know* how to have fear." Leonor's remark was about how the child's behavior characterized her— namely, "She is an open, friendly child." In the future, this unusual little girl might be identified as the one who is so open, who "doesn't *know* how to be wary." Along the same lines, other Migueleros warned Zambrano about unfriendly people who "don't know how to speak (nicely)"; a person with a temper is often described as one who "knows how to get angry"; and a gentle husband might be admired as one who "does not know how to hit his wife."

The conception of knowledge assumed in all of these examples is a knowledge of practice so habitual that it characterizes. The soda pop example points to habitual practice as one of the core meanings of *na'*; the other examples further establish term's reference to the type of knowledge-practice that can be used to characterize a knower–doer. In the latter sense, *na'*-based characterizations assert a relationship between a person's knowledge–practice and her or his reputation in a community.

As a local form of knowledge that is practicable, demonstrable, and habitual to the point of being characteristic, *na'* bears a strong resemblance to Bourdieu's (1977/1986) notion of *habitus* and thus to Bateson's (1936/1958) notion of *ethos* before it. Bourdieu and Bateson are fairly similar in using their terms to refer at once to (a) the social and cultural context itself, (b) the classifying and generative schemes inculcated into the individual, and (c) the resultant practices of the enculturated individual herself or himself, the individual who has been socialized into a culture. It is easy to imagine *habitus* and *ethos* as generalizations about a group's knowledge-related practices and the underlying concepts that generate them. However, the concept of *na'* allows us to consider greater complexity with respect to voice (that is, varying perspectives among the people being studied), history (the origins of conflicting concepts of knowledge), and representation (people's own comments about knowing and knowledge in different settings and situations). These differences make *na'* a more apt term for understanding social change.

Instead of the coherence of local knowledge emphasized in the concepts of *habitus* and *ethos*, *na'* forces one to focus on the roles of local dialogue and cross talk in the construction of culture. As a term used solely by members of a face-to-face community as they try to make sense of and affect each other and the dynamic world around them, *na'* refers to the knowledge link between an individual or subgroup in the community and Mitontik's moral and communicative universe: namely, how she–he–they are known and knowable and the epistemological implications of that knowledge. As a knowledge link, *na'* refers not only to the material, social, and cultural matters (including everyday practices) that *habitus* and *ethos* presume to capture, but also to local commentaries on *na'* and self-representations designed to minimize negative *na'* commentaries. Indeed, it is these commentaries and self-representations that produce those cultural schemes, contexts, and practices.

Na' is thus in line with recent approaches that view culture "as emerging from events as much as underlying them" (Tsing, 1993, p. 105). In other words, the notion is that people produce culture, not vice-versa (Rockwell, 1996). This concept of people producing culture contrasts strongly with the notion foundational to cross-cultural psychology and common in psychology in general: culture as an independent variable that "causes" individual behavior, which is in turn seen as a dependent variable.

Na' characterizations—that is, describing people in terms of their habitual practices—are like gossip in being particularly effective means of constructing knowledge in that they influence community perceptions and other forms of socialization. As Haviland has observed, gossip "helps map the community for its members" (Haviland, 1977, p. 10). For instance, it is through gossip with kin relations and other social networks that individuals can efficiently learn about desirable and undesirable associates and the most profitable way to interact with them. Thus, gossiping about an "unfortunate old man allows the participants to . . . decide together what to think about the man himself, and . . . assess the causes for his misfortune and guide their future actions accordingly" (Haviland, 1977, p.164). The characteristic practice referred to as *na'* (as opposed to knowledge that is unique, one-time only) and its consequences may be a particularly instructive way for local members of a community to learn about any given life situation. The close relationship between a person's habitual behavior (*na'*) and her or his reputation (community-held identity) may also be a particularly effective way of influencing community perceptions (Basso, 1983, 1988, 1996). For example, individuals with particularly extravagant conduct become "social banners" —that is, they come to "signify" and "embody," and thus are seen as challenges to correct behavior in a small, face-to-face community. Stories about them can be read as a "social text on the subject of human decency": They become "effective vehicles of propaganda . . . necessary precisely because the maintenance of a given symbolic order is always as problematic as its change" (Scott, 1985, pp. 22–23). *Na'* commentaries (commentaries about people's characteristic practices) are thus vital forms of intelligence gathering and intelligence making, intelligence that concerns the maintenance of social norms.

One important difference between *na'* and the important notion of "gossip" is that *na'* involves a theory of knowledge—namely, of which knowledge is privileged and recognized and which is not. One clear example from Zambrano's fieldwork is that if she asked a third party about a person's schooling, she would often be told about whether or not that person was ever seen reading or writing. Individuals, especially women, would themselves often report to Zambrano that they had no schooling; however she would later discover that they had completed two or even four years of schooling. This same occurrence was very common in Greenfield's Zinacantec Maya field-site of Nabenchauk. If presented with this contradiction, the most common explanation given to Zambrano was that they had known how to read and write when they were in school, but that they had not continued to practice those skills—that is, because they no longer practiced the school knowledge, they could not be considered (or consider themselves) to be schooled.

In the you-know-only-what-you-practice *na'* world, "doing" knowledge is what is privileged. In the terms of cognitive psychology, procedural knowledge is more highly valued than is declarative knowledge. This preference is indicated in the physicality of the Tzotzil terms for these activities: School is called *chan vun*, "learning paper," and reading is called *k'el vun*, "looking at paper" (Greenfield & Maynard, 1997). If one is not actively "looking at paper," one may be considered illiterate regardless of school experience and previous literacy skills. *Na's* privileging of practiced knowledge results in anomalous social research findings. For instance, the illiteracy rate reported in the 1993 Mitontik census was higher than that indicated in the 1984 school census despite a significant rise in school participation and curricular improvements. In a *na'* world, literacy skills and school attainment do not have the constancy that they have in a "know" world. They can evaporate through disuse.

FROM *NA'* TO *KNOW*: A DISCUSSION OF APPROPRIATE SETTINGS

Zambrano experienced a second, more humbling example of the *na'* world's privileging of observable knowledge. She found that whereas women and men with six or more years of schooling (and especially those with schooling-based jobs) readily recognized her Harvard credentials and went out of their way to associate with her, all others generally considered her a nonentity until she demonstrated that she knew how to behave in a locally meaningful way: for example, participating in community events with well-regarded community members, waking up earlier than others, working long hours, or communicating in Tzotzil. Zambrano found that, even after she had developed friendships and discussed her work, her credentials and her reasons for being in their rural community never gained any further recognition. She was known solely for her observable acts in their local face-to-face world.

This distinction—between the more-schooled people ready to recognize the knowledge value of Zambrano's credentials and the lesser-schooled people demanding to know her through her actions—is a useful metonym for the contrast between *know* and *na'*. Both *na'* and *know* can be used to refer to such things as factual knowledge, theoretical understanding, problem solving, and skills. The point of distinction, as may be evident by this point in the chapter, is that *na's* approach to knowledge goes much beyond mental knowledge or even that knowledge that is occasionally practiced. *Na'* requires that knowledge be, at a minimum, demonstrably practiced. However, it is those practices that are so habitual as to be characteristic of a knower–doer that present the most irrefutable evidence that a *na'* standard of knowledge has been attained.

It is not coincidental that Zambrano discovered the significance of *na'* while researching the expansion of mass schooling into Mitontik. The distinction is between the kind of knowledge that is privileged in small face-to-face contexts (indexed by the word *na'*) and the kind of credential-centered knowledge that prevails in large-scale systems (indexed by the word *know*).

Unlike Zambrano's older friends in Mitontik, the little toddler who "did not know how" to fear her at the graduation ceremony will probably not "know how" to use *na'* when she describes others to her in the future. Zambrano later discovered the missing piece to the puzzle of the Mitontik toddler who "didn't know how to fear": namely, that the little girl's father was a schooled man with sufficient ambition to occupy the lower reaches of the government's schooling-based reward system (e.g., he has been responsible for the local *Conasupo*, a government-subsidized store, and INEA, a program to promote adult literacy). Even at one-and-a-half, he had already taught his daughter to have an eagerness for personal interaction (with a much diminished concern with family boundaries) previously rare in Mitontik children. Like the children of all of Mitontik's school teachers, Zambrano's charming graduation dinner companion presents an example of the shift away from the use of *na'*. In this particular example, to know a person could now be a one-time occasion, rather than an habitual long-term acquaintance. This shift is a useful index of how schools are transforming socialization in Mitontik. The community's primary language is still Tzotzil but more and more men and, gradually, women are gaining Spanish fluency in school, and with it, exposure to Spanish-based vocabulary, concepts, and values.

Since the 1920s, schools have contributed to increasing intracommunity variation along three axes of experience: schooling, Spanish fluency, and travel outside of the *municipio* or community. At either extreme, one finds individuals who speak in only one language register. At one end are the adults who are firmly tied to the community: *na'* expresses their life-based experience that others will act on what these people "know" and confidence that they can be "known" in that way. *What* is to be known is also very circumscribed, for as Haviland (1977, pp. 179–80) noted:

> Within the Zinacanteco universe it makes little sense to talk about rules governing these skills [male corn hoeing, accepting drink, entering a house; female tortilla-making, skirt and hair tying]. Departures from standard behavior no longer constitute behavior at all: Nonnormal action conveys no messages (except the ultimate message: "I am no longer a Zinacanteco [or a human being]"). Only when there are alternatives can behaving a certain way have meaning.

At the other extreme are people who are progressively distancing themselves from their community. Especially prominent here are the young people who have lived and studied in San Cristóbal, the regional city of Spanish colonial origins, and who would almost never speak in Tzotzil or even use the Spanish word, *saber*, with the meaning of *na'*.

In between, it may be that the use varies with the extent to which a person is vulnerable to being "knowable"—that is, vulnerable to the moral community of humbler Mitontik (discussed below). The invitations of the more-schooled and less-tied-to-Mitontik are like any one might hear at a Cambridge cocktail party: "Would you like something to drink?"

LEARNING MODELS

Researchers have conceptualized this type of schooling-related transformation as moving from an apprenticeship-type pattern of socialization to a more pedagogical pattern. This dichotomy was useful to Zambrano's early conceptualization of the *na'–know* distinction (Greenfield & Lave, 1982; Rogoff, 1990). It remains a good starting point for discussing how the two concepts of knowledge are socialized and how they are manifest in different kinds of learning processes.

The *apprenticeship* model, and its infancy and early childhood version known as the protective style, are based on the assumption that the developing person will learn through observation and gradual participation. The Childs and Greenfield (1980) video study of weaving apprenticeship in Zinacantán (a highland Maya community) presents a clear example of how central observation is to the acquisition of knowledge in Maya culture. Gaskins (1999) similarly highlights the importance of observation in children's everyday learning in a lowland Maya community:

> Much of a Maya child's time is spent observing the other actors in the compound. Before the age of two, a child can spend 40% of his time looking at other people and things. Between the ages of 2 and 3, as the child is becoming more engaged in the larger social world, they still focus on the observation of activities. During this period, their ability to understand events and monitor actions at a distance improves. By three, a child can usually report accurately where every member of her household is and what he or she is doing. The child often appears to be keeping sort of a running tab on compound activities through careful observation. This kind of behavior is similar to that of the adults, who are careful observers and monitor village activity in the same way. . . . Up until age 15, between 70 to 80% of the socially oriented behavior is observation, not interaction. . . .
>
> To the Western eye, this looks a lot like withdrawal or a lack of engagement. But such pervasive social observation as that found in Maya children . . . actually represents a strong engagement with the world through focused observation.

Gaskins thus convincingly repeats the finding that Mayas believe that children learn best by watching. Watching exposes you to the practice of others. It is a logical form of socialization for the practice-based knowledge that is central to the Mayan *na'*.

In terms of participation, the other key facet of apprenticeship learning, Gaskins (1999) notes that Mayan children in the Yucatan Peninsula are included in adult work from an early age. She finds that Mayan parents believe that "chores help their children to grow up to be competent and motivated workers" and thus that "engaging children in adult work is responsible parenting."

In highland Chiapas, only a few hours drive from Mitontik, Maynard (2002) carried out a developmental study of child-to-child teaching in informal play groups in the Zinacantec village of Nabenchauk. Teaching, in Maynard's study, was frequently not a dyadic activity but instead a cross-age group activity involving active participation by all present. Even children as young as 4 can be seen guiding the learning of their 2-year-old siblings in the informal participatory settings that characterize apprenticeship-style learning. The level of teaching sophistication among the children guiding the apprenticeship of younger learners develops as children make social and cognitive advances from age 3 to 11.

Most important for present purposes, Maynard has found that virtually all of the cross-age play sequences in her videotaped sample involved cultural teaching and cultural learning. Unlike U.S. culture, in which each new generation is encouraged to "do their own thing," older Zinacantec children were constantly providing experiences so that their younger siblings could gain the knowledge that defines Zinacantec work and life: knowledge of washing, making tortillas, caring for babies, buying and selling. In other words, what was taught was expected habit and practice, that is, *na'*. The practice of teaching, started at such a young age, is itself an important body of habitual knowledge by adulthood. This expertise at teaching in turn leads to no-failure learning of culturally central skills such as weaving (Childs & Greenfield, 1980).

The apprenticeship model is very different from the *pedagogical* approach toward childhood as a time for play and mental learning. For children who have learned in the pedagogical model, work can come as a sudden shock to which they have not had prior practice. Pedagogically trained individuals may require additional instruction before they can perform work skills and routines—for example, short-term problem-solving strategies, additional verbal instruction, and even manual-based learning. In other words, we often learn our work through the epistemological framework of *know* rather than *na'*. In contrast, the Mayan practice of integrating children into work early on and bit by bit transforms work into habitual practice by the time it must be carried out as an adult task.

The pedagogical style has, in contrast to the apprenticeship style, been associated with mothers whose goal is to promote verbal communication (Feiring & Lewis, 1981; LeVine et al., 1991). It is characterized by distal responses, such as smile, vocalization, and gaze. In the pedagogical model, the adult or skilled person bears more responsibility for the novice's learning. Thus, an important element of this pattern is that the adult or expert stop her or his work and production to give full attention to instructing the novice.

The LeVine research in central Mexico found that the more-schooled mothers in their sample adopted a more pedagogical style of responsiveness (LeVine et al., 1991, p. 488). Similarly, research on socioeconomic status effects on children's cognitive development in the United States has yielded associations between mother's education and an increase in distal interaction with her infant. Indeed, some studies (e.g., Feiring & Lewis, 1981) suggest that it is the ratio of distal to proximal maternal responses that produces the relationships that have long been reported between socioeconomic status and performance on cognitive measures. Namely, distal maternal responses promote the type of verbal achievement recognized in most cognitive tests.

LeVine argues that schooled women have more decontextualized language skills that allow them to interact with institutional agents such as school teachers, health professionals, and government officials. In their research with Vai (Liberian) men, Cole and Scribner (1974; also see Scribner & Cole, 1981) similarly concluded that the tasks showing the most consistent schooling effects were those requiring expository talk in contrived situations.

Maynard's developmental study also reveals how schooling affects teaching style. Maynard (2002) finds that, older Zinacantec siblings with just a few years of schooling, in comparison to their unschooled siblings, are more likely to allow their 2-year-old learners to go it alone on tasks. These older, more-schooled siblings are significantly more likely to teach from a distance that is large enough that they cannot directly participate with the learner in the task being taught. Even a few years of schooling seem to produce a more pedagogical teaching style in these Zinacantec children.

Similarly, formal education seems to move the teaching style of Mayan mothers in Guatemala in a pedagogical direction. In an informal, albeit experimental, situation with a group of children, including their own, less-schooled mothers guided the children's puzzle construction using more shared multiparty engagement (the whole group focusing on a single aspect of the puzzle); more-schooled mothers guided the children more toward division of labor in which individuals or dyads work separately on different task components (Chavajay & Rogoff, 2002). This is the style of cooperative learning seen in school contexts in the United States, a style in which each individual works independently on a piece of the whole (as in so-called "jigsaw learning"; Aronson, Blaney, Stephin, Sikes, & Snapp, 1978). In short, formal schooling is associated with a more individualistic mode of apprenticeship with greater separation of teacher from learner and learners from each other.

In conclusion, the pedagogical versus apprenticeship dichotomy is a good starting point. It is useful to consider how the universe of behaviors that characterizes the pedagogical model is an apprenticeship of sorts. For instance, it is habituating the novice to touch others proportionately more through words and consequently proportionately less through physical means. The behavior can be seen as well through seeing adults as being responsible for children (as oppose to seeing children as responsible for adults). It is particularly useful to conceive of pedagogically trained children as apprentices because their social positions are so easy to view as frivolous and completely irrelevant to the survival of their family and to work in their society. As with all apprentices, these pedagogically trained novices will participate in the production and maintenance of the socio-cultural context into which they are apprenticing just as they participate in its disruption and change.

A person can be said to *na'* that subset of the knowledge that she or he has acquired pedagogically or inferentially that is practicable and recognized by the commentator (even if the commentary is by the individual). The following section presents a collection of epistemology-related findings as captured by researchers working in Maya communities from the 1950s to the present.

UNDERSTANDING *NA'* AND ITS DEVELOPMENT IN A MAYA MORAL COMMUNITY

Without *na'* as a guide, it would be difficult to see the epistemology implicit in Manuel Arias' words to anthropologist Calixta Gutieras-Holmes (1961) in the late 1950s. Arias, a leading man and shaman from the highland Maya community of Chenalhó, sought to have Gutieras-Holmes understand that "that which is learned through the mouth is forgotten; it is through the soul that we learn. The soul repeats it in the heart, not in the mind, and only then do we know what to do" (Gutieras-Holmes, 1961, p. 149).

Arias clearly privileged the knowledge that he associated with the soul, which links heart and mind. If, using the constructions presented here, *na'*-type knowledge is understood to be a reference to a person's soul (*ch'ulel*), the differentiation of *na'* from purely or principally mental knowledge becomes even more self-evident. Because *ch'ulel* or soul is also part of Maya religious beliefs, Arias introduces a moral element into knowledge.

But the moral and the pragmatic are closely linked. Thus, Zinacantecs believe that a young girl will start to weave when she has enough "soul" or "spirit" (*ch'ulel*). Spirit is necessary because weaving is so hard: frustrating, taxing, time consuming, and intellectually demanding. With soul, a girl will weave of her own volition (Haviland Devereaux, 1991). The word *na'* is always used to describe a girl who knows (or who does not know) how to weave. If a girl has enough soul, she is ready for the process of weaving apprenticeship: namely, the knowledge gained through observation and practice (what Greenfield & Lave [1982] and Rogoff [1990] have called apprenticeship-style learning). Hence, weaving in Zinacantán manifests close links between the soul, *na'* as a type of knowledge, and the apprenticeship style of learning. Without *na'*, it would be difficult to recognize the possibility that a discussion of *ch'ulel* (soul) could at once apply to both cosmology and epistemology.

Relevant to the Mayan ethnotheory of human development and socialization, soul acquisition is conceived as part of a lifelong learning process. Two decades after Manuel Arias' conversation with Calixta Gutieras-Holmes, his Princeton-educated son, Jacinto Arias (1973), asserts the same association between knowledge and the soul as his father before him. Jacinto Arias writes that "education is a long process that starts when a child is born and lasts until reaching the summit of his life. It is conceived of as a slow but constant acquisition, bit by bit, of the 'soul' (ch'ulel)" (p. 28). Eber and Rosenbaum (1998) refer to this enculturation–socialization process as "making souls arrive." The socialization process is complemented by a developmental process in which the soul is central. Arias tells Gutieras-Holmes (1961) that although a baby is said to carry its soul before it is born, it accumulates more as it "starts to laugh, to talk, and [as] its mother plays with it"; a child accumulates more soul, becomes more of a person, as she or he engages with the world. Secondly, he indicates that until the age of 7 or even 13 (but especially before the age of 3), a child is especially vulnerable to losing its ch'ulel (soul) because it does not yet know the waking human world ('osilbalamil). Again there is an explicit connection between knowledge and the soul. The younger the person, the more vulnerable she or he is to losing her or his soul. The parents must take great pains to make it remain here—they must pray for the child to have more time (her or his "hour") and make the human world more attractive by avoiding conflicts and doting on the child. They must also prevent the child from falling or otherwise becoming susceptible to having the soul leave the body (for fear of the soul passing to another realm).

De Leon (1999) describes still other routines designed to make children's souls "arrive" by imparting knowledge of the na' type. On the basis of her video data, she carefully describes "toughening routines that arouse angry displays and help infants develop interactive skills for managing conflict. These routines are repeated so that children can practice affect-loaded toughening interactions that strengthen the soul (ch'ulel). The repetitive character of this socialization process indicates that Zinacantec adults want the child to gain control of his or her emotions in a way that will, indeed, become habitual, habit being a central, defining feature of na'.

Child-rearing patterns in this area reflect these concerns. Maya mothers in Mitontik and elsewhere continue to carry their children in their rebozo (shawl draped diagonally across the torso) from birth until the next child is born, usually 2 to 2.5 years. Children must endure the rough, jerky motions of their mother's body as she scrubs clothes, kneads dough, or cleans her milpa. The comfort and nurturing response of the idle Mitontik mother may become a task-dictated response if she is engaged in work. Women joke that the child is also working in these cases, and a child may indeed be learning the rhythms of work as she or he is moved with her or his mother's body. In this sense, the participatory process of apprenticeship-style learning begins early. Anschuetz (1966) describes a traditional birth ritual that involves placing the tools of adulthood in a neonate's hand. At least symbolically, participation in work—that is, apprenticeship—seems literally to begin at birth.

Indeed, Anschuetz (1966) and Blanco and Chodorow (1964) have argued that individual life stages are defined by the work a person can perform. Eber and Rosenbaum (1998) present a clear vision of how the two discourses—child development as ch'ulel acquisition and child development as work apprenticeship—complement one another as a person gains na'. They argue that a child's soul is finally said to have "come" when she becomes a reliable contributor to her family's well-being. For instance, Luch, a Chamulan woman, tells them of the "coming" of her spirit in the following way:

> When my spirit came, I was about eleven or twelve.
>   I learned to work.
>   I took on spinning.
>   I learned how to fluff wool,
>   and then I would spin.
>   I took it seriously,
>   I worked well.
>   It was because my spirit came.
>   Because when I was little
>   I just spent my time playing.
>   I learned to weave well.
>   I wove two white tunics for my father and my brother,
>   I wove a skirt for my mother,
>   I wove my own clothes.
>   (as quoted in Eber and Rosenbaum, 1998, p. 15)

This lyric quote summarizes the argument we presented from the beginning of the chapter. As we argued, na' is not simply about learning to spin or weave, it is also about taking work seriously, working well and with spirit. That is, na' does not just refer to what a person "knows" but also to how she or he is "knowable" by the enveloping moral community—it is also about a person's character.

The descriptions of an apprenticeship-type enculturation presented in this section can be viewed as progressive commitments elicited and made over a lifetime in face-to-face, Maya na' communities. It is crucial to note that participation in a na' "community" need not be so enduring or the persuasion campaigns so overt.

NA' IN NON-MAYA CONTEXTS

When Zambrano began to think about na', she conceptualized it as an "alternative" to pedagogical approaches to knowledge in the rural Maya context where she was conducting her research. A dichotomous approach—na' versus know, apprenticeship versus pedagogical—seemed like a good fit for analyzing the social changes associated with mass school expansion into Mitontik.

As her analysis progressed, it became clear that this either–or approach was too simplified to accurately reflect the complex social changes associated with the expansion of the government-sponsored institutional world of roads, schools, and clinics into a previously remote rural community. Her analysis agreed with Ashcroft and colleagues' (1995, p. 4) observation that

> Critical accounts emphasising the "silencing" effect of the metropolitan forms and institutional practices . . . and the resulting forces of "hybridisation" make an important point. But they neglect the fact that for many people in post-colonial societies the pre-colonial languages and cultures . . . continue to provide the effective framework for their daily lives.

Instead of a "silencing" effect in which *know* was suppressing or even supplanting *na'* in the public discourse and in local culture, what Zambrano observed in Mitontik was an expansion of the communicative and epistemological continuum to encompass the range from *na'* to *know*.

Having witnessed the expansion of *know* into a previously *na'* context, Zambrano is now interested in pursuing the existence of *na'* forms of knowledge in *know*-dominated contexts. Just as emotional, social, and practical intelligence have recently begun to complement IQ (e.g., as a determinant of success; e.g., Goleman 1995; Grigorenko et al., 2001; Sternberg & Grigorenko, 2000), the bias of *na'* toward practiced knowledge and local responsibility balances *know*'s bias toward word-focused mental knowledge and educational credentials.

Most important, the contrast between *know* and *na'* allows us to acknowledge the cross-talk and converse representations from parents, local communities, and schools. We should especially expect critiques when the *know* world violates core beliefs. In one example, Eber and Rosenbaum (1998, p. 11) find three elements of children's experiences to be most valued in the late 20th-century Maya contexts they studied:

1. Receiving love and guidance from a large network of kin and neighbors.
2. Learning to work hard and well.
3. Feeling the abiding and tangible presence of deities in daily life.

It is crucial to recognize that these core beliefs will vary over time and will vary within any population.

Nonetheless, the Spanish word *educación*, as used by immigrants from Mexico and Central America, has a difference in meaning from its cognate, "education." In many ways, this difference parallels the difference between *know* and *na'* (Goldenberg & Gallimore, 1995). In contrast to education, *educación* puts more emphasis on heart than on head. This is true in the sense that *educación* is training for the habitual practice of correct social behavior.

Relations with a kin network are an essential aspect of *educación*. In line with the notion of cross-talk and value conflicts between home and school, Latino immigrant families complain that education takes place at the expense of *educación* in U.S. classrooms (Greenfield, Quiroz, & Raeff, 2000).

The value of the concept of *na'* is that it gives us the opportunity to not only ask "which and how much knowledge or skill?" but also "according to whom?" Whose assessments of correct social behavior are most powerful in a given context or to a particular individual? For instance, *na'*-centered analyses of appeals to *educación* may be expected to reveal conscious or unconscious attempts to stem the tide of changes in social behavior. It is important to recognize the power struggles underlying all constructions of knowledge.

COGNITIVE DEVELOPMENT AND COGNITIVE PSYCHOLOGY: *KNOW* OR *NA'*?

Relating the contrast between *know* and *na'* to the world of psychology, we submit that the word *knowledge* in the fields of cognitive development and cognitive psychology belongs in the category of *know* rather than that of *na'*. For example, Piaget's conception of knowing and knowledge belongs to *know* rather than *na'*. Our theories of cognitive development stem from *our* epistemology; they do not represent the kind of knowledge that is most important in Maya culture. The nature of our own cultural epistemology leads to particular kinds of developmental and cognitive theories, which, in turn, lead to the collection of particular kinds of empirical data. For example, Piaget's tests of conservation (1952), Vygotsky's tests of concept formation (1962), DeLoache's tests of spatial representation (1987), or information-processing tests of memory are all tests of *novel cognitive problems*, problems the child, in principle, has never seen before. In other words, *know* cares only that novel problem has been solved once; *na'* requires that it be practicably and even habitually solved and implemented. Similarly, Chi's studies of memory in the information-processing framework put the emphasis on remembering novel information. All of these theories both assume and privilege *know* rather than *na'*.

In short, a wide array of developmental theories have focused on the development and socialization of our school-based modes of knowing: the mental learning of facts for a test and the mind's construction of novel forms of knowledge. The brief discussion of the Mayan concept of *na'* that we have presented in this chapter makes it evident that the pedagogical *know* concept of knowledge is woefully narrow and inadequate to the challenge of understanding knowledge in the practical contexts of culture and competence. The concept of *na'* breaks the binds of this construction of knowledge that would recognize only academic practitioners and instead embraces a broader conception of knowledge (and thus intelligence) that presses us to admit that the academic world produces but a small amount of the knowledge and intelligence in the world. The great complexity of this topic is that understanding knowledge in practice comprises not only the material, social, and cultural matters that motivate people to know about their world but also the knowledge-access and knowledge-making of that endeavor. It is essential that researchers develop a concept like *na'* that will permit them to recognize the knowledge and intelligence required for people to make sense of and affect each other and the dynamic world around them.

REFERENCES

Anschuetz, M. H. (1966). *To be born in Zinacantan*. Summer Field Report, Harvard University.

Arias, J. (1973). *El mundo numinoso de los Mayas: Estructura y cambios contemporáneos* [The luminous world of the Mayas: Structure and contemporary changes]. México City: Secretaría de Educación Pública.

Aronson, E., Blaney, N., Stephin, C., Sikes, J., & Snapp, M. (1978). *The jigsaw classroom*. Beverly Hills, CA: Sage.

Ashcroft, B., Griffiths, G., & Tiffin, H. (1995). *The post-colonial studies reader*. New York: Routledge.

Basso, K. H. (1983). Stalking with stories: Names, places, and moral narratives among the western Apache. *Proceedings of the American Ethnological Society, 1983*, 19–55.

Basso, K. H. (1988). Speaking with names: Language and landscape among the western Apache. *Cultural Anthropology, 3*(2), 99–130.

Basso, K. H. (1996). Wisdom sits in places: Notes on a western Apache landscape. In S. Field & K. H. Basso (Eds.), *Senses of place* (pp. 53–90). Santa Fe, NM: School of American Research Press.

Bateson, G. (1958). *Naven*. Stanford, CA: Stanford University Press. (Original work published in 1936)

Blanco, M. H., & Chodorow, N. J. (1964). *Children's work and obedience in Zinacantan*. Summer Field Report, Harvard University.

Bourdieu, P. (1986). *Outline of a theory of practice* (R. Nice, Trans.). New York: Cambridge University Press. (Original work published in 1977)

Chavajay, P., & Rogoff, B. (2002). Schooling and traditional collaborative social organization of problem solving by Mayan mothers and children. *Developmental Psychology, 38*, 55–66.

Childs, C. P., & Greenfield, P. M. (1980). Informal modes of learning and teaching: The case of Zinacanteco weaving. In N. Warren (Ed.), *Studies in cross-cultural psychology* (Vol. 2, pp. 269–316). London: Academic Press.

Cole, M., & Scribner, S. (1974). *Culture and thought: A psychological introduction*. New York: Wiley.

Dasen, P. R. (1984). The cross-cultural study of intelligence: Piaget and the Baole. In P. S. Fry (Ed.), *Changing conceptions of intelligence and intellectual functioning: Current theory and research* (pp. 107–134). New York: North-Holland.

de Leon, L. (1999, June). Language, emotion, and moral development in Zinacantec Mayan children. In P. M. Greenfield (Chair), *Cultural context and developmental theory*. Symposium conducted at the 29th Conference of the Jean Piaget Society for the Study of Knowledge and Development, Mexico City, Mexico.

DeLoache, J. S. (1987). Rapid change in the symbolic functioning of very young children. *Science, 238*, 1556–1557.

Duranti, A. (1997). *Linguistic anthropology*. Cambridge, England: Cambridge University Press.

Eber, C., & Rosenbaum, B. P. (1998). *Making souls arrive: Enculturation and identity in two highland Chiapas towns*. Unpublished manuscript.

Feiring, C., & Lewis, M. (1981). Middle-class differences in the mother–child interaction and the child's cognitive development. In T. M. Field (Ed.), *Culture and early interactions* (pp. 63–94). Hillsdale, NJ: Erlbaum.

Gaskins, S. (1999, June). Children's daily lives in a Maya community. In P. M. Greenfield (Chair), *Cultural context and developmental theory*. Symposium conducted at the 29th Conference of the Jean Piaget Society for the Study of Knowledge and Development, Mexico City, Mexico.

Gill, R., & Keats, D. M. (1980). Elements of intellectual competence: Judgments by Australian and Malay university students. *Journal of Cross-Cultural Psychology, 11*, 233–243.

Goldenberg, C., & Gallimore, R. (1995). Immigrant Latino parents' values and beliefs about their children's education: Continuities and discontinuities across cultures and generations. In P. Pintrich & M. Maehr (Eds.), *Advances in achievement motivation* (Vol. 9, pp. 183–228). Greenwich, CT: JAI Press.

Goleman, D. (1995). *Emotional intelligence*. New York: Bantam Books.

Greenfield, P. M. (1974). Cross-cultural research and Piagetian theory: Paradox and progress. In K. F. Riegel & J. A. Meacham (Eds.), *The developing individual in a changing world: Vol. 1. Historical and cultural issues* (pp. 322–333). Paris: Mouton.

Greenfield, P. M. (1997). Culture as process: Empirical methods for cultural psychology. In J. W. Berry, Y. Poortinga, & J. Pandey (Eds.), *Handbook of cross-cultural psychology: Vol. 1. Theory and method* (pp. 301–346). Boston: Allyn & Bacon.

Greenfield, P. M. (1999). Historical change and cognitive change: A two-decade follow-up study in Zinacantan, a Maya community in Chiapas, Mexico. *Mind, Culture, and Activity, 6*, 92–108.

Greenfield, P. M. (in press). *Weaving generations together: Evolving creativity in the Maya of Chiapas*. Santa Fe, NM: SAR Press.

Greenfield, P. M., & Lave, J. (1982). Cognitive aspects of informal education. In D. Wagner & H. Stevenson (Eds.), *Cultural perspectives on child development* (pp. 181–207). San Francisco: Freeman.

Greenfield, P. M., & Maynard, A. E. (1997, November). Women, girls, apprentice-ship, and schooling: A longitudinal study of historical charge among the Zinacantecan Maya. Paper presented in a symposium organized by I. Zambrano, American Anthropological Association, Washington, DC.

Greenfield, P. M., Maynard, A. E., & Childs, C. P. (in press). Historical change, cultural learning, and cognitive representation in Zinacantec Maya children.

Greenfield, P. M., Quiroz, B., & Raeff, C. (2000). Cross-cultural conflict and har-mony in the social construction of the child. In S. Harkness, C. Raeff, & C. R. Super (Eds.), *The social construction of the child: New directions in child develop-ment* (pp.93–108). San Francisco: Jossey-Bass.

Grigorenko, E. L., Geissler, P. W., Prince, R., Okatcha, F., Nokes, C., Kenny, D. A., et al. (2001). The organisation of Luo conceptions of intelligence: A study of implicit theories in a Kenyan village. *International Journal of Behavioral Develop-ment, 25*, 367–378.

Gutieras-Holmes, C. (1961). *Perils of the soul: The world-view of a Tzotzil Indian*. New York: Free Press.

Haviland, J. B. (1977). *Gossip, reputation, and knowledge in Zinacantan*. Chicago: University of Chicago Press.

Haviland Devereaux, L. (1991). Unpublished field notes, Nabenchauk, Chiapas, Mexico.

Inhelder, B., & Piaget, J. (1958). *The growth of logical thinking from childhood to adoles-cence: An essay on the construction of formal operational structures*. Oxford, En-gland: Basic Books.

Laughlin, R. M. (1975). The great Tzotzil dictionary of San Lorenzo Zinacantán. *Smithsonian Contributions to Anthropology, No. 19*. Washington, DC: Smithsonian Institution Press.

LeVine, R., LeVine, S., Richman, A., Tapia Uribe, F., Sunderland Correa, C., & Miller, P. (1991). Women's schooling and child care in demographic transi-tion: A Mexican case study. *Population and Development Review, 17*, 459–496.

Li, J. (2002). A cultural model of learning: Chinese "heart and mind for wanting to learn." *Journal of Cross-Cultural Psychology, 33*, 248–269.

Maynard, A. E. (1999). The development of teaching in social context. In P. M. Greenfield (Chair), *Cultural context and developmental theory*. Symposium con-ducted at the 29th Conference of the Jean Piaget Society for the Study of Knowl-edge and Development, Mexico City, Mexico.

Maynard, A. E. (2002). Cultural teaching: The development of teaching skills in Zinacantec Maya sibling interactions. *Child Development, 73*, 969–982.

Nsamenang, A. B. (1992). *Human development in cultural context: A third world per-spective*. Newbury Park, CA: Sage.

Piaget, J. (1952). *The child's conception of number*. New York: Norton.

Piaget, J. (1977). *The development of thought: Equilibration of cognitive structures* (A. Rosin, Trans.). Oxford, England: Viking Press.

Rockwell, E. (1996). Keys to appropriation: Rural schooling in Mexico. In B. A. Levinson, D. E. Foley, & D. Holland (Eds.), *The cultural production of the educated person* (pp. 301–324). Albany: State University of New York Press.

Rogoff, B. (1990). *Apprenticeship in thinking: Cognitive development in social context.* New York: Oxford University Press.

Scott, J. (1985). *Weapons of the weak: Everyday forms of peasant resistance.* New Haven: Yale University Press.

Scribner, S., & Cole, M. (1981). *The psychology of literacy.* Cambridge, MA: Harvard University Press.

Serpell, R. (1993). *The significance of schooling: Life journeys in an African society.* Cambridge, England: Cambridge University Press.

Sternberg, R. J., & Grigorenko, E. L. (2000). Practical intelligence and its development. In R. Baron & J. D. A. Parker (Eds.), *The handbook of emotional intelligence* (pp. 215–243). San Francisco: Jossey-Bass.

Super, C. M. (1983). Cultural variation in the meaning and uses of children's "intelligence." In J. Deregowski, S. Dziurawiec, & R. Annis (Eds.), *Explorations in cross-cultural psychology* (pp. 199–212). Amsterdam: Swets & Zeitlinger.

Tsing, A. L. (1993). *In the realm of the diamond queen: Marginality in an out-of-the-way place.* Princeton, NJ: Princeton University Press.

Vygotsky, L. S. (1962). Thought and language. Cambridge, MA: MIT Press.

Wober, J. M. (1974). Toward an understanding of the Kiganda concept of intelligence. In J. W. Berry & P. R. Dasen (Eds.), *Culture and cognition* (pp. 261–280). London: Methuen.

Zambrano, I. (1999). *From na' to know: Power, epistemology and the everyday forms of state formation in Mitontik, Chiapas (Mexico).* Unpublished doctoral dissertation, Harvard University.

12

REFLECTIONS ON CULTURE AND COMPETENCE

DAVID MATSUMOTO

This book is a compendium of the works of some of the finest researchers in the field of culture and competence. In this final chapter I discuss four areas of future theoretical and empirical work in the area based on the information provided collectively by the chapters. Although each of the research programs described in the chapters will of course lead to its own line of future research and theorizing, I hope to provide some views of the big picture concerning culture and competence and in the process raise questions about the nature of competence and intelligence, definitions of culture, universal aspects of competence and biological contributions, and the psychological skills underlying the development of competence. Although much of the message of the book is focused on cultural differences, my goal is to gain some perspective on what that big picture may be so that we move not only toward increasing specificity in each of the individual research areas but also toward increasing integration across seemingly disparate views and findings. First it is important to take stock of what we know about this topic by providing a brief summary of the readings in this book.

WHAT WE KNOW ABOUT CULTURE AND COMPETENCE

Competence is often associated with intelligence and "innate" abilities, and the chapters by Grigorenko and O'Keefe (chap. 2); Shapiro and

Azuma (chap. 8); Sternberg and Grigorenko (chap. 9); Wang, Ceci, Williams, and Kopko (chap. 10); and Zambrano and Greenfield (chap. 11) all speak to the importance of intelligence and cognitive competence in all cultures. But another message imparted by the chapters in this book is that there are many different types of competence and that competence itself involves a combination of knowledge, skills, and abilities. Lonner and Hayes (chap. 4), for instance, discuss intercultural competence, whereas Kitayama and Duffy (chap. 3) focus on tacit cognitive competence associated with self-enhancement and self-criticism, folk beliefs and social inference, and perception. Grigorenko and O'Keefe (chap. 2); Miller (chap. 5); Shapiro and Azuma (chap. 8); and Zambrano and Greenfield (chap. 11) all discuss the importance of social, moral, and interpersonal competence.

Not only are there many different types of competence, but cultures differ in the relative importance of, functions, and meanings derived from the various types of competence. Grigorenko and O'Keefe (chap. 2), for example, discuss competencies in children who do not go to school and make the point that competencies develop regardless of the sociopolitical context in which children develop. Even in underdeveloped countries children develop an amazing array of competencies—cognitive, social, emotional, and psychomotor. One of the roles of socialization is the acquisition of key competencies that are necessary for successful life adjustment.

Likewise, Shapiro and Azuma (chap. 8) discuss Japanese views of competence that go beyond intellectual competence to include issues of the heart: interpersonal competence, self-regulation, modesty, empathy, and sympathy. Miller (chap. 5) discusses how different cultures develop different competencies because of differences in the deep structures associated with the theme of autonomy versus relatedness that underlies cultural differences in attachment, child rearing, self-motivation, parenting, and interpersonal morality. Zambrano and Greenfield (chap. 11) discuss the importance of the concept of *na'* in Mayan culture and contrast it with *know* in traditional views of intelligence and competence. *Na'* suggests the importance of the development of character, interpersonal skills, and morality, and these are more important in Mayan culture than knowing.

Several chapters of the book also make important theoretical contributions and highlight different, seemingly antithetical stances to understanding the relationship between culture and competence. On one hand, Berry's chapter (chap. 1) provides a theoretical basis for understanding universal and culture-specific features of competence with his use of an ecocultural framework. This framework posits ecological and sociopolitical influences on biological and cultural adaptations that then lead to psychological outcomes including competence. He suggests a framework that identifies different levels of analysis, differentiating process from competence and performance.

Poortinga and van de Vijver's (chap. 6) chapter complements Berry's in that it demonstrates the cross-cultural invariance of structural organization of cognition based on ability tests in schooled populations. They report that observed differences among cultures may not be as large as often thought, and that carefully designed studies of cognitive processes and outcomes that attempt to control for alternative interpretations frequently report only small performance differences. Also the focus on differences has occurred at the neglect of examining what may be culturally common in human cognition.

On the other hand Wang, Ceci, Williams, and Kopko (chap. 10) argue that competence results from the adaptation of individual abilities to socio-cultural environments. They suggest that four factors shape competence—cultural artifacts, cognitive domains, interpersonal contexts, and individual schemata—and that they are embedded within a person's competence. Because different cultures represent different living environments, people of different cultures possess cognitive competencies unique to those environments. Cognitive competence therefore is relative to the particular cognitive spheres or domains valued in a culture, to the social and physical contexts in which the child participates in organized activities, and to the cultural and societal demands perceived by the child himself or herself. As such these authors suggest that there are no invariant, core competencies universal to every human child.

Finally, although all of the chapters certainly imply the difficulties inherent in testing competence and intelligence across cultures, the chapter by Serpell and Haynes (chap. 7) speaks directly to this issue. They discuss the assumptions underlying the practice of intelligence testing in American society and demonstrate that those assumptions are much less widely shared in contemporary African societies. These authors argue that the process of institutionalizing intelligence testing in Africa threatens to distort important aspects of education in dysfunctional ways rather than enhancing its precision and efficiency. It is a message that is probably applicable to many other cultures as well.

REFLECTIONS ON CULTURE AND COMPETENCE: FOUR AREAS OF FUTURE THEORETICAL AND EMPIRICAL WORK

As shown by the contributions to this volume, the study of culture and competence has resulted in a vibrant range of findings and theories. Many questions remain unanswered, and some of the answers proffered thus far warrant further inquiry. In an effort to explore these avenues of inquiry, I would like to outline four potentially rich areas for new research and theory.

Definitions of Competence and Intelligence and Their Relationship

Although the title of this book is *Culture and Competence*, many of the chapters in the book discussed not only the topic of competence but also the topic of intelligence. Indeed the study of intelligence across cultures has a considerable history in psychology, especially concerning intelligence testing. It is clear that the field has gone well beyond this history and the questions raised by cultural bias in testing to encompass many different aspects of intelligence and competence.

One question that arises in this volume's chapters concerns the relationship between competence and intelligence. What are their definitions and how do they relate to one another? Clearly this book has shown that those definitions may differ from culture to culture, and that preferred modes of competence or intelligence also differ from culture to culture. But are they different constructs or do they refer to the same psychological constructs? And if they are different, what is their relationship? Is that relationship different in different cultures, and do they relate to other constructs and behaviors differently in different cultures?

I am not an expert in this area and perhaps my confusion on this issue comes from not being completely versed in the terminology and research on this topic. It is clear that there are different types of intelligences (e.g., cognitive versus social and interpersonal) and that they can be tapped and represented in different ways (fluid versus crystallized intelligence). It also is clear that there are different representations of competence (e.g., tacit versus explicit competence). But how these areas relate to one another, and their degree of overlap, is not clear.

Clarifying these issues is probably important for future theoretical and empirical work examining the relationship among culture, competence, and intelligence. Knowing where the boundaries start and end, and whether or not there are boundaries to begin with, is information that will help sort the field and make it more understandable.

Definitions and the Role of Culture

Clearly culture influences the definition, role, and function of competence. But what exactly is it about cultures that produce these influences? *Culture* is really a catchall term that is used to represent influence on psychological processes from multiple sources. These sources include ecological (e.g., geography and climate) and sociopolitical factors (e.g., sociocultural history, government and laws, religion, etc.) as well as familial and communal customs, norms, beliefs, opinions, and rituals (cf. Berry and Poortinga and Van de Vijver, chapters 1 and 6, respectively). We know that people who live in different communities and countries have different cultures, and we know that competence is different in these different cultural contexts. But what sources of culture produce those differences and why they produce them are questions that we have yet to address adequately. Future research may endeavor to link cultural dimensions (Hofstede, 2001) or cultural value systems (Schwartz, 1994, 1999; Schwartz & Bardi, 2001) or even universal psychological processes (McCrae & Costa, 1997; McCrae, Costa, del Pilar, Rolland, & Parker, 1998) with cultural differences in competence. Unpacking studies (Matsumoto, 2003a) will be able to identify specific psychological variables that may account for cultural differences in competence. Studies of contextual variables that are external to the individual (Markus & Kitayama, 1998) may give us clues to their contribution to cultural differences in competence.

Future theoretical and empirical work will also need to give attention to the nature of the culture–competence relationship. Culture can enable competence-related behaviors, providing the platform to create new behaviors and competencies; at the same time culture can restrict behaviors, providing guidelines for "shoulds" and "oughts" (Adamopoulous & Lonner, 2001). Also culture can be antecedent to behavior, "causing" behavior in some fashion much like an independent variable; and culture can be a product of behavior, much like a dependent variable (Adamopoulous & Lonner, 2001). And culture and competence may be mutually constituting (Markus & Kitayama, 1998; Shweder, 1999). These variations in the nature of the culture–competence relationship need to be teased out better in the future for a more comprehensive understanding of the relationship.

Finally a dimension of culture that has been overlooked in most considerations of it has to do with the how cultures deal with the discrepancy between cultural norms and individual realities (Matsumoto, 2003b). Cultural norms exist in all cultures, both implicitly and explicitly; individual-level behaviors, however, may or may not conform to those norms. Thus a dynamic tension exists between cultural norms and individual behaviors, and cultures deal differently with these tensions. Some cultures are tolerant and even encouraging of these discrepancies whereas others are less forgiving. How this cultural dimension interacts with competence and competence-related behaviors is an area that can be explored in the future.

Are There Universal Aspects to Competence?

When psychologists consider the relationship between culture and psychology, the discussion often focuses on cultural differences. Of course identifying and understanding cultural differences is an important task in today's multicultural, pluralistic, and increasingly borderless world. As I suggest above, those differences need to be studied even more in the future.

At the same time one needs to keep a healthy perspective and not forget the possibility that there may be many universal aspects of competence as well. In fact neither the existence of cultural differences nor indigenous concepts of competence rules out the possibility of universality in competence-related processes. Berry's chapter (chap. 1) clearly pointed out how cultural differences and pancultural similarities can coexist. And Poortinga and Van de Vijver's chapter (chap. 6) indicated that the most carefully controlled studies produce only small performance differences in competence-related behaviors in schooled populations across cultures; these authors argued for a more balanced view of examining culturally common aspects of competence.

The suggestion of universality in competence-related processes, using such frameworks as that suggested by Berry in his chapter, seems on the surface to be antithetical to arguments for the cultural specificity of competence discussed by Wang and colleagues in their chapter (chap. 10). These differences, in fact, highlight differences in the approaches afforded by the perspectives of cross-cultural and cultural psychology (Adamopoulous & Lonner, 2001; Matsumoto, 2001). Yet despite these apparent differences, these approaches do not necessarily have to be antithetical to each other, in the realm of competence or any other psychological process, if one adopts different levels of analysis in understanding the relationship between culture and psychological processes.

A levels-of-analysis approach differentiates between the form and function of competence across cultures. The underlying goals and functions of the development of competence at some level of abstraction may in fact be culture-constant, whereas the behaviors adopted to achieve those goals may take different forms across cultures. This viewpoint is not unlike the distinctions between process, competence, and performance described in Berry's chapter (chap. 1). Such a viewpoint would allow for indigenous or culture-specific concepts of competence. There may be multiple levels of form as well as function, and culture-constant versus culture-specific effects may be found at different levels. Future theorizing and empirical work may successfully incorporate such models at multiple levels of analysis to bring together these seemingly disparate views.

Related to the topic of universality is the need to also incorporate research and theory highlighting the contribution of biology, and more specifically behavioral genetics, to the development of competence and intelligence and cultural influences on them. Of course, ample research, especially from twin studies, demonstrates that much of intelligence may be biologically and genetically based and thus cross-generationally inherited (McGue, Bouchard, Iacono, & Lykken, 1993). The relative contributions of biological versus cultural factors and how they interact in the creation of competence is an area that is yet to be explored.

To be sure universality in any psychological process does not necessarily have to imply an underlying biological substrate. Pancultural similarities can occur because of nonbiologically based culture-constant learning. Thus when considering universal aspects of competence the issue will become even more complex because some part of these aspects may be associated with an underlying biological process whereas some other parts will not.

Nevertheless discussions of cultural influences on competence (and many other psychological processes for that matter) not only often focus on cultural differences to the exclusion of universality but also forget about the biological bases of competence and intelligence. It is easy to think about how competence can be entirely constructed by culture (or genes). The difficult work in the future is to figure out and study how they all work together—at times complementing each other whereas at other times at odds with each other—to produce the real differences and similarities we observe across individuals and groups and levels of analysis.

This approach is similar to that which characterizes evolutionary psychology (Buss, 1991, 2001), and it also has a place also for universal and culture-specific understanding of personality processes (McCrae & Costa, 1997; McCrae et al., 1998). Because personality, intelligence, and competence are intimate partners in the individual's psychological composition, it only makes sense for future theoretical and empirical work to begin the tough task of putting these pieces back together into a single, coherent whole.

What Are the Psychological Skills That Underlie the Development of Competence Regardless of Cultural Context?

A final topic that all of the chapters touch on but that research has yet to link explicitly with competence has to do with the psychological skills that underlie the development of competence. There is a difference between maturation and development, and in all likelihood competence does not just mature as the body physically does with minimal stimulation; rather it develops according to the complex interaction among person, environment, and biology. As such, some psychological skills are probably necessary for this development to occur.

This topic has been informed considerably by recent research in the area of intercultural competence (cf. Lonner and Hayes, chap. 4). Whereas research had previously suggested that factors such as language proficiency, ethnocentrism, and knowledge of host and home cultures were the most important in predicting intercultural competence and adjustment (Matsumoto, 1999), the most recent research has indicated that skills such as emotion regulation, openness, flexibility, and critical thinking are in fact important skills that allow or do not allow such knowledge or proficiencies to be used in the development of intercultural competence (Matsumoto, 1999; Matsumoto, LeRoux, Bernhard, & Gray, 2001; Matsumoto et al., in press; Matsumoto, LeRoux, Ratzlaff, et al., 2001; Matsumoto & Takeuchi, 1998; Van der Zee & Van Oudenhoven, 2000, 2001).

Emotion regulation in particular has been shown to be the "gatekeeper" skill. The path to developing intercultural competence is laden with many obstacles, often stirring up complex and negative emotions and feelings in participants. If individuals cannot regulate their emotional reactions in a constructive way that allows them to use their knowledge and skills, it is very difficult to develop intercultural competence. If they are able to put their emotions on hold temporarily and to channel their energies to constructive purposes, then they are able to create new cognitive schemas and new competences through their interactions. Essentially they turn minuses into pluses, negatives into positives. The skill that underlies this process is emotional regulation.

Emotional regulation has been shown to be extremely useful in predicting not only intercultural competence and adjustment, but adjustment in a wide variety of contexts. Emotional regulation can predict academic success, development and proficiency of a second language, and income (Matsumoto, LeRoux, Bernhard, et al., 2001; Matsumoto et al., in press; Matsumoto, LeRoux, Ratzlaff, et al., 2001; Van der Zee & Van Oudenhoven, 2000, 2001). Its close relative emotional intelligence has also been shown to be related to many positive adjustment outcomes (George, 2001; Martinez-Pons, 1997; Morand, 2001; Salovey & Mayer, 1990; Schutte et al., 2001).

Moreover, the available evidence appears to suggest that this role of emotional regulation is culturally invariant (Matsumoto et al., in press). That is, emotional regulation appears to be a gatekeeper skill in the prediction of adjustment for people of many different cultural backgrounds. This is a particularly interesting finding as it suggests that emotional regulation may be a psychological skill that is universally important in the development of competence. Its close relation to the personality dimension of neuroticism, which has been shown to exist universally (McCrae & Costa, 1989; McCrae & Costa, 1997; McCrae et al., 1998), also bolsters this suggestion.

Thus it makes sense that emotional regulation plays a role in the development of competence and that this role may be played out in similar fashion across cultures. Future research and theorizing should incorporate emotional regulation and its close associates openness, flexibility, autonomy, creativity, and critical thinking in examining their roles in the development of competence and intelligence across cultures.

CONCLUSION

There are, of course, many other questions and areas for future work, both conceptual and empirical. Each of the lines of research reported individually in each of the chapters deserves to be followed to their logical conclusions, and all of them provide an important piece of the big puzzle of competence. What I hope to have accomplished here is to provide integrative, big-picture view of this area of research based on the chapters reported in this book, in the hope that researchers not lose sight of what that big picture may be. Like many areas in psychology, it is easy to mistake the forest for the trees. In this area, as in so many others, we need to be able someday to put all of the pieces of the puzzle together to form an integrated and comprehensive theory of competence that is meaningful and applicable to as broad a spectrum of the world as possible.

REFERENCES

Adamopoulous, J., & Lonner, W. J. (2001). Culture and psychology at a crossroad: Historical perspective and theoretical analysis. In D. Matsumoto (Ed.), *The handbook of culture and psychology* (pp. 11–34). New York: Oxford University Press.

Buss, D. M. (1991). Evolutionary personality psychology. *Annual Review of Psychology, 42,* 459–491.

Buss, D. M. (2001). Human nature and culture: An evolutionary psychological perspective. *Journal of Personality, 69,* 955–978.

George, J. M. (2001). Emotions and leadership: The role of emotional intelligence. *Human Relations, 53,* 1027–1055.

Hofstede, G. (2001). *Culture's consequences: Comparing values, behaviors, institutions and organizations across nations* (2nd ed.). Thousand Oaks, CA: Sage.

Markus, H. R., & Kitayama, S. (1998). The cultural psychology of personality. *Journal of Cross-Cultural Psychology, 29*(1), 63–87.

Martinez-Pons, M. (1997). The relation of emotional intelligence with selected areas of personal functioning. *Imagination, Cognition, and Personality, 17*(1), 3–13.

Matsumoto, D. (1999). *Nihonjin no Kokusai Tekiouryoku* [The intercultural adjustment potential of the Japanese]. Tokyo: Hon no Tomosha.

Matsumoto, D. (Ed.). (2001). *The handbook of culture and psychology.* New York: Oxford University Press.

Matsumoto, D. (2003a). Cross-cultural research. In S. Davis (Ed.), *The handbook of research methods in experimental psychology* (pp. 189–208). Oxford, England: Blackwell.

Matsumoto, D. (2003b). The discrepancy between consensual-level culture and individual-level culture is an important aspect of culture. *Culture and Psychology, 9,* 89–95.

Matsumoto, D., LeRoux, J. A., Bernhard, R., & Gray, H. (2001). *Personality and behavioral correlates of intercultural adjustment potential.* Manuscript submitted for publication.

Matsumoto, D., LeRoux, J. A., Iwamoto, M., Choi, J. W., Rogers, D., Tatani, H., & Uchida, H. (in press). The robustness of the Intercultural Adjustment Potential Scale (ICAPS). *International Journal of Intercultural Relations.*

Matsumoto, D., LeRoux, J. A., Ratzlaff, C., Tatani, H., Uchida, H., Kim, C., & Araki, S. (2001). Development and validation of a measure of intercultural adjustment potential in Japanese sojourners: The Intercultural Adjustment Potential Scale (ICAPS). *International Journal of Intercultural Relations, 25,* 483–510.

Matsumoto, D., & Takeuchi, S. (1998). Emotions and intercultural communication. *Ibunka communication kenkyu* [Intercultural Communication Research, Kanda University of International Studies Intercultural Communication Institute], *11,* 1–32.

McCrae, R. R., & Costa, P. T. (1989). The structure of interpersonal traits: Wiggin's circumplex and the five-factor model. *Journal of Personality and Social Psychology, 56,* 559–586.

McCrae, R. R., & Costa, P. T. (1997). Personality trait structure as a human universal. *American Psychologist, 52*, 509–516.

McCrae, R. R., Costa, P. T., del Pilar, G. H., Rolland, J.-P., & Parker, W. D. (1998). Cross-cultural assessment of the five-factor model: The revised NEO Personality Inventory. *Journal of Cross-Cultural Psychology, 29*(1), 171–188.

McGue, M., Bouchard, T. J. J., Iacono, W. G., & Lykken, D. T. (1993). Behavioral genetics of cognitive ability: A life-span perspective. In R. Plomin & G. E. McClearn (Eds.), *Nature, nurture, and psychology* (pp. 59–76). Washington, DC: American Psychological Association.

Morand, D. A. (2001). The emotional intelligence of managers: Assessing the construct validity of a nonverbal measure of "people skills." *Journal of Business and Psychology, 16*(1), 21–33.

Salovey, P., & Mayer, J. D. (1990). Emotional intelligence. *Imagination, Cognition, and Personality, 9*(3), 185–211.

Schutte, N. S., Malouff, J. M., Bobik, C., Coston, T. D., Greeson, C., Jedlicka, C., Rhodes, E., & Wendorf, G. (2001). Emotional intelligence and interpersonal relations. *Journal of Social Psychology, 141*, 523–536.

Schwartz, S. H. (1994). Beyond individualism/collectivism: New cultural dimensions of values. In U. E. Kim, H. Triandis, C. Kagitcibasi, S-C. Choi, & G. Yoon (Eds.), *Individualism and collectivism: Theory, method, and applications* (Vol. 18, pp. 85–119). Newbury Park, CA: Sage.

Schwartz, S. H. (1999). A theory of cultural values and some implications for work. *Applied Psychology: An International Review, 48*(1), 23–47.

Schwartz, S. H., & Bardi, A. (2001). Value hierarchies across cultures: Taking a similarities perspective. *Journal of Cross-Cultural Psychology, 32*, 268–290.

Shweder, R. A. (1999). Why cultural psychology? *Ethos, 27*(1), 62–73.

Van der Zee, K. I., & Van Oudenhoven, J. P. (2000). The Multicultural Personality Questionnaire: A multidimensional instrument of multicultural effectiveness. *European Journal of Personality, 14*, 291–309.

Van der Zee, K. I., & Van Oudenhoven, J. P. (2001). The Multicultural Personality Questionnaire: Reliability and validity of self- and other ratings of multicultural effectiveness. *Journal of Research in Personality, 35*, 278–288.

INDEX

Chen, H. C., 210
Chen, M. J., 210
Chenalhó (Mexico), 254, 264
Chewa, 211
Chiao shun, 129
Chiapas (Mexico), 254, 255, 262
Chicago school system, 175
Child, I., 13
Child development
    competence in early, 198–200
    and expectations of mothers, 152
Childhood memories, 239
Child labor, 43–45
Child-rearing. *See* Parenting
Children, 23–46
    and attachment theory, 118–120
    and chores, 261
    development of competencies by, 25–
      30
    motivation in, 128
    out-of-school, 30–45
    as refugees, 31
    and war, 30–35
Children of the streets, 36
Childs, C. P., 261
Child soldiers, 29, 30–35
Chinese culture, ix
    conceptions of intelligence in, 210, 253
    context sensitivity in, 72, 77
    dialectical thinking in, 143
    domains in, 233
    ebb and flow of, 95
    memories in, 239
    morality in, 129
    mothers in, 236
    parenting in, 129
Chinese languages, 142, 230, 241
Chiu, C.-Y., 240
Chiu, L. H., 237
Chodorow, N. J., 266
Choice, 60
Chores, 261
Christian Bible, 166
Chronic stress, 33
Chronic violence, 33
Ch'ulel, 264–266
Civil conflicts, 30–35
Civilian war victims, 31
Closed mind, 101
Coatsworth, D., 226
Coercive recruitment, 32
Cognition

cultural variations in, 67–78
culture related to, 154–156
equivalence factor in, 143–144
and folk beliefs/social inference, 68–71
and framed line test, 71–75
and perception of object/context, 71
and perception of object/size, 75–78
performance differences in. *See* Performance differences
and self-management, 57–58
"Cognition in practice," 40
Cognitive acculturation, 75
Cognitive alacrity, 168
Cognitive anthropologists, 240
Cognitive competence, 17, 226–227
Cognitive context, 76
Cognitive development, 166, 268–269
Cognitive psychology, 268–269
Cognized environment, 7
Cole, M., 142, 148, 154, 155, 164, 179, 263
Collaborators, model cross-cultural, 105–106
Collective, individual vs., 117
Collectivist cultures, 125, 127, 129
Collectivists, 103
Collectivity, 5
College admissions tests, 114
Colonial America, 95
Columbia, 36
Colvin, S. S., 208
Commercial slavery, 44
Communion, 117
Communities, 97, 128
Community well-being, 99
Compassion, 64
Competence
    acquisition of, 190–193
    and context, 12–15
    and culture, 273–275
    definition of, 90
    in early years, 198–200
    education leading to, 95–100
    factors shaping, 225
    framework for cultural. *See* Framework for cultural competence
    and intelligence, 275–276
    intercultural. *See* Intercultural competence
    interpersonal, ix, 188, 189
    intrapersonal, ix
    in Japanese culture, 188–190
    life-span, 200–202
    need for, x

competence of children in, 26
street children in, 37
Developing expertise, 216–217
Developmental goals, 13–14
Developmental niche, 13
Developmental pressure, 29
Developmental psychology, 26
Devlieger, P. J., 166
Dewey, John, 95–97
Dharma, 130
Dholuo language, 213
Dialectical thinking, 143
Differential contexts, 9
Differentiation in thinking, 143
Diligence, 192, 194, 198, 199
Dinges, N. G., 92
Discipline, 191
"Disorganized/disorganized" attachment pattern, 119*n*.1
Domains, 231–233
Domestic workers, 43–44
Donald, Merlin, 239
Drenth, P. J. D., 148
Drinking water, 24
The Duality of Human Existence (D. Bakan), 117
Duffy, S., 72
Dukha, 130
Durojaiye, M. O., 172
Duty, 127, 129
Dynamic testing, 215

East Asian culture
context-dependence/-independence in, 72–77
dispositional/situational factors in, 68–69
industry in, 178
interdependent self in, 59
modes of being in, 79
modes of thinking in, 238
school enrollment in, 24
self-enhancement/-criticism in, 60–63
Eastern culture, self in, 56
Eber, C., 254, 265–267
Ecocultural perspective, 3–4
and adaptation, 7–8
and competence in context, 12–15
and cultural transmission, 9–12
framework for, 6, 8–9
issues in, 5–7
as term, 8

Ecocultural studies, 16
Ecological context, 10–11
Economic development, 170–173
Ecosystem approach, 7
Educacino, 267
Educación, 267–268
Education. *See also* Schooling
inter-cultural competence, 94–100
testing as source of distortion in public, 173–174
Educational selection, 170–173
Egypt, 95
Elders, reinforcement of, 96
Elgin, S. H., 230
Elitism, 173
El Salvador, 31
Emic inclusion strategy, 17
Emotional control, 265
Emotional intelligence, 92, 96–97
Emotional warmth, 202
"Emotion-criticizing" style, 236
"Emotion-explaining" style, 236
Emotion knowledge, 236
Emotion regulation, 279–280
Empathy, 126, 194, 202
Engaged attitude, 198
English language, 142, 176, 189, 210, 213, 230, 241
"Enlightenment," 173
Environmental determinism, 7
Epigenetic development of self, 101
Episodic competence, 239
Equivalence, 143–147, 154
Erikson, Erik, 101
Eskimo culture, 214
Ethiopia, 31, 32, 41, 167
Ethnic differences, 149
Ethnic validity, 106
Ethnocentrism, 92
Ethnoepistemologies, 251–269
and appropriate settings, 259–260
and cultural conceptions of intelligence, 252–253
and know vs. *na'*, 268–269
and learning models, 261–264
methodology of, 254–256
and morality, 264–266
and *na'* concept, 256–259, 266–268
Ethnographic methods, 15
Ethnography, 254
Ethnotheory, 253
Ethos, 257

Liberia, 31, 142, 263
Libya, 150, 151
LIC (less industrialized country), 172
Life adjustment, 27–28
Life situation, 11
Life space, 11
Life span, 200–202, 239
Linguistic capacities, 26
Literacy, 143, 146, 166
Little, A., 172
Lobel, S., 126
Logical reasoning, 151–152
Logistic linear model, 145
Lonner, W. J., 94
Lopez, R., 175
Love, 129
Low-income countries, 148
Lucknow (India), 38
Luoro, 212
Luria, A. R., 141–142

Madlala, C. F. M., 176
Malaysia, 211
Mali, 44, 211
Malleability, 79–80
Malnutrition, 24
Manpower, 170
Maori culture, 232
Markus, H. R., 58, 154, 238
Martins, R. A., 36
Marxist thinking, 141
Masai culture, 27
Mashima, M., 190
Maslow, Abraham, 101
Massacres, 31
Masten, A., 226
Master–apprentice-style relationship, 191
Masuda, T., 71
Maternal interaction style, 199
Mathematics
    competence in, 230
    Kumon method for studying, 191, 192
    street, 39–40, 232
Matrices subtest, 217
Mayan culture, 252–268
    apprentice-style learning in, 266
    child rearing in, 265
    morality in, 264–266
    mothers in, 262–263
Maynard, A. E., 254, 262, 263
Means of survival, 32
Measurement unit equivalence, 144

Meier, Elisa, 38n.2
Memory, 150–151, 237–240
Memory span, 150–151
Mental health, 218
Mental testing, 166
Mentoring process, 177
Meritocracy, 170
Metacognition, 209
Metamemory, 151
Metric equivalence, 144, 146, 147
Mexico, 254–255, 262, 267
MIC. *See* More industrialized country
Middle-class culture, 58–59
Middle-class European American culture,
    111–112, 114–115, 117
Migrant families, 37
Militarized schooling, 32, 35
Mill, John Stuart, 121
Miller, K., 230
Miller, P., 154
Minarai kikan, 191
Misra, G., 99
Mission in life, 34
Mitontik (Mexico), 252–257, 259–260, 265,
    266
Miyamoto, Y., 64, 69
Modeling, 191
Model(s) of cultural competencies
    and critical role of nonsocial
        competences, 80–81
    development over time, 27
Modes of being, 56
Modus operandi, 56
Money-making skills, 28–29. *See also* In-
    come-earning activities
Morality, interpersonal, 122–123, 129–130
More industrialized country (MIC), 172, 173
Morling, B., 64
Mothers, 125
    American, 195–197
    aspirations of, for their preschoolers, 199
    education levels of, 262–263
    expectations of, 152
    and infants, 235
    Japanese, 193–195
Motivation
    for learning, 95–96
    social, 126–128
    in social development, 120–121
Mozambique, 29, 31
Mpofu, E., 176–178, 180
Music, 191–193

and culture/cognition relationship, 154–156
history of, 140–143
in information processing, 152–153
with invariant background, 149–153
in memory, 150–151
and organization of cognitive factors, 143–149
patterns in, 147–149
Permissiveness, 121, 122
Persistence, 191, 192
Personal agency, 120
Personality research, 140
Personal validity, 106
Persuasion, 64
Peru, 32
Peterson, J., 208
Phonemic learning, 80
Phonological loop hypothesis, 150
Physical fitness, 34
Physical health, 216, 218
Piaget, Jean, 141, 167, 252–253, 268
Pintner, R., 112, 208
Plath, D. W., 117
Play, 198
Police, 37
Poortinga, Y. H., 141, 153
Population control, 32
Portfolio Assessment, 177
Possiblism, 7
Posttraumatic stress, 33, 34
Poverty, 36, 37, 39, 41, 128
Practical intelligence, 217–218
Practice, habitual, 256–258
Practiced knowledge, 258–259
Practice (term), 164
Preperceptual world, 10
Pressey, S. L., 209
Primary control, 63, 64, 189
Primary school enrollment, 24–25
Priming, 79–80
Prince, R., 213
Privileged knowledge, 258
Probabilistic functionalism, 9
Problem Solving factor, 188
Problem-solving tasks, 194–195
Procedural knowledge, 258
Process, adaptation as, 7
Processes (term), 13
Program plan, 166
Protagonists (in folk tales), 189–190

Protocols I and II (1977) to the Geneva Conventions, 30
Psychological differentiation, 102–103
Psychological skills, 279–280
Psychological world, 11
Psychologists, 93–94, 100, 165, 176–178
Psychology
cognitive, 268–269
cross-cultural, 4, 6
cultural, 56, 254
developmental, 26
instructors of, 93–94
in Japan, 176
theme-park, 226
Western, 178
Psychometrics, 113–115, 143–149, 151, 164, 167
Public education, 173–174
Puerto Rican culture, 125
Pygmies, 146

Quran, 142

Racism, 180
Rasch item difficulties, 145–146
Ratings, testing, 164–165
Raven scores, 139
Raven's Matrices, 147
Reading, 195, 258–259
Reading speed, 150
Reading/Writing factor, 188
Rebozo, 265
Recall, 226, 232
Receptive Social Competence factor, 188, 202
Receptivity, interpersonal, 193
Recruitment (of soldiers), 32
Refugees, 31, 153
Regulation of internal attitude, 189, 190
Regulations, 166
Rehearsal strategy, 150–151
Reinforcement of elders, 96
Relatedness, autonomy, 117–119, 121–123, 125
Relational self, 56
Relationship-focused approach, 192, 194
Relationships, 11–12
Relative task, 73
Relativism, 4, 6
Repertoire, 11–12
Reputation, 258
Research, 15–16, 166–170